Praise for Samba-3 by Example

"*Samba-3 by Example* provides useful, thoroughly documented explanations for all aspects of a Samba deployment. They're the same kind of patient answers I got when my dad taught me how to ride a bike without training wheels. Now, if only dad knew active Directory...."
—*Will Enestvedt, UNIX System Administrator, Johnson & Wales University*

"When my colleague and I were first reading John Terpstra's *Samba-3 by Example*, we were impressed by how easy it was to find the chapter we wanted to implement, and the ease of following his step-by-step approach. We always felt Terpstra was there with us, for every configuration line. It was like having our own personal tutor. I always take his book to every client that uses Samba. Additionally, Terpstra does something most authors don't, he keeps his documentation up to date. When we were doing our first implementation, he just released the update that morning; we downloaded it, printed it, and implemented it. Now, to me, that is cutting-edge technology at its best."

—*Steven C. Henry*

"A cook learns to follow a recipe until he has mastered the art. This is your cookbook to successful Windows networks. I followed this recipe to migrate our NT4 domain to Samba-3, and the recipe just worked great. I could not have completed this project without the *Samba-3 by Example* book—it brings dry, lifeless man-pages down to the reality IT support people face."

—*Geoff Scott, IT Systems Administrator, Guests Furniture Hire Pty Ltd*

"I used the book *Samba-3 by Example* to get started at 8:30 last night. I finished my complete PDC and it was up and running in six hours with Windows 2000 and XP Pro clients ready for work in the morning. That's from someone who is brand new to Linux. This book is awesome!"

—*Jesse Knudsen, Windows Systems Administrator*

Samba-3 by Example

Second Edition

Bruce Perens' Open Source Series

http://www.phptr.com/perens

Samba-3 by Example

Practical Exercises to Successful Deployment

Second Edition

John H. Terpstra

Prentice Hall Professional Technical Reference

Upper Saddle River, NJ • Boston • Indianapolis • San Francisco
New York • Toronto • Montreal • London • Munich • Paris • Madrid
Capetown • Sydney • Tokyo • Singapore • Mexico City

Library of Congress Control Number: 2005928103

Printed in the United States of America.

ISBN 0-13-188221-X
Text printed in the United States on recycled paper at Courier in Stoughton, Massachusetts.
First printing, August 2005

ABOUT THE COVER ARTWORK

The cover artwork of this book continues the freedom theme of the first edition of "Samba-3 by Example." The history of civilization demonstrates the fragile nature of freedom. It can be lost in a moment, and once lost, the cost of recovering liberty can be incredible. The previous edition cover featured Alfred the Great who liberated England from the constant assault of Vikings and Norsemen. Events in England that finally liberated the common people came about in small steps, but the result should not be under-estimated. Today, as always, freedom and liberty are seldom appreciated until they are lost. If we can not quantify what is the value of freedom, we shall be little motivated to protect it.

Samba-3 by Example Cover Artwork: The British houses of parliament are a symbol of the Westminster system of government. This form of government permits the people to govern themselves at the lowest level, yet it provides for courts of appeal that are designed to protect freedom and to hold back all forces of tyranny. The clock is a pertinent symbol of the importance of time and place.

The information technology industry is being challenged by the imposition of new laws, hostile litigation, and the imposition of significant constraint of practice that threatens to remove the freedom to develop and deploy open source software solutions. Samba is a software solution that epitomizes freedom of choice in network interoperability for Microsoft Windows clients.

I hope you will take the time needed to deploy it well, and that you may realize the greatest benefits that may be obtained. You are free to use it in ways never considered, but in doing so there may be some obstacles. Every obstacle that is overcome adds to the freedom you can enjoy. Use Samba well, and it will serve you well.

ACKNOWLEDGMENTS

Samba-3 by Example would not have been written except as a result of feedback provided by reviewers and readers of the book *The Official Samba-3 HOWTO and Reference Guide.* This second edition was made possible by generous feedback from Samba users. I hope this book more than answers the challenge and needs of many more networks that are languishing for a better networking solution.

I am deeply indebted to a large group of diligent people. Space prevents me from listing all of them, but a few stand out as worthy of mention. Jelmer Vernooij made the notable contribution of building the XML production environment and thereby made possible the typesetting of this book.

Samba would not have come into existence if Andrew Tridgell had not taken the first steps. He continues to lead the project. Under the shadow of his mantle are some great folks who never give up and are always ready to help. Thank you to: Jeremy Allison, Jerry Carter, Andrew Bartlett, Jelmer Vernooij, Alexander Bokovoy, Volker Lendecke, and other team members who answered my continuous stream of questions — all of which resulted in improved content in this book.

My heartfelt thanks go out also to a small set of reviewers (alphabetically listed) who gave substantial feedback and significant suggestions for improvement: Tony Earnshaw, William Enestvedt, Eric Hines, Roland Gruber, Gavin Henry, Steven Henry, Luke Howard, Tarjei Huse, Jon Johnston, Alan Munter, Mike MacIsaac, Scott Mann, Ed Riddle, Geoff Scott, Santos Soler, Misty Stanley-Jones, Mark Taylor, and Jérôme Tournier.

My appreciation is extended to a team of more than 30 additional reviewers who helped me to find my way around dark corners.

Particular mention is due to Lyndell, Amos, and Melissa who gave me the latitude necessary to spend nearly an entire year writing Samba documentation, and then gave more so this second edition could be created.

CONTENTS

Part I   Example Network Configurations

EXAMPLE NETWORK CONFIGURATIONS

Part II   Domain Members, Updating Samba and Migration

DOMAIN MEMBERS, UPDATING SAMBA AND MIGRATION

Part III   Reference Section

REFERENCE SECTION

LIST OF EXAMPLES

Chapter 5

Chapter 6

Chapter 7

Chapter 9

Chapter 10

Chapter 12

Chapter 15

LIST OF FIGURES

LIST OF TABLES

FOREWORD

By John M. Weathersby, Executive Director, OSSI

The Open Source Software Institute (OSSI) is comprised of representatives from a broad spectrum of business and non-business organizations that share a common interest in the promotion of development and implementation of open source software solutions globally, and in particular within the United States of America.

The OSSI has global affiliations with like-minded organizations. Our affiliate in the United Kingdom is the Open Source Consortium (OSC). Both the OSSI and the OSC share a common objective to expand the use of open source software in federal, state, and municipal government agencies; and in academic institutions. We represent businesses that provide professional support services that answer the needs of our target organizational information technology consumers in an effective and cost-efficient manner.

Open source software has matured greatly over the past five years with the result that an increasing number of people who hold key decisionmaking positions want to know how the business model works. They want to understand how problems get resolved, how questions get answered, and how the development model is sustained. Information and communications technology directors in defense organizations, and in other government agencies that deal with sensitive information, want to become familiar with development road-maps and, in particular, seek to evaluate the track record of the mainstream open source project teams.

Wherever the OSSI gains entrance to new opportunities we find that Microsoft Windows technologies are the benchmark against which open source software solutions are measured. Two open source software projects are key to our ability to present a structured and convincing proposition that there are alternatives to the incumbent proprietary means of meeting information technology needs. They are the Apache Web Server and Samba.

Just as the Apache Web Server is the standard in web serving technology, Samba is the definitive standard for providing interoperability with UNIX systems and other non-Microsoft operating system platforms. Both open source applications have a truly remarkable track record that extends for more than a decade. Both have demonstrated the unique capacity to innovate and maintain a level of development that has not only kept pace with demands, but, in many areas, each project has also proven to be an industry leader.

One of the areas in which the Samba project has demonstrated key leadership is in documentation. The OSSI was delighted when we saw the Samba Team, and John H. Terpstra in particular, release two amazingly well-written books to help Samba software users deploy, maintain, and troubleshoot Windows networking installations. We were concerned that, given the large volume of documentation, the challenge to maintain it and keep it current might prove difficult.

This second edition of the book, *Samba-3 by Example*, barely one year following the release of the first edition, has removed all concerns and is proof that open source solutions are a compelling choice. The first edition was released shortly following the release of Samba version 3.0 itself, and has become the authoritative instrument for training and for guiding deployment.

I am personally aware of how much effort has gone into this second edition. John Terpstra has worked with government bodies and with large organizations that have deployed Samba-3 since it was released. He also worked to ensure that this book gained community following. He asked those who have worked at the coalface of large and small organizations alike, to contribute their experiences. He has captured that in this book and has succeeded yet again. His recipe is persistence, intuition, and a high level of respect for the people who use Samba.

This book is the first source you should turn to before you deploy Samba and as you are mastering its deployment. I am proud and excited to be associated in a small way with such a useful tool. This book has reached maturity that is demonstrated by reiteration that every step in deployment must be validated. This book makes it easy to succeed, and difficult to fail, to gain a stable network environment.

I recommend this book for use by all IT managers and network administrators.

PREFACE

Network administrators live busy lives. We face distractions and pressures that drive us to seek proven, working case scenarios that can be easily implemented. Often this approach lands us in trouble. There is a saying that, geometrically speaking, the shortest distance between two points is a straight line, but practically we find that the quickest route to a stable network solution is the long way around.

This book is your means to the straight path. It provides step-by-step, proven, working examples of Samba deployments. If you want to deploy Samba-3 with the least effort, or if you want to become an expert at deploying Samba-3 without having to search through lots of documentation, this book is the ticket to your destination.

Samba is software that can be run on a platform other than Microsoft Windows, for example, UNIX, Linux, IBM System 390, OpenVMS, and other operating systems. Samba uses the TCP/IP protocol that is installed on the host server. When correctly configured, it allows that host to interact with a Microsoft Windows client or server as if it is a Windows file and print server. This book will help you to implement Windows-compatible file and print services.

The examples presented in this book are typical of various businesses and reflect the problems and challenges they face. Care has been taken to preserve attitudes, perceptions, practices, and demands from real network case studies. The maximum benefit may be obtained from this book by working carefully through each exercise. You may be in a hurry to satisfy a specific need, so feel free to locate the example that most closely matches your need, copy it, and innovate as much as you like. Above all, enjoy the process of learning the secrets of MS Windows networking that is truly liberated by Samba.

The focus of attention in this book is Samba-3. Specific notes are made in respect of how Samba may be made secure. This book does not attempt to provide detailed information regarding secure operation and configuration of peripheral services and applications such as OpenLDAP, DNS and DHCP, the need for which can be met from other resources that are dedicated to the subject.

Why Is This Book Necessary?

This book is the result of observations and feedback. The feedback from the Samba-HOWTO-Collection has been positive and complimentary. There have been requests for far more worked examples, a "Samba Cookbook," and for training materials to help kick-start the process of mastering Samba.

The Samba mailing lists users have asked for sample configuration files that work. It is natural to question one's own ability to correctly configure a complex tool such as Samba until a minimum necessary knowledge level has been attained.

The Samba-HOWTO-Collection — as does *The Official Samba-3 HOWTO and Reference Guide* — documents Samba features and functionality in a topical context. This book takes a completely different approach. It walks through Samba network configurations that are working within particular environmental contexts, providing documented step-by-step implementations. All example case configuration files, scripts, and other tools are provided on the CD-ROM. This book is descriptive, provides detailed diagrams, and makes deployment of Samba-3 a breeze.

Samba 3.0.20 Update Edition

The Samba 3.0.x series has been remarkably popular. At the time this book first went to print samba-3.0.2 was being released. There have been significant modifications and enhancements between samba-3.0.2 and samba-3.0.14 (the current release) that necessitate this documentation update. This update has the specific intent to refocus this book so that its guidance can be followed for samba-3.0.20 and beyond. Further changes are expected as Samba-3 matures further and will be reflected in future updates.

The changes shown in Table 1 are incorporated in this update.

Prerequisites

This book is not a tutorial on UNIX or Linux administration. UNIX and Linux training is best obtained from books dedicated to the subject. This book assumes that you have at least the basic skill necessary to use these operating systems, and that you can use a basic system editor to edit and configure files. It has been written with the assumption that you have experience with Samba, have read *The Official Samba-3 HOWTO and Reference Guide* and the Samba-HOWTO-Collection, or that you have familiarity with Microsoft Windows.

If you do not have this experience, you can follow the examples in this book but may find yourself at times intimidated by assumptions made. In this situation, you may need to refer to administrative guides or manuals for your operating system platform to find what is the best method to achieve what the text of this book describes.

Approach

The first chapter deals with some rather thorny network analysis issues. Do not be put off by this. The information you glean, even without a detailed understanding of network protocol analysis, can help you understand how Windows networking functions.

Each following chapter of this book opens with the description of a networking solution sought by a hypothetical site. Bob Jordan is a hypothetical decision maker for an imaginary company, `Abmas Biz NL`. We will use the non-existent domain name `abmas.biz`. All *facts* presented regarding this company are fictitious and have been drawn from a variety of real business scenarios over many years. Not one of these reveal the identify of the real-world company from which the scenario originated.

Table 1 Samba Changes — 3.0.2 to 3.0.20

New Feature	Description
Winbind Case Handling	User and group names returned by **winbindd** are now converted to lower case for better consistency. Samba implementations that depend on the case of information returned by winbind (such as %u and %U) must now convert the dependency to expecting lower case values. This affects mail spool files, home directories, valid user lines in the `smb.conf` file, etc.
Schema Changes	Addition of code to handle password aging, password uniqueness controls, bad password instances at logon time, have made necessary extensions to the SambaSAM schema. This change affects all sites that use LDAP and means that the directory schema must be updated.
Username Map Handling	Samba-3.0.8 redefined the behavior: Local authentication results in a username map file lookup before authenticating the connection. All authentication via an external domain controller will result in the use of the fully qualified name (i.e.: DOMAIN\username) after the user has been successfully authenticated.
UNIX Extension Handling	Symbolically linked files and directories on the UNIX host to absolute paths will now be followed. This can be turned off using "wide links = No" in the share stanza in the `smb.conf` file. Turning off "wide links" support will degrade server performance because each path must be checked.
Privileges Support	Versions of Samba prior to samba-3.0.11 required the use of the UNIX `root` account from network Windows clients. The new "enable privileges = Yes" capability means that functions such as adding machines to the domain, managing printers, etc. can now be delegated to normal user accounts or to groups of users.

In any case, Mr. Jordan likes to give all his staff nasty little assignments. Stanley Saroka is one of his proteges; Christine Roberson is the network administrator Bob trusts. Jordan is inclined to treat other departments well because they finance Abmas IT operations.

Each chapter presents a summary of the network solution we have chosen to demonstrate together with a rationale to help you to understand the thought process that drove that solution. The chapter then documents in precise detail all configuration files and steps that must be taken to implement the example solution. Anyone wishing to gain serious value from this book will do well to take note of the implications of points made, so watch out for the *this means that* notations.

Each chapter has a set of questions and answers to help you to to understand and digest key attributes of the solutions presented.

Summary of Topics

The contents of this second edition of *Samba-3 by Example* have been rearranged based on feedback from purchasers of the first edition.

Clearly the first edition contained most of what was needed and that was missing from other books that cover this difficult subject. The new arrangement adds additional material to meet consumer requests and includes changes that originated as suggestions for improvement.

Chapter 1 now dives directly into the heart of the implementation of Windows file and print server networks that use Samba at the heart.

Chapter 1 — No Frills Samba Servers. Here you design a solution for three different business scenarios, each for a company called Abmas. There are two simple networking problems and one slightly more complex networking challenge. In the first two cases, Abmas has a small simple office, and they want to replace a Windows 9x peer-to-peer network. The third example business uses Windows 2000 Professional. This must be simple, so let's see how far we can get. If successful, Abmas grows quickly and soon needs to replace all servers and workstations.

TechInfo — This chapter demands:

- Case 1: The simplest `smb.conf` file that may reasonably be used. Works with Samba-2.x also. This configuration uses Share Mode security. Encrypted passwords are not used, so there is no `smbpasswd` file.

- Case 2: Another simple `smb.conf` file that adds WINS support and printing support. This case deals with a special requirement that demonstrates how to deal with purpose-built software that has a particular requirement for certain share names and printing demands. This configuration uses Share Mode security and also works with Samba-2.x. Encrypted passwords are not used, so there is no `smbpasswd` file.

- Case 3: This `smb.conf` configuration uses User Mode security. The file share configuration demonstrates the ability to provide master access to an administrator while restricting all staff to their own work areas. Encrypted passwords are used, so there is an implicit `smbpasswd` file.

Chapter 2 — Small Office Networking. Abmas is a successful company now. They have 50 network users and want a little more varoom from the network. This is a typical small office and they want better systems to help them to grow. This is your chance to really give advanced users a bit more functionality and usefulness.

TechInfo — This `smb.conf` file makes use of encrypted passwords, so there is an `smbpasswd` file. It also demonstrates use of the *valid users* and *valid groups* to restrict share access. The Windows clients access the server as Domain members. Mobile users log onto the Domain while in the office, but use a local machine account while on the road. The result is an environment that answers mobile computing user needs.

Chapter 3 — Secure Office Networking. Abmas is growing rapidly now. Money is a little tight, but with 130 network users, security has become a concern. They have many new machines to install and the old equipment will be retired. This time they want the new network to scale and grow for at least two years. Start with a sufficient system and allow room for growth. You are now implementing an Internet connection and have a few reservations about user expectations.

TechInfo — This `smb.conf` file makes use of encrypted passwords, and you can use a `tdbsam` password backend. Domain logons are introduced. Applications are served from the central server. Roaming profiles are mandated. Access to the server is tightened up so that only domain members can access server resources. Mobile computing needs still are catered to.

Chapter 4 — The 500 User Office. The two-year projections were met. Congratulations, you are a star. Now Abmas needs to replace the network. Into the existing user base, they need to merge a 280-user company they just acquired. It is time to build a serious network. There are now three buildings on one campus and your assignment is to keep everyone working while a new network is rolled out. Oh, isn't it nice to roll out brand new clients and servers! Money is no longer tight, you get to buy and install what you ask for. You will install routers and a firewall. This is exciting!

TechInfo — This `smb.conf` file makes use of encrypted passwords, and a `tdbsam` password backend is used. You are not ready to launch into LDAP yet, so you accept the limitation of having one central Domain Controller with a Domain Member server in two buildings on your campus. A number of clever techniques are used to demonstrate some of the smart options built into Samba.

Chapter 5 — Making Happy Users. Congratulations again. Abmas is happy with your services and you have been given another raise. Your users are becoming much more capable and are complaining about little things that need to be fixed. Are you up to the task? Mary says it takes her 20 minutes to log onto the network and it is killing her productivity. Email is a bit *unreliable* — have you been sleeping on the job? We do not discuss the technology of email but when the use of mail clients breaks because of networking problems, you had better get on top of it. It's time for a change.

TechInfo — This `smb.conf` file makes use of encrypted passwords; a distributed `ldap-sam` password backend is used. Roaming profiles are enabled. Desktop profile controls are introduced. Check out the techniques that can improve the user experience of network performance. As a special bonus, this chapter documents how to configure smart downloading of printer drivers for drag-and-drop printing support. And, yes, the secret of configuring CUPS is clearly documented. Go for it; this one will tease you, too.

Chapter 6 — A Distributed 2000 User Network. Only eight months have passed, and Abmas has acquired another company. You now need to expand the network further. You have to deal with a network that spans several countries. There are three new networks in addition to the original three buildings at the head-office campus. The head office is in New York and you have branch offices in Washington, Los Angeles, and London. Your desktop standard is Windows XP Professional. In many ways, everything has changed and yet it must remain the same. Your team is primed for another roll-out. You know there are further challenges ahead.

TechInfo — Slave LDAP servers are introduced. Samba is configured to use multiple LDAP backends. This is a brief chapter; it assumes that the technology has been mastered and gets right down to concepts and how to deploy them.

Chapter 7 — Adding UNIX/Linux Servers and Clients. Well done, Bob, your team has achieved much. Now help Abmas integrate the entire network. You want central control and central support and you need to cut costs. How can you reduce administrative overheads and yet get better control of the network?

This chapter has been contributed by Mark Taylor <`mark.taylor@siriusit.co.uk`>[1] and is based on a live site. For further information regarding this example case, please contact Mark directly.

TechInfo — It is time to consider how to add Samba servers and UNIX and Linux network clients. Users who convert to Linux want to be able to log on using Windows network accounts. You explore nss_ldap, pam_ldap, winbind, and a few neat techniques for taking control. Are you ready for this?

Chapter 8 — Updating Samba-3. This chapter is the result of repeated requests for better documentation of the steps that must be followed when updating or upgrading a Samba server. It attempts to cover the entire subject in broad-brush but at the same time provides detailed background information that is not covered elsewhere in the Samba documentation.

TechInfo — Samba stores a lot of essential network information in a large and growing collection of files. This chapter documents the essentials of where those files may be located and how to find them. It also provides an insight into inter-related matters that affect a Samba installation.

Chapter 9 — Migrating NT4 Domain to Samba-3. Another six months have passed. Abmas has acquired yet another company. You will find a way to migrate all users off the old network onto the existing network without loss of passwords and will effect the change-over during one weekend. May the force (and caffeine) be with you, may you keep your back to the wind and may the sun shine on your face.

---

[1]<`mailto:mark.taylor@siriusit.co.uk`>

TechInfo — This chapter demonstrates the use of the **net rpc migrate** facility using an LDAP ldapsam backend, and also using a tdbsam passdb backend. Both are much-asked-for examples of NT4 Domain migration.

Chapter 10 — Migrating NetWare 4.11 Server to Samba. Misty Stanley-Jones has contributed information that summarizes her experience at migration from a NetWare server to Samba-3.

TechInfo — The documentation provided demonstrates how one site migrated from NetWare to Samba. Some alternatives tools are mentioned. These could be used to provide another pathway to a successful migration.

Chapter 11 — Active Directory, Kerberos and Security. Abmas has acquired another company that has just migrated to running Windows Server 2003 and Active Directory. One of your staff makes offhand comments that land you in hot water. A network security auditor is hired by the head of the new business and files a damning report, and you must address the *defects* reported. You have hired new network engineers who want to replace Microsoft Active Directory with a pure Kerberos solution. How will you handle this?

TechInfo — This chapter is your answer. Learn about share access controls, proper use of UNIX/Linux file system access controls, and Windows 200x Access Control Lists. Follow these steps to beat the critics.

Chapter 12 — Integrating Additional Services. The battle is almost over, Samba-3 has won the day. Your team are delighted and now you find yourself at yet another cross-roads. Abmas have acquired a snack food business, you made promises you must keep. IT costs must be reduced, you have new resistance, but you will win again. This time you choose to install the Squid proxy server to validate the fact that Samba is far more than just a file and print server. SPNEGO authentication support means that your Microsoft Windows clients gain transparent proxy access.

TechInfo — Samba provides the **ntlm_auth** module that makes it possible for MS Windows Internet Explorer to connect via the Squid Web and FTP proxy server. You will configure Samba-3 as well as Squid to deliver authenticated access control using the Active Directory Domain user security credentials.

Chapter 13 — Performance, Reliability and Availability. Bob, are you sure the new Samba server is up to the load? Your network is serving many users who risk becoming unproductive. What can you do to keep ahead of demand? Can you keep the cost under control also? What can go wrong?

TechInfo — Hot tips that put chili into your network. Avoid name resolution problems, identify potential causes of network collisions, avoid Samba configuration options that will weigh the server down. MS distributed file services to make your network fly and much more. This chapter contains a good deal of "Did I tell you about this...?" type of hints to help keep your name on the top performers list.

Chapter 14 — Samba Support. This chapter has been added specifically to help those who are seeking professional paid support for Samba. The critics of Open Source Software often assert that there is no support for free software. Some critics argue that free software undermines the service that proprietary commercial software vendors depend on. This chapter explains what are the support options for Samba and the fact that a growing number of businesses make money by providing commercial paid-for Samba support.

Chapter 15 — A Collection of Useful Tid-bits. Sometimes it seems that there is not a good place for certain odds and ends that impact Samba deployment. Some readers would argue that everyone can be expected to know this information, or at least be able to find it easily. So to avoid offending a reader's sensitivities, the tid-bits have been placed in this chapter. Do check out the contents, you may find something of value among the loose ends.

Chapter 16 — Windows Networking Primer. Here we cover practical exercises to help us to understand how MS Windows network protocols function. A network protocol analyzer helps you to appreciate the fact that Windows networking is highly dependent on broadcast messaging. Additionally, you can look into network packets that a Windows client sends to a network server to set up a network connection. On completion, you should have a basic understanding of how network browsing functions and have seen some of the information a Windows client sends to a file and print server to create a connection over which file and print operations may take place.

Conventions Used

The following notation conventions are used throughout this book:

- TOSHARG2 is used as an abbreviation for the book, "The Official Samba-3 HOWTO and Reference Guide, Second Edition" Editors: John H. Terpstra and Jelmer R. Vernooij, Publisher: Prentice Hall, ISBN: 0131882228.

- S3bE2 is used as an abbreviation for the book, "Samba-3 by Example, Second Edition" Editors: John H. Terpstra, Publisher: Prentice Hall, ISBN: 013188221X.

- Directories and filenames appear in mono-font. For example, `/etc/pam.conf`.

- Executable names are bolded. For example, **smbd**.

- Menu items and buttons appear in bold. For example, click **Next**.

- Selecting a menu item is indicated as: **Start** → **Control Panel** → **Administrative Tools** → **Active Directory Users and Computers**

Part I

Example Network Configurations

EXAMPLE NETWORK CONFIGURATIONS

This section of *Samba-3 by Example* provides example network configurations that can be copied, or modified as needed, and deployed as-is.

Best use can be made of this book by finding in this section the network design and layout that best approximates your estimated needs. It is recommended that you will implement the design pattern exactly as it appears, then after the installation has been proven to work make any changes or modifications needed at your site.

The examples have been tested with Red Hat Fedora Core 2, Novell SUSE Linux Professional 9.3 and Novell SUSE Linux Enterprise Server (SLES) 9. The principals of implementation apply to all Linux and UNIX systems in general, though some system files and tools will be different and the location of some Samba file locations will be different since these are determined by the person who packages Samba for each platform.

If you are deploying Samba is a mission-critical environment, or if you simply want to save time and get your Samba network operational with minimal fuss, there is the option to purchase commercial, professional, Samba support. Information regarding commercial support options may be obtained from the commercial support[2] pages from the Samba web site.

---

[2]`<http://www.samba.org/samba/support/>`

Chapter 1

NO-FRILLS SAMBA SERVERS

This is the start of the real journey toward the successful deployment of Samba. For some this chapter is the end of the road because their needs will have been adequately met. For others, this chapter is the beginning of a journey that will take them well past the contents of this book. This book provides example configurations of, for the greater part, complete networking solutions. The intent of this book is to help you to get your Samba installation working with the least amount of pain and aggravation.

1.1 Introduction

This chapter lays the groundwork for understanding the basics of Samba operation. Instead of a bland technical discussion, each principle is demonstrated by way of a real-world scenario for which a working solution[1] is fully described.

The practical exercises take you on a journey through a drafting office, a charity administration office, and an accounting office. You may choose to apply any or all of these exercises to your own environment.

Every assignment case can be implemented far more creatively, but remember that the solutions you create are designed to demonstrate a particular solution possibility. With experience, you should find much improved solutions compared with those presented here. By the time you complete this book, you should aim to be a Samba expert, so do attempt to find better solutions and try them as you work your way through the examples.

1.2 Assignment Tasks

Each case presented highlights different aspects of Windows networking for which a simple Samba-based solution can be provided. Each has subtly different requirements taken from real-world cases. The cases are briefly reviewed to cover important points. Instructions are based on the assumption that the official Samba Team RPM package has been installed.

---

[1]The examples given mirror those documented in The Official Samba-3 HOWTO and Reference Guide, Second Edition (TOSHARG2) Chapter 2, Section 2.3.1. You may gain additional insight from the standalone server configurations covered in TOSHARG2, sections 2.3.1.2 through 2.3.1.4.

This chapter has three assignments built around fictitious companies:

- A drafting office

- A charity administration office

- An accounting office

Let's get started.

1.2.1   Drafting Office

Our fictitious company is called *Abmas Design, Inc.* This is a three-person computer-aided design (CAD) business that often has more work than can be handled. The business owner hires contract draftspeople from wherever he can. They bring their own notebook computers into the office. There are four permanent drafting machines. Abmas has a collection of over 10 years of plans that must be available for all draftsmen to reference. Abmas hires the services of an experienced network engineer to update the plans that are stored on a central server one day per month. She knows how to upload plans from each machine. The files available from the server must remain read-only. Anyone should be able to access the plans at any time and without barriers or difficulty.

Mr. Bob Jordan has asked you to install the new server as economically as possible. The central server has a Pentium-IV 1.6GHz CPU, 768MB RAM, a 20GB IDE boot drive, a 160GB IDE second disk to store plans, and a 100-base-T Ethernet card. You have already installed Red Hat Fedora CoreX and have upgraded Samba to version 3.0.20 using the RPM package that is provided from the Samba FTP[2] sites. (Note: Fedora CoreX indicates your favorite version.)

The four permanent drafting machines (Microsoft Windows workstations) have attached printers and plotters that are shared on a peer-to-peer basis by any and all network users. The intent is to continue to share printers in this manner. The three permanent staff work together with all contractors to store all new work on one PC. A daily copy is made of the work storage area to another PC for safekeeping. When the network consultant arrives, the weekly work area is copied to the central server and the files are removed from the main weekly storage machine. The office works best with this arrangement and does not want to change anything. Old habits are too ingrained.

1.2.1.1   Dissection and Discussion

The requirements for this server installation demand simplicity. An anonymous read-only file server adequately meets all needs. The network consultant determines how to upload all files from the weekly storage area to the server. This installation should focus only on critical aspects of the installation.

---

[2]<http://www.samba.org>

It is not necessary to have specific users on the server. The site has a method for storing all design files (plans). Each plan is stored in a directory that is named YYYYWW,[3] where YYYY is the year, and WW is the week of the year. This arrangement allows work to be stored by week of year to preserve the filing technique the site is familiar with. There is also a customer directory that is alphabetically listed. At the top level are 26 directories (A-Z), in each is a second-level of directory for the first plus second letters of the name (A-Z); inside each is a directory by the customers' name. Inside each directory is a symbolic link to each design drawing or plan. This way of storing customer data files permits all plans to be located both by customer name and by the date the work was performed, without demanding the disk space that would be needed if a duplicate file copy were to be stored. The share containing the plans is called *Plans*.

1.2.1.2   Implementation

It is assumed that the server is fully installed and ready for installation and configuration of Samba 3.0.20 and any support files needed. All TCP/IP addresses have been hard-coded. In our case the IP address of the Samba server is `192.168.1.1` and the netmask is `255.255.255.0`. The hostname of the server used is `server`.

SAMBA SERVER CONFIGURATION

1. Download the Samba-3 RPM packages for Red Hat Fedora Core2 from the Samba FTP servers.[4]

2. Install the RPM package using either the Red Hat Linux preferred GUI tool or the **rpm**:

   ```
   root#  rpm -Uvh samba-3.0.20-1.i386.rpm
   ```

3. Create a mount point for the file system that will be used to store all data files. You can create a directory called `/plans`:

   ```
   root#  mkdir /plans
   root#  chmod 755 /plans
   ```

   The 755 permissions on this directory (mount point) permit the owner to read, write, and execute, and the group and everyone else to read and execute only. Use Red Hat Linux system tools (refer to Red Hat instructions) to format the 160GB hard drive with a suitable file system. An Ext3 file system is suitable. Configure this drive to automatically mount using the `/plans` directory as the mount point.

4. Install the `smb.conf` file shown in Example 1.2.1 in the `/etc/samba` directory.

---

[3]This information is given purely as an example of how data may be stored in such a way that it will be easy to locate records at a later date. The example is not meant to imply any instructions that may be construed as essential to the design of the solution; this is something you will almost certainly want to determine for yourself.

[4]<http://www.samba.org>

Example 1.2.1 Drafting Office smb.conf File

```
# Global Parameters
 [global]
        workgroup = MIDEARTH
        security = SHARE
 [Plans]
        path = /plans
        read only = Yes
        guest ok = Yes
```

5. Verify that the `/etc/hosts` file contains the following entry:

    ```
    192.168.1.1 server
    ```

6. Use the standard system tool to start Samba and to configure it to restart automatically at every system reboot. For example,

    ```
    root#  chkconfig smb on
    root#  /etc/rc.d/init.d/smb restart
    ```

WINDOWS CLIENT CONFIGURATION

1. Make certain that all clients are set to the same network address range as used for the Samba server. For example, one client might have an IP address 192.168.1.10.

2. Ensure that the netmask used on the Windows clients matches that used for the Samba server. All clients must have the same netmask, such as 255.255.255.0.

3. Set the workgroup name on all clients to MIDEARTH.

4. Verify on each client that the machine called SERVER is visible in the **Network Neighborhood**, that it is possible to connect to it and see the share **Plans**, and that it is possible to open that share to reveal its contents.

1.2.1.3   Validation

The first priority in validating the new Samba configuration should be to check that Samba answers on the loop-back interface. Then it is time to check that Samba answers its own name correctly. Last, check that a client can connect to the Samba server.

1. To check the ability to access the **smbd** daemon services, execute the following:

    ```
    root#  smbclient -L localhost -U%
            Sharename      Type       Comment
    ```

```
    ---------        ----       -------
    Plans            Disk
    IPC$             IPC        IPC Service (Samba 3.0.20)
    ADMIN$           IPC        IPC Service (Samba 3.0.20)

    Server                      Comment
    ---------                   -------
    SERVER                      Samba 3.0.20

    Workgroup                   Master
    ---------                   --------
    MIDEARTH                    SERVER
```

This indicates that Samba is able to respond on the loopback interface to a NULL connection. The *-U%* means send an empty username and an empty password. This command should be repeated after Samba has been running for 15 minutes.

2. Now verify that Samba correctly handles being passed a username and password, and that it answers its own name. Execute the following:

```
root#  smbclient -L server -Uroot%password
```

The output should be identical to the previous response. Samba has been configured to ignore all usernames given; instead it uses the *guest account* for all connections.

3. From the Windows 9x/Me client, launch Windows Explorer: **[Desktop: right-click] Network Neighborhood+Explore** → **[Left Panel] [+] Entire Network** → **[Left Panel] [+] Server** → **[Left Panel] [+] Plans**. In the right panel you should see the files and directories (folders) that are in the **Plans** share.

1.2.2   Charity Administration Office

The fictitious charity organization is called *Abmas Vision NL*. This office has five networked computers. Staff are all volunteers, staff changes are frequent. Ms. Amy May, the director of operations, wants a no-hassle network. Anyone should be able to use any PC. Only two Windows applications are used: a custom funds tracking and management package that stores all files on the central server and Microsoft Word. The office prepares mail-out letters, invitations, and thank-you notes. All files must be stored in perpetuity. The custom funds tracking and management (FTM) software is configured to use a server named SERVER, a share named FTMFILES, and a printer queue named PRINTQ that uses preprinted stationery, thus demanding a dedicated printer. This printer does not need to be mapped to a local printer on the workstations.

The FTM software has been in use since the days of Windows 3.11. The software was configured by the vendor who has since gone out of business. The identities of the file server and the printer are hard-coded in a configuration file that was created using a setup tool that the vendor did not provide to Abmas Vision NL or to its predecessors. The company that produced the software is no longer in business. In order to avoid risk of any incompatibilities, the share name and the name of the target print queue must be set precisely as the application expects. In fact, share names and print queue names should be treated as case insensitive (i.e., case does not matter), but Abmas Vision advises that if the share name is not in lowercase, the application claims it cannot find the file share.

Printer handling in Samba results in a significant level of confusion. Samba presents to the MS Windows client only a print queue. The Samba **smbd** process passes a print job sent to it from the Windows client to the native UNIX printing system. The native UNIX printing system (spooler) places the job in a print queue from which it is delivered to the printer. In this book, network diagrams refer to a printer by the name of the print queue that services that printer. It does not matter what the fully qualified name (or the hostname) of a network-attached printer is. The UNIX print spooler is configured to correctly deliver all jobs to the printer.

This organization has a policy forbidding use of privately owned computers on site as a measure to prevent leakage of confidential information. Only the five PCs owned by Abmas Vision NL are used on this network.

The central server was donated by a local computer store. It is a dual processor Pentium-III server, has 1GB RAM, a 3-Ware IDE RAID Controller that has four 200GB IDE hard drives, and a 100-base-T network card. The office has 100-base-T permanent network connections that go to a central hub, and all equipment is new. The five network computers all are equipped with Microsoft Windows Me. Funding is limited, so the server has no operating system on it. You have approval to install Samba on Linux, provided it works without problems. There are two HP LaserJet 5 PS printers that are network connected. The second printer is to be used for general office and letter printing. Your recommendation to allow only the Linux server to print directly to the printers was accepted. You have supplied SUSE Enterprise Linux Server 9 and have upgraded Samba to version 3.0.20.

1.2.2.1 Dissection and Discussion

This installation demands simplicity. Frequent turnover of volunteer staff indicates that a network environment that requires users to logon might be problematic. It is suggested that the best solution for this office would be one where the user can log onto any PC with any username and password. Samba can accommodate an office like this by using the *force user* parameter in share and printer definitions. Using the *force user* parameter ensures that all files are owned by same user identifier (UID) and thus that there will never be a problem with file access due to file access permissions. Additionally, you elect to use the *nt acl support* = *No* option to ensure that access control lists (Posix type) cannot be written to any file or directory. This prevents an inadvertent ACL from overriding actual file permissions.

This organization is a prime candidate for Share Mode security. The *force user* allows all files to be owned by the same user and group. In addition, it would not hurt to set SUID and set SGID shared directories. This means that all new files that are created, no matter who creates it, are owned by the owner or group of the directory in which they are created. For further information regarding the significance of the SUID/SGID settings, see Chapter 15, "A Collection of Useful Tidbits", Section 15.8.

All client workstations print to a print queue on the server. This ensures that print jobs continue to print in the event that a user shuts down the workstation immediately after sending a job to the printer. Today, both Red Hat Linux and SUSE Linux use CUPS-based printing. Older Linux systems offered a choice between the LPRng printing system or CUPS. It appears, however, that CUPS has become the leading UNIX printing technology.

The print queues are set up as `Raw` devices, which means that CUPS will not do intelligent print processing, and vendor-supplied drivers must be installed locally on the Windows clients.

The hypothetical software, FTM, is representative of custom-built software that directly uses a NetBIOS interface. Most such software originated in the days of MS/PC DOS. NetBIOS names are uppercase (and functionally are case insensitive), so some old software applications would permit only uppercase names to be entered. Some such applications were later ported to MS Windows but retain the uppercase network resource naming conventions because customers are familiar with that. We made the decision to name shares and print queues for this application in uppercase for the same reason. Nothing would break if we were to use lowercase names, but that decision might create a need to retrain staff — something well avoided at this time.

NetBIOS networking does not print directly to a printer. Instead, all printing is done to a print queue. The print spooling system is responsible for communicating with the physical printer. In this example, therefore, the resource called `PRINTQ` really is just a print queue. The name of the print queue is representative of the device to which the print spooler delivers print jobs.

1.2.2.2   Implementation

It is assumed that the server is fully installed and ready for configuration of Samba 3.0.20 and for necessary support files. All TCP/IP addresses should be hard-coded. In our case, the IP address of the Samba server is 192.168.1.1 and the netmask is 255.255.255.0. The hostname of the server used is `server`. The office network is built as shown in Figure 1.1.

SAMBA SERVER CONFIGURATION

1. Create a group account for office file storage:

   ```
   root#  groupadd office
   ```

2. Create a user account for office file storage:

   ```
   root#  useradd -m abmas
   root#  passwd abmas
   Changing password for abmas.
   New password: XXXXXXXX
   ```

Figure 1.1 Charity Administration Office Network

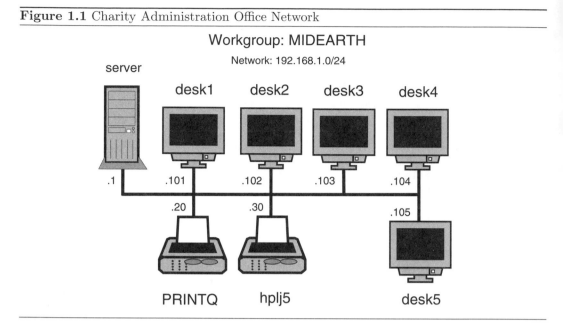

Workgroup: MIDEARTH

Network: 192.168.1.0/24

```
Re-enter new password: XXXXXXXX
Password changed
```

where XXXXXXXX is a secret password.

3. Use the 3-Ware IDE RAID Controller firmware utilities to configure the four 200GB drives as a single RAID level 5 drive, with one drive set aside as the hot spare. (Refer to the 3-Ware RAID Controller Manual for the manufacturer's preferred procedure.) The resulting drive has a capacity of approximately 500GB of usable space.

4. Create a mount point for the file system that can be used to store all data files. Create a directory called /data:

```
root#  mkdir /data
root#  chmod 755 /data
```

The 755 permissions on this directory (mount point) permit the owner to read, write, and execute, and the group and everyone else to read and execute only.

5. Use SUSE Linux system tools (refer to the SUSE Administrators Guide for correct procedures) to format the partition with a suitable file system. The reiserfs file system is suitable. Configure this drive to automount using the /data directory as the mount point. It must be mounted before proceeding.

6. Under the directory called /data, create two directories named ftmfiles and officefiles, and set ownership and permissions:

```
root#   mkdir -p /data/{ftmfiles,officefiles/{letters,invitations,misc}}
root#   chown -R abmas:office /data
root#   chmod -R ug+rwxs,o-w,o+rx /data
```

These demonstrate compound operations. The **mkdir** command creates in one step these directories:

```
/data/fmtfiles
/data/officefiles
/data/officefiles/letters
/data/officefiles/invitations
/data/officefiles/misc
```

The **chown** operation sets the owner to the user **abmas** and the group to **office** on all directories just created. It recursively sets the permissions so that the owner and group have SUID/SGID with read, write, and execute permission, and everyone else has read and execute permission. This means that all files and directories are created with the same owner and group as the directory in which they are created. Any new directories created still have the same owner, group, and permissions as the directory they are in. This should eliminate all permissions-based file access problems. For more information on this subject, refer to TOSHARG2[5] or refer to the UNIX man page for the **chmod** and the **chown** commands.

7. Install the smb.conf file shown in Example 1.2.2 in the /etc/samba directory. This newer smb.conf file uses user-mode security and is more suited to the mode of operation of Samba-3 than the older share-mode security configuration that was shown in the first edition of this book. Note: If you want to use the older-style configuration that uses share-mode security, you can install the file shown in Example 1.2.3 in the /etc/samba directory.

8. We must ensure that the **smbd** can resolve the name of the Samba server to its IP address. Verify that the /etc/hosts file contains the following entry:

```
192.168.1.1 server
```

9. Configure the printers with the IP address as shown in Figure 1.1. Follow the instructions in the manufacturer's manual to permit printing to port 9100 so that the CUPS spooler can print using raw mode protocols.

10. Configure the CUPS Print Queues:

```
root#   lpadmin -p PRINTQ -v socket://192.168.1.20:9100 -E
```

---

[5]The Official Samba-3 HOWTO and Reference Guide, Chapter 15, File, Directory and Share Access Controls.

```
root#  lpadmin -p hplj5 -v socket://192.168.1.30:9100 -E
```

This creates the necessary print queues with no assigned print filter.

11. Edit the file /etc/cups/mime.convs to uncomment the line:

```
application/octet-stream     application/vnd.cups-raw        0       -
```

12. Edit the file /etc/cups/mime.types to uncomment the line:

```
application/octet-stream
```

13. Use the standard system tool to start Samba and CUPS to configure them to restart automatically at every system reboot. For example,

```
root#   chkconfig smb on
root#   chkconfig cups on
root#   /etc/rc.d/init.d/smb restart
root#   /etc/rc.d/init.d/cups restart
```

WINDOWS CLIENT CONFIGURATION

1. Configure clients to the network settings shown in Figure 1.1.

2. Ensure that the netmask used on the Windows clients matches that used for the Samba server. All clients must have the same netmask, such as 255.255.255.0.

3. On all Windows clients, set the WINS Server address to 192.168.1.1, the IP address of the server.

4. Set the workgroup name on all clients to MIDEARTH.

5. Install the "Client for Microsoft Networks." Ensure that the only option enabled in its properties is the option "Logon and restore network connections."

6. Click **OK** when you are prompted to reboot the system. Reboot the system, then log on using any username and password you choose.

7. Verify on each client that the machine called SERVER is visible in **My Network Places**, that it is possible to connect to it and see the share **office**, and that it is possible to open that share to reveal its contents.

8. Disable password caching on all Windows 9x/Me machines using the registry change file shown in Example 1.2.4. Be sure to remove all files that have the PWL extension that are in the C:\WINDOWS directory.

   The best way to apply this change is to save the patch in a file called ME-dpwc.reg and then execute:

Example 1.2.2 Charity Administration Office smb.conf New-style File

```
# Global Parameters - Newer Configuration
[global]
        workgroup = MIDEARTH
        printing = CUPS
        printcap name = CUPS
        map to guest = Bad User
        show add printer wizard = No
        wins support = yes
[FTMFILES]
        comment = Funds Tracking & Management Files
        path = /data/ftmfiles
        read only = No
        force user = abmas
        force group = office
        guest ok = Yes
        nt acl support = No
[office]
        comment = General Office Files
        path = /data/officefiles
        read only = No
        force user = abmas
        force group = office
        guest ok = Yes
        nt acl support = No
[printers]
        comment = Print Temporary Spool Configuration
        path = /var/spool/samba
        printable = Yes
        guest ok = Yes
        use client driver = Yes
        browseable = No
```

```
C:\WINDOWS: regedit ME-dpwc.reg
```

9. Instruct all users to log onto the workstation using a name and password of their own choosing. The Samba server has been configured to ignore the username and password given.

10. On each Windows Me workstation, configure a network drive mapping to drive G: that redirects to the uniform naming convention (UNC) resource \\server\office. Make this a permanent drive connection:

   (a) **My Network → Map Network Drive...**

   (b) In the box labeled "Drive:", type G.

Example 1.2.3 Charity Administration Office smb.conf Old-style File

```
# Global Parameters - Older Style Configuration
[global]
        workgroup = MIDEARTH
        security = SHARE
        printing = CUPS
        printcap name = CUPS
        disable spoolss = Yes
        show add printer wizard = No
        wins support = yes
[FTMFILES]
        comment = Funds Tracking & Management Files
        path = /data/ftmfiles
        read only = No
        force user = abmas
        force group = office
        guest ok = Yes
        nt acl support = No
[office]
        comment = General Office Files
        path = /data/officefiles
        read only = No
        force user = abmas
        force group = office
        guest ok = Yes
        nt acl support = No
[printers]
        comment = Print Temporary Spool Configuration
        path = /var/spool/samba
        printable = Yes
        guest ok = Yes
        use client driver = Yes
        browseable = No
```

(c) In the box labeled "Path:", enter \\server\officefiles.

(d) Click **Reconnect at logon**. Click **OK**.

11. On each workstation, install the FTM software following the manufacturer's instructions.

   (a) During installation, you are prompted for the name of the Windows 98 server. Enter the name SERVER.

   (b) You are prompted for the name of the data share. The prompt defaults to FTMFILES. Press enter to accept the default value.

   (c) You are now prompted for the print queue name. The default prompt is the name of the server you entered (SERVER as follows: \\SERVER\PRINTQ). Simply

---

Example 1.2.4 Windows Me — Registry Edit File: Disable Password Caching

---

```
REGEDIT4

[HKEY_LOCAL_MACHINE\SOFTWARE\Microsoft\
   Windows\CurrentVersion\Policies\Network]
   "DisablePwdCaching"=dword:00000001
```

---

accept the default and press enter to continue. The software now completes the installation.

12. Install an office automation software package of the customer's choice. Either Microsoft Office 2003 Standard or OpenOffice 1.1.0 suffices for any functions the office may need to perform. Repeat this on each workstation.

13. Install a printer on each workstation using the following steps:

    (a) Click **Start** → **Settings** → **Printers**+**Add Printer**+**Next**. Do not click **Network printer**. Ensure that **Local printer** is selected.

    (b) Click **Next**. In the Manufacturer: panel, select HP. In the Printers: panel, select the printer called HP LaserJet 5/5M Postscript. Click **Next**.

    (c) In the Available ports: panel, select FILE:. Accept the default printer name by clicking **Next**. When asked, "Would you like to print a test page?", click **No**. Click **Finish**.

    (d) You may be prompted for the name of a file to print to. If so, close the dialog panel. Right-click **HP LaserJet 5/5M Postscript** → **Properties** → **Details (Tab)** → **Add Port**.

    (e) In the Network panel, enter the name of the print queue on the Samba server as follows: \\SERVER\hplj5. Click **OK**+**OK** to complete the installation.

    (f) It is a good idea to test the functionality of the complete installation before handing the newly configured network over to the Charity Administration Office for production use.

1.2.2.3   Validation

Use the same validation process as was followed in Section 1.2.1.3.

1.2.3   Accounting Office

Abmas Accounting is a 40-year-old family-run business. There are nine permanent computer users. The network clients were upgraded two years ago. All computers run Windows 2000 Professional. This year the server will be upgraded from an old Windows NT4 server (actually running Windows NT4 Workstation, which worked fine for fewer than 10 users) that has run in workgroup (standalone) mode, to a new Linux server running Samba.

The office does not want a Domain Server. Mr. Alan Meany wants to keep the Windows 2000 Professional clients running as workgroup machines so that any staff member can take a machine home and keep working. It has worked well so far, and your task is to replace the old server. All users have their own workstation logon (you configured it that way when the machines were installed). Mr. Meany wants the new system to operate the same way as the old Windows NT4 server — users cannot access each others' files, but he can access everyone's files. Each person's work files are in a separate share on the server. Users log on to their Windows workstation with their username and enter an assigned password; they do not need to enter a password when accessing their files on the server.

The new server will run Red Hat Fedora Core2. You should install Samba-3.0.20 and copy all files from the old system to the new one. The existing Windows NT4 server has a parallel port HP LaserJet 4 printer that is shared by all. The printer driver is installed on each workstation. You must not change anything on the workstations. Mr. Meany gave instructions to replace the server, "but leave everything else alone to avoid staff unrest."

You have tried to educate Mr. Meany and found that he has no desire to understand networking. He believes that Windows for Workgroups 3.11 was "the best server Microsoft ever sold" and that Windows NT and 2000 are "too fang-dangled complex!"

1.2.3.1   Dissection and Discussion

The requirements of this network installation are not unusual. The staff are not interested in the details of networking. Passwords are never changed. In this example solution, we demonstrate the use of User Mode security in a simple context. Directories should be set SGID to ensure that members of a common group can access the contents. Each user has his or her own share to which only they can connect. Mr. Meany's share will be a top-level directory above the share point for each employee. Mr. Meany is a member of the same group as his staff and can access their work files. The well-used HP LaserJet 4 is available as a service called `hplj`.

You have finished configuring the new hardware and have just completed installation of Red Hat Fedora Core2. Roll up your sleeves and let's get to work.

1.2.3.2   Implementation

The workstations have fixed IP addresses. The old server runs Windows NT4 Workstation, so it cannot be running as a WINS server. It is best that the new configuration preserves the same configuration. The office does not use Internet access, so security really is not an issue.

The core information regarding the users, their passwords, the directory share point, and the share name is given in Table 1.1. The overall network topology is shown in Figure 1.2. All machines have been configured as indicated prior to the start of Samba configuration. The following prescriptive steps may now commence.

MIGRATION FROM WINDOWS NT4 WORKSTATION SYSTEM TO SAMBA-3

Figure 1.2 Accounting Office Network Topology

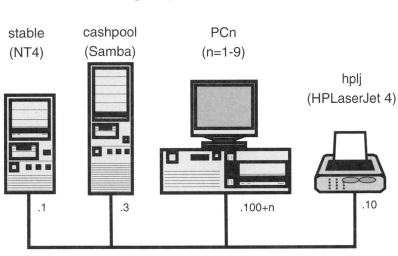

Workgroup: BILLMORE

stable (NT4) — .1
cashpool (Samba) — .3
PCn (n=1-9) — .100+n
hplj (HPLaserJet 4) — .10

Network: 192.168.1.0/24

Table 1.1 Accounting Office Network Information

User	Login-ID	Password	Share Name	Directory	Wkst
Alan Meany	alan	alm1961	alan	/data	PC1
James Meany	james	jimm1962	james	/data/james	PC2
Jeannie Meany	jeannie	jema1965	jeannie	/data/jeannie	PC3
Suzy Millicent	suzy	suzy1967	suzy	/data/suzy	PC4
Ursula Jenning	ujen	ujen1974	ursula	/data/ursula	PC5
Peter Pan	peter	pete1984	peter	/data/peter	PC6
Dale Roland	dale	dale1986	dale	/data/dale	PC7
Bertrand E Paoletti	eric	eric1993	eric	/data/eric	PC8
Russell Lewis	russ	russ2001	russell	/data/russell	PC9

1. Rename the old server from CASHPOOL to STABLE by logging onto the console as the Administrator. Restart the machine following system prompts.

2. Name the new server CASHPOOL using the standard configuration method. Restart the machine following system prompts.

3. Install the latest Samba-3 binary Red Hat Linux RPM that is available from the Samba FTP site.

4. Add a group account for the office to use. Execute the following:

```
root#  groupadd accts
```

5. Install the smb.conf file shown[6] in Example 1.2.5.

6. For each user who uses this system (see Table 1.1), execute the following:

```
root#  useradd -m -G accts -c "Name of User" "LoginID"
root#  passwd "LoginID"
Changing password for user "LoginID"
New Password: XXXXXXXX <-- the password from the table
Retype new password: XXXXXXXX
root#  smbpasswd -a "LoginID"
New SMB password: XXXXXXXX <-- the password from the table
Retype new SMB password: XXXXXXXX
Added user "LoginID"
```

7. Create the directory structure for the file shares by executing the following:

```
root#  mkdir -p /data
root#  chown alan /data
root#  for i in james suzy ursula peter dale eric jeannie russell
> do
>   mkdir -p /data/$i
>   chown $i /data/$i
> done
root#  chgrp -R accts /data
root#  chmod -R ug+rwxs,o-r+x /data
```

The data storage structure is now prepared for use.

8. Configure the CUPS Print Queues:

```
root#  lpadmin -p hplj -v parallel:/dev/lp0 -E
```

This creates the necessary print queues with no assigned print filter.

9. Edit the file /etc/cups/mime.convs to uncomment the line:

```
application/octet-stream      application/vnd.cups-raw      0      -
```

---

[6]This example uses the *smbpasswd* file in an obtuse way, since the use of the *passdb backend* has not been specified in the smb.conf file. This means that you are depending on correct default behavior.

10. Edit the file /etc/cups/mime.types to uncomment the line:

    ```
    application/octet-stream
    ```

11. Use the standard system tool to start Samba and CUPS to configure them to restart automatically at every system reboot. For example,

    ```
    root#   chkconfig smb on
    root#   chkconfig cups on
    root#   /etc/rc.d/init.d/smb restart
    root#   /etc/rc.d/init.d/cups restart
    ```

12. On Alan's workstation, use Windows Explorer to migrate the files from the old server to the new server. The new server should appear in the **Network Neighborhood** with the name of the old server (CASHPOOL).

    (a) Log on to Alan's workstation as the user alan.

    (b) Launch a second instance of Windows Explorer and navigate to the share called **files** on the server called **STABLE**.

    (c) Click in the right panel, and press **Ctrl-A** to select all files and directories. Press **Ctrl-C** to instruct Windows that you wish to copy all selected items.

    (d) Launch the Windows Explorer, and navigate to the share called **files** on the server called **CASHPOOL**. Click in the right panel, and then press **Ctrl-V** to commence the copying process.

13. Verify that the files are being copied correctly from the Windows NT4 machine to the Samba-3 server. This is best done on the Samba-3 server. Check the contents of the directory tree under /data by executing the following command:

    ```
    root#   ls -aR /data
    ```

    Make certain to check the ownership and permissions on all files. If in doubt, execute the following:

    ```
    root#   chown alan /data
    root#   for i in james suzy ursula peter dale eric jeannie russell
    >   do
    >     chown $i /data/$i
    >   done
    root#   chgrp -R accts /data
    root#   chmod -R ug+rwxs,o-r+x /data
    ```

14. The migration of all data should now be complete. It is time to validate the installation. For this, you should make sure all applications, including printing, work before asking the customer to test drive the new network.

Example 1.2.5 Accounting Office Network smb.conf Old Style Configuration File

```
# Global parameters
[global]
        workgroup = BILLMORE
        printcap name = CUPS
        disable spoolss = Yes
        show add printer wizard = No
        printing = cups
[files]
        comment = Work area files
        path = /data/%U
        read only = No
[master]
        comment = Master work area files
        path = /data
        valid users = alan
        read only = No
[printers]
        comment = Print Temporary Spool Configuration
        path = /var/spool/samba
        printable = Yes
        guest ok = Yes
        use client driver = Yes
        browseable = No
```

1.3   Questions and Answers

The following questions and answers draw from the examples in this chapter. Many design decisions are impacted by the configurations chosen. The intent is to expose some of the hidden implications.

F.A.Q.

1. **Q:** *What makes an anonymous Samba server more simple than a non-anonymous Samba server?*
A: In the anonymous server, the only account used is the `guest` account. In a non-anonymous configuration, it is necessary to add real user accounts to both the UNIX system and to the Samba configuration. Non-anonymous servers require additional administration.

2. **Q:** *How is the operation of the parameter* `force user` *different from setting the root directory of the share SUID?*
A: The parameter `force user` causes all operations on the share to assume the UID of the forced user. The new default GID that applies is the primary GID of the forced user. This gives all users of this resource the actual privilege of the forced user.

When a directory is set SUID, the operating system forces files that are written within it to be owned by the owner of the directory. While this happens, the user who is using the share has only the level of privilege he or she is assigned within the operating system context.

The parameter `force user` has potential security implications that go beyond the actual share root directory. Be careful and wary of using this parameter.

3. **Q:** *When would you both use the per share parameter* `force user` *and set the share root directory SUID?*
A: You would use both parameters when it is necessary to guarantee that all share handling operations are conducted as the forced user, while all file and directory creation are done as the SUID directory owner.

4. **Q:** *What is better about CUPS printing than LPRng printing?*
A: CUPS is a print spooling system that has integrated remote management facilities, provides completely automated print processing/preprocessing, and can be configured to automatically apply print preprocessing filters to ensure that a print job submitted is correctly rendered for the target printer. CUPS includes an image file RIP that supports printing of image files to non-PostScript printers. CUPS has lots of bells and whistles and is more like a supercharged MS Windows NT/200x print monitor and processor. Its complexity can be eliminated or turbocharged to suit any fancy.

The LPRng software is an enhanced, extended, and portable implementation of the Berkeley LPR print spooler functionality. It provides the same interface and meets RFC1179 requirements. LPRng can be configured to act like CUPS, but it is in principle a replacement for the old Berkeley lpr/lpd spooler. LPRng is generally preferred by those who are familiar with Berkeley lpr/lpd.

Which spooling system is better is a matter of personal taste. It depends on what you want to do and how you want to do it and manage it. Most modern Linux systems ship with CUPS as the default print management system.

5. **Q:** *When should Windows client IP addresses be hard-coded?*
A: When there are few MS Windows clients, little client change, no mobile users, and users are not inclined to tamper with network settings, it is a safe and convenient matter to hard-code Windows client TCP/IP settings. Given that it is possible to lock down the Windows desktop and remove user ability to access network configuration controls, fixed configuration eliminates the need for a DHCP server. This reduces maintenance overheads and eliminates a possible point of network failure.

6. **Q:** *Under what circumstances is it best to use a DHCP server?*
A: In network configurations where there are mobile users, or where Windows client PCs move around (particularly between offices or between subnets), it makes complete sense to control all Windows client configurations using a DHCP server. Additionally, when users do tamper with the network settings, DHCP can be used to normalize all client settings.

One underappreciated benefit of using a DHCP server to assign all network client device TCP/IP settings is that it makes it a pain-free process to change network TCP/IP settings, change network addressing, or enhance the ability of client devices to benefit from new network services.

Another benefit of modern DHCP servers is their ability to register dynamically assigned IP addresses with the DNS server. The benefits of Dynamic DNS (DDNS) are considerable in a large Windows network environment.

7. **Q:** *What is the purpose of setting the parameter* **guest ok** *on a share?*
A: If this parameter is set to yes for a service, then no password is required to connect to the service. Privileges are those of the guest account.

8. **Q:** *When would you set the global parameter* **disable spoolss***?*
A: Setting this parameter to **Yes** disables Samba's support for the SPOOLSS set of MS-RPCs and yields behavior identical to Samba 2.0.x. Windows NT/2000 clients can downgrade to using LanMan style printing commands. Windows 9x/Me are unaffected by the parameter. However, this disables the ability to upload printer drivers to a Samba server via the Windows NT/200x Add Printer Wizard or by using the NT printer properties dialog window. It also disables the capability of Windows NT/200x clients to download print drivers from the Samba host on demand. Be extremely careful about setting this parameter.

The alternate parameter **use client driver** applies only to Windows NT/200x clients. It has no effect on Windows 95/98/Me clients. When serving a printer to Windows NT/200x clients without first installing a valid printer driver on the Samba host, the client is required to install a local printer driver. From this point on, the client treats the printer as a local printer and not a network printer connection. This is much the same behavior that occurs when **disable spoolss = yes**.

Under normal circumstances, the NT/200x client attempts to open the network printer using MS-RPC. Because the client considers the printer to be local, it attempts to issue the **OpenPrinterEx()** call requesting access rights associated with the logged on user. If the user possesses local administrator rights but not root privilege on the Samba host (often the case), the **OpenPrinterEx()** call fails. The result is that the client now displays an "Access Denied; Unable to connect" message in the printer queue window (even though jobs may be printed successfully). This parameter MUST not be enabled on a print share that has a valid print driver installed on the Samba server.

9. **Q:** *Why would you disable password caching on Windows 9x/Me clients?*

A: Windows 9x/Me workstations that are set at default (password caching enabled) store the username and password in files located in the Windows master directory. Such files can be scavenged (read off a client machine) and decrypted, thus revealing the user's access credentials for all systems the user may have accessed. It is most insecure to allow any Windows 9x/Me client to operate with password caching enabled.

10. **Q:** *The example of Abmas Accounting uses User Mode security. How does this provide anonymous access?*

A: The example used does not provide anonymous access. Since the clients are all Windows 2000 Professional, and given that users are logging onto their machines, by default the client attempts to connect to a remote server using currently logged in user credentials. By ensuring that the user's login ID and password are the same as those set on the Samba server, access is transparent and does not require separate user authentication.

Chapter 2

SMALL OFFICE NETWORKING

Chapter 1, "No-Frills Samba Servers" focused on the basics of simple yet effective network solutions. Network administrators who take pride in their work (that's most of us, right?) take care to deliver what our users want, but not too much more. If we make things too complex, we confound our users and increase costs of network ownership. A professional network manager avoids the temptation to put too much pizazz into the way that the network operates. Some creativity is helpful, but keep it under control — good advice that the following two scenarios illustrate.

In one case the network administrator of a mid-sized company spent three months building a new network to replace an old Netware server. What he delivered had all the bells and whistles he could muster. There were a few teething problems during the changeover, nothing serious but a little disruptive all the same. Users were exposed to many changes at once. The network administrator was asked to resign two months after implementing the new system because so many staff complained they had lost time and were not happy with the new network. Everything was automated, and he delivered more features than any advanced user could think of. He was just too smart for his own good.

In the case of the other company, a new network manager was appointed to oversee the replacement of a LanTastic network with an MS Windows NT 4.0 network. He had the replacement installed and operational within two weeks. Before installation and changeover, he called a meeting to explain to all users what was going to happen, how it would affect them, and that he would be available 24 hours a day to help them transition. One week after conversion, he held another meeting asking for cooperation in the introduction of a few new features that would help to make life easier. Network users were thrilled with the help he provided. The network he implemented was nowhere near as complex as in the first example, had fewer features, and yet he had happy users. Months later he was still adding new innovations. He always asked the users if a particular feature was what they wanted. He asked his boss for a raise and got it. He often told me, "Always keep a few new tricks up your sleeves for when you need them." Was he smart? You decide. Let's get on with our next exercise.

2.1   Introduction

Abmas Accounting has grown. Mr. Meany likes you and says he knew you were the right person for the job. That's why he asked you to install the new server. The past few months have been hard work. You advised Mr. Meany that it is time for a change. Abmas now has 52 users, having acquired an investment consulting business recently. The new users were added to the network without any problems.

Some of the Windows clients are nearly past their use-by date. You found damaged and unusable software on some of the workstations that came with the acquired business and found some machines in need of both hardware and software maintenance.

2.1.1   Assignment Tasks

Mr. Meany is retiring in 12 months. Before he goes, he wants you to help ensure that the business is running efficiently. Many of the new staff want notebook computers. They visit customer business premises and need to use local network facilities; these users are technically competent. The company uses a business application that requires Windows XP Professional. In short, a complete client upgrade is about to happen. Mr. Meany told you that he is working on another business acquisition and that by the time he retires there will be 80 to 100 users.

Mr. Meany is not concerned about security. He wants to make it easier for staff to do their work. He has hired you to help him appoint a full-time network manager before he retires. Above all, he says he is investing in the ability to grow. He is determined to live his lifelong dream and hand the business over to a bright and capable executive who can make things happen. This means your network design must cope well with growth.

In a few months, Abmas will require an Internet connection for email and so that staff can easily obtain software updates. Mr. Meany is warming up to the installation of antivirus software but is not yet ready to approve this expense. He told you to spend the money a virus scanner costs on better quality notebook computers for mobile users.

One of Mr. Meany's golfing partners convinced him to buy new laser printers, one black only, the other a color laser printer. Staff support the need for a color printer so they can present more attractive proposals and reports.

Mr. Meany also asked if it would be possible for one of the staff to manage user accounts from the Windows desktop. That person will be responsible for basic operations.

2.2   Dissection and Discussion

What are the key requirements in this business example? A quick review indicates a need for

- Scalability, from 52 to over 100 users in 12 months
- Mobile computing capability

- Improved reliability and usability

- Easier administration

In this instance the installed Linux system is assumed to be a Red Hat Linux Fedora Core2 server (as in Section 1.2.3).

2.2.1   Technical Issues

It is time to implement a domain security environment. You will use the `smbpasswd` (default) backend. You should implement a DHCP server. There is no need to run DNS at this time, but the system will use WINS. The domain name will be `BILLMORE`. This time, the name of the server will be `SLEETH`.

All printers will be configured as DHCP clients. The DHCP server will assign the printer a fixed IP address by way of its Ethernet interface (MAC) address. See Example 2.3.2.

NOTE

The `smb.conf` file you are creating in this exercise can be used with equal effectiveness with Samba-2.2.x series releases. This is deliberate so that in the next chapter it is possible to start with the installation that you have created here, migrate it to a Samba-3 configuration, and then secure the system further. Configurations following this one utilize features that may not be supported in Samba-2.2.x releases. However, you should note that the examples in each chapter start with the assumption that a fresh new installation is being effected.

Later on, when the Internet connection is implemented, you will add DNS as well as other enhancements. It is important that you plan accordingly.

You have split the network into two separate areas. Each has its own Ethernet switch. There are 20 users on the accounting network and 32 users on the financial services network. The server has two network interfaces, one serving each network. The network printers will be located in a central area. You plan to install the new printers and keep the old printer in use also.

You will provide separate file storage areas for each business entity. The old system will go away, accounting files will be handled under a single directory, and files will be stored under customer name, not under a personal work area. Staff will be made responsible for file location, so the old share point must be maintained.

Given that DNS will not be used, you will configure WINS name resolution for UNIX hostname name resolution.

It is necessary to map Windows Domain Groups to UNIX groups. It is advisable to also map Windows Local Groups to UNIX groups. Additionally, the two key staff groups in the firm are accounting staff and financial services staff. For these, it is necessary to create UNIX groups as well as Windows Domain Groups.

In the sample `smb.conf` file, you have configured Samba to call the UNIX **groupadd** to add group entries. This utility does not permit the addition of group names that contain uppercase characters or spaces. This is considered a bug. The **groupadd** is part of the **shadow-utils** open source software package. A later release of this package may have been patched to resolve this bug. If your operating platform has this bug, it means that attempts to add a Windows Domain Group that has either a space or uppercase characters in it will fail. See *TOSHARG2*, Chapter 11, Section 11.3.1, Example 11.1, for more information.

Vendor-supplied printer drivers will be installed on each client. The CUPS print spooler on the UNIX host will be operated in `raw` mode.

2.2.2   Political Issues

Mr. Meany is an old-school manager. He sets the rules and wants to see compliance. He is willing to spend money on things he believes are of value. You need more time to convince him of real priorities.

Go ahead, buy better notebooks. Wouldn't it be neat if they happened to be supplied with antivirus software? Above all, demonstrate good purchase value and remember to make your users happy.

2.3   Implementation

In this example, the assumption is made that this server is being configured from a clean start. The alternate approach could be to demonstrate the migration of the system that is documented in Section 1.2.3.2 to meet the new requirements. The decision to treat this case, as with future examples, as a new installation is based on the premise that you can determine the migration steps from the information provided in Chapter 9, "Migrating NT4 Domain to Samba-3". Additionally, a fresh installation makes the example easier to follow.

Each user will be given a home directory on the UNIX system, which will be available as a private share. Two additional shares will be created, one for the accounting department and the other for the financial services department. Network users will be given access to these shares by way of group membership.

UNIX group membership is the primary mechanism by which Windows Domain users will be granted rights and privileges within the Windows environment.

The user **alanm** will be made the owner of all files. This will be preserved by setting the sticky bit (set UID/GID) on the top-level directories.

SERVER INSTALLATION STEPS

   1. Using UNIX/Linux system tools, name the server `sleeth`.

Figure 2.1 Abmas Accounting — 52-User Network Topology

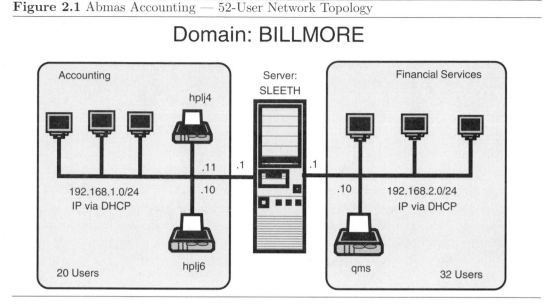

2. Place an entry for the machine `sleeth` in the `/etc/hosts`. The printers are network attached, so there should be entries for the network printers also. An example `/etc/hosts` file is shown here:

```
192.168.1.1     sleeth sleeth1
192.168.2.1     sleeth2
192.168.1.10    hplj6
192.168.1.11    hplj4
192.168.2.10    qms
```

3. Install the Samba-3 binary RPM from the Samba-Team FTP site.

4. Install the ISC DHCP server using the UNIX/Linux system tools available to you.

5. Because Samba will be operating over two network interfaces and clients on each side may want to be able to reach clients on the other side, it is imperative that IP forwarding is enabled. Use the system tool of your choice to enable IP forwarding. In the absence of such a tool on the Linux system, add to the `/etc/rc.d/rc.local` file an entry as follows:

```
echo 1 > /proc/sys/net/ipv4/ip_forward
```

This causes the Linux kernel to forward IP packets so that it acts as a router.

6. Install the `smb.conf` file as shown in Example 2.3.3 and Example 2.3.4. Combine these two examples to form a single `/etc/samba/smb.conf` file.

7. Add the user **root** to the Samba password backend:

```
root#  smbpasswd -a root
New SMB password: XXXXXXX
Retype new SMB password: XXXXXXX
root#
```

This is the Windows Domain Administrator password. Never delete this account from the password backend after Windows Domain Groups have been initialized. If you delete this account, your system is crippled. You cannot restore this account, and your Samba server can no longer be administered.

8. Create the username map file to permit the **root** account to be called **Administrator** from the Windows network environment. To do this, create the file **/etc/samba/ smbusers** with the following contents:

```
####
# User mapping file
####
# File Format
# -----------
# Unix_ID = Windows_ID
#
# Examples:
# root = Administrator
# janes = "Jane Smith"
# jimbo = Jim Bones
#
# Note: If the name contains a space it must be double quoted.
#       In the example above the name 'jimbo' will be mapped to Windows
#       user names 'Jim' and 'Bones' because the space was not quoted.
######################################################################
root = Administrator
####
# End of File
####
```

9. Create and map Windows Domain Groups to UNIX groups. A sample script is provided in Example 2.3.1. Create a file containing this script. We called ours **/etc/ samba/initGrps.sh**. Set this file so it can be executed, and then execute the script. Sample output should be as follows:

```
root#  chmod 755 initGrps.sh
root#  cd /etc/samba
root#  ./initGrps.sh
```

Example 2.3.1 Script to Map Windows NT Groups to UNIX Groups

```bash
#!/bin/bash
#
# initGrps.sh
#

# Create UNIX groups
groupadd acctsdep
groupadd finsrvcs

# Map Windows Domain Groups to UNIX groups
net groupmap modify ntgroup="Domain Admins"  unixgroup=root
net groupmap modify ntgroup="Domain Users"   unixgroup=users
net groupmap modify ntgroup="Domain Guests"  unixgroup=nobody

# Add Functional Domain Groups
net groupmap add ntgroup="Accounts Dept"  unixgroup=acctsdep type=d
net groupmap add ntgroup="Financial Services" unixgroup=finsrvcs type=d
```

```
Updated mapping entry for Domain Admins
Updated mapping entry for Domain Users
Updated mapping entry for Domain Guests
No rid or sid specified, choosing algorithmic mapping
Successfully added group Accounts Dept to the mapping db
No rid or sid specified, choosing algorithmic mapping
Successfully added group Domain Guests to the mapping db

root#  cd /etc/samba
root#  net groupmap list | sort
Account Operators (S-1-5-32-548) -> -1
Accounts Dept (S-1-5-21-194350-25496802-3394589-2003) -> acctsdep
Administrators (S-1-5-32-544) -> -1
Backup Operators (S-1-5-32-551) -> -1
Domain Admins (S-1-5-21-194350-25496802-3394589-512) -> root
Domain Guests (S-1-5-21-194350-25496802-3394589-514) -> nobody
Domain Users (S-1-5-21-194350-25496802-3394589-513) -> users
Financial Services (S-1-5-21-194350-25496802-3394589-2005) -> finsrvcs
Guests (S-1-5-32-546) -> -1
Power Users (S-1-5-32-547) -> -1
Print Operators (S-1-5-32-550) -> -1
Replicators (S-1-5-32-552) -> -1
System Operators (S-1-5-32-549) -> -1
Users (S-1-5-32-545) -> -1
```

10. For each user who needs to be given a Windows Domain account, make an entry in the `/etc/passwd` file as well as in the Samba password backend. Use the system tool of your choice to create the UNIX system accounts, and use the Samba **smbpasswd** program to create the Domain user accounts. There are a number of tools for user management under UNIX, such as **useradd** and **adduser**, as well as a plethora of custom tools. With the tool of your choice, create a home directory for each user.

11. Using the preferred tool for your UNIX system, add each user to the UNIX groups created previously, as necessary. File system access control will be based on UNIX group membership.

12. Create the directory mount point for the disk subsystem that is mounted to provide data storage for company files. In this case the mount point is indicated in the `smb.conf` file is `/data`. Format the file system as required, mount the formatted file system partition using **mount**, and make the appropriate changes in `/etc/fstab`.

13. Create the top-level file storage directories are follows:

```
root#   mkdir -p /data/{accounts,finsvcs}
root#   chown -R root:root /data
root#   chown -R alanm:accounts /data/accounts
root#   chown -R alanm:finsvcs /data/finsvcs
root#   chmod -R ug+rwx,o+rx-w /data
```

Each department is responsible for creating its own directory structure within its share. The directory root of the **accounts** share is `/data/accounts`. The directory root of the **finsvcs** share is `/data/finsvcs`.

14. Configure the printers with the IP addresses as shown in Figure 2.1. Follow the instructions in the manufacturers' manuals to permit printing to port 9100. This allows the CUPS spooler to print using raw mode protocols.

15. Configure the CUPS Print Queues as follows:

```
root#   lpadmin -p hplj4 -v socket://192.168.1.11:9100 -E
root#   lpadmin -p hplj6 -v socket://192.168.1.10:9100 -E
root#   lpadmin -p qms -v socket://192.168.2.10:9100 -E
```

This creates the necessary print queues with no assigned print filter.

16. Edit the file `/etc/cups/mime.convs` to uncomment the line:

```
application/octet-stream     application/vnd.cups-raw     0     -
```

17. Edit the file `/etc/cups/mime.types` to uncomment the line:

```
application/octet-stream
```

18. Using your favorite system editor, create an `/etc/dhcpd.conf` with the contents as shown in Example 2.3.2.

19. Use the standard system tool to start Samba and CUPS and configure them to start automatically at every system reboot. For example,

```
root#  chkconfig dhcp on
root#  chkconfig smb on
root#  chkconfig cups on
root#  /etc/rc.d/init.d/dhcp restart
root#  /etc/rc.d/init.d/smb restart
root#  /etc/rc.d/init.d/cups restart
```

20. Configure the name service switch (NSS) to handle WINS-based name resolution. Since this system does not use a DNS server, it is safe to remove this option from the NSS configuration. Edit the `/etc/nsswitch.conf` file so that the `hosts:` entry looks like this:

```
hosts:    files wins
```

2.3.1   Validation

Does everything function as it ought? That is the key question at this point. Here are some simple steps to validate your Samba server configuration.

VALIDATION STEPS

1. If your `smb.conf` file has bogus options or parameters, this may cause Samba to refuse to start. The first step should always be to validate the contents of this file by running:

```
root#  testparm -s
Load smb config files from smb.conf
Processing section "[homes]"
Processing section "[printers]"
Processing section "[netlogon]"
Processing section "[accounts]"
Processing section "[service]"
Loaded services file OK.
# Global parameters
[global]
        workgroup = BILLMORE
```

```
            passwd chat = *New*Password* \
        %n\n *Re-enter*new*password* %n\n *Password*changed*
            username map = /etc/samba/smbusers
            syslog = 0
            name resolve order = wins bcast hosts
            printcap name = CUPS
            show add printer wizard = No
            add user script = /usr/sbin/useradd -m '%u'
            delete user script = /usr/sbin/userdel -r '%u'
            add group script = /usr/sbin/groupadd '%g'
            delete group script = /usr/sbin/groupdel '%g'
            add user to group script = /usr/sbin/usermod -G '%g' '%u'
            add machine script = /usr/sbin/useradd
                -s /bin/false -d /var/lib/nobody '%u'
            logon script = scripts\logon.bat
            logon path =
            logon drive = X:
            domain logons = Yes
            preferred master = Yes
            wins support = Yes
    ...
### Remainder cut to save space ###
```

The inclusion of an invalid parameter (say one called dogbert) would generate an error as follows:

```
Unknown parameter encountered: "dogbert"
Ignoring unknown parameter "dogbert"
```

Clear away all errors before proceeding, and start or restart samba as necessary.

2. Check that the Samba server is running:

```
root#  ps ax | grep mbd
14244 ?         S       0:00 /usr/sbin/nmbd -D
14245 ?         S       0:00 /usr/sbin/nmbd -D
14290 ?         S       0:00 /usr/sbin/smbd -D

$rootprompt; ps ax | grep winbind
14293 ?         S       0:00 /usr/sbin/winbindd -B
14295 ?         S       0:00 /usr/sbin/winbindd -B
```

The **winbindd** daemon is running in split mode (normal), so there are also two instances of it. For more information regarding **winbindd**, see *TOSHARG2*, Chapter 23, Section 23.3. The single instance of **smbd** is normal.

3. Check that an anonymous connection can be made to the Samba server:

```
root#  smbclient -L localhost -U%

        Sharename       Type        Comment
        ---------       ----        -------
        netlogon        Disk        Network Logon Service
        accounts        Disk        Accounting Files
        finsvcs         Disk        Financial Service Files
        IPC$            IPC         IPC Service (Samba3)
        ADMIN$          IPC         IPC Service (Samba3)
        hplj4           Printer     Hewlett-Packard LaserJet 4
        hplj6           Printer     Hewlett-Packard LaserJet 6
        qms             Printer     QMS Magicolor Laser Printer XXXX


        Server                  Comment
        ---------               -------
        SLEETH                  Samba 3.0.20

        Workgroup               Master
        ---------               -------
        BILLMORE                SLEETH
```

This demonstrates that an anonymous listing of shares can be obtained. This is the equivalent of browsing the server from a Windows client to obtain a list of shares on the server. The -U% argument means to send a NULL username and a NULL password.

4. Verify that the printers have the IP addresses assigned in the DHCP server configuration file. The easiest way to do this is to ping the printer name. Immediately after the ping response has been received, execute **arp -a** to find the MAC address of the printer that has responded. Now you can compare the IP address and the MAC address of the printer with the configuration information in the /etc/dhcpd.conf file. They should, of course, match. For example,

```
root#  ping hplj4
PING hplj4 (192.168.1.11) 56(84) bytes of data.
64 bytes from hplj4 (192.168.1.11): icmp_seq=1 ttl=64 time=0.113 ms

root#  arp -a
hplj4 (192.168.1.11) at 08:00:46:7A:35:E4 [ether] on eth0
```

The MAC address 08:00:46:7A:35:E4 matches that specified for the IP address from which the printer has responded and the entry for it in the /etc/dhcpd.conf file.

5. Make an authenticated connection to the server using the **smbclient** tool:

```
root#  smbclient //sleeth/accounts -U alanm
Password: XXXXXXX
smb: \> dir
  .                              D          0  Sun Nov  9 01:28:34 2003
  ..                             D          0  Sat Aug 16 17:24:26 2003
  .mc                           DH          0  Sat Nov  8 21:57:38 2003
  .qt                           DH          0  Fri Sep  5 00:48:25 2003
  SMB                            D          0  Sun Oct 19 23:04:30 2003
  Documents                      D          0  Sat Nov  1 00:31:51 2003
  xpsp1a_en_x86.exe                 131170400  Sun Nov  2 01:25:44 2003

        65387 blocks of size 65536. 28590 blocks available
smb: \> q
```

WINDOWS XP PROFESSIONAL CLIENT CONFIGURATION

1. Configure clients to the network settings shown in Figure 2.1. All clients use DHCP for TCP/IP protocol stack configuration. DHCP configures all Windows clients to use the WINS Server address 192.168.1.1.

2. Join the Windows Domain called BILLMORE. Use the Domain Administrator username root and the SMB password you assigned to this account. A detailed step-by-step procedure for joining a Windows 200x/XP Professional client to a Windows Domain is given in Chapter 15, "A Collection of Useful Tidbits", Section 15.1. Reboot the machine as prompted and then log on using a Domain User account.

3. Verify on each client that the machine called SLEETH is visible in **My Network Places**, that it is possible to connect to it and see the shares **accounts** and **finsvcs**, and that it is possible to open that share to reveal its contents.

4. Instruct all users to log onto the workstation using their assigned username and password.

5. Install a printer on each using the following steps:

    (a) Click **Start** → **Settings** → **Printers**+**Add Printer**+**Next**. Do not click **Network printer**. Ensure that **Local printer** is selected.

    (b) Click **Next**. In the **Manufacturer:** panel, select HP. In the **Printers:** panel, select the printer called HP LaserJet 4. Click **Next**.

    (c) In the **Available ports:** panel, select FILE:. Accept the default printer name by clicking **Next**. When asked, "Would you like to print a test page?", click **No**. Click **Finish**.

    (d) You may be prompted for the name of a file to print to. If so, close the dialog panel. Right-click **HP LaserJet 4** → **Properties** → **Details (Tab)** → **Add Port**.

    (e) In the **Network** panel, enter the name of the print queue on the Samba server as follows: \\SERVER\hplj4. Click **OK**+**OK** to complete the installation.

(f) Repeat the printer installation steps above for the HP LaserJet 6 printer as well as for the QMS Magicolor XXXX laser printer.

2.3.2 Notebook Computers: A Special Case

As a network administrator, you already know how to create local machine accounts for Windows 200x/XP Professional systems. This is the preferred solution to provide continuity of work for notebook users so that absence from the office network environment does not become a barrier to productivity.

By creating a local machine account that has the same username and password as you create for that user in the Windows Domain environment, the user can log onto the machine locally and still transparently access network resources as if logged onto the domain itself. There are some trade-offs that mean that as the network is more tightly secured, it becomes necessary to modify Windows client configuration somewhat.

2.3.3 Key Points Learned

In this network design and implementation exercise, you created a Windows NT4-style Domain Controller using Samba-3.0.20. Following these guidelines, you experienced and implemented several important aspects of Windows networking. In the next chapter, you build on the experience. These are the highlights from this chapter:

- You implemented a DHCP server, and Microsoft Windows clients were able to obtain all necessary network configuration settings from this server.

- You created a Windows Domain Controller. You were able to use the network logon service and successfully joined Windows 200x/XP Professional clients to the Domain.

- You created raw print queues in the CUPS printing system. You maintained a simple printing system so that all users can share centrally managed printers. You installed native printer drivers on the Windows clients.

- You experienced the benefits of centrally managed user accounts on the server.

- You offered Mobile notebook users a solution that allows them to continue to work while away from the office and not connected to the corporate network.

2.4 Questions and Answers

Your new Domain Controller is ready to serve you. What does it mean? Here are some questions and answers that may help.

F.A.Q.

1. **Q:** *What is the key benefit of using DHCP to configure Windows client TCP/IP stacks?*
A: First and foremost, portability. It means that notebook users can move between the

Abmas office and client offices (so long as they, too, use DHCP) without having to manually reconfigure their machines. It also means that when they work from their home environments either using DHCP assigned addressing or when using dial-up networking, settings such as default routes and DNS server addresses that apply only to the Abmas office environment do not interfere with remote operations. This is an extremely important feature of DHCP.

2. **Q:** *Are there any DHCP server configuration parameters in the* `/etc/dhcpd.conf` *that should be noted in particular?*
A: Yes. The configuration you created automatically provides each client with the IP address of your WINS server. It also configures the client to preferentially register NetBIOS names with the WINS server, and then instructs the client to first query the WINS server when a NetBIOS machine name needs to be resolved to an IP Address. This configuration results in far lower UDP broadcast traffic than would be the case if WINS was not used.

3. **Q:** *Is it possible to create a Windows Domain account that is specifically called* `Administrator`?
A: You can surely create a Windows Domain account called `Administrator`. It is also possible to map that account so that it has the effective UNIX UID of 0. This way it isn't necessary to use the *username map* facility to map this account to the UNIX account called `root`.

4. **Q:** *Why is it necessary to give the Windows Domain* `Administrator` *a UNIX UID of 0?*
A: The Windows Domain `Administrator` account is the most privileged account that exists on the Windows platform. This user can change any setting, add, delete, or modify user accounts, and completely reconfigure the system. The equivalent to this account in the UNIX environment is the `root` account. If you want to permit the Windows Domain Administrator to manage accounts as well as permissions, privileges, and security settings within the Domain and on the Samba server, equivalent rights must be assigned. This is achieved with the `root` UID equal to 0.

5. **Q:** *One of my junior staff needs the ability to add machines to the Domain, but I do not want to give him* `root` *access. How can we do this?*
A: Users who are members of the `Domain Admins` group can add machines to the Domain. This group is mapped to the UNIX group account called `root` (or the equivalent `wheel` on some UNIX systems) that has a GID of 0. This must be the primary GID of the account of the user who is a member of the Windows `Domain Admins` account.

6. **Q:** *Why must I map Windows Domain Groups to UNIX groups?*
A: Samba-3 does not permit a Domain Group to become visible to Domain network clients unless the account has a UNIX group account equivalent. The Domain groups that should be given UNIX equivalents are **Domain Guests**, **Domain Users**, and **Domain Admins**.

7. **Q:** *I deleted my* `root` *account and now I cannot add it back! What can I do?*
A: This is a nasty problem. Fortunately, there is a solution.

1. Back up your existing configuration files in case you need to restore them.

2. Rename the `group_mapping.tdb` file.

3. Use the **smbpasswd** to add the root account.

4. Restore the `group_mapping.tdb` file.

8. **Q:** *When I run* **net groupmap list***, it reports a group called* **Administrators** *as well as* **Domain Admins***. What is the difference between them?*
A: The group called **Administrators** is representative of the same account that would be present as the Local Group account on a Domain Member server or workstation. Samba uses only Domain Groups at this time. A Workstation or Server Local Group has no meaning in a Samba context. This may change at some later date. These accounts are provided only so that security objects are correctly shown.

9. **Q:** *What is the effect of changing the name of a Samba server or of changing the Domain name?*
A: If you elect to change the name of the Samba server, on restarting **smbd**, Windows security identifiers are changed. In the case of a standalone server or a Domain Member server, the machine SID is changed. This may break Domain membership. In the case of a change of the Domain name (Workgroup name), the Domain SID is changed. This affects all Domain memberships.

If it becomes necessary to change either the server name or the Domain name, be sure to back up the respective SID before the change is made. You can back up the SID using the **net getlocalsid** (Samba-3) or the **smbpasswd** (Samba-2.2.x). To change the SID, you use the same tool. Be sure to check the man page for this command for detailed instructions regarding the steps involved.

10. **Q:** *How can I manage user accounts from my Windows XP Professional workstation?*
A: Samba-3 implements a Windows NT4-style security domain architecture. This type of Domain cannot be managed using tools present on a Windows XP Professional installation. You may download from the Microsoft Web site the SRVTOOLS.EXE package. Extract it into the directory from which you wish to use it. This package extracts the tools: **User Manager for Domains**, **Server Manager**, and **Event Viewer**. You may use the **User Manager for Domains** to manage your Samba-3 Domain user and group accounts. Of course, you do need to be logged on as the `Administrator` for the Samba-3 Domain. It may help to log on as the `root` account.

Example 2.3.2 Abmas Accounting DHCP Server Configuration File — /etc/dhcpd.conf

```
default-lease-time 86400;
max-lease-time 172800;
default-lease-time 86400;

option ntp-servers 192.168.1.1;
option domain-name "abmas.biz";
option domain-name-servers 192.168.1.1, 192.168.2.1;
option netbios-name-servers 192.168.1.1, 192.168.2.1;
option netbios-node-type 8;
### NOTE ###
# netbios-node-type=8 means set clients to Hybrid Mode
#    so they will use Unicast communication with the WINS
#    server and thus reduce the level of UDP broadcast
#    traffic by up to 90%.
############

subnet 192.168.1.0 netmask 255.255.255.0 {
   range dynamic-bootp 192.168.1.128 192.168.1.254;
   option subnet-mask 255.255.255.0;
   option routers 192.168.1.1;
   allow unknown-clients;
   host hplj4 {
      hardware ethernet 08:00:46:7a:35:e4;
      fixed-address 192.168.1.10;
      }
   host hplj6 {
      hardware ethernet 00:03:47:cb:81:e0;
      fixed-address 192.168.1.11;
      }
   }
subnet 192.168.2.0 netmask 255.255.255.0 {
   range dynamic-bootp 192.168.2.128 192.168.2.254;
   option subnet-mask 255.255.255.0;
   option routers 192.168.2.1;
   allow unknown-clients;
   host qms {
      hardware ethernet 01:04:31:db:e1:c0;
      fixed-address 192.168.1.10;
      }
   }
subnet 127.0.0.0 netmask 255.0.0.0 {
   }
```

Example 2.3.3 Accounting Office Network smb.conf File — [globals] Section

```
# Global parameters
  [global]
          workgroup = BILLMORE
          passwd chat = *New*Password* %n\n*Re-enter*new*password* %n\  ↵
              n *Password*changed*
          username map = /etc/samba/smbusers
          syslog = 0
          name resolve order = wins bcast hosts
          printcap name = CUPS
          show add printer wizard = No
          add user script = /usr/sbin/useradd -m '%u'
          delete user script = /usr/sbin/userdel -r '%u'
          add group script = /usr/sbin/groupadd '%g'
          delete group script = /usr/sbin/groupdel '%g'
          add user to group script = /usr/sbin/usermod -G '%g' '%u'
          add machine script = /usr/sbin/useradd -s /bin/false -d /var  ↵
              /lib/nobody '%u'
          logon script = scripts\login.bat
          logon path =
          logon drive = X:
          domain logons = Yes
          preferred master = Yes
          wins support = Yes
          printing = CUPS
```

Example 2.3.4 Accounting Office Network smb.conf File — Services and Shares Section

```
[homes]
        comment = Home Directories
        valid users = %S
        read only = No
        browseable = No
[printers]
        comment = SMB Print Spool
        path = /var/spool/samba
        printable = Yes
        guest ok = Yes
        use client driver = Yes
        browseable = No
[netlogon]
        comment = Network Logon Service
        path = /data/%U
        valid users = %S
        read only = No
[accounts]
        comment = Accounting Files
        path = /data/accounts
        valid users = %G
        read only = No
[finsvcs]
        comment = Financial Service Files
        path = /data/finsvcs
        valid users = %G
        read only = No
```

Chapter 3

SECURE OFFICE NETWORKING

Congratulations, your Samba networking skills are developing nicely. You started out with three simple networks in Chapter 1, "No-Frills Samba Servers", and then in Chapter 2, "Small Office Networking" you designed and built a network that provides a high degree of flexibility, integrity, and dependability. It was enough for the basic needs each was designed to fulfill. In this chapter you address a more complex set of needs. The solution you explore introduces you to basic features that are specific to Samba-3.

You should note that a working and secure solution could be implemented using Samba-2.2.x. In the exercises presented here, you are gradually using more Samba-3-specific features, so caution is advised for anyone who tries to use Samba-2.2.x with the guidance here given. To avoid confusion, this book is all about Samba-3. Let's get the exercises in this chapter underway.

3.1 Introduction

You have made Mr. Meany a very happy man. Recently he paid you a fat bonus for work well done. It is one year since the last network upgrade. You have been quite busy. Two months ago Mr. Meany gave approval to hire Christine Roberson, who has taken over general network management. Soon she will provide primary user support. You have demonstrated that you can delegate responsibility and can plan and execute according to that plan. Above all, you have shown Mr. Meany that you are a responsible person. Today is a big day. Mr. Meany called you to his office at 9 a.m. for news you never expected: You are going to take charge of business operations. Mr. Meany is retiring and has entrusted the business to your capable hands.

Mr. Meany may be retiring from this company, but not from work. He is taking the opportunity to develop Abmas Accounting into a larger and more substantial company. He says that it took him many years to learn that there is no future in just running a business. He now realizes there is great personal satisfaction in the creation of career opportunities for people in the local community. He wants to do more for others, as he is doing for you. Today he spent a lot of time talking about his grand plan for growth, which you will deal with in the chapters ahead.

Over the past year, the growth projections were exceeded. The network has grown to meet the needs of 130 users. Along with growth, the demand for improved services and better functionality has also developed. You are about to make an interim improvement and then hand over all Help desk and network maintenance to Christine. Christine has professional certifications in Microsoft Windows as well as in Linux; she is a hard worker and quite likable. Christine does not want to manage the department (although she manages well). She gains job satisfaction when left to sort things out. Occasionally she wants to work with you on a challenging problem. When you told her about your move, she almost resigned, although she was reassured that a new manager would be hired to run Information Technology, and she would be responsible only for operations.

3.1.1   Assignment Tasks

You promised the staff Internet services including Web browsing, electronic mail, virus protection, and a company Web site. Christine is eager to help turn the vision into reality. Let's see how close you can get to the promises made.

The network you are about to deliver will service 130 users today. Within a year, Abmas will aquire another company. Mr. Meany claims that within 2 years there will be well over 500 users on the network. You have bought into the big picture, so prepare for growth. You have purchased a new server and will implement a new network infrastructure.

You have decided to not recycle old network components. The only items that will be carried forward are notebook computers. You offered staff new notebooks, but not one person wanted the disruption for what was perceived as a marginal update. You decided to give everyone, even the notebook user, a new desktop computer.

You procured a DSL Internet connection that provides 1.5 Mb/sec (bidirectional) and a 10 Mb/sec ethernet port. You registered the domain `abmas.us`, and the Internet Service Provider (ISP) is supplying secondary DNS. Information furnished by your ISP is shown in Table 3.1.

It is of paramount priority that under no circumstances will Samba offer service access from an Internet connection. You are paying an ISP to give, as part of its value-added services, full firewall protection for your connection to the outside world. The only services allowed in from the Internet side are the following destination ports: `http/https` (`ports 80 and 443`), `email` (`port 25`), DNS (`port 53`). All Internet traffic will be allowed out after network address translation (NAT). No internal IP addresses are permitted through the NAT filter because complete privacy of internal network operations must be assured.

Christine recommended that desktop systems should be installed from a single cloned master system that has a minimum of locally installed software and loads all software off a central application server. The benefit of having the central application server is that it allows single-point maintenance of all business applications, a more efficient way to manage software. She further recommended installation of antivirus software on workstations as well as on the Samba server. Christine knows the dangers of potential virus infection and insists on a comprehensive approach to detective as well as corrective action to protect network operations.

Table 3.1 Abmas.US ISP Information

Parameter	Value
Server IP Address	123.45.67.66
DSL Device IP Address	123.45.67.65
Network Address	123.45.67.64/30
Gateway Address	123.45.54.65
Primary DNS Server	123.45.54.65
Secondary DNS Server	123.45.54.32
Forwarding DNS Server	123.45.12.23

Figure 3.1 Abmas Network Topology — 130 Users

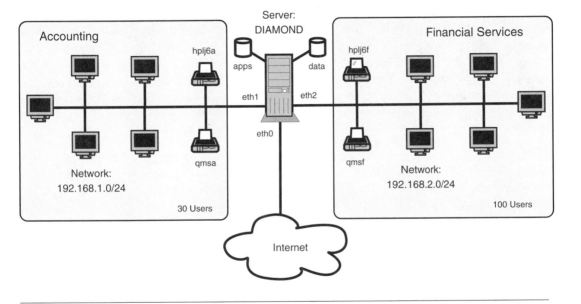

A significant concern is the problem of managing company growth. Recently, a number of users had to share a PC while waiting for new machines to arrive. This presented some problems with desktop computers and software installation into the new users' desktop profiles.

3.2   Dissection and Discussion

Many of the conclusions you draw here are obvious. Some requirements are not very clear or may simply be your means of drawing the most out of Samba-3. Much can be done more simply than you will demonstrate here, but keep in mind that the network must scale to at least 500 users. This means that some functionality will be overdesigned for the current

130-user environment.

3.2.1   Technical Issues

In this exercise we use a 24-bit subnet mask for the two local networks. This, of course, limits our network to a maximum of 253 usable IP addresses. The network address range chosen is one assigned by RFC1918 for private networks. When the number of users on the network begins to approach the limit of usable addresses, it is a good idea to switch to a network address specified in RFC1918 in the 172.16.0.0/16 range. This is done in subsequent chapters.

The high growth rates projected are a good reason to use the `tdbsam` passdb backend. The use of `smbpasswd` for the backend may result in performance problems. The `tdbsam` passdb backend offers features that are not available with the older, flat ASCII-based `smbpasswd` database.

The proposed network design uses a single server to act as an Internet services host for electronic mail, Web serving, remote administrative access via SSH, Samba-based file and print services. This design is often chosen by sites that feel they cannot afford or justify the cost or overhead of having separate servers. It must be realized that if security of this type of server should ever be violated (compromised), the whole network and all data is at risk. Many sites continue to choose this type of solution; therefore, this chapter provides detailed coverage of key implementation aspects.

Samba will be configured to specifically not operate on the Ethernet interface that is directly connected to the Internet.

You know that your ISP is providing full firewall services, but you cannot rely on that. Always assume that human error will occur, so be prepared by using Linux firewall facilities based on **iptables** to effect NAT. Block all incoming traffic except to permitted well-known ports. You must also allow incoming packets to establish outgoing connections. You will permit all internal outgoing requests.

The configuration of Web serving, Web proxy services, electronic mail, and the details of generic antivirus handling are beyond the scope of this book and therefore are not covered except insofar as this affects Samba-3.

Notebook computers are configured to use a network login when in the office and a local account to log in while away from the office. Users store all work done in transit (away from the office) by using a local share for work files. Standard procedures dictate that on completion of the work that necessitates mobile file access, all work files are moved back to secure storage on the office server. Staff is instructed to not carry on any company notebook computer any files that are not absolutely required. This is a preventative measure to protect client information as well as private business records.

All applications are served from the central server from a share called **apps**. Microsoft Office XP Professional and OpenOffice 1.1.0 will be installed using a network (or administrative) installation. Accounting and financial management software can also be run only from the central application server. Notebook users are provided with locally installed applications on a need-to-have basis only.

The introduction of roaming profiles support means that users can move between desktop computer systems without constraint while retaining full access to their data. The desktop travels with them as they move.

The DNS server implementation must now address both internal and external needs. You forward DNS lookups to your ISP-provided server as well as the `abmas.us` external secondary DNS server.

Compared with the DHCP server configuration in Chapter 2, "Small Office Networking", Example 2.3.2, the configuration used in this example has to deal with the presence of an Internet connection. The scope set for it ensures that no DHCP services will be offered on the external connection. All printers are configured as DHCP clients so that the DHCP server assigns the printer a fixed IP address by way of the Ethernet interface (MAC) address. One additional feature of this DHCP server configuration file is the inclusion of parameters to allow dynamic DNS (DDNS) operation.

This is the first implementation that depends on a correctly functioning DNS server. Comprehensive steps are included to provide for a fully functioning DNS server that also is enabled for DDNS operation. This means that DHCP clients can be autoregistered with the DNS server.

You are taking the opportunity to manually set the netbios name of the Samba server to a name other than what will be automatically resolved. You are doing this to ensure that the machine has the same NetBIOS name on both network segments.

As in the previous network configuration, printing in this network configuration uses direct raw printing (i.e., no smart printing and no print driver autodownload to Windows clients). Printer drivers are installed on the Windows client manually. This is not a problem because Christine is to install and configure one single workstation and then clone that configuration, using Norton Ghost, to all workstations. Each machine is identical, so this should pose no problem.

3.2.1.1 Hardware Requirements

This server runs a considerable number of services. From similarly configured Linux installations, the approximate calculated memory requirements are as shown in Example 3.2.1.

You should add a safety margin of at least 50% to these estimates. The minimum system memory recommended for initial startup 1 GB, but to permit the system to scale to 500 users, it makes sense to provision the machine with 4 GB memory. An initial configuration with only 1 GB memory would lead to early performance complaints as the system load builds up. Given the low cost of memory, it does not make sense to compromise in this area.

Aggregate input/output loads should be considered for sizing network configuration as well as disk subsystems. For network bandwidth calculations, one would typically use an estimate of 0.1 MB/sec per user. This suggests that 100-Base-T (approx. 10 MB/sec) would deliver below acceptable capacity for the initial user load. It is therefore a good idea to begin with 1 Gb Ethernet cards for the two internal networks, each attached to a 1 Gb Ethernet switch that provides connectivity to an expandable array of 100-Base-T switched ports.

Example 3.2.1 Estimation of Memory Requirements

Application Name	Memory per User (MBytes)	130 Users Total MBytes	500 Users Total MBytes
DHCP	2.5	3	3
DNS	16.0	16	16
Samba (nmbd)	16.0	16	16
Samba (winbind)	16.0	16	16
Samba (smbd)	4.0	520	2000
Apache	10.0 (20 User)	200	200
CUPS	3.5	16	32
Basic OS	256.0	256	256
Total:		1043 MBytes	2539 MBytes

Considering the choice of 1 Gb Ethernet interfaces for the two local network segments, the aggregate network I/O capacity will be 2100 Mb/sec (about 230 MB/sec), an I/O demand that would require a fast disk storage I/O capability. Peak disk throughput is limited by the disk subsystem chosen. It is desirable to provide the maximum I/O bandwidth affordable. If a low-cost solution must be chosen, 3Ware IDE RAID Controllers are a good choice. These controllers can be fitted into a 64-bit, 66 MHz PCI-X slot. They appear to the operating system as a high-speed SCSI controller that can operate at the peak of the PCI-X bandwidth (approximately 450 MB/sec). Alternative SCSI-based hardware RAID controllers should also be considered. Alternately, it makes sense to purchase well-known, branded hardware that has appropriate performance specifications. As a minimum, one should attempt to provide a disk subsystem that can deliver I/O rates of at least 100 MB/sec.

Disk storage requirements may be calculated as shown in Example 3.2.2.

The preferred storage capacity should be approximately 1 Terabyte. Use of RAID level 5 with two hot spare drives would require an 8-drive by 200 GB capacity per drive array.

3.2.2   Political Issues

Your industry is coming under increasing accountability pressures. Increased paranoia is necessary so you can demonstrate that you have acted with due diligence. You must not trust your Internet connection.

Apart from permitting more efficient management of business applications through use of an application server, your primary reason for the decision to implement this is that it gives you greater control over software licensing.

You are well aware that the current configuration results in some performance issues as the size of the desktop profile grows. Given that users use Microsoft Outlook Express, you know that the storage implications of the .PST file is something that needs to be addressed later.

Example 3.2.2 Estimation of Disk Storage Requirements

```
Corporate Data: 100 MBytes/user per year
Email Storage:  500 MBytes/user per year
Applications:   5000 MBytes
Safety Buffer:  At least 50%


Given 500 Users and 2 years:
------------------------------
          Corporate Data:  2 x 100 x 500 = 100000 MBytes = 100 GBytes
          Email Storage:   2 x 500 x 500 = 500000 MBytes = 500 GBytes
          Applications:                      5000 MBytes =   5 GBytes
                                           ----------------------------
                      Total:                             605 GBytes
             Add 50% buffer                              303 GBytes
                    Recommended Storage:                 908 GBytes
```

3.3   Implementation

Figure 3.1 demonstrates the overall design of the network that you will implement.

The information presented here assumes that you are already familiar with many basic steps. As this stands, the details provided already extend well beyond just the necessities of Samba configuration. This decision is deliberate to ensure that key determinants of a successful installation are not overlooked. This is the last case that documents the finite minutiae of DHCP and DNS server configuration. Beyond the information provided here, there are many other good reference books on these subjects.

The `smb.conf` file has the following noteworthy features:

- The NetBIOS name of the Samba server is set to `DIAMOND`.

- The Domain name is set to `PROMISES`.

- Ethernet interface `eth0` is attached to the Internet connection and is externally exposed. This interface is explicitly not available for Samba to use. Samba listens on this interface for broadcast messages but does not broadcast any information on `eth0`, nor does it accept any connections from it. This is achieved by way of the *interfaces* parameter and the *bind interfaces only* entry.

- The *passdb backend* parameter specifies the creation and use of the `tdbsam` password backend. This is a binary database that has excellent scalability for a large number of user account entries.

- WINS serving is enabled by the *wins support* = Yes, and name resolution is set to use it by means of the *name resolve order* = wins bcast hosts entry.

- The Samba server is configured for use by Windows clients as a time server.

- Samba is configured to directly interface with CUPS via the direct internal interface that is provided by CUPS libraries. This is achieved with the *printing* = CUPS as well as the *printcap name* = CUPS entries.

- External interface scripts are provided to enable Samba to interface smoothly to essential operating system functions for user and group management. This is important to enable workstations to join the Domain and is also important so that you can use the Windows NT4 Domain User Manager as well as the Domain Server Manager. These tools are provided as part of the `SRVTOOLS.EXE` toolkit that can be downloaded from the Microsoft FTP site[1].

- The `smb.conf` file specifies that the Samba server will operate in (default) *security = user* mode[2] (User Mode).

- Domain logon services as well as a Domain logon script are specified. The logon script will be used to add robustness to the overall network configuration.

- Roaming profiles are enabled through the specification of the parameter, *logon path* = \\%L\profiles\%U. The value of this parameter translates the %L to the name by which the Samba server is called by the client (for this configuration, it translates to the name `DIAMOND`), and the %U will translate to the name of the user within the context of the connection made to the profile share. It is the administrator's responsibility to ensure there is a directory in the root of the profile share for each user. This directory must be owned by the user also. An exception to this requirement is when a profile is created for group use.

- Precautionary veto is effected for particular Windows file names that have been targeted by virus-related activity. Additionally, Microsoft Office files are vetoed from opportunistic locking controls. This should help to prevent lock contention-related file access problems.

- Every user has a private home directory on the UNIX/Linux host. This is mapped to a network drive that is the same for all users.

The configuration of the server is the most complex so far. The following steps are used:

1 Basic System Configuration

2 Samba Configuration

3 DHCP and DNS Server Configuration

4 Printer Configuration

5 Process Start-up Configuration

6 Validation

7 Application Share Configuration

8 Windows Client Configuration

---

[1]<ftp://ftp.microsoft.com/Softlib/MSLFILES/SRVTOOLS.EXE>

[2]See *TOSHARG2*, Chapter 3. This is necessary so that Samba can act as a Domain Controller (PDC); see *TOSHARG2*, Chapter 4, for additional information.

The following sections cover each step in logical and defined detail.

3.3.1   Basic System Configuration

The preparation in this section assumes that your SUSE Enterprise Linux Server 8.0 system has been freshly installed. It prepares basic files so that the system is ready for comprehensive operation in line with the network diagram shown in Figure 3.1.

SERVER CONFIGURATION STEPS

1. Using the UNIX/Linux system tools, name the server `server.abmas.us`. Verify that your hostname is correctly set by running:

```
root#  uname -n
server
```

   An alternate method to verify the hostname is:

```
root#  hostname -f
server.abmas.us
```

2. Edit your `/etc/hosts` file to include the primary names and addresses of all network interfaces that are on the host server. This is necessary so that during startup the system can resolve all its own names to the IP address prior to startup of the DNS server. An example of entries that should be in the `/etc/hosts` file is:

```
127.0.0.1        localhost
192.168.1.1      sleeth1.abmas.biz sleeth1 diamond
192.168.2.1      sleeth2.abmas.biz sleeth2
123.45.67.66     server.abmas.us server
```

   You should check the startup order of your system. If the CUPS print server is started before the DNS server (**named**), you should also include an entry for the printers in the `/etc/hosts` file, as follows:

```
192.168.1.20     qmsa.abmas.biz qmsa
192.168.1.30     hplj6a.abmas.biz hplj6a
192.168.2.20     qmsf.abmas.biz qmsf
192.168.2.30     hplj6f.abmas.biz hplj6f
```

   The printer entries are not necessary if **named** is started prior to startup of **cupsd**, the CUPS daemon.

3. The host server is acting as a router between the two internal network segments as
   well as for all Internet access. This necessitates that IP forwarding be enabled. This
   can be achieved by adding to the `/etc/rc.d/boot.local` an entry as follows:

```
echo 1 > /proc/sys/net/ipv4/ip_forward
```

To ensure that your kernel is capable of IP forwarding during configuration, you may
wish to execute that command manually also. This setting permits the Linux system
to act as a router.[3]

4. Installation of a basic firewall and NAT facility is necessary. The following script can
   be installed in the `/usr/local/sbin` directory. It is executed from the `/etc/rc.d/`
   `boot.local` startup script. In your case, this script is called **abmas-netfw.sh**. The
   script contents are shown in Example 3.3.1.

5. Execute the following to make the script executable:

```
root#  chmod 755 /usr/local/sbin/abmas-natfw.sh
```

You must now edit `/etc/rc.d/boot.local` to add an entry that runs your **abmas-natfw.sh** script. The following entry works for you:

```
#! /bin/sh
#
# Copyright (c) 2002 SUSE Linux AG Nuernberg, Germany.
# All rights reserved.
#
# Author: Werner Fink, 1996
#         Burchard Steinbild, 1996
#
# /etc/init.d/boot.local
#
# script with local commands to be executed from init on system startup
#
# Here you should add things that should happen directly after booting
# before we're going to the first run level.
#
/usr/local/sbin/abmas-natfw.sh
```

The server is now ready for Samba configuration. During the validation step, you remove
the entry for the Samba server `diamond` from the `/etc/hosts` file. This is done after you
are satisfied that DNS-based name resolution is functioning correctly.

---

[3]You may want to do the echo command last and include "0" in the init scripts, since it opens up your
network for a short time.

3.3.2   Samba Configuration

When you have completed this section, the Samba server is ready for testing and validation; however, testing and validation have to wait until DHCP, DNS, and printing (CUPS) services have been configured.

Samba Configuration Steps

1. Install the Samba-3 binary RPM from the Samba-Team FTP site. Assuming that the binary RPM file is called `samba-3.0.20-1.i386.rpm`, one way to install this file is as follows:

   ```
   root#  rpm -Uvh samba-3.0.20-1.i386.rpm
   ```

   This operation must be performed while logged in as the **root** user. Successful operation is clearly indicated. If this installation should fail for any reason, refer to the operating system manufacturer's documentation for guidance.

2. Install the `smb.conf` file shown in Example 3.3.2, Example 3.3.3, and Example 3.3.4. Concatenate (join) all three files to make a single `smb.conf` file. The final, fully qualified path for this file should be `/etc/samba/smb.conf`.

3. Add the `root` user to the password backend as follows:

   ```
   root#  smbpasswd -a root
   New SMB password: XXXXXXXX
   Retype new SMB password: XXXXXXXX
   root#
   ```

   The `root` account is the UNIX equivalent of the Windows Domain Administrator. This account is essential in the regular maintenance of your Samba server. It must never be deleted. If for any reason the account is deleted, you may not be able to recreate this account without considerable trouble.

4. Create the username map file to permit the `root` account to be called `Administrator` from the Windows network environment. To do this, create the file `/etc/samba/smbusers` with the following contents:

   ```
   ####
   # User mapping file
   ####
   # File Format
   # -----------
   # Unix_ID = Windows_ID
   #
   # Examples:
   # root = Administrator
   ```

```
# janes = "Jane Smith"
# jimbo = Jim Bones
#
# Note: If the name contains a space it must be double quoted.
#       In the example above the name 'jimbo' will be mapped to Windows
#       user names 'Jim' and 'Bones' because the space was not quoted.
###################################################################
root = Administrator
####
# End of File
####
```

5. Create and map Windows Domain Groups to UNIX groups. A sample script is provided in Chapter 2, "Small Office Networking", Example 2.3.1. Create a file containing this script. We called ours /etc/samba/initGrps.sh. Set this file so it can be executed, and then execute the script. Sample output should be as follows:

```
root#  chmod 755 initGrps.sh
root#  /etc/samba # ./initGrps.sh
Updated mapping entry for Domain Admins
Updated mapping entry for Domain Users
Updated mapping entry for Domain Guests
No rid or sid specified, choosing algorithmic mapping
Successfully added group Accounts Dept to the mapping db
No rid or sid specified, choosing algorithmic mapping
Successfully added group Domain Guests to the mapping db

root#  /etc/samba # net groupmap list | sort
Account Operators (S-1-5-32-548) -> -1
Accounts Dept (S-1-5-21-179504-2437109-488451-2003) -> acctsdep
Administrators (S-1-5-32-544) -> -1
Backup Operators (S-1-5-32-551) -> -1
Domain Admins (S-1-5-21-179504-2437109-488451-512) -> root
Domain Guests (S-1-5-21-179504-2437109-488451-514) -> nobody
Domain Users (S-1-5-21-179504-2437109-488451-513) -> users
Financial Services (S-1-5-21-179504-2437109-488451-2005) -> finsrvcs
Guests (S-1-5-32-546) -> -1
Power Users (S-1-5-32-547) -> -1
Print Operators (S-1-5-32-550) -> -1
Replicators (S-1-5-32-552) -> -1
System Operators (S-1-5-32-549) -> -1
Users (S-1-5-32-545) -> -1
```

6. There is one preparatory step without which you will not have a working Samba network environment. You must add an account for each network user. For each user

who needs to be given a Windows Domain account, make an entry in the /etc/passwd file as well as in the Samba password backend. Use the system tool of your choice to create the UNIX system account, and use the Samba **smbpasswd** to create a Domain user account. There are a number of tools for user management under UNIX, such as **useradd**, and **adduser**, as well as a plethora of custom tools. You also want to create a home directory for each user. You can do this by executing the following steps for each user:

```
root#  useradd -m username
root#  passwd username
Changing password for username.
New password: XXXXXXXX
Re-enter new password: XXXXXXXX
Password changed
root#  smbpasswd -a username
New SMB password: XXXXXXXX
Retype new SMB password: XXXXXXXX
Added user username.
```

You do of course use a valid user login ID in place of *username*.

7. Using the preferred tool for your UNIX system, add each user to the UNIX groups created previously as necessary. File system access control will be based on UNIX group membership.

8. Create the directory mount point for the disk subsystem that can be mounted to provide data storage for company files. In this case the mount point is indicated in the smb.conf file is /data. Format the file system as required, and mount the formatted file system partition using appropriate system tools.

9. Create the top-level file storage directories for data and applications as follows:

```
root#  mkdir -p /data/{accounts,finsvcs}
root#  mkdir -p /apps
root#  chown -R root:root /data
root#  chown -R root:root /apps
root#  chown -R bjordan:accounts /data/accounts
root#  chown -R bjordan:finsvcs /data/finsvcs
root#  chmod -R ug+rwxs,o-rwx /data
root#  chmod -R ug+rwx,o+rx-w /apps
```

Each department is responsible for creating its own directory structure within the departmental share. The directory root of the **accounts** share is /data/accounts. The directory root of the **finsvcs** share is /data/finsvcs. The /apps directory is the root of the **apps** share that provides the application server infrastructure.

10. The `smb.conf` file specifies an infrastructure to support roaming profiles and network logon services. You can now create the file system infrastructure to provide the locations on disk that these services require. Adequate planning is essential, since desktop profiles can grow to be quite large. For planning purposes, a minimum of 200 MB of storage should be allowed per user for profile storage. The following commands create the directory infrastructure needed:

```
root#  mkdir -p /var/spool/samba
root#  mkdir -p /var/lib/samba/{netlogon/scripts,profiles}
root#  chown -R root:root /var/spool/samba
root#  chown -R root:root /var/lib/samba
root#  chmod a+rwxt /var/spool/samba
```

For each user account that is created on the system, the following commands should be executed:

```
root#  mkdir /var/lib/samba/profiles/'username'
root#  chown 'username':users /var/lib/samba/profiles/'username'
root#  chmod ug+wrx,o+rx,-w /var/lib/samba/profiles/'username'
```

11. Create a logon script. It is important that each line is correctly terminated with a carriage return and line-feed combination (i.e., DOS encoding). The following procedure works if the right tools (`unix2dos` and `dos2unix`) are installed. First, create a file called `/var/lib/samba/netlogon/scripts/logon.bat.unix` with the following contents:

```
net time \\diamond /set /yes
net use h: /home
net use p: \\diamond\apps
```

Convert the UNIX file to a DOS file using the **unix2dos** as shown here:

```
root#  unix2dos < /var/lib/samba/netlogon/scripts/logon.bat.unix \
    > /var/lib/samba/netlogon/scripts/logon.bat
```

3.3.3   Configuration of DHCP and DNS Servers

DHCP services are a basic component of the entire network client installation. DNS operation is foundational to Internet access as well as to trouble-free operation of local networking. When you have completed this section, the server should be ready for solid duty operation.

DHCP AND DNS SERVER CONFIGURATION STEPS

1. Create a file called `/etc/dhcpd.conf` with the contents as shown in Example 3.3.6.

2. Create a file called `/etc/named.conf` that has the combined contents of the Example 3.3.7, Example 3.3.8, and Example 3.3.9 files that are concatenated (merged) in this specific order.

3. Create the files shown in their respective directories as shown in Table 3.2.

Table 3.2 DNS (named) Resource Files

Reference	File Location
Example 15.4.1	/var/lib/named/localhost.zone
Example 15.4.2	/var/lib/named/127.0.0.zone
Example 15.4.3	/var/lib/named/root.hint
Example 3.3.12	/var/lib/named/master/abmas.biz.hosts
Example 3.3.13	/var/lib/named/abmas.us.hosts
Example 3.3.10	/var/lib/named/192.168.1.0.rev
Example 3.3.11	/var/lib/named/192.168.2.0.rev

4. All DNS name resolution should be handled locally. To ensure that the server is configured correctly to handle this, edit `/etc/resolv.conf` to have the following content:

```
search abmas.us abmas.biz
nameserver 127.0.0.1
nameserver 123.45.54.23
```

This instructs the name resolver function (when configured correctly) to ask the DNS server that is running locally to resolve names to addresses. In the event that the local name server is not available, ask the name server provided by the ISP. The latter, of course, does not resolve purely local names to IP addresses.

5. The final step is to edit the `/etc/nsswitch.conf` file. This file controls the operation of the various resolver libraries that are part of the Linux Glibc libraries. Edit this file so that it contains the following entries:

```
hosts:      files dns wins
```

The basic DHCP and DNS services are now ready for validation testing. Before you can proceed, there are a few more steps along the road. First, configure the print spooling and print processing system. Then you can configure the server so that all services start automatically on reboot. You must also manually start all services prior to validation testing.

3.3.4   Printer Configuration

Network administrators who are new to CUPS based-printing typically experience some
difficulty mastering its powerful features. The steps outlined in this section are designed to
navigate around the distractions of learning CUPS. Instead of implementing smart features
and capabilities, our approach is to use it as a transparent print queue that performs no
filtering, and only minimal handling of each print job that is submitted to it. In other words,
our configuration turns CUPS into a raw-mode print queue. This means that the correct
printer driver must be installed on all clients.

PRINTER CONFIGURATION STEPS

1. Configure each printer to be a DHCP client, carefully following the manufacturer's
   guidelines.

2. Follow the instructions in the printer manufacturer's manuals to permit printing to
   port 9100. Use any other port the manufacturer specifies for direct-mode raw printing,
   and adjust the port as necessary in the following example commands. This allows the
   CUPS spooler to print using raw mode protocols.

3. Configure the CUPS Print Queues as follows:

   ```
   root#  lpadmin -p qmsa -v socket://qmsa.abmas.biz:9100 -E
   root#  lpadmin -p hplj6a -v socket://hplj6a.abmas.biz:9100 -E
   root#  lpadmin -p qmsf -v socket://qmsf.abmas.biz:9100 -E
   root#  lpadmin -p hplj6f -v socket://hplj6f.abmas.biz:9100 -E
   ```

   This creates the necessary print queues with no assigned print filter.

4. Print queues may not be enabled at creation. Use **lpc stat** to check the status of the
   print queues and, if necessary, make certain that the queues you have just created are
   enabled by executing the following:

   ```
   root#  /usr/bin/enable qmsa
   root#  /usr/bin/enable hplj6a
   root#  /usr/bin/enable qmsf
   root#  /usr/bin/enable hplj6f
   ```

5. Even though your print queues may be enabled, it is still possible that they are not
   accepting print jobs. A print queue services incoming printing requests only when
   configured to do so. Ensure that your print queues are set to accept incoming jobs by
   executing the following commands:

   ```
   root#  /usr/bin/accept qmsa
   root#  /usr/bin/accept hplj6a
   root#  /usr/bin/accept qmsf
   ```

```
root#  /usr/bin/accept hplj6f
```

6. Edit the file **/etc/cups/mime.convs** to uncomment the line:

```
application/octet-stream      application/vnd.cups-raw      0      -
```

7. Edit the file **/etc/cups/mime.types** to uncomment the line:

```
application/octet-stream
```

8. Printing drivers are installed on each network client workstation.

Note: If the parameter *cups options* = *Raw* is specified in the **smb.conf** file, the last two steps can be omitted with CUPS version 1.1.18, or later.

The UNIX system print queues have been configured and are ready for validation testing.

3.3.5 Process Startup Configuration

There are two essential steps to process startup configuration. First, the process must be configured so that it automatically restarts each time the server is rebooted. This step involves use of the **chkconfig** tool that creates the appropriate symbolic links from the master daemon control file that is located in the **/etc/rc.d** directory, to the **/etc/rc'x'.d** directories. Links are created so that when the system run level is changed, the necessary start or kill script is run.

In the event that a service is not run as a daemon, but via the internetworking super daemon (**inetd** or **xinetd**), then the **chkconfig** tool makes the necessary entries in the **/etc/xinetd.d** directory and sends a hang-up (HUP) signal to the the the super daemon, thus forcing it to re-read its control files.

Last, each service must be started to permit system validation to proceed.

1. Use the standard system tool to configure each service to restart automatically at every system reboot. For example,

```
root#  chkconfig dhpc on
root#  chkconfig named on
root#  chkconfig cups on
root#  chkconfig smb on
```

2. Now start each service to permit the system to be validated. Execute each of the following in the sequence shown:

```
root#  /etc/rc.d/init.d/dhcp restart
```

```
root#   /etc/rc.d/init.d/named restart
root#   /etc/rc.d/init.d/cups restart
root#   /etc/rc.d/init.d/smb restart
```

3.3.6   Validation

Complex networking problems are most often caused by simple things that are poorly or incorrectly configured. The validation process adopted here should be followed carefully; it is the result of the experience gained from years of making and correcting the most common mistakes. Shortcuts often lead to basic errors. You should refrain from taking shortcuts, from making basic assumptions, and from not exercising due process and diligence in network validation. By thoroughly testing and validating every step in the process of network installation and configuration, you can save yourself from sleepless nights and restless days. A well debugged network is a foundation for happy network users and network administrators. Later in this book you learn how to make users happier. For now, it is enough to learn to validate. Let's get on with it.

SERVER VALIDATION STEPS

1. One of the most important facets of Samba configuration is to ensure that name resolution functions correctly. You can check name resolution with a few simple tests. The most basic name resolution is provided from the /etc/hosts file. To test its operation, make a temporary edit to the /etc/nsswitch.conf file. Using your favorite editor, change the entry for hosts to read:

   ```
   hosts:      files
   ```

   When you have saved this file, execute the following command:

   ```
   root#  ping diamond
   PING sleeth1.abmas.biz (192.168.1.1) 56(84) bytes of data.
   64 bytes from sleeth1 (192.168.1.1): icmp_seq=1 ttl=64 time=0.131 ms
   64 bytes from sleeth1 (192.168.1.1): icmp_seq=2 ttl=64 time=0.179 ms
   64 bytes from sleeth1 (192.168.1.1): icmp_seq=3 ttl=64 time=0.192 ms
   64 bytes from sleeth1 (192.168.1.1): icmp_seq=4 ttl=64 time=0.191 ms

   --- sleeth1.abmas.biz ping statistics ---
   4 packets transmitted, 4 received, 0% packet loss, time 3016ms
   rtt min/avg/max/mdev = 0.131/0.173/0.192/0.026 ms
   ```

   This proves that name resolution via the /etc/hosts file is working.

2. So far, your installation is going particularly well. In this step we validate DNS server and name resolution operation. Using your favorite UNIX system editor, change the /etc/nsswitch.conf file so that the hosts entry reads:

```
hosts:          dns
```

3. Before you test DNS operation, it is a good idea to verify that the DNS server is running by executing the following:

```
root#  ps ax | grep named
  437 ?          S       0:00 /sbin/syslogd -a /var/lib/named/dev/log
  524 ?          S       0:00 /usr/sbin/named -t /var/lib/named -u named
  525 ?          S       0:00 /usr/sbin/named -t /var/lib/named -u named
  526 ?          S       0:00 /usr/sbin/named -t /var/lib/named -u named
  529 ?          S       0:00 /usr/sbin/named -t /var/lib/named -u named
  540 ?          S       0:00 /usr/sbin/named -t /var/lib/named -u named
 2552 pts/2      S       0:00 grep named
```

This means that we are ready to check DNS operation. Do so by executing:

```
root#  ping diamond
PING sleeth1.abmas.biz (192.168.1.1) 56(84) bytes of data.
64 bytes from sleeth1 (192.168.1.1): icmp_seq=1 ttl=64 time=0.156 ms
64 bytes from sleeth1 (192.168.1.1): icmp_seq=2 ttl=64 time=0.183 ms

--- sleeth1.abmas.biz ping statistics ---
2 packets transmitted, 2 received, 0% packet loss, time 999ms
rtt min/avg/max/mdev = 0.156/0.169/0.183/0.018 ms
```

You should take a few more steps to validate DNS server operation, as follows:

```
root#  host -f diamond.abmas.biz
sleeth1.abmas.biz has address 192.168.1.1
```

You may now remove the entry called `diamond` from the `/etc/hosts` file. It does not hurt to leave it there, but its removal reduces the number of administrative steps for this name.

4. WINS is a great way to resolve NetBIOS names to their IP address. You can test the operation of WINS by starting **nmbd** (manually or by way of the Samba startup method shown in Section 3.3.5). You must edit the `/etc/nsswitch.conf` file so that the `hosts` entry is as follows:

```
hosts:          wins
```

The next step is to make certain that Samba is running using **ps ax|grep mbd**, and then execute the following:

```
root#  ping diamond
PING diamond (192.168.1.1) 56(84) bytes of data.
64 bytes from 192.168.1.1: icmp_seq=1 ttl=64 time=0.094 ms
64 bytes from 192.168.1.1: icmp_seq=2 ttl=64 time=0.479 ms
```

Now that you can relax with the knowledge that all three major forms of name resolution to IP address resolution are working, edit the /etc/nsswitch.conf again. This time you add all three forms of name resolution to this file. Your edited entry for hosts should now look like this:

```
hosts:        files dns wins
```

The system is looking good. Let's move on.

5. It would give you peace of mind to know that the DHCP server is running and available for service. You can validate DHCP services by running:

```
root#  ps ax | grep dhcp
 2618 ?          S       0:00 /usr/sbin/dhcpd ...
 8180 pts/2      S       0:00 grep dhcp
```

This shows that the server is running. The proof of whether or not it is working comes when you try to add the first DHCP client to the network.

6. This is a good point at which to start validating Samba operation. You are content that name resolution is working for basic TCP/IP needs. Let's move on. If your smb.conf file has bogus options or parameters, this may cause Samba to refuse to start. The first step should always be to validate the contents of this file by running:

```
root#  testparm -s
Load smb config files from smb.conf
Processing section "[homes]"
Processing section "[printers]"
Processing section "[netlogon]"
Processing section "[profiles]"
Processing section "[accounts]"
Processing section "[service]"
Processing section "[apps]"
Loaded services file OK.
# Global parameters
[global]
```

```
    workgroup = PROMISES
    netbios name = DIAMOND
    interfaces = eth1, eth2, lo
    bind interfaces only = Yes
    passdb backend = tdbsam
    pam password change = Yes
    passwd program = /usr/bin/passwd '%u'
    passwd chat = *New*Password* %n\n \
            *Re-enter*new*password* %n\n *Password*changed*
    username map = /etc/samba/smbusers
    unix password sync = Yes
    log level = 1
    syslog = 0
    log file = /var/log/samba/%m
    max log size = 50
    smb ports = 139
    name resolve order = wins bcast hosts
    time server = Yes
    printcap name = CUPS
    show add printer wizard = No
    add user script = /usr/sbin/useradd -m '%u'
    delete user script = /usr/sbin/userdel -r '%u'
    add group script = /usr/sbin/groupadd '%g'
    delete group script = /usr/sbin/groupdel '%g'
    add user to group script = /usr/sbin/usermod -G '%g' '%u'
    add machine script = /usr/sbin/useradd \
                            -s /bin/false -d /dev/null '%u'
    shutdown script = /var/lib/samba/scripts/shutdown.sh
    abort shutdown script = /sbin/shutdown -c
    logon script = scripts\logon.bat
    logon path = \\%L\profiles\%U
    logon drive = X:
    logon home = \\%L\%U
    domain logons = Yes
    preferred master = Yes
    wins support = Yes
    utmp = Yes
    winbind use default domain = Yes
    map acl inherit = Yes
    cups options = Raw
    veto files = /*.eml/*.nws/*.{*}/
    veto oplock files = /*.doc/*.xls/*.mdb/

[homes]
    comment = Home Directories
    valid users = %S
    read only = No
```

```
      browseable = No
  ...
  ### Remainder cut to save space ###
```

Clear away all errors before proceeding.

7. Check that the Samba server is running:

```
root#  ps ax | grep mbd
14244 ?          S      0:00 /usr/sbin/nmbd -D
14245 ?          S      0:00 /usr/sbin/nmbd -D
14290 ?          S      0:00 /usr/sbin/smbd -D

$rootprompt; ps ax | grep winbind
14293 ?          S      0:00 /usr/sbin/winbindd -B
14295 ?          S      0:00 /usr/sbin/winbindd -B
```

The **winbindd** daemon is running in split mode (normal), so there are also two instances[4] of it.

8. Check that an anonymous connection can be made to the Samba server:

```
root#  smbclient -L localhost -U%

        Sharename       Type        Comment
        ---------       ----        -------
        IPC$            IPC         IPC Service (Samba 3.0.20)
        netlogon        Disk        Network Logon Service
        profiles        Disk        Profile Share
        accounts        Disk        Accounting Files
        service         Disk        Financial Services Files
        apps            Disk        Application Files
        ADMIN$          IPC         IPC Service (Samba 3.0.20)
        hplj6a          Printer     hplj6a
        hplj6f          Printer     hplj6f
        qmsa            Printer     qmsa
        qmsf            Printer     qmsf

        Server                  Comment
        ---------               -------
        DIAMOND                 Samba 3.0.20

        Workgroup               Master
```

---

[4]For more information regarding winbindd, see *TOSHARG2*, Chapter 23, Section 23.3. The single instance of **smbd** is normal. One additional **smbd** slave process is spawned for each SMB/CIFS client connection.

```
        ---------                   -------
        PROMISES                    DIAMOND
```

This demonstrates that an anonymous listing of shares can be obtained. This is the equivalent of browsing the server from a Windows client to obtain a list of shares on the server. The -U% argument means to send a NULL username and a NULL password.

9. Verify that each printer has the IP address assigned in the DHCP server configuration file. The easiest way to do this is to ping the printer name. Immediately after the ping response has been received, execute **arp -a** to find the MAC address of the printer that has responded. Now you can compare the IP address and the MAC address of the printer with the configuration information in the /etc/dhcpd.conf file. They should, of course, match. For example,

```
root#  ping hplj6
PING hplj6a (192.168.1.30) 56(84) bytes of data.
64 bytes from hplj6a (192.168.1.30): icmp_seq=1 ttl=64 time=0.113 ms

root#  arp -a
hplj6a (192.168.1.30) at 00:03:47:CB:81:E0 [ether] on eth0
```

The MAC address 00:03:47:CB:81:E0 matches that specified for the IP address from which the printer has responded and with the entry for it in the /etc/dhcpd.conf file. Repeat this for each printer configured.

10. Make an authenticated connection to the server using the **smbclient** tool:

```
root#  smbclient //diamond/accounts -U gholmes
Password: XXXXXXX
smb: \> dir
  .                           D        0  Thu Nov 27 15:07:09 2003
  ..                          D        0  Sat Nov 15 17:40:50 2003
  zakadmin.exe                    161424  Thu Nov 27 15:06:52 2003
  zak.exe                        6066384  Thu Nov 27 15:06:52 2003
  dhcpd.conf                        1256  Thu Nov 27 15:06:52 2003
  smb.conf                          2131  Thu Nov 27 15:06:52 2003
  initGrps.sh                 A     1089  Thu Nov 27 15:06:52 2003
  POLICY.EXE                       86542  Thu Nov 27 15:06:52 2003

            55974 blocks of size 65536. 33968 blocks available
smb: \> q
```

11. Your new server is connected to an Internet-accessible connection. Before you start your firewall, you should run a port scanner against your system. You should repeat that after the firewall has been started. This helps you understand to what extent the

server may be vulnerable to external attack. One way you can do this is by using an external service, such as the DSL Reports[5] tools. Alternately, if you can gain root-level access to a remote UNIX/Linux system that has the **nmap** tool, you can run the following:

```
root#  nmap -v -sT server.abmas.us

Starting nmap V. 3.00 ( www.insecure.org/nmap/ )
Host server.abmas.us (123.45.67.66) appears to be up ... good.
Initiating Connect() Scan against server.abmas.us (123.45.67.66)
Adding open port 6000/tcp
Adding open port 873/tcp
Adding open port 445/tcp
Adding open port 10000/tcp
Adding open port 901/tcp
Adding open port 631/tcp
Adding open port 25/tcp
Adding open port 111/tcp
Adding open port 32770/tcp
Adding open port 3128/tcp
Adding open port 53/tcp
Adding open port 80/tcp
Adding open port 443/tcp
Adding open port 139/tcp
Adding open port 22/tcp
The Connect() Scan took 0 seconds to scan 1601 ports.
Interesting ports on server.abmas.us (123.45.67.66):
(The 1587 ports scanned but not shown below are in state: closed)
Port        State       Service
22/tcp      open        ssh
25/tcp      open        smtp
53/tcp      open        domain
80/tcp      open        http
111/tcp     open        sunrpc
139/tcp     open        netbios-ssn
443/tcp     open        https
445/tcp     open        microsoft-ds
631/tcp     open        ipp
873/tcp     open        rsync
901/tcp     open        samba-swat
3128/tcp    open        squid-http
6000/tcp    open        X11
10000/tcp   open        snet-sensor-mgmt
32770/tcp   open        sometimes-rpc3
```

---

[5]<http://www.dslreports.com/scan>

```
Nmap run completed -- 1 IP address (1 host up) scanned in 1 second
```

The above scan was run before the external interface was locked down with the NAT-firewall script you created above. The following results are obtained after the firewall rules have been put into place:

```
root#  nmap -v -sT server.abmas.us

Starting nmap V. 3.00 ( www.insecure.org/nmap/ )
Host server.abmas.us (123.45.67.66) appears to be up ... good.
Initiating Connect() Scan against server.abmas.us (123.45.67.66)
Adding open port 53/tcp
Adding open port 22/tcp
The Connect() Scan took 168 seconds to scan 1601 ports.
Interesting ports on server.abmas.us (123.45.67.66):
(The 1593 ports scanned but not shown below are in state: filtered)
Port       State        Service
22/tcp     open         ssh
25/tcp     closed       smtp
53/tcp     open         domain
80/tcp     closed       http
443/tcp    closed       https

Nmap run completed -- 1 IP address (1 host up) scanned in 168 seconds
```

3.3.7   Application Share Configuration

The use of an application server is a key mechanism by which desktop administration overheads can be reduced. Check the application manual for your software to identify how best to create an administrative installation.

Some Windows software will only run locally on the desktop computer. Such software is typically not suited for administrative installation. Administratively installed software permits one or more of the following installation choices:

- Install software fully onto a workstation, storing data files on the same workstation.

- Install software fully onto a workstation with central network data file storage.

- Install software to run off a central application server with data files stored on the local workstation. This is often called a minimum installation, or a network client installation.

- Install software to run off a central application server with data files stored on a central network share. This type of installation often prevents storage of work files on the local workstation.

A common application deployed in this environment is an office suite. Enterprise editions of Microsoft Office XP Professional can be administratively installed by launching the installation from a command shell. The command that achieves this is **setup /a**. It results in a set of prompts through which various installation choices can be made. Refer to the Microsoft Office Resource SDK and Resource Kit for more information regarding this mode of installation of MS Office XP Professional. The full administrative installation of MS Office XP Professional requires approximately 650 MB of disk space.

When the MS Office XP Professional product has been installed to the administrative network share, the product can be installed onto a workstation by executing the normal setup program. The installation process now provides a choice to either perform a minimum installation or a full local installation. A full local installation takes over 100 MB of disk space. A network workstation (minimum) installation requires typically 10 MB to 15 MB of local disk space. In the latter case, when the applications are used, they load over the network.

Microsoft Office Service Packs can be unpacked to update an administrative share. This makes it possible to update MS Office XP Professional for all users from a single installation of the service pack and generally circumvents the need to run updates on each network Windows client.

The default location for MS Office XP Professional data files can be set through registry editing or by way of configuration options inside each Office XP Professional application.

OpenOffice.Org OpenOffice Version 1.1.0 can be installed locally. It can also be installed to run off a network share. The latter is a most desirable solution for office-bound network users and for administrative staff alike. It permits quick and easy updates to be rolled out to all users with a minimum of disruption and with maximum flexibility.

The process for installation of administrative shared OpenOffice involves download of the distribution ZIP file, followed by extraction of the ZIP file into a temporary disk area. When fully extracted using the unzipping tool of your choosing, change into the Windows installation files directory then execute **setup -net**. You are prompted on screen for the target installation location. This is the administrative share point. The full administrative OpenOffice share takes approximately 150 MB of disk space.

3.3.7.1 Comments Regarding Software Terms of Use

Many single-user products can be installed into an administrative share, but personal versions of products such as Microsoft Office XP Professional do not permit this. Many people do not like terms of use typical with commercial products, so a few comments regarding software licensing seem important.

Please do not use an administrative installation of proprietary and commercially licensed software products to violate the copyright holders' property. All software is licensed, particularly software that is licensed for use free of charge. All software is the property of the copyright holder unless the author and/or copyright holder has explicitly disavowed ownership and has placed the software into the public domain.

Software that is under the GNU General Public License, like proprietary software, is licensed in a way that restricts use. For example, if you modify GPL software and then distribute the binary version of your modifications, you must offer to provide the source code as well. This restriction is designed to maintain the momentum of the diffusion of technology and to protect against the withholding of innovations.

Commercial and proprietary software generally restrict use to those who have paid the license fees and who comply with the licensee's terms of use. Software that is released under the GNU General Public License is restricted to particular terms and conditions also. Whatever the licensing terms may be, if you do not approve of the terms of use, please do not use the software.

Samba is provided under the terms of the GNU GPL Version 2, a copy of which is provided with the source code.

3.3.8   Windows Client Configuration

Christine needs to roll out 130 new desktop systems. There is no doubt that she also needs to reinstall many of the notebook computers that will be recycled for use with the new network configuration. The smartest way to handle the challenge of the roll-out program is to build a staged system for each type of target machine, and then use an image replication tool such as Norton Ghost (enterprise edition) to replicate the staged machine to its target desktops. The same can be done with notebook computers as long as they are identical or sufficiently similar.

WINDOWS CLIENT CONFIGURATION PROCEDURE

1. Install MS Windows XP Professional. During installation, configure the client to use DHCP for TCP/IP protocol configuration. DHCP configures all Windows clients to use the WINS Server address that has been defined for the local subnet.

2. Join the Windows Domain `PROMISES`. Use the Domain Administrator username `root` and the SMB password you assigned to this account. A detailed step-by-step procedure for joining a Windows 200x/XP Professional client to a Windows Domain is given in Chapter 15, "A Collection of Useful Tidbits", Section 15.1. Reboot the machine as prompted and then log on using the Domain Administrator account (`root`).

3. Verify `DIAMOND` is visible in **My Network Places**, that it is possible to connect to it and see the shares **accounts**, **apps**, and **finsvcs**, and that it is possible to open each share to reveal its contents.

4. Create a drive mapping to the **apps** share on the server `DIAMOND`.

5. Perform an administrative installation of each application to be used. Select the options that you wish to use. Of course, you can choose to run applications over the network, correct?

6. Now install all applications to be installed locally. Typical tools include Adobe Acrobat, NTP-based time synchronization software, drivers for specific local devices such as fingerprint scanners, and the like. Probably the most significant application for local installation is antivirus software.

7. Now install all four printers onto the staging system. The printers you install include the accounting department HP LaserJet 6 and Minolta QMS Magicolor printers. You will also configure identical printers that are located in the financial services department. Install printers on each machine following the steps shown in the Windows client printer preparation procedure below.

8. When you are satisfied that the staging systems are complete, use the appropriate procedure to remove the client from the domain. Reboot the system and then log on as the local administrator and clean out all temporary files stored on the system. Before shutting down, use the disk defragmentation tool so that the file system is in optimal condition before replication.

9. Boot the workstation using the Norton (Symantec) Ghosting diskette (or CD-ROM) and image the machine to a network share on the server.

10. You may now replicate the image to the target machines using the appropriate Norton Ghost procedure. Make sure to use the procedure that ensures each machine has a unique Windows security identifier (SID). When the installation of the disk image has completed, boot the PC.

11. Log on to the machine as the local Administrator (the only option), and join the machine to the Domain, following the procedure set out in Chapter 15, "A Collection of Useful Tidbits", Section 15.1. The system is now ready for the user to log on, provided you have created a network logon account for that user, of course.

12. Instruct all users to log on to the workstation using their assigned username and password.

WINDOWS CLIENT PRINTER PREPARATION PROCEDURE

1. Click **Start** → **Settings** → **Printers+Add Printer+Next**. Do not click **Network printer**. Ensure that **Local printer** is selected.

2. Click **Next**. In the **Manufacturer:** panel, select HP. In the **Printers:** panel, select the printer called HP LaserJet 6. Click **Next**.

3. In the **Available ports:** panel, select FILE:. Accept the default printer name by clicking **Next**. When asked, "Would you like to print a test page?," click **No**. Click **Finish**.

4. You may be prompted for the name of a file to print to. If so, close the dialog panel. Right-click **HP LaserJet 6** → **Properties** → **Details (Tab)** → **Add Port**.

5. In the **Network** panel, enter the name of the print queue on the Samba server as follows: \\DIAMOND\hplj6a. Click **OK+OK** to complete the installation.

6. Repeat the printer installation steps above for both HP LaserJet 6 printers as well as for both QMS Magicolor laser printers.

3.3.9   Key Points Learned

How do you feel? You have built a capable network, a truly ambitious project. Future network updates can be handled by your staff. You must be a satisfied manager. Let's review the achievements.

- A simple firewall has been configured to protect the server in the event that the ISP firewall service should fail.

- The Samba configuration uses measures to ensure that only local network users can connect to SMB/CIFS services.

- Samba uses the new `tdbsam` passdb backend facility. Considerable complexity was added to Samba functionality.

- A DHCP server was configured to implement dynamic DNS (DDNS) updates to the DNS server.

- The DNS server was configured to permit DDNS only for local network clients. This server also provides primary DNS services for the company Internet presence.

- You introduced an application server as well as the concept of cloning a Windows client in order to effect improved standardization of desktops and to reduce the costs of network management.

3.4   Questions and Answers

F.A.Q.

1. **Q:** *What is the maximum number of account entries that the* `tdbsam` *passdb backend can handle?*
A: The tdb data structure and support system can handle more entries than the number of accounts that are possible on most UNIX systems. A practical limit would come into play long before a performance boundary would be anticipated. That practical limit is controlled by the nature of Windows networking. There are few Windows file and print servers that can handle more than a few hundred concurrent client connections. The key limiting factors that predicate offloading of services to additional servers are memory capacity, the number of CPUs, network bandwidth, and disk I/O limitations. All of these are readily exhausted by just a few hundred concurrent active users. Such bottlenecks can best be removed by segmentation of the network (distributing network load across multiple networks).

As the network grows, it becomes necessary to provide additional authentication servers (domain controllers). The tdbsam is limited to a single machine and cannot be reliably replicated. This means that practical limits on network design dictate the point at which a distributed passdb backend is required; at this time, there is no real alternative other than ldapsam (LDAP).

The guideline provided in *TOSHARG2*, Chapter 10, Section 10.1.2, is to limit the number of accounts in the tdbsam backend to 250. This is the point at which most networks tend to want backup domain controllers (BDCs). Samba-3 does not provide a mechanism for replicating tdbsam data so it can be used by a BDC. The limitation of 250 users per tdbsam is predicated only on the need for replication, not on the limits[6] of the tdbsam backend itself.

2. **Q:** *Would Samba operate any better if the OS level is set to a value higher than 35?*
A: No. MS Windows workstations and servers do not use a value higher than 33. Setting this to a value of 35 already assures Samba of precedence over MS Windows products in browser elections. There is no gain to be had from setting this higher.

3. **Q:** *Why in this example have you provided UNIX group to Windows Group mappings for only Domain Groups?*
A: At this time, Samba has the capacity to use only Domain Groups mappings. It is possible that at a later date Samba may make use of Windows Local Groups, as well as of the Active Directory special Groups. Proper operation requires Domain Groups to be mapped to valid UNIX groups.

4. **Q:** *Why has a path been specified in the IPC$ share?*
A: This is done so that in the event that a software bug may permit a client connection to the IPC$ share to obtain access to the file system, it does so at a location that presents least risk. Under normal operation this type of paranoid step should not be necessary. The use of this parameter should not be necessary.

5. **Q:** *Why does the* `smb.conf` *file in this exercise include an entry for* smb ports?
A: The default order by which Samba-3 attempts to communicate with MS Windows clients is via port 445 (the TCP port used by Windows clients when NetBIOS-less SMB over TCP/IP is in use). TCP port 139 is the primary port used for NetBIOS over TCP/IP. In this configuration Windows network operations are predicated around NetBIOS over TCP/IP. By specifying the use of only port 139, the intent is to reduce unsuccessful service connection attempts. The result of this is improved network performance. Where Samba-3 is installed as an Active Directory Domain member, the default behavior is highly beneficial and should not be changed.

6. **Q:** *What is the difference between a print queue and a printer?*
A: A printer is a physical device that is connected either directly to the network or to a computer via a serial, parallel, or USB connection so that print jobs can be submitted to it to create a hard copy printout. Network-attached printers that use TCP/IP-based printing generally accept a single print data stream and block all secondary attempts to dispatch jobs concurrently to the same device. If many clients were to concurrently print directly via

---

[6]Bench tests have shown that tdbsam is a very effective database technology. There is surprisingly little performance loss even with over 4000 users.

TCP/IP to the same printer, it would result in a huge amount of network traffic through continually failing connection attempts.

A print server (like CUPS or LPR/LPD) accepts multiple concurrent input streams or print requests. When the data stream has been fully received, the input stream is closed, and the job is then submitted to a sequential print queue where the job is stored until the printer is ready to receive the job.

7. Q: *Can all MS Windows application software be installed onto an application server share?*
A: Much older Windows software is not compatible with installation to and execution from an application server. Enterprise versions of Microsoft Office XP Professional can be installed to an application server. Retail consumer versions of Microsoft Office XP Professional do not permit installation to an application server share and can be installed and used only to/from a local workstation hard disk.

8. Q: *Why use dynamic DNS (DDNS)?*
A: When DDNS records are updated directly from the DHCP server, it is possible for network clients that are not NetBIOS-enabled, and thus cannot use WINS, to locate Windows clients via DNS.

9. Q: *Why would you use WINS as well as DNS-based name resolution?*
A: WINS is to NetBIOS names as DNS is to fully qualified domain names (FQDN). The FQDN is a name like "myhost.mydomain.tld" where *tld* means `top-level domain`. A FQDN is a longhand but easy-to-remember expression that may be up to 1024 characters in length and that represents an IP address. A NetBIOS name is always 16 characters long. The 16th character is a name type indicator. A specific name type is registered[7] for each type of service that is provided by the Windows server or client and that may be registered where a WINS server is in use.

WINS is a mechanism by which a client may locate the IP Address that corresponds to a NetBIOS name. The WINS server may be queried to obtain the IP Address for a NetBIOS name that includes a particular registered NetBIOS name type. DNS does not provide a mechanism that permits handling of the NetBIOS name type information.

DNS provides a mechanism by which TCP/IP clients may locate the IP address of a particular hostname or service name that has been registered in the DNS database for a particular domain. A DNS server has limited scope of control and is said to be authoritative for the zone over which it has control.

Windows 200x Active Directory requires the registration in the DNS zone for the domain it controls of service locator[8] records that Windows clients and servers will use to locate Kerberos and LDAP services. ADS also requires the registration of special records that are

---

[7]See *TOSHARG2*, Chapter 9, for more information.
[8]See TOSHARG2, Chapter 9, Section 9.3.3.

called global catalog (GC) entries and site entries by which domain controllers and other essential ADS servers may be located.

10. **Q:** *What are the major benefits of using an application server?*
A: The use of an application server can significantly reduce application update maintenance. By providing a centralized application share, software updates need be applied to only one location for all major applications used. This results in faster update roll-outs and significantly better application usage control.

Example 3.3.1 NAT Firewall Configuration Script

```
#!/bin/sh
echo -e "\n\nLoading NAT firewall.\n"
IPTABLES=/usr/sbin/iptables
EXTIF="eth0"
INTIFA="eth1"
INTIFB="eth2"

/sbin/depmod -a
/sbin/modprobe ip_tables
/sbin/modprobe ip_conntrack
/sbin/modprobe ip_conntrack_ftp
/sbin/modprobe iptable_nat
/sbin/modprobe ip_nat_ftp
$IPTABLES -P INPUT DROP
$IPTABLES -F INPUT
$IPTABLES -P OUTPUT ACCEPT
$IPTABLES -F OUTPUT
$IPTABLES -P FORWARD DROP
$IPTABLES -F FORWARD

$IPTABLES -A INPUT -i lo -j ACCEPT
$IPTABLES -A INPUT -i $INTIFA -j ACCEPT
$IPTABLES -A INPUT -i $INTIFB -j ACCEPT
$IPTABLES -A INPUT -i $EXTIF -m state --state ESTABLISHED,RELATED -j ACCEPT
# Enable incoming traffic for: SSH, SMTP, DNS(tcp), HTTP, HTTPS
for i in 22 25 53 80 443
do
        $IPTABLES -A INPUT -i $EXTIF -p tcp --dport $i  -j ACCEPT
done
# Allow DNS(udp)
$IPTABLES -A INPUT -i $EXTIF -p udp -dport 53  -j ACCEPT
echo "Allow all connections OUT and only existing and specified ones IN"
$IPTABLES -A FORWARD -i $EXTIF -o $INTIFA -m state \
                                --state ESTABLISHED,RELATED -j ACCEPT
$IPTABLES -A FORWARD -i $EXTIF -o $INTIFB -m state \
                                --state ESTABLISHED,RELATED -j ACCEPT
$IPTABLES -A FORWARD -i $INTIFA -o $EXTIF -j ACCEPT
$IPTABLES -A FORWARD -i $INTIFB -o $EXTIF -j ACCEPT
$IPTABLES -A FORWARD -j LOG
echo "   Enabling SNAT (MASQUERADE) functionality on $EXTIF"
$IPTABLES -t nat -A POSTROUTING -o $EXTIF -j MASQUERADE
echo "1" > /proc/sys/net/ipv4/ip_forward
echo -e "\nNAT firewall done.\n"
```

Example 3.3.2 130 User Network with *tdbsam* — [globals] Section

```
# Global parameters
[global]
        workgroup = PROMISES
        netbios name = DIAMOND
        interfaces = eth1, eth2, lo
        bind interfaces only = Yes
        passdb backend = tdbsam
        pam password change = Yes
        passwd program = /usr/bin/passwd %u
        passwd chat = *New*Password* %n\n *Re-enter*new*password*%n\  ←
            n *Password*changed*
        username map = /etc/samba/smbusers
        unix password sync = Yes
        log level = 1
        syslog = 0
        log file = /var/log/samba/%m
        max log size = 50
        smb ports = 139
        name resolve order = wins bcast hosts
        time server = Yes
        printcap name = CUPS
        show add printer wizard = No
        add user script = /usr/sbin/useradd -m '%u'
        delete user script = /usr/sbin/userdel -r '%u'
        add group script = /usr/sbin/groupadd '%g'
        delete group script = /usr/sbin/groupdel '%g'
        add user to group script = /usr/sbin/usermod -G '%g' '%u'
        add machine script = /usr/sbin/useradd -s /bin/false -d /tmp  ←
            '%u'
        shutdown script = /var/lib/samba/scripts/shutdown.sh
        abort shutdown script = /sbin/shutdown -c
        logon script = scripts\logon.bat
        logon path = \\%L\profiles\%U
        logon drive = X:
        logon home = \\%L\%U
        domain logons = Yes
        preferred master = Yes
        wins support = Yes
        utmp = Yes
        map acl inherit = Yes
        printing = cups
        cups options = Raw
        veto files = /*.eml/*.nws/*.{*}/
        veto oplock files = /*.doc/*.xls/*.mdb/
```

Example 3.3.3 130 User Network with *tdbsam* — Services Section Part A

```
[homes]
        comment = Home Directories
        valid users = %S
        read only = No
        browseable = No
[printers]
        comment = SMB Print Spool
        path = /var/spool/samba
        guest ok = Yes
        printable = Yes
        use client driver = Yes
        default devmode = Yes
        browseable = No
[netlogon]
        comment = Network Logon Service
        path = /var/lib/samba/netlogon
        guest ok = Yes
        locking = No
[profiles]
        comment = Profile Share
        path = /var/lib/samba/profiles
        read only = No
        profile acls = Yes
[accounts]
        comment = Accounting Files
        path = /data/accounts
        read only = No
```

Example 3.3.4 130 User Network with *tdbsam* — Services Section Part B

```
[service]
        comment = Financial Services Files
        path = /data/service
        read only = No
[pidata]
        comment = Property Insurance Files
        path = /data/pidata
        read only = No
[apps]
        comment = Application Files
        path = /apps
        read only = Yes
        admin users = bjordan
```

Example 3.3.5 Script to Map Windows NT Groups to UNIX Groups

```bash
#!/bin/bash
#
# initGrps.sh
#

# Create UNIX groups
groupadd acctsdep
groupadd finsrvcs

# Map Windows Domain Groups to UNIX groups
net groupmap modify ntgroup="Domain Admins"  unixgroup=root
net groupmap modify ntgroup="Domain Users"   unixgroup=users
net groupmap modify ntgroup="Domain Guests"  unixgroup=nobody

# Add Functional Domain Groups
net groupmap add ntgroup="Accounts Dept"  unixgroup=acctsdep type=d
net groupmap add ntgroup="Financial Services" unixgroup=finsrvcs type=d
net groupmap add ntgroup="Insurance Group"     unixgroup=piops type=d

# Map Windows NT machine local groups to local UNIX groups
# Mapping of local groups is not necessary and not functional
# for this installation.
```

Example 3.3.6 DHCP Server Configuration File — /etc/dhcpd.conf

```
# Abmas Accounting Inc.
default-lease-time 86400;
max-lease-time 172800;
default-lease-time 86400;
option ntp-servers 192.168.1.1;
option domain-name "abmas.biz";
option domain-name-servers 192.168.1.1, 192.168.2.1;
option netbios-name-servers 192.168.1.1, 192.168.2.1;
option netbios-node-type 8;        ### Node type = Hybrid ###
ddns-updates on;               .        ### Dynamic DNS enabled ###
ddns-update-style interim;

subnet 192.168.1.0 netmask 255.255.255.0 {
        range dynamic-bootp 192.168.1.128 192.168.1.254;
        option subnet-mask 255.255.255.0;
        option routers 192.168.1.1;
        allow unknown-clients;
        host qmsa {
                hardware ethernet 08:00:46:7a:35:e4;
                fixed-address 192.168.1.20;
                }
        host hplj6a {
                hardware ethernet 00:03:47:cb:81:e0;
                fixed-address 192.168.1.30;
                }
        }
subnet 192.168.2.0 netmask 255.255.255.0 {
        range dynamic-bootp 192.168.2.128 192.168.2.254;
        option subnet-mask 255.255.255.0;
        option routers 192.168.2.1;
        allow unknown-clients;
        host qmsf {
                hardware ethernet 01:04:31:db:e1:c0;
                fixed-address 192.168.1.20;
          }
        host hplj6f {
                hardware ethernet 00:03:47:cf:83:e2;
                fixed-address 192.168.2.30;
                }
    }
subnet 127.0.0.0 netmask 255.0.0.0 {
        }
subnet 123.45.67.64 netmask 255.255.255.252 {
        }
```

Example 3.3.7 DNS Master Configuration File — /etc/named.conf Master Section

```
###
# Abmas Biz DNS Control File
###
# Date: November 15, 2003
###
options {
   directory "/var/lib/named";
   forwarders {
      123.45.12.23;
      };
   forward first;
   listen-on {
      mynet;
      };
   auth-nxdomain yes;
   multiple-cnames yes;
   notify no;
};

zone "." in {
   type hint;
   file "root.hint";
};

zone "localhost" in {
   type master;
   file "localhost.zone";
};

zone "0.0.127.in-addr.arpa" in {
   type master;
   file "127.0.0.zone";
};

acl mynet {
   192.168.1.0/24;
   192.168.2.0/24;
   127.0.0.1;
};

acl seconddns {
   123.45.54.32;
};
```

Example 3.3.8 DNS Master Configuration File — /etc/named.conf Forward Lookup Definition Section

```
zone "abmas.biz" {
    type master;
    file "/var/lib/named/master/abmas.biz.hosts";
    allow-query {
        mynet;
    };
    allow-transfer {
        mynet;
    };
    allow-update {
        mynet;
    };
};

zone "abmas.us" {
    type master;
    file "/var/lib/named/master/abmas.us.hosts";
    allow-query {
        all;
    };
    allow-transfer {
        seconddns;
    };
};
```

Example 3.3.9 DNS Master Configuration File — /etc/named.conf Reverse Lookup Definition Section

```
zone "1.168.192.in-addr.arpa" {
    type master;
    file "/var/lib/named/master/192.168.1.0.rev";
    allow-query {
        mynet;
    };
    allow-transfer {
        mynet;
    };
    allow-update {
        mynet;
    };
};

zone "2.168.192.in-addr.arpa" {
    type master;
    file "/var/lib/named/master/192.168.2.0.rev";
    allow-query {
        mynet;
    };
    allow-transfer {
        mynet;
    };
    allow-update {
        mynet;
    };
};
```

Example 3.3.10 DNS 192.168.1 Reverse Zone File

```
$ORIGIN .
$TTL 38400   ; 10 hours 40 minutes
1.168.192.in-addr.arpa   IN SOA   sleeth.abmas.biz. root.abmas.biz. (
             2003021825 ; serial
             10800        ; refresh (3 hours)
             3600         ; retry (1 hour)
             604800       ; expire (1 week)
             38400        ; minimum (10 hours 40 minutes)
             )
         NS sleeth1.abmas.biz.
$ORIGIN 1.168.192.in-addr.arpa.
1        PTR    sleeth1.abmas.biz.
20       PTR    qmsa.abmas.biz.
30       PTR    hplj6a.abmas.biz.
```

Example 3.3.11 DNS 192.168.2 Reverse Zone File

```
$ORIGIN .
$TTL 38400   ; 10 hours 40 minutes
2.168.192.in-addr.arpa   IN SOA   sleeth.abmas.biz. root.abmas.biz. (
             2003021825 ; serial
             10800        ; refresh (3 hours)
             3600         ; retry (1 hour)
             604800       ; expire (1 week)
             38400        ; minimum (10 hours 40 minutes)
             )
         NS sleeth2.abmas.biz.
$ORIGIN 2.168.192.in-addr.arpa.
1        PTR    sleeth2.abmas.biz.
20       PTR    qmsf.abmas.biz.
30       PTR    hplj6f.abmas.biz.
```

Example 3.3.12 DNS Abmas.biz Forward Zone File

```
$ORIGIN .
$TTL 38400        ; 10 hours 40 minutes
abmas.biz        IN SOA   sleeth1.abmas.biz. root.abmas.biz. (
                                 2003021833 ; serial
                                 10800      ; refresh (3 hours)
                                 3600       ; retry (1 hour)
                                 604800     ; expire (1 week)
                                 38400      ; minimum (10 hours 40 minutes)
                                 )
                         NS      dns.abmas.biz.
                         MX      10 mail.abmas.biz.
$ORIGIN abmas.biz.
sleeth1                  A       192.168.1.1
sleeth2                  A       192.168.2.1
qmsa                     A       192.168.1.20
hplj6a                   A       192.168.1.30
qmsf                     A       192.168.2.20
hplj6f                   A       192.168.2.30
dns                      CNAME   sleeth1
diamond                  CNAME   sleeth1
mail                     CNAME   sleeth1
```

Example 3.3.13 DNS Abmas.us Forward Zone File

```
$ORIGIN .
$TTL 38400        ; 10 hours 40 minutes
abmas.us         IN SOA   server.abmas.us. root.abmas.us. (
                                 2003021833 ; serial
                                 10800      ; refresh (3 hours)
                                 3600       ; retry (1 hour)
                                 604800     ; expire (1 week)
                                 38400      ; minimum (10 hours 40 minutes)
                                 )
                         NS      dns.abmas.us.
                         NS      dns2.abmas.us.
                         MX      10 mail.abmas.us.
$ORIGIN abmas.us.
server                   A       123.45.67.66
dns2                     A       123.45.54.32
gw                       A       123.45.67.65
www                      CNAME   server
mail                     CNAME   server
dns                      CNAME   server
```

Chapter 4

THE 500-USER OFFICE

The Samba-3 networking you explored in Chapter 3, "Secure Office Networking" covers the finer points of configuration of peripheral services such as DHCP and DNS, and WINS. You experienced implementation of a simple configuration of the services that are important adjuncts to successful deployment of Samba.

An analysis of the history of postings to the Samba mailing list easily demonstrates that the two most prevalent Samba problem areas are

- Defective resolution of a NetBIOS name to its IP address
- Printing problems

The exercises so far in this book have focused on implementation of the simplest printing processes involving no print job processing intelligence. In this chapter, you maintain that same approach to printing, but Chapter 5, "Making Happy Users" presents an opportunity to make printing more complex for the administrator while making it easier for the user.

Chapter 3, "Secure Office Networking" demonstrates operation of a DHCP server and a DNS server as well as a central WINS server. You validated the operation of these services and saw an effective implementation of a Samba domain controller using the *tdbsam* passdb backend.

The objective of this chapter is to introduce more complex techniques that can be used to improve manageability of Samba as networking needs grow. In this chapter, you implement a distributed DHCP server environment, a distributed DNS server arrangement, a centralized WINS server, and a centralized Samba domain controller.

A note of caution is important regarding the Samba configuration that is used in this chapter. The use of a single domain controller on a routed, multisegment network is a poor design choice that leads to potential network user complaints. This chapter demonstrates some successful techniques in deployment and configuration management. This should be viewed as a foundation chapter for complex Samba deployments.

As you master the techniques presented here, you may find much better methods to improve network management and control while reducing human resource overheads. You should take the opportunity to innovate and expand on the methods presented here and explore them to the fullest.

4.1   Introduction

Business continues to go well for Abmas. Mr. Meany is driving your success and the network continues to grow thanks to the hard work Christine has done. You recently hired Stanley Soroka as manager of information systems. Christine recommended Stan to the role. She told you Stan is so good at handling Samba that he can make a cast iron rocking horse that is embedded in concrete kick like a horse at a rodeo. You need skills like his. Christine and Stan get along just fine. Let's see what you can get out of this pair as they plot the next-generation networks.

Ten months ago Abmas closed an acquisition of a property insurance business. The founder lost interest in the business and decided to sell it to Mr. Meany. Because they were former university classmates, the purchase was concluded with mutual assent. The acquired business is located at the other end of town in much larger facilities. The old Abmas building has become too small. Located on the same campus as the newly acquired business are two empty buildings that are ideal to provide Abmas with opportunity for growth.

Abmas has now completed the purchase of the two empty buildings, and you are to install a new network and relocate staff in nicely furnished new facilities. The new network is to be used to fully integrate company operations. You have decided to locate the new network operations control center in the larger building in which the insurance group is located to take advantage of an ideal floor space and to allow Stan and Christine to fully stage the new network and test it before it is rolled out. Your strategy is to complete the new network so that it is ready for operation when the old office moves into the new premises.

4.1.1   Assignment Tasks

The acquired business had 280 network users. The old Abmas building housed 220 network users in unbelievably cramped conditions. The network that initially served 130 users now handles 220 users quite well.

The two businesses will be fully merged to create a single campus company. The Property Insurance Group (PIG) houses 300 employees, the new Accounting Services Group (ASG) will be in a small building (BLDG1) that houses 50 employees, and the Financial Services Group (FSG) will be housed in a large building that has capacity for growth (BLDG2). Building 2 houses 150 network users.

You have decided to connect the building using fiber optic links between new routers. As a backup, the buildings are interconnected using line-of-sight high-speed infrared facilities. The infrared connection provides a secondary route to be used during periods of high demand for network bandwidth.

The Internet gateway is upgraded to 15 Mb/sec service. Your ISP provides on your premises a fully managed Cisco PIX firewall. You no longer need to worry about firewall facilities on your network.

Stanley and Christine have purchased new server hardware. Christine wants to roll out a network that has whistles and bells. Stan wants to start off with a simple to manage, not-too-complex network. He believes that network users need to be gradually introduced to new features and capabilities and not rushed into an environment that may cause disorientation and loss of productivity.

Your intrepid network team has decided to implement a network configuration that closely mirrors the successful system you installed in the old Abmas building. The new network infrastructure is owned by Abmas, but all desktop systems are being procured through a new out-source services and leasing company. Under the terms of a deal with Mr. M. Proper (CEO), DirectPointe, Inc., provides all desktop systems and includes full level-one help desk support for a flat per-machine monthly fee. The deal allows you to add workstations on demand. This frees Stan and Christine to deal with deeper issues as they emerge and permits Stan to work on creating new future value-added services.

DirectPointe Inc. receives from you a new standard desktop configuration every four months. They automatically roll that out to each desktop system. You must keep DirectPointe informed of all changes.

The new network has a single Samba Primary Domain Controller (PDC) located in the Network Operation Center (NOC). Buildings 1 and 2 each have a local server for local application servicing. It is a domain member. The new system uses the *tdbsam* passdb backend.

Printing is based on raw pass-through facilities just as it has been used so far. All printer drivers are installed on the desktop and notebook computers.

4.2   Dissection and Discussion

The example you are building in this chapter is of a network design that works, but this does not make it a design that is recommended. As a general rule, there should be at least one Backup Domain Controller (BDC) per 150 Windows network clients. The principle behind this recommendation is that correct operation of MS Windows clients requires rapid network response to all SMB/CIFS requests. The same rule says that if there are more than 50 clients per domain controller, they are too busy to service requests. Let's put such rules aside and recognize that network load affects the integrity of domain controller responsiveness. This network will have 500 clients serviced by one central domain controller. This is not a good omen for user satisfaction. You, of course, address this very soon (see Chapter 5, "Making Happy Users").

4.2.1   Technical Issues

Stan has talked you into a horrible compromise, but it is addressed. Just make certain that the performance of this network is well validated before going live.

Design decisions made in this design include the following:

- A single PDC is being implemented. This limitation is based on the choice not to use LDAP. Many network administrators fear using LDAP because of the perceived complexity of implementation and management of an LDAP-based backend for all user identity management as well as to store network access credentials.

- Because of the refusal to use an LDAP (ldapsam) passdb backend at this time, the only choice that makes sense with 500 users is to use the tdbsam passwd backend. This type of backend is not receptive to replication to BDCs. If the tdbsam `passdb.tdb` file is replicated to BDCs using **rsync**, there are two potential problems: (1) data that is in memory but not yet written to disk will not be replicated, and (2) domain member machines periodically change the secret machine password. When this happens, there is no mechanism to return the changed password to the PDC.

- All domain user, group, and machine accounts are managed on the PDC. This makes for a simple mode of operation but has to be balanced with network performance and integrity of operations considerations.

- A single central WINS server is being used. The PDC is also the WINS server. Any attempt to operate a routed network without a WINS server while using NetBIOS over TCP/IP protocols does not work unless on each client the name resolution entries for the PDC are added to the `LMHOSTS`. This file is normally located on the Windows XP Professional client in the `C:\WINDOWS\SYSTEM32\ETC\DRIVERS` directory.

- At this time the Samba WINS database cannot be replicated. That is why a single WINS server is being implemented. This should work without a problem.

- BDCs make use of **winbindd** to provide access to domain security credentials for file system access and object storage.

- Configuration of Windows XP Professional clients is achieved using DHCP. Each subnet has its own DHCP server. Backup DHCP serving is provided by one alternate DHCP server. This necessitates enabling of the DHCP Relay agent on all routers. The DHCP Relay agent must be programmed to pass DHCP Requests from the network directed at the backup DHCP server.

- All network users are granted the ability to print to any printer that is network-attached. All printers are available from each server. Print jobs that are spooled to a printer that is not on the local network segment are automatically routed to the print spooler that is in control of that printer. The specific details of how this might be done are demonstrated for one example only.

- The network address and subnetmask chosen provide 1022 usable IP addresses in each subnet. If in the future more addresses are required, it would make sense to add further subnets rather than change addressing.

4.2.2   Political Issues

This case gets close to the real world. You and I know the right way to implement domain control. Politically, we have to navigate a minefield. In this case, the need is to get the PDC rolled out in compliance with expectations and also to be ready to save the day by having the real solution ready before it is needed. That real solution is presented in Chapter 5, "Making Happy Users".

4.3 Implementation

The following configuration process begins following installation of Red Hat Fedora Core2 on the three servers shown in the network topology diagram in Figure 4.1. You have selected hardware that is appropriate to the task.

Figure 4.1 Network Topology — 500 User Network Using tdbsam passdb backend.

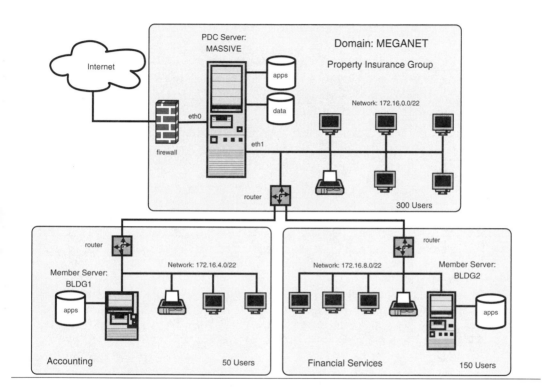

4.3.1 Installation of DHCP, DNS, and Samba Control Files

Carefully install the configuration files into the correct locations as shown in Table 4.1. You should validate that the full file path is correct as shown.

The abbreviation shown in this table as {VLN} refers to the directory location beginning with /var/lib/named.

4.3.2 Server Preparation: All Servers

The following steps apply to all servers. Follow each step carefully.

SERVER PREPARATION STEPS

Table 4.1 Domain: MEGANET, File Locations for Servers

File Information		Server Name		
Source	**Target Location**	**MASSIVE**	**BLDG1**	**BLDG2**
Example 4.3.1	/etc/samba/smb.conf	Yes	No	No
Example 4.3.2	/etc/samba/dc-common.conf	Yes	No	No
Example 4.3.3	/etc/samba/common.conf	Yes	Yes	Yes
Example 4.3.4	/etc/samba/smb.conf	No	Yes	No
Example 4.3.5	/etc/samba/smb.conf	No	No	Yes
Example 4.3.6	/etc/samba/dommem.conf	No	Yes	Yes
Example 4.3.7	/etc/dhcpd.conf	Yes	No	No
Example 4.3.8	/etc/dhcpd.conf	No	Yes	No
Example 4.3.9	/etc/dhcpd.conf	No	No	Yes
Example 4.3.10	/etc/named.conf (part A)	Yes	No	No
Example 4.3.11	/etc/named.conf (part B)	Yes	No	No
Example 4.3.12	/etc/named.conf (part C)	Yes	No	No
Example 4.3.13	{VLN}/master/abmas.biz.hosts	Yes	No	No
Example 4.3.14	{VLN}/master/abmas.us.hosts	Yes	No	No
Example 4.3.15	/etc/named.conf (part A)	No	Yes	Yes
Example 4.3.16	/etc/named.conf (part B)	No	Yes	Yes
Example 15.4.1	{VLN}/localhost.zone	Yes	Yes	Yes
Example 15.4.2	{VLN}/127.0.0.zone	Yes	Yes	Yes
Example 15.4.3	{VLN}/root.hint	Yes	Yes	Yes

1. Using the UNIX/Linux system tools, set the name of the server as shown in the network topology diagram in Figure 4.1. For SUSE Linux products, the tool that permits this is called **yast2**; for Red Hat Linux products, you can use the **netcfg** tool. Verify that your hostname is correctly set by running:

```
root#  uname -n
```

An alternate method to verify the hostname is:

```
root#  hostname -f
```

2. Edit your /etc/hosts file to include the primary names and addresses of all network interfaces that are on the host server. This is necessary so that during startup the system is able to resolve all its own names to the IP address prior to startup of the DNS server. You should check the startup order of your system. If the CUPS print server is started before the DNS server (**named**), you should also include an entry for the printers in the /etc/hosts file.

3. All DNS name resolution should be handled locally. To ensure that the server is

configured correctly to handle this, edit /etc/resolv.conf so it has the following content:

```
search abmas.us abmas.biz
nameserver 127.0.0.1
```

This instructs the name resolver function (when configured correctly) to ask the DNS server that is running locally to resolve names to addresses.

4. Add the **root** user to the password backend:

```
root#  smbpasswd -a root
New SMB password: XXXXXXXX
Retype new SMB password: XXXXXXXX
root#
```

The **root** account is the UNIX equivalent of the Windows domain administrator. This account is essential in the regular maintenance of your Samba server. It must never be deleted. If for any reason the account is deleted, you may not be able to recreate this account without considerable trouble.

5. Create the username map file to permit the **root** account to be called **Administrator** from the Windows network environment. To do this, create the file /etc/samba/ **smbusers** with the following contents:

```
####
# User mapping file
####
# File Format
# -----------
# Unix_ID = Windows_ID
#
# Examples:
# root = Administrator
# janes = "Jane Smith"
# jimbo = Jim Bones
#
# Note: If the name contains a space it must be double quoted.
#        In the example above the name 'jimbo' will be mapped to Windows
#        user names 'Jim' and 'Bones' because the space was not quoted.
################################################################################
root = Administrator
####
# End of File
```

```
####
```

6. Configure all network-attached printers to have a fixed IP address.

7. Create an entry in the DNS database on the server `MASSIVE` in both the forward lookup database for the zone `abmas.biz.hosts` and in the reverse lookup database for the network segment that the printer is located in. Example configuration files for similar zones were presented in Chapter 3, "Secure Office Networking", Example 3.3.12 and Example 3.3.11.

8. Follow the instructions in the printer manufacturer's manuals to permit printing to port 9100. Use any other port the manufacturer specifies for direct mode, raw printing. This allows the CUPS spooler to print using raw mode protocols.

9. Only on the server to which the printer is attached configure the CUPS Print Queues as follows:

```
root#  lpadmin -p printque -v socket://printer-name.abmas.biz:9100 -E
```

This step creates the necessary print queue to use no assigned print filter. This is ideal for raw printing, that is, printing without use of filters. The name *printque* is the name you have assigned for the particular printer.

10. Print queues may not be enabled at creation. Make certain that the queues you have just created are enabled by executing the following:

```
root#  /usr/bin/enable printque
```

11. Even though your print queue may be enabled, it is still possible that it does not accept print jobs. A print queue services incoming printing requests only when configured to do so. Ensure that your print queue is set to accept incoming jobs by executing the following command:

```
root#  /usr/bin/accept printque
```

12. This step, as well as the next one, may be omitted where CUPS version 1.1.18 or later is in use. Although it does no harm to follow it anyway, and may help to avoid time spent later trying to figure out why print jobs may be disappearing without a trace. Look at these two steps as *insurance* against lost time. Edit file `/etc/cups/mime.convs` to uncomment the line:

```
application/octet-stream    application/vnd.cups-raw    0    -
```

13. Edit the file `/etc/cups/mime.types` to uncomment the line:

```
application/octet-stream
```

14. Refer to the CUPS printing manual for instructions regarding how to configure CUPS so that print queues that reside on CUPS servers on remote networks route print jobs to the print server that owns that queue. The default setting on your CUPS server may automatically discover remotely installed printers and may permit this functionality without requiring specific configuration.

15. As part of the roll-out program, you need to configure the application's server shares. This can be done once on the central server and may then be replicated using a tool such as **rsync**. Refer to the man page for **rsync** for details regarding use. The notes in Section 3.3.7 may help in your decisions to use an application server facility.

NOTE

Logon scripts that are run from a domain controller (PDC or BDC) are capable of using semi-intelligent processes to automap Windows client drives to an application server that is nearest to the client. This is considerably more difficult when a single PDC is used on a routed network. It can be done, but not as elegantly as you see in the next chapter.

4.3.3 Server-Specific Preparation

There are some steps that apply to particular server functionality only. Each step is critical to correct server operation. The following step-by-step installation guidance will assist you in working through the process of configuring the PDC and then both BDC's.

4.3.3.1 Configuration for Server: MASSIVE

The steps presented here attempt to implement Samba installation in a generic manner. While some steps are clearly specific to Linux, it should not be too difficult to apply them to your platform of choice.

PRIMARY DOMAIN CONTROLLER PREPARATION

1. The host server acts as a router between the two internal network segments as well as for all Internet access. This necessitates that IP forwarding be enabled. This can be achieved by adding to the `/etc/rc.d/boot.local` an entry as follows:

```
echo 1 > /proc/sys/net/ipv4/ip_forward
```

To ensure that your kernel is capable of IP forwarding during configuration, you may wish to execute that command manually also. This setting permits the Linux system to act as a router.

2. This server is dual hosted (i.e., has two network interfaces) — one goes to the Internet and the other to a local network that has a router that is the gateway to the remote networks. You must therefore configure the server with route table entries so that it can find machines on the remote networks. You can do this using the appropriate system tools for your Linux server or using static entries that you place in one of the system startup files. It is best to always use the tools that the operating system vendor provided. In the case of SUSE Linux, the best tool to do this is YaST (refer to SUSE Administration Manual); in the case of Red Hat, this is best done using the graphical system configuration tools (see the Red Hat documentation). An example of how this may be done manually is as follows:

```
root#  route add net 172.16.4.0 netmask 255.255.252.0 gw 172.16.0.128
root#  route add net 172.16.8.0 netmask 255.255.252.0 gw 172.16.0.128
```

If you just execute these commands manually, the route table entries you have created are not persistent across system reboots. You may add these commands directly to the local startup files as follows: (SUSE) /etc/rc.d/boot.local, (Red Hat) /etc/rc.d/init.d/rc.local.

3. The final step that must be completed is to edit the /etc/nsswitch.conf file. This file controls the operation of the various resolver libraries that are part of the Linux Glibc libraries. Edit this file so that it contains the following entries:

```
hosts:      files dns wins
```

4. Create and map Windows domain groups to UNIX groups. A sample script is provided in Example 4.3.17. Create a file containing this script. You called yours /etc/samba/initGrps.sh. Set this file so it can be executed and then execute the script. An example of the execution of this script as well as its validation are shown in Section 4.3.2, Step 5.

5. For each user who needs to be given a Windows domain account, make an entry in the /etc/passwd file as well as in the Samba password backend. Use the system tool of your choice to create the UNIX system account, and use the Samba **smbpasswd** to create a domain user account. There are a number of tools for user management under UNIX, such as **useradd**, **adduser**, as well as a plethora of custom tools. With the tool of your choice, create a home directory for each user.

6. Using the preferred tool for your UNIX system, add each user to the UNIX groups created previously as necessary. File system access control is based on UNIX group membership.

7. Create the directory mount point for the disk subsystem that is to be mounted to provide data storage for company files, in this case, the mount point indicated in the smb.conf file is /data. Format the file system as required and mount the formatted file system partition using appropriate system tools.

8. Create the top-level file storage directories for data and applications as follows:

```
root#  mkdir -p /data/{accounts,finsvcs,pidata}
root#  mkdir -p /apps
root#  chown -R root:root /data
root#  chown -R root:root /apps
root#  chown -R bjordan:accounts /data/accounts
root#  chown -R bjordan:finsvcs /data/finsvcs
root#  chown -R bjordan:finsvcs /data/pidata
root#  chmod -R ug+rwxs,o-rwx /data
root#  chmod -R ug+rwx,o+rx-w /apps
```

Each department is responsible for creating its own directory structure within the departmental share. The directory root of the **accounts** share is /data/accounts. The directory root of the **finsvcs** share is /data/finsvcs. The /apps directory is the root of the **apps** share that provides the application server infrastructure.

9. The smb.conf file specifies an infrastructure to support roaming profiles and network logon services. You can now create the file system infrastructure to provide the locations on disk that these services require. Adequate planning is essential because desktop profiles can grow to be quite large. For planning purposes, a minimum of 200 MB of storage should be allowed per user for profile storage. The following commands create the directory infrastructure needed:

```
root#  mkdir -p /var/spool/samba
root#  mkdir -p /var/lib/samba/{netlogon/scripts,profiles}
root#  chown -R root:root /var/spool/samba
root#  chown -R root:root /var/lib/samba
root#  chmod a+rwxt /var/spool/samba
```

For each user account that is created on the system, the following commands should be executed:

```
root#  mkdir /var/lib/samba/profiles/'username'
root#  chown 'username':users /var/lib/samba/profiles/'username'
root#  chmod ug+wrx,o+rx,-w /var/lib/samba/profiles/'username'
```

10. Create a logon script. It is important that each line is correctly terminated with a carriage return and line-feed combination (i.e., DOS encoding). The following procedure works if the right tools (unxi2dos and dos2unix) are installed. First, create a

file called /var/lib/samba/netlogon/scripts/logon.bat.unix with the following
contents:

```
net time \\massive /set /yes
net use h: /home
```

Convert the UNIX file to a DOS file:

```
root#  dos2unix < /var/lib/samba/netlogon/scripts/logon.bat.unix \
       > /var/lib/samba/netlogon/scripts/logon.bat
```

11. There is one preparatory step without which you cannot have a working Samba net-
    work environment. You must add an account for each network user. You can do this
    by executing the following steps for each user:

```
root#  useradd -m username
root#  passwd username
Changing password for username.
New password: XXXXXXXX
Re-enter new password: XXXXXXXX
Password changed
root#  smbpasswd -a username
New SMB password: XXXXXXXX
Retype new SMB password: XXXXXXXX
Added user username.
```

You do, of course, use a valid user login ID in place of *username*.

12. Follow the processes shown in Section 4.3.4 to start all services.

13. Your server is ready for validation testing. Do not proceed with the steps in Sec-
    tion 4.3.3.2 until after the operation of the server has been validated following the
    same methods as outlined in Chapter 3, "Secure Office Networking", Section 3.3.6.

4.3.3.2   Configuration Specific to Domain Member Servers: BLDG1, BLDG2

The following steps will guide you through the nuances of implementing BDCs for the
broadcast isolated network segments. Remember that if the target installation platform is
not Linux, it may be necessary to adapt some commands to the equivalent on the target
platform.

BACKUP DOMAIN CONTROLLER CONFIGURATION STEPS

1. The final step that must be completed is to edit the `/etc/nsswitch.conf` file. This
   file controls the operation of the various resolver libraries that are part of the Linux
   Glibc libraries. Edit this file so that it contains the following entries:

   ```
   passwd:     files winbind
   group:      files winbind
   hosts:      files dns wins
   ```

2. Follow the steps outlined in Section 4.3.4 to start all services. Do not start Samba at
   this time. Samba is controlled by the process called **smb**.

3. You must now attempt to join the domain member servers to the domain. The following instructions should be executed to effect this:

   ```
   root#  net rpc join
   ```

4. You now start the Samba services by executing:

   ```
   root#  service smb start
   ```

5. Your server is ready for validation testing. Do not proceed with the steps in Section 4.3.3.2 until after the operation of the server has been validated following the
   same methods as outlined in Section 3.3.6.

4.3.4   Process Startup Configuration

There are two essential steps to process startup configuration. A process must be configured
so that it is automatically restarted each time the server is rebooted. This step involves
use of the **chkconfig** tool that created appropriate symbolic links from the master daemon
control file that is located in the `/etc/rc.d` directory to the `/etc/rc'x'.d` directories.
Links are created so that when the system run-level is changed, the necessary start or kill
script is run.

In the event that a service is provided not as a daemon but via the internetworking super
daemon (**inetd** or **xinetd**), then the **chkconfig** tool makes the necessary entries in the
`/etc/xinetd.d` directory and sends a hang-up (HUP) signal to the super daemon, thus
forcing it to re-read its control files.

Last, each service must be started to permit system validation to proceed. The following
steps are for a Red Hat Linux system, please adapt them to suit the target OS platform on
which you are installing Samba.

PROCESS STARTUP CONFIGURATION STEPS

1. Use the standard system tool to configure each service to restart automatically at
   every system reboot. For example,

Example 4.3.1 Server: MASSIVE (PDC), File: /etc/samba/smb.conf

```
# Global parameters
[global]
        workgroup = MEGANET
        netbios name = MASSIVE
        interfaces = eth1, lo
        bind interfaces only = Yes
        passdb backend = tdbsam
        smb ports = 139
        add user script = /usr/sbin/useradd -m '%u'
        delete user script = /usr/sbin/userdel -r '%u'
        add group script = /usr/sbin/groupadd '%g'
        delete group script = /usr/sbin/groupdel '%g'
        add user to group script = /usr/sbin/usermod -G '%g' '%u'
        add machine script = /usr/sbin/useradd -s /bin/false -d /var ↩
            /lib/nobody '%u'
        preferred master = Yes
        wins support = Yes
        include = /etc/samba/dc-common.conf
[accounts]
        comment = Accounting Files
        path = /data/accounts
        read only = No
[service]
        comment = Financial Services Files
        path = /data/service
        read only = No
[pidata]
        comment = Property Insurance Files
        path = /data/pidata
        read only = No
```

```
root#   chkconfig dhpc on
root#   chkconfig named on
root#   chkconfig cups on
root#   chkconfig smb on
root#   chkconfig swat on
```

2. Now start each service to permit the system to be validated. Execute each of the following in the sequence shown:

```
root#   service dhcp restart
root#   service named restart
root#   service cups restart
root#   service smb restart
```

Example 4.3.2 Server: MASSIVE (PDC), File: /etc/samba/dc-common.conf

```
# Global parameters
 [global]
        shutdown script = /var/lib/samba/scripts/shutdown.sh
        abort shutdown script = /sbin/shutdown −c
        logon script = scripts\logon.bat
        logon path = \%L\profiles\%U
        logon drive = X:
        logon home = \%L\%U
        domain logons = Yes
        preferred master = Yes
        include = /etc/samba/common.conf
 [homes]
        comment = Home Directories
        valid users = %S
        read only = No
        browseable = No
 [netlogon]
        comment = Network Logon Service
        path = /var/lib/samba/netlogon
        guest ok = Yes
        locking = No
 [profiles]
        comment = Profile Share
        path = /var/lib/samba/profiles
        read only = No
        profile acls = Yes
```

```
root#   service swat restart
```

4.3.5   Windows Client Configuration

The procedure for desktop client configuration for the network in this chapter is similar to that used for the previous one. There are a few subtle changes that should be noted.

WINDOWS CLIENT CONFIGURATION STEPS

1. Install MS Windows XP Professional. During installation, configure the client to use DHCP for TCP/IP protocol configuration. DHCP configures all Windows clients to use the WINS Server address that has been defined for the local subnet.

2. Join the Windows domain MEGANET. Use the domain administrator username root and the SMB password you assigned to this account. A detailed step-by-step procedure for joining a Windows 200x/XP Professional client to a Windows domain is given in Chapter 15, "A Collection of Useful Tidbits", Section 15.1. Reboot the machine as prompted and then log on using the domain administrator account (root).

Example 4.3.3 Common Samba Configuration File: /etc/samba/common.conf

```
[global]
        username map = /etc/samba/smbusers
        log level = 1
        syslog = 0
        log file = /var/log/samba/%m
        max log size = 50
        smb ports = 139
        name resolve order = wins bcast hosts
        time server = Yes
        printcap name = CUPS
        show add printer wizard = No
        shutdown script = /var/lib/samba/scripts/shutdown.sh
        abort shutdown script = /sbin/shutdown -c
        utmp = Yes
        map acl inherit = Yes
        printing = cups
        veto files = /*.eml/*.nws/*.{*}/
        veto oplock files = /*.doc/*.xls/*.mdb/
        include =
# Share and Service Definitions are common to all servers
[printers]
        comment = SMB Print Spool
        path = /var/spool/samba
        guest ok = Yes
        printable = Yes
        use client driver = Yes
        default devmode = Yes
        browseable = No
[apps]
        comment = Application Files
        path = /apps
        admin users = bjordan
        read only = No
```

3. Verify that the server called MEGANET is visible in **My Network Places**, that it is possible to connect to it and see the shares **accounts**, **apps**, and **finsvcs**, and that it is possible to open each share to reveal its contents.

4. Create a drive mapping to the **apps** share on a server. At this time, it does not particularly matter which application server is used. It is necessary to manually set a persistent drive mapping to the local applications server on each workstation at the time of installation. This step is avoided by the improvements to the design of the network configuration in the next chapter.

5. Perform an administrative installation of each application to be used. Select the options that you wish to use. Of course, you choose to run applications over the network, correct?

Example 4.3.4 Server: BLDG1 (Member), File: smb.conf

```
# Global parameters
 [global]
        workgroup = MEGANET
        netbios name = BLDG1
        include = /etc/samba/dom–mem.conf
```

Example 4.3.5 Server: BLDG2 (Member), File: smb.conf

```
# Global parameters
 [global]
        workgroup = MEGANET
        netbios name = BLDG2
        include = /etc/samba/dom–mem.conf
```

Example 4.3.6 Common Domain Member Include File: dom-mem.conf

```
# Global parameters
 [global]
        shutdown script = /var/lib/samba/scripts/shutdown.sh
        abort shutdown script = /sbin/shutdown -c
        preferred master = Yes
        wins server = 172.16.0.1
        idmap uid = 15000-20000
        idmap gid = 15000-20000
        include = /etc/samba/common.conf
```

---

6. Now install all applications to be installed locally. Typical tools include Adobe Acrobat, NTP-based time synchronization software, drivers for specific local devices such as fingerprint scanners, and the like. Probably the most significant application to be locally installed is antivirus software.

7. Now install all four printers onto the staging system. The printers you install include the accounting department HP LaserJet 6 and Minolta QMS Magicolor printers, and you also configure use of the identical printers that are located in the financial services department. Install printers on each machine using the following steps:

STEPS TO INSTALL PRINTER DRIVERS ON WINDOWS CLIENTS

   (a) Click **Start** → **Settings** → **Printers**+**Add Printer**+**Next**. Do not click **Network printer**. Ensure that **Local printer** is selected.

   (b) Click **Next**. In the **Manufacturer:** panel, select HP. In the **Printers:** panel, select the printer called HP LaserJet 6. Click **Next**.

   (c) In the **Available ports:** panel, select FILE:. Accept the default printer name by clicking **Next**. When asked, "Would you like to print a test page?", click **No**.

Example 4.3.7 Server: MASSIVE, File: dhcpd.conf

```
# Abmas Accounting Inc.

default-lease-time 86400;
max-lease-time 172800;
default-lease-time 86400;
ddns-updates on;
ddns-update-style interim;

option ntp-servers 172.16.0.1;
option domain-name "abmas.biz";
option domain-name-servers 172.16.0.1, 172.16.4.1;
option netbios-name-servers 172.16.0.1;
option netbios-node-type 8;

subnet 172.16.1.0 netmask 255.255.252.0 {
        range dynamic-bootp 172.16.1.0 172.16.2.255;
        option subnet-mask 255.255.252.0;
        option routers 172.16.0.1, 172.16.0.128;
        allow unknown-clients;
    }
subnet 172.16.4.0 netmask 255.255.252.0 {
        range dynamic-bootp 172.16.7.0 172.16.7.254;
        option subnet-mask 255.255.252.0;
        option routers 172.16.4.128;
        allow unknown-clients;
    }
subnet 172.16.8.0 netmask 255.255.252.0 {
        range dynamic-bootp 172.16.11.0 172.16.11.254;
        option subnet-mask 255.255.252.0;
        option routers 172.16.4.128;
        allow unknown-clients;
    }
subnet 127.0.0.0 netmask 255.0.0.0 {
        }
subnet 123.45.67.64 netmask 255.255.255.252 {
        }
```

Click **Finish**.

(d) You may be prompted for the name of a file to print to. If so, close the dialog panel. Right-click **HP LaserJet 6** → **Properties**.

(e) In the **Network** panel, enter the name of the print queue on the Samba server as follows: \\BLDG1\hplj6a. Click **OK+OK** to complete the installation.

Example 4.3.8 Server: BLDG1, File: dhcpd.conf

```
# Abmas Accounting Inc.

default-lease-time 86400;
max-lease-time 172800;
default-lease-time 86400;
ddns-updates on;
ddns-update-style ad-hoc;

option ntp-servers 172.16.0.1;
option domain-name "abmas.biz";
option domain-name-servers 172.16.0.1, 172.16.4.1;
option netbios-name-servers 172.16.0.1;
option netbios-node-type 8;

subnet 172.16.1.0 netmask 255.255.252.0 {
        range dynamic-bootp 172.16.3.0 172.16.3.255;
        option subnet-mask 255.255.252.0;
        option routers 172.16.0.1, 172.16.0.128;
        allow unknown-clients;
    }
subnet 172.16.4.0 netmask 255.255.252.0 {
        range dynamic-bootp 172.16.5.0 172.16.6.255;
        option subnet-mask 255.255.252.0;
        option routers 172.16.4.128;
        allow unknown-clients;
    }
subnet 127.0.0.0 netmask 255.0.0.0 {
        }
```

   (f) Repeat the printer installation steps above for both HP LaserJet 6 printers as well as for both QMS Magicolor laser printers. Remember to install all printers but to set the destination port for each to the server on the local network. For example, a workstation in the accounting group should have all printers directed at the server BLDG1. You may elect to point all desktop workstation configurations at the server called MASSIVE and then in your deployment procedures, it would be wise to document the need to redirect the printer configuration (as well as the applications server drive mapping) to the server on the network segment on which the workstation is to be located.

8. When you are satisfied that the staging systems are complete, use the appropriate procedure to remove the client from the domain. Reboot the system, and then log on as the local administrator and clean out all temporary files stored on the system. Before shutting down, use the disk defragmentation tool so that the file system is in optimal condition before replication.

Example 4.3.9 Server: BLDG2, File: dhcpd.conf

```
# Abmas Accounting Inc.

default-lease-time 86400;
max-lease-time 172800;
default-lease-time 86400;
ddns-updates on;
ddns-update-style interim;

option ntp-servers 172.16.0.1;
option domain-name "abmas.biz";
option domain-name-servers 172.16.0.1, 172.16.4.1;
option netbios-name-servers 172.16.0.1;
option netbios-node-type 8;

subnet 172.16.8.0 netmask 255.255.252.0 {
        range dynamic-bootp 172.16.9.0 172.16.10.255;
        option subnet-mask 255.255.252.0;
        option routers 172.16.8.128;
        allow unknown-clients;
    }
subnet 127.0.0.0 netmask 255.0.0.0 {
        }
```

9. Boot the workstation using the Norton (Symantec) Ghosting disk (or CD-ROM) and image the machine to a network share on the server.

10. You may now replicate the image using the appropriate Norton Ghost procedure to the target machines. Make sure to use the procedure that ensures each machine has a unique Windows security identifier (SID). When the installation of the disk image is complete, boot the PC.

11. Log onto the machine as the local Administrator (the only option), and join the machine to the domain following the procedure set out in Chapter 15, "A Collection of Useful Tidbits", Section 15.1. You must now set the persistent drive mapping to the applications server that the user is to use. The system is now ready for the user to log on, provided you have created a network logon account for that user, of course.

12. Instruct all users to log onto the workstation using their assigned username and password.

4.3.6 Key Points Learned

The network you have just deployed has been a valuable exercise in forced constraint. You have deployed a network that works well, although you may soon start to see performance problems, at which time the modifications demonstrated in Chapter 5, "Making Happy Users" bring the network to life. The following key learning points were experienced:

- The power of using `smb.conf` include files

- Use of a single PDC over a routed network

- Joining a Samba-3 domain member server to a Samba-3 domain

- Configuration of winbind to use domain users and groups for Samba access to resources on the domain member servers

- The introduction of roaming profiles

4.4   Questions and Answers

F.A.Q.

1. **Q:** *The example* `smb.conf` *files in this chapter make use of the* `include` *facility. How may I get to see what the actual working* `smb.conf` *settings are?*
A: You may readily see the net compound effect of the included files by running:

```
root#  testparm -s | less
```

2. **Q:** *Why does the include file* `common.conf` *have an empty include statement?*
A: The use of the empty include statement nullifies further includes. For example, let's say you desire to have just an smb.conf file that is built from the array of include files of which the master control file is called `master.conf`. The following command produces a compound `smb.conf` file.

```
root#  testparm -s /etc/samba/master.conf > /etc/samba/smb.conf
```

If the include parameter was not in the common.conf file, the final `smb.conf` file leaves the include in place, even though the file it points to has already been included. This is a bug that will be fixed at a future date.

3. **Q:** *I accept that the simplest configuration necessary to do the job is the best. The use of* `tdbsam` *passdb backend is much simpler than having to manage an LDAP-based* `ldapsam` *passdb backend. I tried using* **rsync** *to replicate the* `passdb.tdb`, *and it seems to work fine! So what is the problem?*
A: Replication of the *tdbsam* database file can result in loss of currency in its contents between the PDC and BDCs. The most notable symptom is that workstations may not

be able to log onto the network following a reboot and may have to rejoin the domain to recover network access capability.

4. **Q:** *You are using DHCP Relay enabled on the routers as well as a local DHCP server. Will this cause a clash?*
A: No. It is possible to have as many DHCP servers on a network segment as makes sense. A DHCP server offers an IP address lease, but it is the client that determines which offer is accepted, no matter how many offers are made. Under normal operation, the client accepts the first offer it receives.

The only exception to this rule is when the client makes a directed request from a specific DHCP server for renewal of the lease it has. This means that under normal circumstances there is no risk of a clash.

5. **Q:** *How does the Windows client find the PDC?*
A: The Windows client obtains the WINS server address from the DHCP lease information. It also obtains from the DHCP lease information the parameter that causes it to use directed UDP (UDP Unicast) to register itself with the WINS server and to obtain enumeration of vital network information to enable it to operate successfully.

6. **Q:** *Why did you enable IP forwarding (routing) only on the server called MASSIVE?*
A: The server called MASSIVE is acting as a router to the Internet. No other server (BLDG1 or BLDG2) has any need for IP forwarding because they are attached only to their own network. Route table entries are needed to direct MASSIVE to send all traffic intended for the remote network segments to the router that is its gateway to them.

7. **Q:** *You did nothing special to implement roaming profiles. Why?*
A: Unless configured to do otherwise, the default behavior with Samba-3 and Windows XP Professional clients is to use roaming profiles.

8. **Q:** *On the domain member computers, you configured winbind in the /etc/nsswitch. conf file. You did not configure any PAM settings. Is this an omission?*
A: PAM is needed only for authentication. When Samba is using Microsoft encrypted passwords, it makes only marginal use of PAM. PAM configuration handles only authentication. If you want to log onto the domain member servers using Windows networking usernames and passwords, it is necessary to configure PAM to enable the use of winbind. Samba makes use only of the identity resolution facilities of the name service switch (NSS).

9. **Q:** *You are starting SWAT up on this example but have not discussed that anywhere. Why did you do this?*

A: Oh, I did not think you would notice that. It is there so that it can be used. This is more fully discussed in *TOSHARG2*, which has a full chapter dedicated to the subject. While we are on the subject, it should be noted that you should definitely not use SWAT on any system that makes use of `smb.conf` *include* files because SWAT optimizes them out into an aggregated file but leaves in place a broken reference to the top-layer include file. SWAT was not designed to handle this functionality gracefully.

10. **Q:** *The domain controller has an auto-shutdown script. Isn't that dangerous?*
A: Well done, you spotted that! I guess it is dangerous. It is good to know that you can do this, though.

Example 4.3.10 Server: MASSIVE, File: named.conf, Part: A

```
###
# Abmas Biz DNS Control File
###
# Date: November 15, 2003
###
options {
   directory "/var/lib/named";
   forwarders {
      123.45.12.23;
      123.45.54.32;
      };
   forward first;
   listen-on {
      mynet;
      };
   auth-nxdomain yes;
   multiple-cnames yes;
   notify no;
};

zone "." in {
   type hint;
   file "root.hint";
};

zone "localhost" in {
   type master;
   file "localhost.zone";
};

zone "0.0.127.in-addr.arpa" in {
   type master;
   file "127.0.0.zone";
};

acl mynet {
   172.16.0.0/24;
   172.16.4.0/24;
   172.16.8.0/24;
   127.0.0.1;
};

acl seconddns {
      123.45.54.32;
};
```

Example 4.3.11 Server: MASSIVE, File: named.conf, Part: B

```
zone "abmas.biz" {
   type master;
   file "/var/lib/named/master/abmas.biz.hosts";
   allow-query {
      mynet;
   };
   allow-transfer {
      mynet;
   };
   allow-update {
      mynet;
   };
};

zone "abmas.us" {
        type master;
        file "/var/lib/named/master/abmas.us.hosts";
        allow-query {
                all;
        };
        allow-transfer {
                seconddns;
        };
};
```

Example 4.3.12 Server: MASSIVE, File: named.conf, Part: C

```
zone "0.16.172.in-addr.arpa" {
    type master;
    file "/var/lib/named/master/172.16.0.0.rev";
    allow-query {
        mynet;
    };
    allow-transfer {
        mynet;
    };
    allow-update {
        mynet;
    };
};

zone "4.16.172.in-addr.arpa" {
    type master;
    file "/var/lib/named/master/172.16.4.0.rev";
    allow-query {
        mynet;
    };
    allow-transfer {
        mynet;
    };
    allow-update {
        mynet;
    };
};

zone "8.16.172.in-addr.arpa" {
    type master;
    file "/var/lib/named/master/172.16.8.0.rev";
    allow-query {
        mynet;
    };
    allow-transfer {
        mynet;
    };
    allow-update {
        mynet;
    };
};
```

Example 4.3.13 Forward Zone File: abmas.biz.hosts

```
$ORIGIN .
$TTL 38400   ; 10 hours 40 minutes
abmas.biz   IN SOA   massive.abmas.biz. root.abmas.biz. (
            2003021833 ; serial
            10800        ; refresh (3 hours)
            3600         ; retry (1 hour)
            604800       ; expire (1 week)
            38400        ; minimum (10 hours 40 minutes)
            )
        NS massive.abmas.biz.
        NS bldg1.abmas.biz.
        NS bldg2.abmas.biz.
        MX 10 massive.abmas.biz.
$ORIGIN abmas.biz.
massive         A   172.16.0.1
router0             A       172.16.0.128
bldg1               A       172.16.4.1
router4             A       172.16.4.128
bldg2               A       172.16.8.1
router8             A       172.16.8.128
```

Example 4.3.14 Forward Zone File: abmas.biz.hosts

```
$ORIGIN .
$TTL 38400   ; 10 hours 40 minutes
abmas.us IN SOA   server.abmas.us. root.abmas.us. (
            2003021833 ; serial
            10800        ; refresh (3 hours)
            3600         ; retry (1 hour)
            604800       ; expire (1 week)
            38400        ; minimum (10 hours 40 minutes)
            )
        NS dns.abmas.us.
        NS dns2.abmas.us.
        MX 10 mail.abmas.us.
$ORIGIN abmas.us.
server          A   123.45.67.66
dns2         A   123.45.54.32
gw        A   123.45.67.65
www             CNAME server
mail            CNAME server
dns             CNAME server
```

Example 4.3.15 Servers: BLDG1/BLDG2, File: named.conf, Part: A

```
###
# Abmas Biz DNS Control File
###
# Date: November 15, 2003
###
options {
   directory "/var/lib/named";
   forwarders {
      172.16.0.1;
      };
   forward first;
   listen-on {
      mynet;
      };
   auth-nxdomain yes;
   multiple-cnames yes;
   notify no;
};

zone "." in {
   type hint;
   file "root.hint";
};

zone "localhost" in {
   type master;
   file "localhost.zone";
};

zone "0.0.127.in-addr.arpa" in {
   type master;
   file "127.0.0.zone";
};

acl mynet {
   172.16.0.0/24;
   172.16.4.0/24;
   172.16.8.0/24;
   127.0.0.1;
};

acl seconddns {
      123.45.54.32;
};
```

Example 4.3.16 Servers: BLDG1/BLDG2, File: named.conf, Part: B

```
zone "abmas.biz" {
   type slave;
   file "/var/lib/named/slave/abmas.biz.hosts";
   allow-query {
      mynet;
   };
   allow-transfer {
      mynet;
   };
};

zone "0.16.172.in-addr.arpa" {
   type slave;
   file "/var/lib/slave/master/172.16.0.0.rev";
   allow-query {
      mynet;
   };
   allow-transfer {
      mynet;
   };
};

zone "4.16.172.in-addr.arpa" {
   type slave;
   file "/var/lib/named/slave/172.16.4.0.rev";
   allow-query {
      mynet;
   };
   allow-transfer {
      mynet;
   };
};

zone "8.16.172.in-addr.arpa" {
   type slave;
   file "/var/lib/named/slave/172.16.8.0.rev";
   allow-query {
      mynet;
   };
   allow-transfer {
      mynet;
   };
};
```

Example 4.3.17 Initialize Groups Script, File: /etc/samba/initGrps.sh

---

```bash
#!/bin/bash

# Create UNIX groups
groupadd acctsdep
groupadd finsrvcs
groupadd piops

# Map Windows Domain Groups to UNIX groups
net groupmap modify ntgroup="Domain Admins"  unixgroup=root
net groupmap modify ntgroup="Domain Users"   unixgroup=users
net groupmap modify ntgroup="Domain Guests"  unixgroup=nobody

# Add Functional Domain Groups
net groupmap add ntgroup="Accounts Dept"        unixgroup=acctsdep type=d
net groupmap add ntgroup="Financial Services"   unixgroup=finsrvcs type=d
net groupmap add ntgroup="Insurance Group"      unixgroup=piops type=d
```

## Chapter 5

MAKING HAPPY USERS

It is said that "a day that is without troubles is not fulfilling. Rather, give me a day of troubles well handled so that I can be content with my achievements."

In the world of computer networks, problems are as varied as the people who create them or experience them. The design of the network implemented in Chapter 4, "The 500-User Office" may create problems for some network users. The following lists some of the problems that may occur:

CAUTION

A significant number of network administrators have responded to the guidance given here. It should be noted that there are sites that have a single PDC for many hundreds of concurrent network clients. Network bandwidth, network bandwidth utilization, and server load are among the factors that determine the maximum number of Windows clients that can be served by a single domain controller (PDC or BDC) on a network segment. It is possible to operate with only a single PDC over a routed network. What is possible is not necessarily *best practice*. When Windows client network logons begin to fail with the message that the domain controller cannot be found or that the user account cannot be found (when you know it exists), that may be an indication that the domain controller is overloaded or network bandwidth is overloaded. The guidance given for PDC/BDC ratio to Windows clients is conservative and if followed will minimize problems — but it is not absolute.

Users experiencing difficulty logging onto the network When a Windows client logs onto the network, many data packets are exchanged between the client and the server that is providing the network logon services. Each request between the client and the server must complete within a specific time limit. This is one of the primary factors that govern the installation of multiple domain controllers (usually called secondary or backup controllers). As a rough rule, there should be one such backup controller for every 30 to 150 clients. The actual limits are determined by network operational characteristics.

If the domain controller provides only network logon services and all file and print activity is handled by domain member servers, one domain controller per 150 clients on a single network segment may suffice. In any case, it is highly recommended to have a minimum of one domain controller (PDC or BDC) per network segment. It is better to have at least one BDC on the network segment that has a PDC. If the domain controller is also used as a file and print server, the number of clients it can service reliably is reduced, and generally for low powered hardware should not exceed 30 machines (Windows workstations plus domain member servers) per domain controller. Many sites are able to operate with more clients per domain controller, the number of clients that can be supported is limited by the CPU speed, memory and the workload on the Samba server as well as network bandwidth utilization.

Slow logons and log-offs Slow logons and log-offs may be caused by many factors that include:

- Excessive delays in the resolution of a NetBIOS name to its IP address. This may be observed when an overloaded domain controller is also the WINS server. Another cause may be the failure to use a WINS server (this assumes that there is a single network segment).

- Network traffic collisions due to overloading of the network segment. One short-term workaround to this may be to replace network HUBs with Ethernet switches.

- Defective networking hardware. Over the past few years, we have seen on the Samba mailing list a significant increase in the number of problems that were traced to a defective network interface controller, a defective HUB or Ethernet switch, or defective cabling. In most cases, it was the erratic nature of the problem that ultimately pointed to the cause of the problem.

- Excessively large roaming profiles. This type of problem is typically the result of poor user education as well as poor network management. It can be avoided by users not storing huge quantities of email in MS Outlook PST files as well as by not storing files on the desktop. These are old bad habits that require much discipline and vigilance on the part of network management.

- You should verify that the Windows XP WebClient service is not running. The use of the WebClient service has been implicated in many Windows networking-related problems.

Loss of access to network drives and printer resources Loss of access to network resources during client operation may be caused by a number of factors, including:

- Network overload (typically indicated by a high network collision rate)

- Server overload

- Timeout causing the client to close a connection that is in use but has been latent (no traffic) for some time (5 minutes or more)

- Defective networking hardware

No matter what the cause, a sudden loss of access to network resources can result in BSOD (blue screen of death) situations that necessitate rebooting of the client workstation. In the case of a mild problem, retrying to access the network drive of the printer may restore operations, but in any case this is a serious problem that may lead to the next problem, data corruption.

Potential data corruption Data corruption is one of the most serious problems. It leads to uncertainty, anger, and frustration, and generally precipitates immediate corrective demands. Management response to this type of problem may be rational, as well as highly irrational. There have been cases where management has fired network staff for permitting this situation to occur without immediate correction. There have been situations where perfectly functional hardware was thrown out and replaced, only to find the problem caused by a low-cost network hardware item. There have been cases where server operating systems were replaced, or where Samba was updated, only to later isolate the problem due to defective client software.

In this chapter, you can work through a number of measures that significantly arm you to anticipate and combat network performance issues. You can work through complex and thorny methods to improve the reliability of your network environment, but be warned that all such steps demand the price of complexity.

5.1   Regarding LDAP Directories and Windows Computer Accounts

Computer (machine) accounts can be placed wherever you like in an LDAP directory subject to some constraints that are described in this section.

The POSIX and SambaSAMAccount components of computer (machine) accounts are both used by Samba. That is, machine accounts are treated inside Samba in the same way that Windows NT4/200X treats them. A user account and a machine account are indistinguishable from each other, except that the machine account ends in a $ character, as do trust accounts.

The need for Windows user, group, machine, trust, and other such accounts to be tied to a valid UNIX UID is a design decision that was made a long way back in the history of Samba development. It is unlikely that this decision will be reversed or changed during the remaining life of the Samba-3.x series.

The resolution of a UID from the Windows SID is achieved within Samba through a mechanism that must refer back to the host operating system on which Samba is running. The name service switch (NSS) is the preferred mechanism that shields applications (like Samba) from the need to know everything about every host OS it runs on.

Samba asks the host OS to provide a UID via the "passwd", "shadow" and "group" facilities in the NSS control (configuration) file. The best tool for achieving this is left up to the UNIX administrator to determine. It is not imposed by Samba. Samba provides winbindd together with its support libraries as one method. It is possible to do this via LDAP, and for that Samba provides the appropriate hooks so that all account entities can be located in an LDAP directory.

For many the weapon of choice is to use the PADL nss_ldap utility. This utility must be configured so that computer accounts can be resolved to a POSIX/UNIX account UID. That is fundamentally an LDAP design question. The information provided on the Samba list and in the documentation is directed at providing working examples only. The design of an LDAP directory is a complex subject that is beyond the scope of this documentation.

5.2   Introduction

You just opened an email from Christine that reads:

Good morning,

> A few months ago we sat down to design the network. We discussed the challenges ahead and we all agreed to compromise our design to keep it simple. We knew there would be problems, but anticipated that we would have some time to resolve any issues that might be encountered.

> As you now know, we started off on the wrong foot. We have a lot of unhappy users. One of them resigned yesterday afternoon because she was under duress to complete some critical projects. She suffered a blue screen of death situation just as she was finishing four hours of intensive work, all of which was lost. She has a unique requirement that involves storing large files on her desktop. Mary's desktop profile is nearly 1 GB in size. As a result of her desktop configuration, it takes her nearly 15 minutes just to log onto her workstation. But that is not enough. Because all network logon traffic passes over the network links between our buildings, logging on may take three or four attempts due to blue screen problems associated with network timeouts.

> A few of us worked to help her out of trouble. We convinced her to stay and promised to fully resolve the difficulties she is facing. We have no choice. We must implement LDAP and set hard limits on what our users can do with their desktops. Otherwise, we face staff losses that can surely do harm to our growth as well as to staff morale. I am sure we can better deal with the consequences of what we know we must do than we can with the unrest we have now.

> Stan and I have discussed the current situation. We are resolved to help our users and protect the well being of Abmas. Please acknowledge this advice with consent to proceed as required to regain control of our vital IT operations.

> —Christine

Every compromise has consequences. Having a large routed (i.e., multisegment) network with only a single domain controller is a poor design that has obvious operational effects that may frustrate users. Here is your reply:

Christine, Your diligence and attention to detail are much valued. Stan and I fully support your proposals to resolve the issues. I am confident that your plans fully realized will significantly boost staff morale. Please go ahead with your plans. If you have any problems, please let me know. Please let Stan know what the estimated cost will be so I can approve the expense. Do not wait for approval; I appreciate the urgency.

—Bob

5.2.1 Assignment Tasks

The priority of assigned tasks in this chapter is:

1. Implement Backup Domain Controllers (BDCs) in each building. This involves a change from a *tdbsam* backend that was used in the previous chapter to an LDAP-based backend.

   You can implement a single central LDAP server for this purpose.

2. Rectify the problem of excessive logon times. This involves redirection of folders to network shares as well as modification of all user desktops to exclude the redirected folders from being loaded at login time. You can also create a new default profile that can be used for all new users.

You configure a new MS Windows XP Professional workstation disk image that you roll out to all desktop users. The instructions you have created are followed on a staging machine from which all changes can be carefully tested before inflicting them on your network users.

This is the last network example in which specific mention of printing is made. The example again makes use of the CUPS printing system.

5.3 Dissection and Discussion

The implementation of Samba BDCs necessitates the installation and configuration of LDAP. For this site, you use OpenLDAP, the open source software LDAP server platform. Commercial LDAP servers in current use with Samba-3 include:

- Novell eDirectory[1] is being successfully used by some sites. Information on how to use eDirectory can be obtained from the Samba mailing lists or from Novell.

- IBM Tivoli Directory Server[2] can be used to provide the Samba LDAP backend. Example schema files are provided in the Samba source code tarball under the directory `~samba/example/LDAP`.

- Sun ONE Identity Server product suite[3] provides an LDAP server that can be used for Samba. Example schema files are provided in the Samba source code tarball under the directory `~samba/example/LDAP`.

---

[1] <http://www.novell.com/products/edirectory/>
[2] <http://www-306.ibm.com/software/tivoli/products/directory-server/>
[3] <http://www.sun.com/software/software/products/identity_srvr/home_identity.xml>

A word of caution is fully in order. OpenLDAP is purely an LDAP server, and unlike commercial offerings, it requires that you manually edit the server configuration files and manually initialize the LDAP directory database. OpenLDAP itself has only command-line tools to help you to get OpenLDAP and Samba-3 running as required, albeit with some learning curve challenges.

For most sites, the deployment of Microsoft Active Directory from the shrink-wrapped installation is quite adequate. If you are migrating from Microsoft Active Directory, be warned that OpenLDAP does not include GUI-based directory management tools. Even a simple task such as adding users to the OpenLDAP database requires an understanding of what you are doing, why you are doing it, and the tools that you must use.

When installed and configured, an OpenLDAP Identity Management backend for Samba functions well. High availability operation may be obtained through directory replication/synchronization and master/slave server configurations. OpenLDAP is a mature platform to host the organizational directory infrastructure that can include all UNIX accounts, directories for electronic mail, and much more. The price paid through learning how to design an LDAP directory schema in implementation and configuration of management tools is well rewarded by performance and flexibility and the freedom to manage directory contents with greater ability to back up, restore, and modify the directory than is generally possible with Microsoft Active Directory.

A comparison of OpenLDAP with Microsoft Active Directory does not do justice to either. OpenLDAP is an LDAP directory tool-set. Microsoft Active Directory Server is an implementation of an LDAP server that is largely preconfigured for a specific task orientation. It comes with a set of administrative tools that is entirely customized for the purpose of running MS Windows applications that include file and print services, Microsoft Exchange server, Microsoft SQL server, and more. The complexity of OpenLDAP is highly valued by the UNIX administrator who wants to build a custom directory solution. Microsoft provides an application called MS ADAM[4] that provides more generic LDAP services, yet it does not have the vanilla-like services of OpenLDAP.

You may wish to consider outsourcing the development of your OpenLDAP directory to an expert, particularly if you find the challenge of learning about LDAP directories, schemas, configuration, and management tools and the creation of shell and Perl scripts a bit challenging. OpenLDAP can be easily customized, though it includes many ready-to-use schemas. Samba-3 provides an OpenLDAP schema file that is required for use as a passdb backend.

For those who are willing to brave the process of installing and configuring LDAP and Samba-3 interoperability, there are a few nice Web-based tools that may help you to manage your users and groups more effectively. The Web-based tools you might like to consider include the LDAP Account Manager[5] (LAM) and the Webmin-based Webmin[6] Idealx CGI tools[7].

---

[4] <http://www.microsoft.com/windowsserver2003/adam/default.mspx>
[5] <http://lam.sourceforge.net/>
[6] <http://www.webmin.com>
[7] <http://webmin.idealx.org/index.en.html>

Some additional LDAP tools should be mentioned. Every so often a Samba user reports using one of these, so it may be useful to them: GQ[8], a GTK-based LDAP browser; LDAP Browser/Editor[9] ; JXplorer[10] (by Computer Associates); and phpLDAPadmin[11].

NOTE

The following prescriptive guidance is not an LDAP tutorial. The LDAP implementation expressly uses minimal security controls. No form of secure LDAP communications is attempted. The LDAP configuration information provided is considered to consist of the barest essentials only. You are strongly encouraged to learn more about LDAP before attempting to deploy it in a business-critical environment.

Information to help you get started with OpenLDAP is available from the OpenLDAP web site[12]. Many people have found the book *LDAP System Administration*,[13] by Jerry Carter quite useful.

Mary's problems are due to two factors. First, the absence of a domain controller on the local network is the main cause of the errors that result in blue screen crashes. Second, Mary has a large profile that must be loaded over the WAN connection. The addition of BDCs on each network segment significantly improves overall network performance for most users, but it is not enough. You must gain control over user desktops, and this must be done in a way that wins their support and does not cause further loss of staff morale. The following procedures solve this problem.

There is also an opportunity to implement smart printing features. You add this to the Samba configuration so that future printer changes can be managed without need to change desktop configurations.

You add the ability to automatically download new printer drivers, even if they are not installed in the default desktop profile. Only one example of printing configuration is given. It is assumed that you can extrapolate the principles and use them to install all printers that may be needed.

5.3.1   Technical Issues

The solution provided is a minimal approach to getting OpenLDAP running as an identity management directory server for UNIX system accounts as well as for Samba. From the OpenLDAP perspective, UNIX system accounts are stored POSIX schema extensions.

---

[8]<http://biot.com/gq>
[9]<http://www.iit.edu/~gawojar/ldap/>
[10]<http://www.jxplorer.org/>
[11]<http://phpldapadmin.sourceforge.net/>
[12]<http://www.openldap.org/pub/>
[13]<http://www.oreilly.com/catalog/ldapsa/index.html>

Samba provides its own schema to permit storage of account attributes Samba needs. Samba-3 can use the LDAP backend to store:

- Windows Networking User Accounts

- Windows NT Group Accounts

- Mapping Information between UNIX Groups and Windows NT Groups

- ID Mappings for SIDs to UIDs (also for foreign Domain SIDs)

The use of LDAP with Samba-3 makes it necessary to store UNIX accounts as well as Windows Networking accounts in the LDAP backend. This implies the need to use the PADL LDAP tools[14]. The resolution of the UNIX group name to its GID must be enabled from either the /etc/group or from the LDAP backend. This requires the use of the PADL nss_ldap tool-set that integrates with the NSS. The same requirements exist for resolution of the UNIX username to the UID. The relationships are demonstrated in Figure 5.1.

Figure 5.1 The Interaction of LDAP, UNIX Posix Accounts and Samba Accounts

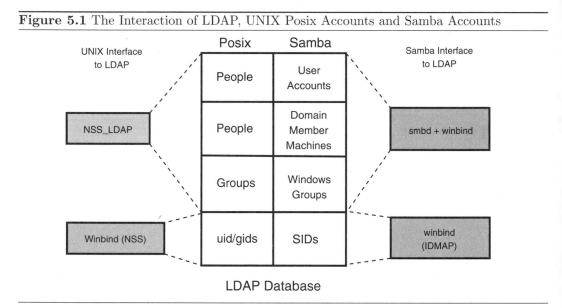

You configure OpenLDAP so that it is operational. Before deploying the OpenLDAP, you really ought to learn how to configure secure communications over LDAP so that site security is not at risk. This is not covered in the following guidance.

When OpenLDAP has been made operative, you configure the PDC called **MASSIVE**. You initialize the Samba **secrets.tdb** file. Then you create the LDAP Interchange Format (LDIF) file from which the LDAP database can be initialized. You need to decide how best to create user and group accounts. A few hints are, of course, provided. You can also find on the enclosed CD-ROM, in the **Chap06** directory, a few tools that help to manage user and group configuration.

---

[14]<http://www.padl.com/Contents/OpenSourceSoftware.html>

In order to effect folder redirection and to add robustness to the implementation, create a network default profile. All network users workstations are configured to use the new profile. Roaming profiles will automatically be deleted from the workstation when the user logs off.

The profile is configured so that users cannot change the appearance of their desktop. This is known as a mandatory profile. You make certain that users are able to use their computers efficiently.

A network logon script is used to deliver flexible but consistent network drive connections.

5.3.1.1   Addition of Machines to the Domain

Samba versions prior to 3.0.11 necessitated the use of a domain administrator account that maps to the UNIX UID=0. The UNIX operating system permits only the `root` user to add user and group accounts. Samba 3.0.11 introduced a new facility known as `Privileges`, which provides five new privileges that can be assigned to users and/or groups; see Table 5.1.

Table 5.1 Current Privilege Capabilities

Privilege	Description
SeMachineAccountPrivilege	Add machines to domain
SePrintOperatorPrivilege	Manage printers
SeAddUsersPrivilege	Add users and groups to the domain
SeRemoteShutdownPrivilege	Force shutdown from a remote system
SeDiskOperatorPrivilege	Manage disk share

In this network example use is made of one of the supported privileges purely to demonstrate how any user can now be given the ability to add machines to the domain using a normal user account that has been given the appropriate privileges.

5.3.1.2   Roaming Profile Background

As XP roaming profiles grow, so does the amount of time it takes to log in and out.

An XP roaming profile consists of the `HKEY_CURRENT_USER` hive file `NTUSER.DAT` and a number of folders (My Documents, Application Data, Desktop, Start Menu, Templates, NetHood, Favorites, and so on). When a user logs onto the network with the default configuration of MS Windows NT/200x/XPP, all this data is copied to the local machine under the `C:\Documents and Settings\%USERNAME%` directory. While the user is logged in, any changes made to any of these folders or to the `HKEY_CURRENT_USER` branch of the registry are made to the local copy of the profile. At logout the profile data is copied back to the server. This behavior can be changed through appropriate registry changes and/or through changes to the default user profile. In the latter case, it updates the registry with the values that are set in the profile `NTUSER.DAT` file.

The first challenge is to reduce the amount of data that must be transferred to and from the profile server as roaming profiles are processed. This includes removing all the shortcuts in the Recent directory, making sure the cache used by the Web browser is not being dumped into the `Application Data` folder, removing the Java plug-ins cache (the .jpi_cache directory in the profile), as well as training the user to not place large files on the desktop and to use his or her mapped home directory instead of the `My Documents` folder for saving documents.

Using a folder other than `My Documents` is a nuisance for some users, since many applications use it by default.

The secret to rapid loading of roaming profiles is to prevent unnecessary data from being copied back and forth, without losing any functionality. This is not difficult; it can be done by making changes to the Local Group Policy on each client as well as changing some paths in each user's `NTUSER.DAT` hive.

Every user profile has its own `NTUSER.DAT` file. This means you need to edit every user's profile, unless a better method can be followed. Fortunately, with the right preparations, this is not difficult. It is possible to remove the `NTUSER.DAT` file from each user's profile. Then just create a Network Default Profile. Of course, it is necessary to copy all files from redirected folders to the network share to which they are redirected.

5.3.1.3   The Local Group Policy

Without an Active Directory PDC, you cannot take full advantage of Group Policy Objects. However, you can still make changes to the Local Group Policy by using the Group Policy editor (**gpedit.msc**).

The *Exclude directories in roaming profile* settings can be found under **User Configuration** → **Administrative Templates** → **System** → **User Profiles**. By default this setting contains "Local Settings; Temporary Internet Files; History; Temp".

Simply add the folders you do not wish to be copied back and forth to this semicolon-separated list. Note that this change must be made on all clients that are using roaming profiles.

5.3.1.4   Profile Changes

There are two changes that should be done to each user's profile. Move each of the directories that you have excluded from being copied back and forth out of the usual profile path. Modify each user's `NTUSER.DAT` file to point to the new paths that are shared over the network instead of to the default path (`C:\Documents and Settings\%USERNAME%`).

The above modifies existing user profiles. So that newly created profiles have these settings, you need to modify the `NTUSER.DAT` in the `C:\Documents and Settings\Default User` folder on each client machine, changing the same registry keys. You could do this by copying `NTUSER.DAT` to a Linux box and using **regedt32**. The basic method is described under Section 5.7.1.

5.3.1.5   Using a Network Default User Profile

If you are using Samba as your PDC, you should create a file share called NETLOGON and within that create a directory called Default User, which is a copy of the desired default user configuration (including a copy of NTUSER.DAT). If this share exists and the Default User folder exists, the first login from a new account pulls its configuration from it. See also the Real Men Don't Click[15] Web site.

5.3.1.6   Installation of Printer Driver Auto-Download

The subject of printing is quite topical. Printing problems run second place to name resolution issues today. So far in this book, you have experienced only what is generally known as "dumb" printing. Dumb printing is the arrangement by which all drivers are manually installed on each client and the printing subsystems perform no filtering or intelligent processing. Dumb printing is easily understood. It usually works without many problems, but it has its limitations also. Dumb printing is better known as **Raw-Print-Through** printing.

Samba permits the configuration of **smart** printing using the Microsoft Windows point-and-click (also called drag-and-drop) printing. What this provides is essentially the ability to print to any printer. If the local client does not yet have a driver installed, the driver is automatically downloaded from the Samba server and installed on the client. Drag-and-drop printing is neat; it means the user never needs to fuss with driver installation, and that is a Good Thing,^{TM} isn't it?

There is a further layer of print job processing that is known as **intelligent** printing that automatically senses the file format of data submitted for printing and then invokes a suitable print filter to convert the incoming data stream into a format suited to the printer to which the job is dispatched.

The CUPS printing subsystem is capable of intelligent printing. It has the capacity to detect the data format and apply a print filter. This means that it is feasible to install on all Windows clients a single printer driver for use with all printers that are routed through CUPS. The most sensible driver to use is one for a PostScript printer. Fortunately, Easy Software Products[16], the authors of CUPS, have released a PostScript printing driver for Windows. It can be installed into the Samba printing backend so that it automatically downloads to the client when needed.

This means that so long as there is a CUPS driver for the printer, all printing from Windows software can use PostScript, no matter what the actual printer language for the physical device is. It also means that the administrator can swap out a printer with a totally different type of device without ever needing to change a client workstation driver.

This book is about Samba-3, so you can confine the printing style to just the smart style of installation. Those interested in further information regarding intelligent printing should review documentation on the Easy Software Products Web site.

---

[15]<http://isg.ee.ethz.ch/tools/realmen/det/skel.en.html>
[16]<http://www.easysw.com>

5.3.1.7   Avoiding Failures: Solving Problems Before They Happen

It has often been said that there are three types of people in the world: those who have sharp minds and those who forget things. Please do not ask what the third group is like! Well, it seems that many of us have company in the second group. There must be a good explanation why so many network administrators fail to solve apparently simple problems efficiently and effectively.

Here are some diagnostic guidelines that can be referred to when things go wrong:

Preliminary Advice: Dangers Can Be Avoided   The best advice regarding how to mend a broken leg is "Never break a leg!"

Newcomers to Samba and LDAP seem to struggle a great deal at first. If you want advice regarding the best way to remedy LDAP and Samba problems: "Avoid them like the plague!"

If you are now asking yourself how problems can be avoided, the best advice is to start out your learning experience with a *known-good configuration*. After you have seen a fully working solution, a good way to learn is to make slow and progressive changes that cause things to break, then observe carefully how and why things ceased to work.

The examples in this chapter (also in the book as a whole) are known to work. That means that they could serve as the kick-off point for your journey through fields of knowledge. Use this resource carefully; we hope it serves you well.

WARNING

Do not be lulled into thinking that you can easily adopt the examples in this book and adapt them without first working through the examples provided. A little thing overlooked can cause untold pain and may permanently tarnish your experience.

The Name Service Caching Daemon   The name service caching daemon (nscd) is a primary cause of difficulties with name resolution, particularly where **winbind** is used. Winbind does its own caching, thus nscd causes double caching which can lead to peculiar problems during debugging. As a rule, it is a good idea to turn off the name service caching daemon.

Operation of the name service caching daemon is controlled by the `/etc/nscd.conf` file. Typical contents of this file are as follows:

```
# /etc/nscd.conf
# An example Name Service Cache config file.  This file is needed by nscd.
# Legal entries are:
#       logfile                 <file>
```

```
#       debug-level             <level>
#       threads                 <threads to use>
#       server-user             <user to run server as instead of root>
#             server-user is ignored if nscd is started with -S parameters
#       stat-user               <user who is allowed to request statistics>
#       reload-count            unlimited|<number>
#
#       enable-cache            <service> <yes|no>
#       positive-time-to-live   <service> <time in seconds>
#       negative-time-to-live   <service> <time in seconds>
#       suggested-size          <service> <prime number>
#       check-files             <service> <yes|no>
#       persistent              <service> <yes|no>
#       shared                  <service> <yes|no>
# Currently supported cache names (services): passwd, group, hosts
#       logfile                 /var/log/nscd.log
#       threads                 6
#       server-user             nobody
#       stat-user               somebody
        debug-level             0
#       reload-count            5
        enable-cache            passwd          yes
        positive-time-to-live   passwd          600
        negative-time-to-live   passwd          20
        suggested-size          passwd          211
        check-files             passwd          yes
        persistent              passwd          yes
        shared                  passwd          yes
        enable-cache            group           yes
        positive-time-to-live   group           3600
        negative-time-to-live   group           60
        suggested-size          group           211
        check-files             group           yes
        persistent              group           yes
        shared                  group           yes
# !!!!!WARNING!!!!! Host cache is insecure!!! The mechanism in nscd to
# cache hosts will cause your local system to not be able to trust
# forward/reverse lookup checks. DO NOT USE THIS if your system relies on
# this sort of security mechanism. Use a caching DNS server instead.
        enable-cache            hosts           no
        positive-time-to-live   hosts           3600
        negative-time-to-live   hosts           20
        suggested-size          hosts           211
        check-files             hosts           yes
        persistent              hosts           yes
        shared                  hosts           yes
```

It is feasible to comment out the `passwd` and `group` entries so they will not be cached. Alternatively, it is often simpler to just disable the **nscd** service by executing (on Novell SUSE Linux):

```
root#  chkconfig nscd off
root#  rcnscd off
```

Debugging LDAP   In the example `/etc/openldap/slapd.conf` control file (see Example 5.4.1) there is an entry for `loglevel 256`. To enable logging via the syslog infrastructure, it is necessary to uncomment this parameter and restart **slapd**.

LDAP log information can be directed into a file that is separate from the normal system log files by changing the `/etc/syslog.conf` file so it has the following contents:

```
# Some foreign boot scripts require local7
#
local0,local1.*                -/var/log/localmessages
local2,local3.*                -/var/log/localmessages
local5.*                       -/var/log/localmessages
local6,local7.*                -/var/log/localmessages
local4.*                       -/var/log/ldaplogs
```

In this case, all LDAP-related logs will be directed to the file `/var/log/ldaplogs`. This makes it easy to track LDAP errors. The snippet provides a simple example of usage that can be modified to suit local site needs. The configuration used later in this chapter reflects such customization with the intent that LDAP log files will be stored at a location that meets local site needs and wishes more fully.

Debugging NSS_LDAP   The basic mechanism for diagnosing problems with the nss_ldap utility involves adding to the `/etc/ldap.conf` file the following parameters:

```
debug 256
logdir /data/logs
```

Create the log directory as follows:

```
root#  mkdir /data/logs
```

The diagnostic process should follow these steps:

NSS_LDAP DIAGNOSTIC STEPS

1. Verify the `nss_base_passwd`, `nss_base_shadow`, `nss_base_group` entries in the `/etc/ldap.conf` file and compare them closely with the directory tree location that was chosen when the directory was first created. One way this can be done is by executing:

```
root#  slapcat | grep Group | grep dn
dn: ou=Groups,dc=abmas,dc=biz
dn: cn=Domain Admins,ou=Groups,dc=abmas,dc=biz
dn: cn=Domain Users,ou=Groups,dc=abmas,dc=biz
dn: cn=Domain Guests,ou=Groups,dc=abmas,dc=biz
dn: cn=Domain Computers,ou=Groups,dc=abmas,dc=biz
dn: cn=Administrators,ou=Groups,dc=abmas,dc=biz
dn: cn=Print Operators,ou=Groups,dc=abmas,dc=biz
dn: cn=Backup Operators,ou=Groups,dc=abmas,dc=biz
dn: cn=Replicators,ou=Groups,dc=abmas,dc=biz
```

The first line is the DIT entry point for the container for POSIX groups. The correct entry for the `/etc/ldap.conf` for the `nss_base_group` parameter therefore is the distinguished name (dn) as applied here:

```
nss_base_group ou=Groups,dc=abmas,dc=biz?one
```

The same process may be followed to determine the appropriate dn for user accounts. If the container for computer accounts is not the same as that for users (see the `smb.conf` file entry for `ldap machine suffix`), it may be necessary to set the following DIT dn in the `/etc/ldap.conf` file:

```
nss_base_passwd dc=abmas,dc=biz?sub
```

This instructs LDAP to search for machine as well as user entries from the top of the DIT down. This is inefficient, but at least should work. Note: It is possible to specify multiple `nss_base_passwd` entries in the `/etc/ldap.conf` file; they will be evaluated sequentially. Let us consider an example of use where the following DIT has been implemented:

- User accounts are stored under the DIT: ou=Users, dc=abmas, dc=biz

- User login accounts are under the DIT: ou=People, ou-Users, dc=abmas, dc=biz

- Computer accounts are under the DIT: ou=Computers, ou=Users, dc=abmas, dc=biz

The appropriate multiple entry for the `nss_base_passwd` directive in the `/etc/ldap.conf` file may be:

```
nss_base_passwd ou=People,ou=Users,dc=abmas,dc=org?one
```

```
nss_base_passwd ou=Computers,ou=Users,dc=abmas,dc=org?one
```

2. Perform lookups such as:

```
root#  getent passwd
```

Each such lookup will create an entry in the /data/log directory for each such process executed. The contents of each file created in this directory may provide a hint as to the cause of the a problem that is under investigation.

3. For additional diagnostic information, check the contents of the /var/log/messages to see what error messages are being generated as a result of the LDAP lookups. Here is an example of a successful lookup:

```
slapd[12164]: conn=0 fd=10 ACCEPT from IP=127.0.0.1:33539
(IP=0.0.0.0:389)
slapd[12164]: conn=0 op=0 BIND dn="" method=128
slapd[12164]: conn=0 op=0 RESULT tag=97 err=0 text=
slapd[12164]: conn=0 op=1 SRCH base="" scope=0 deref=0
filter="(objectClass=*)"
slapd[12164]: conn=0 op=1 SEARCH RESULT tag=101 err=0
nentries=1 text=
slapd[12164]: conn=0 op=2 UNBIND
slapd[12164]: conn=0 fd=10 closed
slapd[12164]: conn=1 fd=10 ACCEPT from
IP=127.0.0.1:33540 (IP=0.0.0.0:389)
slapd[12164]: conn=1 op=0 BIND
dn="cn=Manager,dc=abmas,dc=biz" method=128
slapd[12164]: conn=1 op=0 BIND
dn="cn=Manager,dc=abmas,dc=biz" mech=SIMPLE ssf=0
slapd[12164]: conn=1 op=0 RESULT tag=97 err=0 text=
slapd[12164]: conn=1 op=1 SRCH
base="ou=People,dc=abmas,dc=biz" scope=1 deref=0
filter="(objectClass=posixAccount)"
slapd[12164]: conn=1 op=1 SRCH attr=uid userPassword
uidNumber gidNumber cn
homeDirectory loginShell gecos description objectClass
slapd[12164]: conn=1 op=1 SEARCH RESULT tag=101 err=0
nentries=2 text=
slapd[12164]: conn=1 fd=10 closed
```

4. Check that the bindpw entry in the /etc/ldap.conf or in the /etc/ldap.secrets file is correct, as specified in the /etc/openldap/slapd.conf file.

Debugging Samba   The following parameters in the `smb.conf` file can be useful in tracking down Samba-related problems:

```
[global]
    ...
    log level = 5
    log file = /var/log/samba/%m.log
    max log size = 0
    ...
```

This will result in the creation of a separate log file for every client from which connections are made. The log file will be quite verbose and will grow continually. Do not forget to change these lines to the following when debugging has been completed:

```
[global]
    ...
    log level = 1
    log file = /var/log/samba/%m.log
    max log size = 50
    ...
```

The log file can be analyzed by executing:

```
root#   cd /var/log/samba
root#   grep -v "^\[200" machine_name.log
```

Search for hints of what may have failed by looking for the words *fail* and *error*.

Debugging on the Windows Client   MS Windows 2000 Professional and Windows XP Professional clients can be configured to create a netlogon.log file that can be very helpful in diagnosing network logon problems. Search the Microsoft knowledge base for detailed instructions. The techniques vary a little with each version of MS Windows.

5.3.2   Political Issues

MS Windows network users are generally very sensitive to limits that may be imposed when confronted with locked-down workstation configurations. The challenge you face must be promoted as a choice between reliable, fast network operation and a constant flux of problems that result in user irritation.

5.3.3   Installation Checklist

You are starting a complex project. Even though you went through the installation of a complex network in Chapter 4, "The 500-User Office", this network is a bigger challenge because of the large number of complex applications that must be configured before the first few steps can be validated. Take stock of what you are about to undertake, prepare yourself, and frequently review the steps ahead while making at least a mental note of what has already been completed. The following task list may help you to keep track of the task items that are covered:

- Samba-3 PDC Server Configuration

  1. DHCP and DNS servers

  2. OpenLDAP server

  3. PAM and NSS client tools

  4. Samba-3 PDC

  5. Idealx smbldap scripts

  6. LDAP initialization

  7. Create user and group accounts

  8. Printers

  9. Share point directory roots

  10. Profile directories

  11. Logon scripts

  12. Configuration of user rights and privileges

- Samba-3 BDC Server Configuration

  1. DHCP and DNS servers

  2. PAM and NSS client tools

  3. Printers

  4. Share point directory roots

  5. Profiles directories

- Windows XP Client Configuration

  1. Default profile folder redirection

  2. MS Outlook PST file relocation

  3. Delete roaming profile on logout

  4. Upload printer drivers to Samba servers

  5. Install software

6. Creation of roll-out images

5.4 Samba Server Implementation

The network design shown in Figure 5.2 is not comprehensive. It is assumed that you will install additional file servers and possibly additional BDCs.

Figure 5.2 Network Topology — 500 User Network Using ldapsam passdb backend

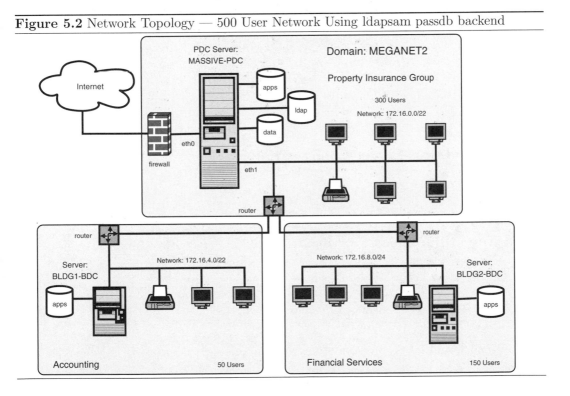

All configuration files and locations are shown for SUSE Linux 9.2 and are equally valid for SUSE Linux Enterprise Server 9. The file locations for Red Hat Linux are similar. You may need to adjust the locations for your particular Linux system distribution/implementation.

NOTE

The following information applies to Samba-3.0.20 when used with the Idealx smbldap-tools scripts version 0.9.1. If using a different version of Samba or of the smbldap-tools tarball, please verify that the versions you are about to use are matching. The smbldap-tools package uses counter-entries in the LDAP directory to avoid duplication of the UIDs and GIDs that are issued for POSIX accounts. The LDAP rdn under which this information is stored are called `uidNumber` and `gidNumber` respectively. These may be located in any convenient part of the directory information tree (DIT). In the examples that follow they have been located under `dn=sambaDomainName=MEGANET2,dc=abmas,dc=org`. They could just as well be located under the rdn `cn=NextFreeUnixId`.

The steps in the process involve changes from the network configuration shown in Chapter 4, "The 500-User Office". Before implementing the following steps, you must have completed the network implementation shown in that chapter. If you are starting with newly installed Linux servers, you must complete the steps shown in Section 4.3.1 before commencing at Section 5.4.1.

5.4.1 OpenLDAP Server Configuration

Confirm that the packages shown in Table 5.2 are installed on your system.

Table 5.2 Required OpenLDAP Linux Packages

SUSE Linux 8.x	SUSE Linux 9.x	Red Hat Linux
nss_ldap	nss_ldap	nss_ldap
pam_ldap	pam_ldap	pam_ldap
openldap2	openldap2	openldap
openldap2-client	openldap2-client	

Samba-3 and OpenLDAP will have a degree of interdependence that is unavoidable. The method for bootstrapping the LDAP and Samba-3 configuration is relatively straightforward. If you follow these guidelines, the resulting system should work fine.

OPENLDAP SERVER CONFIGURATION STEPS

1. Install the file shown in Example 5.4.2 in the directory `/etc/openldap`.

2. Remove all files from the directory `/data/ldap`, making certain that the directory exists with permissions:

```
root#  ls -al /data | grep ldap
```

```
drwx------   2 ldap     ldap          48 Dec 15 22:11 ldap
```

This may require you to add a user and a group account for LDAP if they do not exist.

3. Install the file shown in Example 5.4.1 in the directory **/data/ldap**. In the event that this file is added after **ldap** has been started, it is possible to cause the new settings to take effect by shutting down the LDAP server, executing the **db_recover** command inside the **/data/ldap** directory, and then restarting the LDAP server.

4. Performance logging can be enabled and should preferably be sent to a file on a file system that is large enough to handle significantly sized logs. To enable the logging at a verbose level to permit detailed analysis, uncomment the entry in the **/etc/openldap/slapd.conf** shown as "loglevel 256". Edit the **/etc/syslog.conf** file to add the following at the end of the file:

```
local4.*       -/data/ldap/log/openldap.log
```

Note: The path **/data/ldap/log** should be set at a location that is convenient and that can store a large volume of data.

Example 5.4.1 LDAP DB_CONFIG File

```
set_cachesize         0 150000000 1
set_lg_regionmax      262144
set_lg_bsize          2097152
#set_lg_dir           /var/log/bdb
set_flags             DB_LOG_AUTOREMOVE
```

5.4.2   PAM and NSS Client Configuration

The steps that follow involve configuration of LDAP, NSS LDAP-based resolution of users and groups. Also, so that LDAP-based accounts can log onto the system, the steps ahead configure the Pluggable Authentication Modules (PAM) to permit LDAP-based authentication.

Since you have chosen to put UNIX user and group accounts into the LDAP database, it is likely that you may want to use them for UNIX system (Linux) local machine logons. This necessitates correct configuration of PAM. The **pam_ldap** open source package provides the PAM modules that most people would use. On SUSE Linux systems, the **pam_unix2.so** module also has the ability to redirect authentication requests through LDAP.

You have chosen to configure these services by directly editing the system files, but of course, you know that this configuration can be done using system tools provided by the Linux system vendor. SUSE Linux has a facility in YaST (the system admin tool) through

yast → **system** → **ldap-client** that permits configuration of SUSE Linux as an LDAP client. Red Hat Linux provides the **authconfig** tool for this.

PAM AND NSS CLIENT CONFIGURATION STEPS

1. Execute the following command to find where the **nss_ldap** module expects to find its control file:

```
root#  strings /lib/libnss_ldap.so.2 | grep conf
```

The preferred and usual location is `/etc/ldap.conf`.

2. On the server `MASSIVE`, install the file shown in Example 5.4.4 into the path that was obtained from the step above. On the servers called `BLDG1` and `BLDG2`, install the file shown in Example 5.4.5 into the path that was obtained from the step above.

3. Edit the NSS control file (`/etc/nsswitch.conf`) so that the lines that control user and group resolution will obtain information from the normal system files as well as from **ldap**:

```
passwd: files ldap
shadow: files ldap
group:  files ldap
hosts:  files dns wins
```

Later, when the LDAP database has been initialized and user and group accounts have been added, you can validate resolution of the LDAP resolver process. The inclusion of WINS-based hostname resolution is deliberate so that all MS Windows client hostnames can be resolved to their IP addresses, whether or not they are DHCP clients.

NOTE

Some Linux systems (Novell SUSE Linux in particular) add entries to the `nsswitch.conf` file that may cause operational problems with the configuration methods adopted in this book. It is advisable to comment out the entries `passwd_compat` and `group_compat` where they are found in this file.

Even at the risk of overstating the issue, incorrect and inappropriate configuration of the `nsswitch.conf` file is a significant cause of operational problems with LDAP.

4. For PAM LDAP configuration on this SUSE Linux 9.0 system, the simplest solution is to edit the following files in the `/etc/pam.d` directory: **login**, **password**, **samba**, **sshd**. In each file, locate every entry that has the **pam_unix2.so** entry and add to the line the entry **use_ldap** as shown for the **login** module in this example:

```
#%PAM-1.0
auth       requisite   pam_unix2.so    nullok use_ldap #set_secrpc
auth       required    pam_securetty.so
auth       required    pam_nologin.so
#auth      required    pam_homecheck.so
auth       required    pam_env.so
auth       required    pam_mail.so
account    required    pam_unix2.so    use_ldap
password   required    pam_pwcheck.s   nullok
password   required    pam_unix2.so    nullok use_first_pass \
                                       use_authtok use_ldap
session    required    pam_unix2.so    none use_ldap # debug or trace
session    required    pam_limits.so
```

On other Linux systems that do not have an LDAP-enabled **pam_unix2.so** module,
you must edit these files by adding the **pam_ldap.so** modules as shown here:

```
#%PAM-1.0
auth       required    pam_securetty.so
auth       required    pam_nologin.so
auth       sufficient  pam_ldap.so
auth       required    pam_unix2.so    nullok try_first_pass #set_secrpc
account    sufficient  pam_ldap.so
account    required    pam_unix2.so
password   required    pam_pwcheck.so nullok
password   required    pam_ldap.so     use_first_pass use_authtok
password   required    pam_unix2.so    nullok use_first_pass use_authtok
session    required    pam_unix2.so    none # debug or trace
session    required    pam_limits.so
session    required    pam_env.so
session    optional    pam_mail.so
```

This example does have the LDAP-enabled **pam_unix2.so**, but simply demonstrates
the use of the **pam_ldap.so** module. You can use either implementation, but if the
pam_unix2.so on your system supports LDAP, you probably want to use it rather
than add an additional module.

5.4.3 Samba-3 PDC Configuration

Verify that the Samba-3.0.20 (or later) packages are installed on each SUSE Linux server
before following the steps below. If Samba-3.0.20 (or later) is not installed, you have the
choice to either build your own or obtain the packages from a dependable source. Packages
for SUSE Linux 8.x, 9.x, and SUSE Linux Enterprise Server 9, as well as for Red Hat Fedora

Core and Red Hat Enterprise Linux Server 3 and 4, are included on the CD-ROM that is included with this book.

CONFIGURATION OF PDC CALLED MASSIVE

1. Install the files in Example 5.4.6, Example 5.4.7, Example 5.5.3, and Example 5.5.4 into the `/etc/samba/` directory. The three files should be added together to form the `smb.conf` master file. It is a good practice to call this file something like `smb.conf.master` and then to perform all file edits on the master file. The operational `smb.conf` is then generated as shown in the next step.

2. Create and verify the contents of the `smb.conf` file that is generated by:

```
root#  testparm -s smb.conf.master > smb.conf
```

Immediately follow this with the following:

```
root#  testparm
```

The output that is created should be free from errors, as shown here:

```
Load smb config files from /etc/samba/smb.conf
Processing section "[accounts]"
Processing section "[service]"
Processing section "[pidata]"
Processing section "[homes]"
Processing section "[printers]"
Processing section "[apps]"
Processing section "[netlogon]"
Processing section "[profiles]"
Processing section "[profdata]"
Processing section "[print$]"
Loaded services file OK.
Server role: ROLE_DOMAIN_PDC
Press enter to see a dump of your service definitions
```

3. Delete all runtime files from prior Samba operation by executing (for SUSE Linux):

```
root#  rm /etc/samba/*tdb
root#  rm /var/lib/samba/*tdb
root#  rm /var/lib/samba/*dat
root#  rm /var/log/samba/*
```

4. Samba-3 communicates with the LDAP server. The password that it uses to authenticate to the LDAP server must be stored in the `secrets.tdb` file. Execute the following
   to create the new `secrets.tdb` files and store the password for the LDAP Manager:

```
root#  smbpasswd -w not24get
```

The expected output from this command is:

```
Setting stored password for "cn=Manager,dc=abmas,dc=biz" in secrets.tdb
```

5. Samba-3 generates a Windows Security Identifier (SID) only when **smbd** has been
   started. For this reason, you start Samba. After a few seconds delay, execute:

```
root#  smbclient -L localhost -U%
root#  net getlocalsid
```

A report such as the following means that the domain SID has not yet been written
to the `secrets.tdb` or to the LDAP backend:

```
[2005/03/03 23:19:34, 0] lib/smbldap.c:smbldap_connect_system(852)
   failed to bind to server ldap://massive.abmas.biz
with dn="cn=Manager,dc=abmas,dc=biz" Error: Can't contact LDAP server
        (unknown)
[2005/03/03 23:19:48, 0] lib/smbldap.c:smbldap_search_suffix(1169)
   smbldap_search_suffix: Problem during the LDAP search:
        (unknown) (Timed out)
```

The attempt to read the SID will cause and attempted bind to the LDAP server.
Because the LDAP server is not running, this operation will fail by way of a timeout,
as shown previously. This is normal output; do not worry about this error message.
When the domain has been created and written to the `secrets.tdb` file, the output
should look like this:

```
SID for domain MASSIVE is: S-1-5-21-3504140859-1010554828-2431957765
```

If, after a short delay (a few seconds), the domain SID has still not been written to
the `secrets.tdb` file, it is necessary to investigate what may be misconfigured. In
this case, carefully check the **smb.conf** file for typographical errors (the most common
problem). The use of the **testparm** is highly recommended to validate the contents
of this file.

6. When a positive domain SID has been reported, stop Samba.

7. Configure the NFS server for your Linux system. So you can complete the steps that follow, enter into the /etc/exports the following entry:

```
/home    *(rw,root_squash,sync)
```

This permits the user home directories to be used on the BDC servers for testing purposes. You, of course, decide what is the best way for your site to distribute data drives, and you create suitable backup and restore procedures for Abmas I'd strongly recommend that for normal operation the BDC is completely independent of the PDC. rsync is a useful tool here, as it resembles the NT replication service quite closely. If you do use NFS, do not forget to start the NFS server as follows:

```
root#  rcnfsserver start
```

Your Samba-3 PDC is now ready to communicate with the LDAP password backend. Let's get on with configuration of the LDAP server.

5.4.4   Install and Configure Idealx smbldap-tools Scripts

The Idealx scripts, or equivalent, are necessary to permit Samba-3 to manage accounts on the LDAP server. You have chosen the Idealx scripts because they are the best-known LDAP configuration scripts. The use of these scripts will help avoid the necessity to create custom scripts. It is easy to download them from the Idealx Web site[17]. The tarball may be directly downloaded[18] from this site also. Alternatively, you may obtain the smbldap-tools-0.9.1-1.src.rpm[19] file that may be used to build an installable RPM package for your Linux system.

NOTE

The smbldap-tools scripts can be installed in any convenient directory of your choice, in which case you must change the path to them in your smb.conf file on the PDC (MASSIVE).

The smbldap-tools are located in /opt/IDEALX/sbin. The scripts are not needed on BDC machines because all LDAP updates are handled by the PDC alone.

---

[17]<http://samba.idealx.org/index.en.html>
[18]<http://samba.idealx.org/dist/smbldap-tools-0.9.1.tgz>
[19]<http://samba.idealx.org/dist/smbldap-tools-0.9.1-1.src.rpm>

5.4.4.1   Installation of smbldap-tools from the Tarball

To perform a manual installation of the smbldap-tools scripts, the following procedure may be used:

UNPACKING AND INSTALLATION STEPS FOR THE SMBLDAP-TOOLS TARBALL

1. Create the `/opt/IDEALX/sbin` directory, and set its permissions and ownership as shown here:

```
root#  mkdir -p /opt/IDEALX/sbin
root#  chown root:root /opt/IDEALX/sbin
root#  chmod 755 /opt/IDEALX/sbin
root#  mkdir -p /etc/smbldap-tools
root#  chown root:root /etc/smbldap-tools
root#  chmod 755 /etc/smbldap-tools
```

2. If you wish to use the downloaded tarball, unpack the smbldap-tools in a suitable temporary location. Change into either the directory extracted from the tarball or the smbldap-tools directory in your `/usr/share/doc/packages` directory tree.

3. Copy all the `smbldap-*` and the `configure.pl` files into the `/opt/IDEALX/sbin` directory, as shown here:

```
root#  cd smbldap-tools-0.9.1/
root#  cp smbldap-* configure.pl *pm /opt/IDEALX/sbin/
root#  cp smbldap*conf /etc/smbldap-tools/
root#  chmod 750 /opt/IDEALX/sbin/smbldap-*
root#  chmod 750 /opt/IDEALX/sbin/configure.pl
root#  chmod 640 /etc/smbldap-tools/smbldap.conf
root#  chmod 600 /etc/smbldap-tools/smbldap_bind.conf
```

4. The smbldap-tools scripts master control file must now be configured. Change to the `/opt/IDEALX/sbin` directory, then edit the `smbldap_tools.pm` to affect the changes shown here:

```
...
# ugly funcs using global variables and spawning openldap clients

my $smbldap_conf="/etc/smbldap-tools/smbldap.conf";
my $smbldap_bind_conf="/etc/smbldap-tools/smbldap_bind.conf";
...
```

5. To complete the configuration of the smbldap-tools, set the permissions and ownership by executing the following commands:

```
root#  chown root:root /opt/IDEALX/sbin/*
root#  chmod 755 /opt/IDEALX/sbin/smbldap-*
root#  chmod 640 /opt/IDEALX/sbin/smb*pm
```

The smbldap-tools scripts are now ready for the configuration step outlined in Section 5.4.4.3.

5.4.4.2 Installing smbldap-tools from the RPM Package

In the event that you have elected to use the RPM package provided by Idealx, download the source RPM smbldap-tools-0.9.1-1.src.rpm, then follow this procedure:

INSTALLATION STEPS FOR SMBLDAP-TOOLS RPM'S

1. Install the source RPM that has been downloaded as follows:

   ```
   root#  rpm -i smbldap-tools-0.9.1-1.src.rpm
   ```

2. Change into the directory in which the SPEC files are located. On SUSE Linux:

   ```
   root#  cd /usr/src/packages/SPECS
   ```

   On Red Hat Linux systems:

   ```
   root#  cd /usr/src/redhat/SPECS
   ```

3. Edit the smbldap-tools.spec file to change the value of the _sysconfig macro as shown here:

   ```
   %define _prefix /opt/IDEALX
   %define _sysconfdir /etc
   ```

   Note: Any suitable directory can be specified.

4. Build the package by executing:

   ```
   root#  rpmbuild -ba -v smbldap-tools.spec
   ```

   A build process that has completed without error will place the installable binary files in the directory ../RPMS/noarch.

5. Install the binary package by executing:

```
root#  rpm -Uvh ../RPMS/noarch/smbldap-tools-0.9.1-1.noarch.rpm
```

The Idealx scripts should now be ready for configuration using the steps outlined in Section 5.4.4.3.

5.4.4.3   Configuration of smbldap-tools

Prior to use, the smbldap-tools must be configured to match the settings in the `smb.conf` file and to match the settings in the `/etc/openldap/slapd.conf` file. The assumption is made that the `smb.conf` file has correct contents. The following procedure ensures that this is completed correctly:

The smbldap-tools require that the NetBIOS name (machine name) of the Samba server be included in the `smb.conf` file.

CONFIGURATION STEPS FOR SMBLDAP-TOOLS TO ENABLE USE

1. Change into the directory that contains the `configure.pl` script.

   ```
   root#  cd /opt/IDEALX/sbin
   ```

2. Execute the `configure.pl` script as follows:

   ```
   root#  ./configure.pl
   ```

   The interactive use of this script for the PDC is demonstrated here:

   ```
   root#  /opt/IDEALX/sbin/configure.pl
   -=-=-=-=-=-=-=-=-=-=-=-=-=-=-=-=-=-=-=-=-=-=-=-=-=-=-=-=-=-=-=-=
          smbldap-tools script configuration
          -=-=-=-=-=-=-=-=-=-=-=-=-=-=-=-=-=-=
   Before starting, check
     . if your samba controller is up and running.
     . if the domain SID is defined (you can get it with the
                                            'net getlocalsid')

     . you can leave the configuration using the Crtl-c key combination
     . empty value can be set with the "." character
   -=-=-=-=-=-=-=-=-=-=-=-=-=-=-=-=-=-=-=-=-=-=-=-=-=-=-=-=-=-=-=-=
   Looking for configuration files...

   Samba Config File Location [/etc/samba/smb.conf] >
   smbldap-tools configuration file Location (global parameters)
                   [/etc/opt/IDEALX/smbldap-tools/smbldap.conf] >
   ```

```
smbldap Config file Location (bind parameters)
                    [/etc/opt/IDEALX/smbldap-tools/smbldap_bind.conf] >
-=-=-=-=-=-=-=-=-=-=-=-=-=-=-=-=-=-=-=-=-=-=-=-=-=-=-=-=-=-=-=-=-=-=-=
Let's start configuring the smbldap-tools scripts ...

. workgroup name: name of the domain Samba act as a PDC
  workgroup name [MEGANET2] >
. netbios name: netbios name of the samba controler
  netbios name [MASSIVE] >
. logon drive: local path to which the home directory
                    will be connected (for NT Workstations). Ex: 'H:'
  logon drive [H:] >
. logon home: home directory location (for Win95/98 or NT Workstation)
  (use %U as username) Ex:'\\MASSIVE\%U'
  logon home (press the "." character if you don't want homeDirectory)
                                                       [\\MASSIVE\%U] >
. logon path: directory where roaming profiles are stored.
                                        Ex:'\\MASSIVE\profiles\%U'
  logon path (press the "." character
              if you don't want roaming profile) [\\%L\profiles\%U] >
. home directory prefix (use %U as username)
                                        [/home/%U] > /data/users/%U
. default users' homeDirectory mode [700] >
. default user netlogon script (use %U as username)
                                            [scripts\logon.bat] >
  default password validation time (time in days) [45] > 900
. ldap suffix [dc=abmas,dc=biz] >
. ldap group suffix [ou=Groups] >
. ldap user suffix [ou=People,ou=Users] >
. ldap machine suffix [ou=Computers,ou=Users] >
. Idmap suffix [ou=Idmap] >
. sambaUnixIdPooldn: object where you want to store the next uidNumber
  and gidNumber available for new users and groups
  sambaUnixIdPooldn object (relative to ${suffix})
                                        [sambaDomainName=MEGANET2] >
. ldap master server: IP adress or DNS name of the master
                                        (writable) ldap server
  ldap master server [massive.abmas.biz] >
. ldap master port [389] >
. ldap master bind dn [cn=Manager,dc=abmas,dc=biz] >
. ldap master bind password [] >
. ldap slave server: IP adress or DNS name of the slave ldap server:
                                        can also be the master one
  ldap slave server [massive.abmas.biz] >
. ldap slave port [389] >
. ldap slave bind dn [cn=Manager,dc=abmas,dc=biz] >
. ldap slave bind password [] >
```

```
. ldap tls support (1/0) [0] >
. SID for domain MEGANET2: SID of the domain
                         (can be obtained with 'net getlocalsid MASSIVE')
  SID for domain MEGANET2
                              [S-1-5-21-3504140859-1010554828-2431957765]] >
. unix password encryption: encryption used for unix passwords
  unix password encryption (CRYPT, MD5, SMD5, SSHA, SHA) [SSHA] > MD5
. default user gidNumber [513] >
. default computer gidNumber [515] >
. default login shell [/bin/bash] >
. default skeleton directory [/etc/skel] >
. default domain name to append to mail adress [] > abmas.biz
-=-=-=-=-=-=-=-=-=-=-=-=-=-=-=-=-=-=-=-=-=-=-=-=-=-=-=-=-=-=
backup old configuration files:
  /etc/opt/IDEALX/smbldap-tools/smbldap.conf->
                         /etc/opt/IDEALX/smbldap-tools/smbldap.conf.old
  /etc/opt/IDEALX/smbldap-tools/smbldap_bind.conf->
                         /etc/opt/IDEALX/smbldap-tools/smbldap_bind.conf.old
writing new configuration file:
  /etc/opt/IDEALX/smbldap-tools/smbldap.conf done.
  /etc/opt/IDEALX/smbldap-tools/smbldap_bind.conf done.
```

Since a slave LDAP server has not been configured, it is necessary to specify the IP address of the master LDAP server for both the master and the slave configuration prompts.

3. Change to the directory that contains the `smbldap.conf` file, then verify its contents.

The smbldap-tools are now ready for use.

5.4.5   LDAP Initialization and Creation of User and Group Accounts

The LDAP database must be populated with well-known Windows domain user accounts and domain group accounts before Samba can be used. The following procedures step you through the process.

At this time, Samba-3 requires that on a PDC all UNIX (POSIX) group accounts that are mapped (linked) to Windows domain group accounts must be in the LDAP database. It does not hurt to have UNIX user and group accounts in both the system files as well as in the LDAP database. From a UNIX system perspective, the NSS resolver checks system files before referring to LDAP. If the UNIX system can resolve (find) an account in the system file, it does not need to ask LDAP.

Addition of an account to the LDAP backend can be done in two ways:

- If you always have a user account in the /etc/passwd on every server or in a NIS(+) backend, it is not necessary to add POSIX accounts for them in LDAP. In this case, you can add Windows domain user accounts using the **pdbedit** utility. Use of this tool from the command line adds the SambaSamAccount entry for the user, but does not add the PosixAccount entry for the user.

This is the least desirable method because when LDAP is used as the passwd backend Samba expects the POSIX account to be in LDAP also. It is possible to use the PADL account migration tool to migrate all system accounts from either the /etc/passwd files, or from NIS, to LDAP.

- If you decide that it is probably a good idea to add both the PosixAccount attributes as well as the SambaSamAccount attributes for each user, then a suitable script is needed. In the example system you are installing in this exercise, you are making use of the Idealx smbldap-tools scripts. A copy of these tools, preconfigured for this system, is included on the enclosed CD-ROM under Chap06/Tools.

If you wish to have more control over how the LDAP database is initialized or if you don't want to use the Idealx smbldap-tools, you should refer to Chapter 15, "A Collection of Useful Tidbits", Section 15.5.

The following steps initialize the LDAP database, and then you can add user and group accounts that Samba can use. You use the **smbldap-populate** to seed the LDAP database. You then manually add the accounts shown in Table 5.3. The list of users does not cover all 500 network users; it provides examples only.

NOTE

In the following examples, as the LDAP database is initialized, we do create a container for Computer (machine) accounts. In the Samba-3 smb.conf files, specific use is made of the People container, not the Computers container, for domain member accounts. This is not a mistake; it is a deliberate action that is necessitated by the fact that the resolution of a machine (computer) account to a UID is done via NSS. The only way this can be handled is using the NSS (/etc/nsswitch. conf) entry for passwd, which is resolved using the nss_ldap library. The configuration file for the nss_ldap library is the file /etc/ldap. conf that provides only one possible LDAP search command that is specified by the entry called nss_base_passwd. This means that the search path must take into account the directory structure so that the LDAP search will commence at a level that is above both the Computers container and the Users (or People) container. If this is done, it is necessary to use a search that will descend the directory tree so that the machine account can be found. Alternatively, by placing all machine accounts in the People container, we are able to sidestep this limitation. This is the simpler solution that has been adopted in this chapter.

LDAP DIRECTORY INITIALIZATION STEPS

Table 5.3 Abmas Network Users and Groups

Account Name	Type	ID	Password
Robert Jordan	User	bobj	n3v3r2l8
Stanley Soroka	User	stans	impl13dst4r
Christine Roberson	User	chrisr	S9n0nw4ll
Mary Vortexis	User	maryv	kw13t0n3
Accounts	Group	Accounts	
Finances	Group	Finances	
Insurance	Group	PIOps	

1. Start the LDAP server by executing:

```
root#  rcldap start
Starting ldap-server                                    done
```

2. Change to the /opt/IDEALX/sbin directory.

3. Execute the script that will populate the LDAP database as shown here:

```
root#  ./smbldap-populate -a root -k 0 -m 0
```

The expected output from this is:

```
Using workgroup name from smb.conf: sambaDomainName=MEGANET2
-=-=-=-=-=-=-=-=-=-=-=-=-=-=-=-=-=-=-=-=-=-=-=-=-=-=-=
=> Warning: you must update smbldap.conf configuration file to :
=> sambaUnixIdPooldn parameter must be set
   to "sambaDomainName=MEGANET2,dc=abmas,dc=biz"
-=-=-=-=-=-=-=-=-=-=-=-=-=-=-=-=-=-=-=-=-=-=-=-=-=-=-=
Using builtin directory structure
adding new entry: dc=abmas,dc=biz
adding new entry: ou=People,dc=abmas,dc=biz
adding new entry: ou=Groups,dc=abmas,dc=biz
entry ou=People,dc=abmas,dc=biz already exist.
adding new entry: ou=Idmap,dc=abmas,dc=biz
adding new entry: sambaDomainName=MEGANET2,dc=abmas,dc=biz
adding new entry: uid=root,ou=People,dc=abmas,dc=biz
adding new entry: uid=nobody,ou=People,dc=abmas,dc=biz
adding new entry: cn=Domain Admins,ou=Groups,dc=abmas,dc=biz
adding new entry: cn=Domain Users,ou=Groups,dc=abmas,dc=biz
adding new entry: cn=Domain Guests,ou=Groups,dc=abmas,dc=biz
adding new entry: cn=Domain Computers,ou=Groups,dc=abmas,dc=biz
adding new entry: cn=Administrators,ou=Groups,dc=abmas,dc=biz
```

```
adding new entry: cn=Print Operators,ou=Groups,dc=abmas,dc=biz
adding new entry: cn=Backup Operators,ou=Groups,dc=abmas,dc=biz
adding new entry: cn=Replicators,ou=Groups,dc=abmas,dc=biz
```

4. Edit the /etc/smbldap-tools/smbldap.conf file so that the following information is changed from:

```
# Where to store next uidNumber and gidNumber available
sambaUnixIdPooldn="cn=NextFreeUnixId,${suffix}"
```

to read, after modification:

```
# Where to store next uidNumber and gidNumber available
#sambaUnixIdPooldn="cn=NextFreeUnixId,${suffix}"
sambaUnixIdPooldn="sambaDomainName=MEGANET2,dc=abmas,dc=biz"
```

5. It is necessary to restart the LDAP server as shown here:

```
root#  rcldap restart
Shutting down ldap-server                                    done
Starting ldap-server                                         done
```

6. So that we can use a global IDMAP repository, the LDAP directory must have a container object for IDMAP data. There are several ways you can check that your LDAP database is able to receive IDMAP information. One of the simplest is to execute:

```
root#  slapcat | grep -i idmap
dn: ou=Idmap,dc=abmas,dc=biz
ou: idmap
```

If the execution of this command does not return IDMAP entries, you need to create an LDIF template file (see Example 5.5.5). You can add the required entries using the following command:

```
root#  ldapadd -x -D "cn=Manager,dc=abmas,dc=biz" \
     -w not24get < /etc/openldap/idmap.LDIF
```

Samba automatically populates this LDAP directory container when it needs to.

7. It looks like all has gone well, as expected. Let's confirm that this is the case by running a few tests. First we check the contents of the database directly by running **slapcat** as follows (the output has been cut down):

```
root#  slapcat
dn: dc=abmas,dc=biz
objectClass: dcObject
objectClass: organization
dc: abmas
o: abmas
structuralObjectClass: organization
entryUUID: 5ab02bf6-c536-1027-9d29-b1f32350fb43
creatorsName: cn=Manager,dc=abmas,dc=biz
createTimestamp: 20031217234200Z
entryCSN: 2003121723:42:00Z#0x0001#0#0000
modifiersName: cn=Manager,dc=abmas,dc=biz
modifyTimestamp: 20031217234200Z
...
dn: cn=Domain Computers,ou=Groups,dc=abmas,dc=biz
objectClass: posixGroup
objectClass: sambaGroupMapping
gidNumber: 553
cn: Domain Computers
description: Netbios Domain Computers accounts
sambaSID: S-1-5-21-3504140859-1010554828-2431957765-553
sambaGroupType: 2
displayName: Domain Computers
structuralObjectClass: posixGroup
entryUUID: 5e0a41d8-c536-1027-9d3b-b1f32350fb43
creatorsName: cn=Manager,dc=abmas,dc=biz
createTimestamp: 20031217234206Z
entryCSN: 2003121723:42:06Z#0x0002#0#0000
modifiersName: cn=Manager,dc=abmas,dc=biz
modifyTimestamp: 20031217234206Z
```

This looks good so far.

8. The next step is to prove that the LDAP server is running and responds to a search request. Execute the following as shown (output has been cut to save space):

```
root#  ldapsearch -x -b "dc=abmas,dc=biz" "(ObjectClass=*)"
# extended LDIF
#
# LDAPv3
# base <dc=abmas,dc=biz> with scope sub
# filter: (ObjectClass=*)
```

```
# requesting: ALL
#

# abmas.biz
dn: dc=abmas,dc=biz
objectClass: dcObject
objectClass: organization
dc: abmas
o: abmas

# People, abmas.biz
dn: ou=People,dc=abmas,dc=biz
objectClass: organizationalUnit
ou: People
...
# Domain Computers, Groups, abmas.biz
dn: cn=Domain Computers,ou=Groups,dc=abmas,dc=biz
objectClass: posixGroup
objectClass: sambaGroupMapping
gidNumber: 553
cn: Domain Computers
description: Netbios Domain Computers accounts
sambaSID: S-1-5-21-3504140859-1010554828-2431957765-553
sambaGroupType: 2
displayName: Domain Computers

# search result
search: 2
result: 0 Success

# numResponses: 20
# numEntries: 19
```

Good. It is all working just fine.

9. You must now make certain that the NSS resolver can interrogate LDAP also. Execute the following commands:

```
root#  getent passwd | grep root
root:x:998:512:Netbios Domain Administrator:/home:/bin/false

root#  getent group | grep Domain
Domain Admins:x:512:root
Domain Users:x:513:
Domain Guests:x:514:
Domain Computers:x:553:
```

This demonstrates that the **nss_ldap** library is functioning as it should. If these two steps fail to produce this information, refer to Section 5.3.1.7 for diagnostic procedures that can be followed to isolate the cause of the problem. Proceed to the next step only when the previous steps have been successfully completed.

10. Our database is now ready for the addition of network users. For each user for whom an account must be created, execute the following:

```
root#  ./smbldap-useradd -m -a username
root#  ./smbldap-passwd username
Changing password for username
New password : XXXXXXXX
Retype new password : XXXXXXXX

root#  smbpasswd username
New SMB password: XXXXXXXX
Retype new SMB password: XXXXXXXX
```

where **username** is the login ID for each user.

11. Now verify that the UNIX (POSIX) accounts can be resolved via NSS by executing the following:

```
root#  getent passwd
root:x:0:0:root:/root:/bin/bash
bin:x:1:1:bin:/bin:/bin/bash
...
root:x:0:512:Netbios Domain Administrator:/home:/bin/false
nobody:x:999:514:nobody:/dev/null:/bin/false
bobj:x:1000:513:System User:/home/bobj:/bin/bash
stans:x:1001:513:System User:/home/stans:/bin/bash
chrisr:x:1002:513:System User:/home/chrisr:/bin/bash
maryv:x:1003:513:System User:/home/maryv:/bin/bash
```

This demonstrates that user account resolution via LDAP is working.

12. This step will determine whether or not identity resolution is working correctly. Do not procede is this step fails, rather find the cause of the failure. The **id** command may be used to validate your configuration so far, as shown here:

```
root#  id chrisr
uid=1002(chrisr) gid=513(Domain Users) groups=513(Domain Users)
```

This confirms that the UNIX (POSIX) user account information can be resolved from LDAP by system tools that make a getentpw() system call.

13. The root account must have UID=0; if not, this means that operations conducted from a Windows client using tools such as the Domain User Manager fails under UNIX because the management of user and group accounts requires that the UID=0. Additionally, it is a good idea to make certain that no matter how root account credentials are resolved, the home directory and shell are valid. You decide to effect this immediately as demonstrated here:

```
root#  cd /opt/IDEALX/sbin
root#  ./smbldap-usermod -u 0 -d /root -s /bin/bash root
```

14. Verify that the changes just made to the **root** account were accepted by executing:

```
root#  getent passwd | grep root
root:x:0:0:root:/root:/bin/bash
root:x:0:512:Netbios Domain Administrator:/root:/bin/bash
```

This demonstrates that the changes were accepted.

15. Make certain that a home directory has been created for every user by listing the directories in **/home** as follows:

```
root#  ls -al /home
drwxr-xr-x   8 root    root            176 Dec 17 18:50 ./
drwxr-xr-x  21 root    root            560 Dec 15 22:19 ../
drwx------   7 bobj    Domain Users    568 Dec 17 01:16 bobj/
drwx------   7 chrisr  Domain Users    568 Dec 17 01:19 chrisr/
drwx------   7 maryv   Domain Users    568 Dec 17 01:27 maryv/
drwx------   7 stans   Domain Users    568 Dec 17 01:43 stans/
```

This is precisely what we want to see.

16. The final validation step involves making certain that Samba-3 can obtain the user accounts from the LDAP ldapsam passwd backend. Execute the following command as shown:

```
root#  pdbedit -Lv chrisr
Unix username:       chrisr
NT username:         chrisr
Account Flags:       [U          ]
User SID:            S-1-5-21-3504140859-1010554828-2431957765-3004
Primary Group SID:   S-1-5-21-3504140859-1010554828-2431957765-513
Full Name:           System User
```

```
Home Directory:          \\MASSIVE\homes
HomeDir Drive:           H:
Logon Script:            scripts\login.cmd
Profile Path:            \\MASSIVE\profiles\chrisr
Domain:                  MEGANET2
Account desc:            System User
Workstations:
Munged dial:
Logon time:              0
Logoff time:             Mon, 18 Jan 2038 20:14:07 GMT
Kickoff time:            Mon, 18 Jan 2038 20:14:07 GMT
Password last set:       Wed, 17 Dec 2003 17:17:40 GMT
Password can change:     Wed, 17 Dec 2003 17:17:40 GMT
Password must change:    Mon, 18 Jan 2038 20:14:07 GMT
Last bad password    :   0
Bad password count   :   0
Logon hours          :   FFFFFFFFFFFFFFFFFFFFFFFFFFFFFFFFFFFFFFFFFF
```

This looks good. Of course, you fully expected that it would all work, didn't you?

17. Now you add the group accounts that are used on the Abmas network. Execute the following exactly as shown:

```
root#   ./smbldap-groupadd -a Accounts
root#   ./smbldap-groupadd -a Finances
root#   ./smbldap-groupadd -a PIOps
```

The addition of groups does not involve keyboard interaction, so the lack of console output is of no concern.

18. You really do want to confirm that UNIX group resolution from LDAP is functioning as it should. Let's do this as shown here:

```
root#   getent group
...
Domain Admins:x:512:root
Domain Users:x:513:bobj,stans,chrisr,maryv
Domain Guests:x:514:
...
Accounts:x:1000:
Finances:x:1001:
PIOps:x:1002:
```

The well-known special accounts (Domain Admins, Domain Users, Domain Guests), as well as our own site-specific group accounts, are correctly listed. This is looking good.

19. The final step we need to validate is that Samba can see all the Windows domain groups and that they are correctly mapped to the respective UNIX group account. To do this, just execute the following command:

```
root#  net groupmap list
Domain Admins (S-1-5-21-3504140859-...-2431957765-512) -> Domain Admins
Domain Users (S-1-5-21-3504140859-...-2431957765-513) -> Domain Users
Domain Guests (S-1-5-21-3504140859-...-2431957765-514) -> Domain Guests
...
Accounts (S-1-5-21-3504140859-1010554828-2431957765-3001) -> Accounts
Finances (S-1-5-21-3504140859-1010554828-2431957765-3003) -> Finances
PIOps (S-1-5-21-3504140859-1010554828-2431957765-3005) -> PIOps
```

This is looking good. Congratulations — it works! Note that in the above output the lines were shortened by replacing the middle value (1010554828) of the SID with the ellipsis (...).

20. The server you have so carefully built is now ready for another important step. You start the Samba-3 server and validate its operation. Execute the following to render all the processes needed fully operative so that, on system reboot, they are automatically started:

```
root#   chkconfig named on
root#   chkconfig dhcpd on
root#   chkconfig ldap on
root#   chkconfig nmb on
root#   chkconfig smb on
root#   chkconfig winbind on
root#   rcnmb start
root#   rcsmb start
root#   rcwinbind start
```

21. The next step might seem a little odd at this point, but take note that you are about to start **winbindd**, which must be able to authenticate to the PDC via the localhost interface with the **smbd** process. This account can be easily created by joining the PDC to the domain by executing the following command:

```
root#  net rpc join -S MASSIVE -U root%not24get
```

Note: Before executing this command on the PDC, both **nmbd** and **smbd** must be started so that the **net** command can communicate with **smbd**. The expected output is as follows:

Joined domain MEGANET2.

This indicates that the domain security account for the PDC has been correctly created.

22. At this time it is necessary to restart **winbindd** so that it can correctly authenticate to the PDC. The following command achieves that:

```
root#  rcwinbind restart
```

23. You may now check Samba-3 operation as follows:

```
root#  smbclient -L massive -U%

        Sharename       Type        Comment
        ---------       ----        -------
        IPC$            IPC         IPC Service (Samba 3.0.20)
        accounts        Disk        Accounting Files
        service         Disk        Financial Services Files
        pidata          Disk        Property Insurance Files
        apps            Disk        Application Files
        netlogon        Disk        Network Logon Service
        profiles        Disk        Profile Share
        profdata        Disk        Profile Data Share
        ADMIN$          IPC         IPC Service (Samba 3.0.20)

        Server                  Comment
        ---------               -------
        MASSIVE                 Samba 3.0.20

        Workgroup               Master
        ---------               -------
        MEGANET2                MASSIVE
```

This shows that an anonymous connection is working.

24. For your finale, let's try an authenticated connection:

```
root#  smbclient //massive/bobj -Ubobj%n3v3r218
smb: \> dir
    .                       D        0  Wed Dec 17 01:16:19 2003
    ..                      D        0  Wed Dec 17 19:04:42 2003
    bin                     D        0  Tue Sep  2 04:00:57 2003
    Documents               D        0  Sun Nov 30 07:28:20 2003
```

```
    public_html          D          0  Sun Nov 30 07:28:20 2003
    .urlview             H        311  Fri Jul  7 06:55:35 2000
    .dvipsrc             H        208  Fri Nov 17 11:22:02 1995

        57681 blocks of size 524288. 57128 blocks available
smb: \> q
```

Well done. All is working fine.

The server **MASSIVE** is now configured, and it is time to move onto the next task.

5.4.6   Printer Configuration

The configuration for Samba-3 to enable CUPS raw-print-through printing has already been taken care of in the **smb.conf** file. The only preparation needed for **smart** printing to be possible involves creation of the directories in which Samba-3 stores Windows printing driver files.

PRINTER CONFIGURATION STEPS

1. Configure all network-attached printers to have a fixed IP address.

2. Create an entry in the DNS database on the server **MASSIVE** in both the forward lookup database for the zone **abmas.biz.hosts** and in the reverse lookup database for the network segment that the printer is to be located in. Example configuration files for similar zones were presented in Chapter 3, "Secure Office Networking", Example 3.3.12 and in Example 3.3.11.

3. Follow the instructions in the printer manufacturers' manuals to permit printing to port 9100. Use any other port the manufacturer specifies for direct mode, raw printing. This allows the CUPS spooler to print using raw mode protocols.

4. Only on the server to which the printer is attached, configure the CUPS Print Queues as follows:

```
root#  lpadmin -p printque
    -v socket://printer-name.abmas.biz:9100 -E
```

This step creates the necessary print queue to use no assigned print filter. This is ideal for raw printing, that is, printing without use of filters. The name *printque* is the name you have assigned for the particular printer.

5. Print queues may not be enabled at creation. Make certain that the queues you have just created are enabled by executing the following:

```
root#  /usr/bin/enable printque
```

6. Even though your print queue may be enabled, it is still possible that it may not accept print jobs. A print queue will service incoming printing requests only when configured to do so. Ensure that your print queue is set to accept incoming jobs by executing the following commands:

```
root#  /usr/bin/accept printque
```

7. Edit the file /etc/cups/mime.convs to uncomment the line:

```
application/octet-stream    application/vnd.cups-raw    0    -
```

8. Edit the file /etc/cups/mime.types to uncomment the line:

```
application/octet-stream
```

9. Refer to the CUPS printing manual for instructions regarding how to configure CUPS so that print queues that reside on CUPS servers on remote networks route print jobs to the print server that owns that queue. The default setting on your CUPS server may automatically discover remotely installed printers and may permit this functionality without requiring specific configuration.

10. The following action creates the necessary directory subsystem. Follow these steps to printing heaven:

```
root#  mkdir -p /var/lib/samba/drivers/{W32ALPHA,W32MIPS,W32X86,WIN40}
root#  chown -R root:root /var/lib/samba/drivers
root#  chmod -R ug=rwx,o=rx /var/lib/samba/drivers
```

5.5   Samba-3 BDC Configuration

CONFIGURATION OF BDC CALLED: BLDG1

1. Install the files in Example 5.5.1, Example 5.5.3, and Example 5.5.4 into the /etc/samba/ directory. The three files should be added together to form the smb.conf file.

2. Verify the smb.conf file as in step 2 of Section 5.4.3.

3. Carefully follow the steps outlined in Section 5.4.2, taking particular note to install the correct ldap.conf.

4. Verify that the NSS resolver is working. You may need to cycle the run level to 1 and back to 5 before the NSS LDAP resolver functions. Follow these commands:

```
root#  init 1
```

After the run level has been achieved, you are prompted to provide the **root** password.
Log on, and then execute:

```
root#  init 5
```

When the normal logon prompt appears, log into the system as **root** and then execute
these commands:

```
root#  getent passwd
root:x:0:0:root:/root:/bin/bash
bin:x:1:1:bin:/bin:/bin/bash
daemon:x:2:2:Daemon:/sbin:/bin/bash
lp:x:4:7:Printing daemon:/var/spool/lpd:/bin/bash
mail:x:8:12:Mailer daemon:/var/spool/clientmqueue:/bin/false
...
root:x:0:512:Netbios Domain Administrator:/root:/bin/bash
nobody:x:999:514:nobody:/dev/null:/bin/false
bobj:x:1000:513:System User:/home/bobj:/bin/bash
stans:x:1001:513:System User:/home/stans:/bin/bash
chrisr:x:1002:513:System User:/home/chrisr:/bin/bash
maryv:x:1003:513:System User:/home/maryv:/bin/bash
vaioboss$:x:1005:553:vaioboss$:/dev/null:/bin/false
bldg1$:x:1006:553:bldg1$:/dev/null:/bin/false
```

This is the correct output. If the accounts that have UIDs above 512 are not shown,
there is a problem.

5. The next step in the verification process involves testing the operation of UNIX group
   resolution via the NSS LDAP resolver. Execute these commands:

```
root#  getent group
root:x:0:
bin:x:1:daemon
daemon:x:2:
sys:x:3:
...
Domain Admins:x:512:root
Domain Users:x:513:bobj,stans,chrisr,maryv,jht
Domain Guests:x:514:
Administrators:x:544:
Users:x:545:
```

```
Guests:x:546:nobody
Power Users:x:547:
Account Operators:x:548:
Server Operators:x:549:
Print Operators:x:550:
Backup Operators:x:551:
Replicator:x:552:
Domain Computers:x:553:
Accounts:x:1000:
Finances:x:1001:
PIOps:x:1002:
```

This is also the correct and desired output, because it demonstrates that the LDAP client is able to communicate correctly with the LDAP server (MASSIVE).

6. You must now set the LDAP administrative password into the Samba-3 `secrets.tdb` file by executing this command:

```
root#  smbpasswd -w not24get
Setting stored password for "cn=Manager,dc=abmas,dc=biz" in secrets.tdb
```

7. Now you must obtain the domain SID from the PDC and store it into the `secrets.tdb` file also. This step is not necessary with an LDAP passdb backend because Samba-3 obtains the domain SID from the sambaDomain object it automatically stores in the LDAP backend. It does not hurt to add the SID to the `secrets.tdb`, and if you wish to do so, this command can achieve that:

```
root#  net rpc getsid MEGANET2
Storing SID S-1-5-21-3504140859-1010554828-2431957765 \
                        for Domain MEGANET2 in secrets.tdb
```

When configuring a Samba-3 BDC that has an LDAP backend, there is no need to take any special action to join it to the domain. However, winbind communicates with the domain controller that is running on the localhost and must be able to authenticate, thus requiring that the BDC should be joined to the domain. The process of joining the domain creates the necessary authentication accounts.

8. To join the Samba BDC to the domain, execute the following:

```
root#  net rpc join -U root%not24get
Joined domain MEGANET2.
```

This indicates that the domain security account for the BDC has been correctly created.

9. Verify that user and group account resolution works via Samba-3 tools as follows:

```
root#  pdbedit -L
root:0:root
nobody:65534:nobody
bobj:1000:System User
stans:1001:System User
chrisr:1002:System User
maryv:1003:System User
bldg1$:1006:bldg1$


root#  net groupmap list
Domain Admins (S-1-5-21-3504140859-...-2431957765-512) ->
                                                   Domain Admins
Domain Users (S-1-5-21-3504140859-...-2431957765-513) -> Domain Users
Domain Guests (S-1-5-21-3504140859-...-2431957765-514) ->
                                                   Domain Guests
Administrators (S-1-5-21-3504140859-...-2431957765-544) ->
                                                   Administrators
...
Accounts (S-1-5-21-3504140859-1010554828-2431957765-3001) -> Accounts
Finances (S-1-5-21-3504140859-1010554828-2431957765-3003) -> Finances
PIOps (S-1-5-21-3504140859-1010554828-2431957765-3005) -> PIOps
```

These results show that all things are in order.

10. The server you have so carefully built is now ready for another important step. Now start the Samba-3 server and validate its operation. Execute the following to render all the processes needed fully operative so that, upon system reboot, they are automatically started:

```
root#  chkconfig named on
root#  chkconfig dhcpd on
root#  chkconfig nmb on
root#  chkconfig smb on
root#  chkconfig winbind on
root#  rcnmb start
root#  rcsmb start
root#  rcwinbind start
```

Samba-3 should now be running and is ready for a quick test. But not quite yet!

11. Your new BLDG1, BLDG2 servers do not have home directories for users. To rectify this using the SUSE yast2 utility or by manually editing the /etc/fstab file, add a mount entry to mount the home directory that has been exported from the MASSIVE server. Mount this resource before proceeding. An alternate approach could be to create local

home directories for users who are to use these machines. This is a choice that you, as system administrator, must make. The following entry in the `/etc/fstab` file suffices for now:

```
massive.abmas.biz:/home   /home   nfs      rw 0 0
```

To mount this resource, execute:

```
root#  mount -a
```

Verify that the home directory has been mounted as follows:

```
root#  df | grep home
massive:/home          29532988      283388  29249600    1% /home
```

12. Implement a quick check using one of the users that is in the LDAP database. Here you go:

```
root#  smbclient //bldg1/bobj -Ubobj%n3v3r218
smb: \> dir
  .                         D        0  Wed Dec 17 01:16:19 2003
  ..                        D        0  Wed Dec 17 19:04:42 2003
  bin                       D        0  Tue Sep  2 04:00:57 2003
  Documents                 D        0  Sun Nov 30 07:28:20 2003
  public_html               D        0  Sun Nov 30 07:28:20 2003
  .urlview                  H      311  Fri Jul  7 06:55:35 2000
  .dvipsrc                  H      208  Fri Nov 17 11:22:02 1995

              57681 blocks of size 524288. 57128 blocks available
smb: \> q
```

Now that the first BDC (BDLG1) has been configured it is time to build and configure the second BDC server (BLDG2) as follows:

CONFIGURATION OF BDC CALLED BLDG2

1. Install the files in Example 5.5.2, Example 5.5.3, and Example 5.5.4 into the `/etc/samba/` directory. The three files should be added together to form the `smb.conf` file.

2. Follow carefully the steps shown in Section 5.5, starting at step 2.

5.6   Miscellaneous Server Preparation Tasks

My father would say, "Dinner is not over until the dishes have been done." The makings of a great network environment take a lot of effort and attention to detail. So far, you have completed most of the complex (and to many administrators, the interesting part of server configuration) steps, but remember to tie it all together. Here are a few more steps that must be completed so that your network runs like a well-rehearsed orchestra.

5.6.1   Configuring Directory Share Point Roots

In your `smb.conf` file, you have specified Windows shares. Each has a *path* parameter. Even though it is obvious to all, one of the common Samba networking problems is caused by forgetting to verify that every such share root directory actually exists and that it has the necessary permissions and ownership.

Here is an example, but remember to create the directory needed for every share:

```
root#  mkdir -p /data/{accounts,finsvcs,piops}
root#  mkdir -p /apps
root#  chown -R root:root /data
root#  chown -R root:root /apps
root#  chown -R bobj:Accounts /data/accounts
root#  chown -R bobj:Finances /data/finsvcs
root#  chown -R bobj:PIOps /data/pidata
root#  chmod -R ug+rwxs,o-rwx /data
root#  chmod -R ug+rwx,o+rx-w /apps
```

5.6.2   Configuring Profile Directories

You made a conscious decision to do everything it would take to improve network client performance. One of your decisions was to implement folder redirection. This means that Windows user desktop profiles are now made up of two components: a dynamically loaded part and a set of file network folders.

For this arrangement to work, every user needs a directory structure for the network folder portion of his or her profile as shown here:

```
root#  mkdir -p /var/lib/samba/profdata
root#  chown root:root /var/lib/samba/profdata
root#  chmod 755 /var/lib/samba/profdata

# Per user structure
root#  cd /var/lib/samba/profdata
root#  mkdir -p username
root#  for i in InternetFiles Cookies History AppData \
```

```
                    LocalSettings MyPictures MyDocuments Recent
root#  do
root#  mkdir username/$i
root#  done
root#  chown -R username:Domain\ Users username
root#  chmod -R 750 username
```

You have three options insofar as the dynamically loaded portion of the roaming profile is concerned:

- You may permit the user to obtain a default profile.

- You can create a mandatory profile.

- You can create a group profile (which is almost always a mandatory profile).

Mandatory profiles cannot be overwritten by a user. The change from a user profile to a mandatory profile is effected by renaming the NTUSER.DAT to NTUSER.MAN, that is, just by changing the filename extension.

The location of the profile that a user can obtain is set in the user's account in the LDAP passdb backend. You can manage this using the Idealx smbldap-tools or using the Windows NT4 Domain User Manager[20].

It may not be obvious that you must ensure that the root directory for the user's profile exists and has the needed permissions. Use the following commands to create this directory:

```
root#  mkdir -p /var/lib/samba/profiles/username
root#  chown username:Domain\ Users
       /var/lib/samba/profiles/username
root#  chmod 700  /var/lib/samba/profiles/username
```

5.6.3 Preparation of Logon Scripts

The use of a logon script with Windows XP Professional is an option that every site should consider. Unless you have locked down the desktop so the user cannot change anything, there is risk that a vital network drive setting may be broken or that printer connections may be lost. Logon scripts can help to restore persistent network folder (drive) and printer connections in a predictable manner. One situation in which such breakage may occur in particular is when a mobile PC (notebook) user attaches to another company's network that forces environment changes that are alien to your network.

If you decide to use network logon scripts, by reference to the smb.conf files for the domain controllers, you see that the path to the share point for the NETLOGON share defined is /var/lib/samba/netlogon. The path defined for the logon script inside that share is scripts\logon.bat. This means that as a Windows NT/200x/XP client logs onto the

---

[20]<ftp://ftp.microsoft.com/Softlib/MSLFILES/SRVTOOLS.EXE>

network, it tries to obtain the file `logon.bat` from the fully qualified path `/var/lib/samba/netlogon/scripts`. This fully qualified path should therefore exist whether you install the `logon.bat`.

You can, of course, create the fully qualified path by executing:

```
root#  mkdir -p /var/lib/samba/netlogon/scripts
```

You should research the options for logon script implementation by referring to *TOSHARG2*, Chapter 24, Section 24.4. A quick Web search will bring up a host of options. One of the most popular logon facilities in use today is called KiXtart[21].

5.6.4   Assigning User Rights and Privileges

The ability to perform tasks such as joining Windows clients to the domain can be assigned to normal user accounts. By default, only the domain administrator account (`root` on UNIX systems because it has UID=0) can add accounts. New to Samba 3.0.11 is the ability to grant this privilege in a very limited fashion to particular accounts.

By default, even Samba-3.0.11 does not grant any rights even to the `Domain Admins` group. Here we grant this group all privileges.

Samba limits privileges on a per-server basis. This is a deliberate limitation so that users who are granted rights can be restricted to particular machines. It is left to the network administrator to determine which rights should be provided and to whom.

STEPS FOR ASSIGNMENT OF USER RIGHTS AND PRIVILEGES

1. Log onto the PDC as the `root` account.

2. Execute the following command to grant the `Domain Admins` group all rights and privileges:

```
root#  net -S MASSIVE  -U root%not24get rpc rights grant \
         "MEGANET2\Domain Admins" SeMachineAccountPrivilege \
    SePrintOperatorPrivilege SeAddUsersPrivilege \
    SeDiskOperatorPrivilege SeRemoteShutdownPrivilege
Successfully granted rights.
```

Repeat this step on each domain controller, in each case substituting the name of the server (e.g., BLDG1, BLDG2) in place of the PDC called MASSIVE.

3. In this step the privilege will be granted to Bob Jordan (bobj) to add Windows workstations to the domain. Execute the following only on the PDC. It is not necessary to do this on BDCs or on DMS machines because machine accounts are only ever added by the PDC:

---

[21]<http://www.kixtart.org>

```
root#  net -S MASSIVE  -U root%not24get rpc rights grant \
            "MEGANET2\bobj" SeMachineAccountPrivilege
Successfully granted rights.
```

4. Verify that privilege assignments have been correctly applied by executing:

```
net rpc rights list accounts -Uroot%not24get
MEGANET2\bobj
SeMachineAccountPrivilege

S-0-0
No privileges assigned

BUILTIN\Print Operators
No privileges assigned

BUILTIN\Account Operators
No privileges assigned

BUILTIN\Backup Operators
No privileges assigned

BUILTIN\Server Operators
No privileges assigned

BUILTIN\Administrators
No privileges assigned

Everyone
No privileges assigned

MEGANET2\Domain Admins
SeMachineAccountPrivilege
SePrintOperatorPrivilege
SeAddUsersPrivilege
SeRemoteShutdownPrivilege
SeDiskOperatorPrivilege
```

5.7   Windows Client Configuration

In the next few sections, you can configure a new Windows XP Professional disk image on a staging machine. You will configure all software, printer settings, profile and policy handling, and desktop default profile settings on this system. When it is complete, you copy the contents of the C:\Documents and Settings\Default User directory to a directory with the same name in the NETLOGON share on the domain controllers.

Much can be learned from the Microsoft Support site regarding how best to set up shared profiles. One knowledge-base article in particular stands out: "How to Create a Base Profile for All Users."[22]

5.7.1 Configuration of Default Profile with Folder Redirection

Log onto the Windows XP Professional workstation as the local **Administrator**. It is necessary to expose folders that are generally hidden to provide access to the Default User folder.

EXPOSE HIDDEN FOLDERS

1. Launch the Windows Explorer by clicking **Start → My Computer → Tools → Folder Options → View Tab**. Select **Show hidden files and folders**, and click **OK**. Exit Windows Explorer.

2. Launch the Registry Editor. Click **Start → Run**. Key in **regedt32**, and click **OK**.

REDIRECT FOLDERS IN DEFAULT SYSTEM USER PROFILE

1. Give focus to HKEY_LOCAL_MACHINE hive entry in the left panel. Click **File → Load Hive... → Documents and Settings → Default User → NTUSER → Open**. In the dialog box that opens, enter the key name Default and click **OK**.

2. Browse inside the newly loaded Default folder to:

```
HKEY_LOCAL_MACHINE\Default\Software\Microsoft\Windows\
                    CurrentVersion\Explorer\User Shell Folders\
```

The right panel reveals the contents as shown in Figure 5.3.

3. You edit hive keys. Acceptable values to replace the %USERPROFILE% variable includes:

   - A drive letter such as U:

   - A direct network path such as \\MASSIVE\profdata

   - A network redirection (UNC name) that contains a macro such as

     %LOGONSERVER%\profdata\

4. Set the registry keys as shown in Table 5.4. Your implementation makes the assumption that users have statically located machines. Notebook computers (mobile users) need to be accommodated using local profiles. This is not an uncommon assumption.

5. Click back to the root of the loaded hive Default. Click **File → Unload Hive... → Yes**.

---
[22]<http://support.microsoft.com/default.aspx?scid=kb;EN-US;168475>

6. Click **File** → **Exit**. This exits the Registry Editor.

7. Now follow the procedure given in Section 5.3.1.3. Make sure that each folder you
   have redirected is in the exclusion list.

8. You are now ready to copy[23] the Default User profile to the Samba domain controllers.
   Launch Microsoft Windows Explorer, and use it to copy the full contents of the directory `Default User` that is in the `C:\Documents and Settings` to the root directory
   of the `NETLOGON` share. If the `NETLOGON` share has the defined UNIX path of `/var/`
   `lib/samba/netlogon`, when the copy is complete there must be a directory in there
   called `Default User`.

Before punching out new desktop images for the client workstations, it is perhaps a good idea
that desktop behavior should be returned to the original Microsoft settings. The following
steps achieve that ojective:

RESET FOLDER DISPLAY TO ORIGINAL BEHAVIOR

1. To launch the Windows Explorer, click **Start** → **My Computer** → **Tools** → **Folder**
   Options → **View Tab**. Deselect **Show hidden files and folders**, and click **OK**. Exit
   Windows Explorer.

Figure 5.3 Windows XP Professional — User Shared Folders

Name	Type	Data
(Default)	REG_SZ	(value not set)
AppData	REG_EXPAND_SZ	%USERPROFILE%\Application Data
Cache	REG_EXPAND_SZ	%USERPROFILE%\Internet Files
Cookies	REG_EXPAND_SZ	%USERPROFILE%\Cookies
Desktop	REG_EXPAND_SZ	%USERPROFILE%\Desktop
Favorites	REG_EXPAND_SZ	%USERPROFILE%\Favorites
History	REG_EXPAND_SZ	%USERPROFILE%\Local Settings\History
Local AppData	REG_EXPAND_SZ	%USERPROFILE%\Local Settings\Application Data
Local Settings	REG_EXPAND_SZ	%USERPROFILE%\Local Settings
My Pictures	REG_EXPAND_SZ	%USERPROFILE%\My Documents\My Pictures
NetHood	REG_EXPAND_SZ	%USERPROFILE%\NetHood
Personal	REG_EXPAND_SZ	%USERPROFILE%\My Documents
PrintHood	REG_EXPAND_SZ	%USERPROFILE%\PrintHood
Programs	REG_EXPAND_SZ	%USERPROFILE%\Start Menu\Programs
Recent	REG_EXPAND_SZ	%USERPROFILE%\Recent
SendTo	REG_EXPAND_SZ	%USERPROFILE%\SendTo
Start Menu	REG_EXPAND_SZ	%USERPROFILE%\Start Menu
Startup	REG_EXPAND_SZ	%USERPROFILE%\Start Menu\Programs\Startup
Templates	REG_EXPAND_SZ	%USERPROFILE%\Templates

---

[23]There is an alternate method by which a default user profile can be added to the `NETLOGON` share. This
facility in the Windows System tool permits profiles to be exported. The export target may be a particular
user or group profile share point or else the `NETLOGON` share. In this case, the profile directory must be
named `Default User`.

Table 5.4 Default Profile Redirections

Registry Key	Redirected Value
Cache	%LOGONSERVER%\profdata\%USERNAME%\InternetFiles
Cookies	%LOGONSERVER%\profdata\%USERNAME%\Cookies
History	%LOGONSERVER%\profdata\%USERNAME%\History
Local AppData	%LOGONSERVER%\profdata\%USERNAME%\AppData
Local Settings	%LOGONSERVER%\profdata\%USERNAME%\LocalSettings
My Pictures	%LOGONSERVER%\profdata\%USERNAME%\MyPictures
Personal	%LOGONSERVER%\profdata\%USERNAME%\MyDocuments
Recent	%LOGONSERVER%\profdata\%USERNAME%\Recent

5.7.2   Configuration of MS Outlook to Relocate PST File

Microsoft Outlook can store a Personal Storage file, generally known as a PST file. It is the nature of email storage that this file grows, at times quite rapidly. So that users' email is available to them at every workstation they may log onto, it is common practice in well-controlled sites to redirect the PST folder to the users' home directory. Follow these steps for each user who wishes to do this.

NOTE

 It is presumed that Outlook Express has been configured for use.

Launch Outlook Express 6. Click **Tools** → **Options** → **Maintenance** → **Store Folder** → **Change**.

Follow the on-screen prompts to relocate the PST file to the desired location.

5.7.3   Configure Delete Cached Profiles on Logout

Configure the Windows XP Professional client to auto-delete roaming profiles on logout:

Click **Start** → **Run**. In the dialog box, enter **MMC** and click **OK**.

Follow these steps to set the default behavior of the staging machine so that all roaming profiles are deleted as network users log out of the system. Click **File** → **Add/Remove Snap-in** → **Add** → **Group Policy** → **Add** → **Finish** → **Close** → **OK**.

The Microsoft Management Console now shows the **Group Policy** utility that enables you to set the policies needed. In the left panel, click **Local Computer Policy** → **Administrative Templates** → **System** → **User Profiles**. In the right panel, set the properties shown here by double-clicking on each item as shown:

- Do not check for user ownership of Roaming Profile Folders = Enabled

- Delete cached copies of roaming profiles = Enabled

Close the Microsoft Management Console. The settings take immediate effect and persist onto all image copies made of this system to deploy the new standard desktop system.

5.7.4   Uploading Printer Drivers to Samba Servers

Users want to be able to use network printers. You have a vested interest in making it easy for them to print. You have chosen to install the printer drivers onto the Samba servers and to enable point-and-click (drag-and-drop) printing. This process results in Samba being able to automatically provide the Windows client with the driver necessary to print to the printer chosen. The following procedure must be followed for every network printer:

STEPS TO INSTALL PRINTER DRIVERS ON THE SAMBA SERVERS

1. Join your Windows XP Professional workstation (the staging machine) to the `MEGANET2` domain. If you are not sure of the procedure, follow the guidance given in Chapter 15, "A Collection of Useful Tidbits", Section 15.1.

2. After the machine has rebooted, log onto the workstation as the domain `root` (this is the Administrator account for the operating system that is the host platform for this implementation of Samba.

3. Launch MS Windows Explorer. Navigate in the left panel. Click **My Network Places** → **Entire Network** → **Microsoft Windows Network** → **Meganet2** → **Massive**. Click on **Massive Printers and Faxes**.

4. Identify a printer that is shown in the right panel. Let us assume the printer is called **ps01-color**. Right-click on the **ps01-color** icon and select the **Properties** entry. This opens a dialog box that indicates that "The printer driver is not installed on this computer. Some printer properties will not be accessible unless you install the printer driver. Do you want to install the driver now?" It is important at this point you answer **No**.

5. The printer properties panel for the **ps01-color** printer on the server `MASSIVE` is displayed. Click the **Advanced** tab. Note that the box labeled **Driver** is empty. Click the **New Driver** button that is next to the **Driver** box. This launches the "Add Printer Wizard".

6. The "Add Printer Driver Wizard on `MASSIVE`" panel is now presented. Click **Next** to continue. From the left panel, select the printer manufacturer. In your case, you are adding a driver for a printer manufactured by Lexmark. In the right panel, select the printer (Lexmark Optra Color 40 PS). Click **Next**, and then **Finish** to commence driver upload. A progress bar appears and instructs you as each file is being uploaded and that it is being directed at the network server \\`massive`\\`ps01-color`.

7. The driver upload completes in anywhere from a few seconds to a few minutes. When it completes, you are returned to the **Advanced** tab in the **Properties** panel. You can set the Location (under the **General** tab) and Security settings (under the **Security**

tab). Under the **Sharing** tab it is possible to load additional printer drivers; there is also a check-box in this tab called "List in the directory". When this box is checked, the printer will be published in Active Directory (Applicable to Active Directory use only.)

8. Click **OK**. It will take a minute or so to upload the settings to the server. You are now returned to the **Printers and Faxes on Massive** monitor. Right-click on the printer, click **Properties** → **Device Settings**. Now change the settings to suit your requirements. BE CERTAIN TO CHANGE AT LEAST ONE SETTING and apply the changes even if you need to reverse the changes back to their original settings.

9. This is necessary so that the printer settings are initialized in the Samba printers database. Click **Apply** to commit your settings. Revert any settings you changed just to initialize the Samba printers database entry for this printer. If you need to revert a setting, click **Apply** again.

10. Verify that all printer settings are at the desired configuration. When you are satisfied that they are, click the **General** tab. Now click the **Print Test Page** button. A test page should print. Verify that it has printed correctly. Then click **OK** in the panel that is newly presented. Click **OK** on the **ps01-color on massive Properties** panel.

11. You must repeat this process for all network printers (i.e., for every printer on each server). When you have finished uploading drivers to all printers, close all applications. The next task is to install software your users require to do their work.

5.7.5   Software Installation

Your network has both fixed desktop workstations as well as notebook computers. As a general rule, it is a good idea to not tamper with the operating system that is provided by the notebook computer manufacturer. Notebooks require special handling that is beyond the scope of this chapter.

For desktop systems, the installation of software onto administratively centralized application servers make a lot of sense. This means that you can manage software maintenance from a central perspective and that only minimal application stubware needs to be installed onto the desktop systems. You should proceed with software installation and default configuration as far as is humanly possible and so long as it makes sense to do so. Make certain to thoroughly test and validate every aspect of software operations and configuration.

When you believe that the overall configuration is complete, be sure to create a shared group profile and migrate that to the Samba server for later reuse when creating custom mandatory profiles, just in case a user may have specific needs you had not anticipated.

5.7.6   Roll-out Image Creation

The final steps before preparing the distribution Norton Ghost image file you might follow are:

Unjoin the domain — Each workstation requires a unique name and must be independently joined into domain membership.

Defragment the hard disk — While not obvious to the uninitiated, defragmentation results in better performance and often significantly reduces the size of the compressed disk image. That also means it will take less time to deploy the image onto 500 workstations.

5.8   Key Points Learned

This chapter introduced many new concepts. Is it a sad fact that the example presented deliberately avoided any consideration of security. Security does not just happen; you must design it into your total network. Security begins with a systems design and implementation that anticipates hostile behavior from users both inside and outside the organization. Hostile and malicious intruders do not respect barriers; they accept them as challenges. For that reason, if not simply from a desire to establish safe networking practices, you must not deploy the design presented in this book in an environment where there is risk of compromise.

As a minimum, the LDAP server must be protected by way of Access Control Lists (ACLs), and it must be configured to use secure protocols for all communications over the network. Of course, secure networking does not result just from systems design and implementation but involves constant user education training and, above all, disciplined attention to detail and constant searching for signs of unfriendly or alien activities. Security is itself a topic for a whole book. Please do consult appropriate sources. Jerry Carter's book *LDAP System Administration*[24] is a good place to start reading about OpenLDAP as well as security considerations.

The substance of this chapter that has been deserving of particular attention includes:

- Implementation of an OpenLDAP-based passwd backend, necessary to support distributed domain control.

- Implementation of Samba primary and secondary domain controllers with a common LDAP backend for user and group accounts that is shared with the UNIX system through the PADL nss_ldap and pam_ldap tool-sets.

- Use of the Idealx smbldap-tools scripts for UNIX (POSIX) account management as well as to manage Samba Windows user and group accounts.

- The basics of implementation of Group Policy controls for Windows network clients.

- Control over roaming profiles, with particular focus on folder redirection to network drives.

- Use of the CUPS printing system together with Samba-based printer driver auto-download.

---

[24]<http://www.booksense.com/product/info.jsp&isbn=1565924916>

5.9   Questions and Answers

Well, here we are at the end of this chapter and we have only ten questions to help you to remember so much. There are bound to be some sticky issues here.

F.A.Q.

1. **Q:** *Why did you not cover secure practices? Isn't it rather irresponsible to instruct network administrators to implement insecure solutions?*
A: Let's get this right. This is a book about Samba, not about OpenLDAP and secure communication protocols for subjects other than Samba. Earlier on, you note, that the dynamic DNS and DHCP solutions also used no protective secure communications protocols. The reason for this is simple: There are so many ways of implementing secure protocols that this book would have been even larger and more complex.

The solutions presented here all work (at least they did for me). Network administrators have the interest and the need to be better trained and instructed in secure networking practices and ought to implement safe systems. I made the decision, right or wrong, to keep this material as simple as possible. The intent of this book is to demonstrate a working solution and not to discuss too many peripheral issues.

This book makes little mention of backup techniques. Does that mean that I am recommending that you should implement a network without provision for data recovery and for disaster management? Back to our focus: The deployment of Samba has been clearly demonstrated.

2. **Q:** *You have focused much on SUSE Linux and little on the market leader, Red Hat. Do you have a problem with Red Hat Linux? Doesn't that make your guidance irrelevant to the Linux I might be using?*
A: Both Red Hat Linux and SUSE Linux comply with the Linux Standards Base specifications for a standard Linux distribution. The differences are marginal. Surely you know your Linux platform, and you do have access to administration manuals for it. This book is not a Linux tutorial; it is a Samba tutorial. Let's keep the focus on the Samba part of the book; all the other bits are peripheral (but important) to creation of a total network solution.

What I find interesting is the attention reviewers give to Linux installation and to the look and feel of the desktop, but does that make for a great server? In this book, I have paid particular attention to the details of creating a whole solution framework. I have not tightened every nut and bolt, but I have touched on all the issues you need to be familiar with. Over the years many people have approached me wanting to know the details of exactly how to implement a DHCP and dynamic DNS server with Samba and WINS. In this chapter, it is plain to see what needs to be configured to provide transparent interoperability. Likewise for CUPS and Samba interoperation. These are key stumbling areas for many people.

At every critical junction, I have provided comparative guidance for both SUSE and Red
Hat Linux. Both manufacturers have done a great job in furthering the cause of open
source software. I favor neither and respect both. I like particular features of both products
(companies also). No bias in presentation is intended. Oh, before I forget, I particularly
like Debian Linux; that is my favorite playground.

3. **Q:** *You did not use SWAT to configure Samba. Is there something wrong with it?*
A: That is a good question. As it is, the `smb.conf` file configurations are presented in
as direct a format as possible. Adding SWAT into the equation would have complicated
matters. I sought simplicity of implementation. The fact is that I did use SWAT to create
the files in the first place.

There are people in the Linux and open source community who feel that SWAT is dangerous
and insecure. Many will not touch it with a barge-pole. By not introducing SWAT, I hope
to have brought their interests on board. SWAT is well covered is *TOSHARG2*.

4. **Q:** *You have exposed a well-used password* not24get. *Is that not irresponsible?*
A: Well, I had to use a password of some sort. At least this one has been consistently used
throughout. I guess you can figure out that in a real deployment it would make sense to use
a more secure and original password.

5. **Q:** *The Idealx smbldap-tools create many domain group accounts that are not used. Is
that a good thing?*
A: I took this up with Idealx and found them most willing to change that in the next
version. Let's give Idealx some credit for the contribution they have made. I appreciate
their work and, besides, it does no harm to create accounts that are not now used — at
some time Samba may well use them.

6. **Q:** *Can I use LDAP just for Samba accounts and not for UNIX system accounts?*
A: Yes, you can do that for user accounts only. Samba requires there to be a POSIX
(UNIX) group account for every Windows domain group account. But if you put your users
into the system password account, how do you plan to keep all domain controller system
password files in sync? I think that having everything in LDAP makes a lot of sense for the
UNIX administrator who is still learning the craft and is migrating from MS Windows.

7. **Q:** *Why are the Windows domain RID portions not the same as the UNIX UID?*
A: Samba uses a well-known public algorithm for assigning RIDs from UIDs and GIDs.
This algorithm ought to ensure that there will be no clashes with well-known RIDs. Well-
known RIDs have special significance to MS Windows clients. The automatic assignment
used the calculation: RID = UID x 2 + 1000. Of course, Samba does permit you to override
that to some extent. See the `smb.conf` man page entry for `algorithmic rid base`.

8. Q: *Printer configuration examples all show printing to the HP port 9100. Does this mean that I must have HP printers for these solutions to work?*
A: No. You can use any type of printer and must use the interfacing protocol supported by the printer. Many networks use LPR/LPD print servers to which are attached PCL printers, inkjet printers, plotters, and so on. At home I use a USB-attached inkjet printer. Use the appropriate device URI (Universal Resource Interface) argument to the `lpadmin` `-v` option that is right for your printer.

9. Q: *Is folder redirection dangerous? I've heard that you can lose your data that way.*
A: The only loss of data I know of that involved folder redirection was caused by manual misuse of the redirection tool. The administrator redirected a folder to a network drive and said he wanted to migrate (move) the data over. Then he changed his mind, so he moved the folder back to the roaming profile. This time, he declined to move the data because he thought it was still in the local profile folder. That was not the case, so by declining to move the data back, he wiped out the data. You cannot hold the tool responsible for that. Caveat emptor still applies.

10. Q: *Is it really necessary to set a local Group Policy to exclude the redirected folders from the roaming profile?*
A: Yes. If you do not do this, the data will still be copied from the network folder (share) to the local cached copy of the profile.

Example 5.4.2 LDAP Master Configuration File — /etc/openldap/slapd.conf Part A

```
include      /etc/openldap/schema/core.schema
include      /etc/openldap/schema/cosine.schema
include      /etc/openldap/schema/inetorgperson.schema
include      /etc/openldap/schema/nis.schema
include      /etc/openldap/schema/samba3.schema

pidfile      /var/run/slapd/slapd.pid
argsfile /var/run/slapd/slapd.args

access to dn.base=""
     by self write
     by * auth

access to attr=userPassword
     by self write
     by * auth

access to attr=shadowLastChange
     by self write
     by * read

access to *
               by * read
               by anonymous auth

#loglevel    256

schemacheck      on
idletimeout 30
backend      bdb
database bdb
checkpoint       1024 5
cachesize        10000

suffix       "dc=abmas,dc=biz"
rootdn       "cn=Manager,dc=abmas,dc=biz"

# rootpw = not24get
rootpw           {SSHA}86kTavd9Dw3FAz6qzWTrCOKX/c0Qe+UV

directory    /data/ldap
```

Example 5.4.3 LDAP Master Configuration File — /etc/openldap/slapd.conf Part B

```
# Indices to maintain
index objectClass              eq
index cn                       pres,sub,eq
index sn                       pres,sub,eq
index uid                      pres,sub,eq
index displayName              pres,sub,eq
index uidNumber                eq
index gidNumber                eq
index memberUID                eq
index sambaSID                 eq
index sambaPrimaryGroupSID     eq
index sambaDomainName          eq
index default                  sub
```

Example 5.4.4 Configuration File for NSS LDAP Support — /etc/ldap.conf

```
host 127.0.0.1

base dc=abmas,dc=biz

binddn cn=Manager,dc=abmas,dc=biz
bindpw not24get

timelimit 50
bind_timelimit 50
bind_policy hard

idle_timelimit 3600

pam_password exop

nss_base_passwd ou=People,dc=abmas,dc=biz?one
nss_base_shadow ou=People,dc=abmas,dc=biz?one
nss_base_group  ou=Groups,dc=abmas,dc=biz?one

ssl off
```

Example 5.4.5 Configuration File for NSS LDAP Clients Support — /etc/ldap.conf

---

```
host 172.16.0.1

base dc=abmas,dc=biz

binddn cn=Manager,dc=abmas,dc=biz
bindpw not24get

timelimit 50
bind_timelimit 50
bind_policy hard

idle_timelimit 3600

pam_password exop

nss_base_passwd ou=People,dc=abmas,dc=biz?one
nss_base_shadow ou=People,dc=abmas,dc=biz?one
nss_base_group  ou=Groups,dc=abmas,dc=biz?one

ssl off
```

Example 5.4.6 LDAP Based smb.conf File, Server: MASSIVE — global Section: Part A

```
# Global parameters
[global]
        unix charset = LOCALE
        workgroup = MEGANET2
        netbios name = MASSIVE
        interfaces = eth1, lo
        bind interfaces only = Yes
        passdb backend = ldapsam:ldap://massive.abmas.biz
        enable privileges = Yes
        username map = /etc/samba/smbusers
        log level = 1
        syslog = 0
        log file = /var/log/samba/%m
        max log size = 50
        smb ports = 139
        name resolve order = wins bcast hosts
        time server = Yes
        printcap name = CUPS
        show add printer wizard = No
        add user script = /opt/IDEALX/sbin/smbldap-useradd -m "%u"
        delete user script = /opt/IDEALX/sbin/smbldap-userdel "%u"
        add group script = /opt/IDEALX/sbin/smbldap-groupadd -p "%g"
        delete group script = /opt/IDEALX/sbin/smbldap-groupdel "%g"
        add user to group script = /opt/IDEALX/sbin/smbldap-groupmod ↩
            -m "%u" "%g"
        delete user from group script = /opt/IDEALX/sbin/smbldap- ↩
            groupmod -x "%u" "%g"
        set primary group script = /opt/IDEALX/sbin/smbldap-usermod ↩
            -g "%g" "%u"
        add machine script = /opt/IDEALX/sbin/smbldap-useradd -w "%u ↩
            "
```

Example 5.4.7 LDAP Based smb.conf File, Server: MASSIVE — global Section: Part B

```
logon script = scripts\logon.bat
logon path = \\%L\profiles\%U
logon drive = X:
domain logons = Yes
preferred master = Yes
wins support = Yes
ldap suffix = dc=abmas,dc=biz
ldap machine suffix = ou=People
ldap user suffix = ou=People
ldap group suffix = ou=Groups
ldap idmap suffix = ou=Idmap
ldap admin dn = cn=Manager,dc=abmas,dc=biz
idmap backend = ldap:ldap://massive.abmas.biz
idmap uid = 10000-20000
idmap gid = 10000-20000
map acl inherit = Yes
printing = cups
printer admin = root, chrisr
```

Example 5.5.1 LDAP Based smb.conf File, Server: BLDG1

```
# Global parameters
[global]
        unix charset = LOCALE
        workgroup = MEGANET2
        netbios name = BLDG1
        passdb backend = ldapsam:ldap://massive.abmas.biz
        enable privileges = Yes
        username map = /etc/samba/smbusers
        log level = 1
        syslog = 0
        log file = /var/log/samba/%m
        max log size = 50
        smb ports = 139
        name resolve order = wins bcast hosts
        printcap name = CUPS
        show add printer wizard = No
        logon script = scripts\logon.bat
        logon path = \\%L\profiles\%U
        logon drive = X:
        domain logons = Yes
        domain master = No
        wins server = 172.16.0.1
        ldap suffix = dc=abmas,dc=biz
        ldap machine suffix = ou=People
        ldap user suffix = ou=People
        ldap group suffix = ou=Groups
        ldap idmap suffix = ou=Idmap
        ldap admin dn = cn=Manager,dc=abmas,dc=biz
        idmap backend = ldap:ldap://massive.abmas.biz
        idmap uid = 10000-20000
        idmap gid = 10000-20000
        printing = cups
        printer admin = root, chrisr
```

Example 5.5.2 LDAP Based smb.conf File, Server: BLDG2

```
# Global parameters
[global]
        unix charset = LOCALE
        workgroup = MEGANET2
        netbios name = BLDG2
        passdb backend = ldapsam:ldap://massive.abmas.biz
        enable privileges = Yes
        username map = /etc/samba/smbusers
        log level = 1
        syslog = 0
        log file = /var/log/samba/%m
        max log size = 50
        smb ports = 139
        name resolve order = wins bcast hosts
        printcap name = CUPS
        show add printer wizard = No
        logon script = scripts\logon.bat
        logon path = \\%L\profiles\%U
        logon drive = X:
        domain logons = Yes
        domain master = No
        wins server = 172.16.0.1
        ldap suffix = dc=abmas,dc=biz
        ldap machine suffix = ou=People
        ldap user suffix = ou=People
        ldap group suffix = ou=Groups
        ldap idmap suffix = ou=Idmap
        ldap admin dn = cn=Manager,dc=abmas,dc=biz
        idmap backend = ldap:ldap://massive.abmas.biz
        idmap uid = 10000-20000
        idmap gid = 10000-20000
        printing = cups
        printer admin = root, chrisr
```

Example 5.5.3 LDAP Based smb.conf File, Shares Section — Part A

```
[accounts]
        comment = Accounting Files
        path = /data/accounts
        read only = No
[service]
        comment = Financial Services Files
        path = /data/service
        read only = No
[pidata]
        comment = Property Insurance Files
        path = /data/pidata
        read only = No
[homes]
        comment = Home Directories
        valid users = %S
        read only = No
        browseable = No
[printers]
        comment = SMB Print Spool
        path = /var/spool/samba
        guest ok = Yes
        printable = Yes
        browseable = No
```

Example 5.5.4 LDAP Based smb.conf File, Shares Section — Part B

```
[apps]
        comment = Application Files
        path = /apps
        admin users = bjordan
        read only = No
[netlogon]
        comment = Network Logon Service
        path = /var/lib/samba/netlogon
        guest ok = Yes
        locking = No
[profiles]
        comment = Profile Share
        path = /var/lib/samba/profiles
        read only = No
        profile acls = Yes
[profdata]
        comment = Profile Data Share
        path = /var/lib/samba/profdata
        read only = No
        profile acls = Yes
[print$]
        comment = Printer Drivers
        path = /var/lib/samba/drivers
        browseable = yes
        guest ok = no
        read only = yes
        write list = root, chrisr
```

Example 5.5.5 LDIF IDMAP Add-On Load File — File: /etc/openldap/idmap.LDIF

```
dn: ou=Idmap,dc=abmas,dc=biz
objectClass: organizationalUnit
ou: idmap
structuralObjectClass: organizationalUnit
```

## Chapter 6

A DISTRIBUTED 2000-USER NETWORK

There is something indeed mystical about things that are big. Large networks exhibit a certain magnetism and exude a sense of importance that obscures reality. You and I know that it is no more difficult to secure a large network than it is a small one. We all know that over and above a particular number of network clients, the rules no longer change; the only real dynamic is the size of the domain (much like a kingdom) over which the network ruler (oops, administrator) has control. The real dynamic then transforms from the technical to the political. Then again, that point is often reached well before the kingdom (or queendom) grows large.

If you have systematically worked your way to this chapter, hopefully you have found some gems and techniques that are applicable in your world. The network designs you have worked with in this book have their strong points as well as weak ones. That is to be expected given that they are based on real business environments, the specifics of which are molded to serve the purposes of this book.

This chapter is intent on wrapping up issues that are central to implementation and design of progressively larger networks. Are you ready for this chapter? Good, it is time to move on.

In previous chapters, you made the assumption that your network administration staff need detailed instruction right down to the nuts and bolts of implementing the solution. That is still the case, but they have graduated now. You decide to document only those issues, methods, and techniques that are new or complex. Routine tasks such as implementing a DNS or a DHCP server are under control. Even the basics of Samba are largely under control. So in this section you focus on the specifics of implementing LDAP changes, Samba changes, and approach and design of the solution and its deployment.

6.1 Introduction

Abmas is a miracle company. Most businesses would have collapsed under the weight of rapid expansion that this company has experienced. Samba is flexible, so there is no need to reinstall the whole operating system just because you need to implement a new network design. In fact, you can keep an old server running right up to the moment of cutover and then do a near-live conversion. There is no need to reinstall a Samba server just to change the way your network should function.

Network growth is common to all organizations. In this exercise, your preoccupation is with the mechanics of implementing Samba and LDAP so that network users on each network segment can work without impediment.

6.1.1 Assignment Tasks

Starting with the configuration files for the server called `MASSIVE` in Chapter 5, "Making Happy Users", you now deal with the issues that are particular to large distributed networks. Your task is simple — identify the challenges, consider the alternatives, and then design and implement a solution.

Remember, you have users based in London (UK), Los Angeles, Washington. DC, and, three buildings in New York. A significant portion of your workforce have notebook computers and roam all over the world. Some dial into the office, others use VPN connections over the Internet, and others just move between buildings.i

What do you say to an employee who normally uses a desktop system but must spend six weeks on the road with a notebook computer? She is concerned about email access and how to keep coworkers current with changing documents.

To top it all off, you have one network support person and one help desk person based in London, a single person dedicated to all network operations in Los Angeles, five staff for user administration and help desk in New York, plus one *floater* for Washington.

You have outsourced all desktop deployment and management to DirectPointe. Your concern is server maintenance and third-level support. Build a plan and show what must be done.

6.2   Dissection and Discussion

In Chapter 5, "Making Happy Users", you implemented an LDAP server that provided the *passdb backend* for the Samba servers. You explored ways to accelerate Windows desktop profile handling and you took control of network performance.

The implementation of an LDAP-based passdb backend (known as *ldapsam* in Samba parlance), or some form of database that can be distributed, is essential to permit the deployment of Samba Primary and Backup Domain Controllers (PDC/BDCs). You see, the problem is that the *tdbsam*-style passdb backend does not lend itself to being replicated. The older plain-text-based *smbpasswd*-style passdb backend can be replicated using a tool such as **rsync**, but *smbpasswd* suffers the drawback that it does not support the range of account facilities demanded by modern network managers.

The new *tdbsam* facility supports functionality that is similar to an *ldapsam*, but the lack of distributed infrastructure sorely limits the scope for its deployment. This raises the following questions: Why can't I just use an XML-based backend, or for that matter, why not use an SQL-based backend? Is support for these tools broken? Answers to these questions require a bit of background.

What is a directory? A directory is a collection of information regarding objects that can be accessed to rapidly find information that is relevant in a particular and consistent manner. A directory differs from a database in that it is generally more often searched (read) than updated. As a consequence, the information is organized to facilitate read access rather than to support transaction processing.

The Lightweight Directory Access Protocol (LDAP) differs considerably from a traditional database. It has a simple search facility that uniquely makes a highly preferred mechanism for managing user identities. LDAP provides a scalable mechanism for distributing the data repository and for keeping all copies (slaves) in sync with the master repository.

Samba is a flexible and powerful file and print sharing technology. It can use many external authentication sources and can be part of a total authentication and identity management infrastructure. The two most important external sources for large sites are Microsoft Active Directory and LDAP. Sites that specifically wish to avoid the proprietary implications of Microsoft Active Directory naturally gravitate toward OpenLDAP.

In Chapter 5, "Making Happy Users", you had to deal with a locally routed network. All deployment concerns focused around making users happy, and that simply means taking control over all network practices and usage so that no one user is disadvantaged by any other. The real lesson is one of understanding that no matter how much network bandwidth you provide, bandwidth remains a precious resource.

In this chapter, you must now consider how the overall network must function. In particular, you must be concerned with users who move between offices. You must take into account the way users need to access information globally. And you must make the network robust enough so that it can sustain partial breakdown without causing loss of productivity.

6.2.1   Technical Issues

There are at least three areas that need to be addressed as you approach the challenge of designing a network solution for the newly expanded business:

- User needs such as mobility and data access

- The nature of Windows networking protocols

- Identity management infrastructure needs

Let's look at each in turn.

6.2.1.1   User Needs

The new company has three divisions. Staff for each division are spread across the company. Some staff are office-bound and some are mobile users. Mobile users travel globally. Some spend considerable periods working in other offices. Everyone wants to be able to work without constraint of productivity.

The challenge is not insignificant. In some parts of the world, even dial-up connectivity is poor, while in other regions political encumbrances severely curtail user needs. Parts of the global Internet infrastructure remain shielded off for reasons outside the scope of this discussion.

Decisions must be made regarding where data is to be stored, how it will be replicated (if at all), and what the network bandwidth implications are. For example, one decision that can be made is to give each office its own master file storage area that can be synchronized to a central repository in New York. This would permit global data to be backed up from a single location. The synchronization tool could be **rsync,** run via a cron job. Mobile users may use off-line file storage under Windows XP Professional. This way, they can synchronize all files that have changed since each logon to the network.

No matter which way you look at this, the bandwidth requirements for acceptable performance are substantial even if only 10 percent of staff are global data users. A company with 3,500 employees, 280 of whom are mobile users who use a similarly distributed network, found they needed at least 2 Mb/sec connectivity between the UK and US offices. Even over 2 Mb/sec bandwidth, this company abandoned any attempt to run roaming profile usage for mobile users. At that time, the average roaming profile took 480 KB, while today the minimum Windows XP Professional roaming profile involves a transfer of over 750 KB from the profile server to and from the client.

Obviously then, user needs and wide-area practicalities dictate the economic and technical aspects of your network design as well as for standard operating procedures.

6.2.1.2   The Nature of Windows Networking Protocols

Network logons that include roaming profile handling requires from 140 KB to 2 MB. The inclusion of support for a minimal set of common desktop applications can push the size of a complete profile to over 15 MB. This has substantial implications for location of user profiles. Additionally, it is a significant factor in determining the nature and style of mandatory profiles that may be enforced as part of a total service-level assurance program that might be implemented.

One way to reduce the network bandwidth impact of user logon traffic is through folder redirection. In Chapter 5, "Making Happy Users", you implemented this in the new Windows XP Professional standard desktop configuration. When desktop folders such as **My Documents** are redirected to a network drive, they should also be excluded from synchronization to and from the server on logon or logout. Redirected folders are analogous to network drive connections.

Of course, network applications should only be run off local application servers. As a general rule, even with 2 Mb/sec network bandwidth, it would not make sense at all for someone who is working out of the London office to run applications off a server that is located in New York.

When network bandwidth becomes a precious commodity (that is most of the time), there is a significant demand to understand network processes and to mold the limits of acceptability around the constraints of affordability.

When a Windows NT4/200x/XP Professional client user logs onto the network, several important things must happen.

- The client obtains an IP address via DHCP. (DHCP is necessary so that users can roam between offices.)

- The client must register itself with the WINS and/or DNS server.

- The client must locate the closest domain controller.

- The client must log onto a domain controller and obtain as part of that process the location of the user's profile, load it, connect to redirected folders, and establish all network drive and printer connections.

- The domain controller must be able to resolve the user's credentials before the logon process is fully implemented.

Given that this book is about Samba and that it implements the Windows NT4-style domain semantics, it makes little sense to compare Samba with Microsoft Active Directory insofar as the logon protocols and principles of operation are concerned. The following information pertains exclusively to the interaction between a Windows XP Professional workstation and a Samba-3.0.20 server. In the discussion that follows, use is made of DHCP and WINS.

As soon as the Windows workstation starts up, it obtains an IP address. This is immediately followed by registration of its name both by broadcast and Unicast registration that is directed at the WINS server.

Given that the client is already a domain member, it then sends a directed (Unicast) request to the WINS server seeking the list of IP addresses for domain controllers (NetBIOS name type 0x1C). The WINS server replies with the information requested.

The client sends two netlogon mailslot broadcast requests to the local network and to each of the IP addresses returned by the WINS server. Whichever answers this request first appears to be the machine that the Windows XP client attempts to use to process the network logon. The mailslot messages use UDP broadcast to the local network and UDP Unicast directed at each machine that was listed in the WINS server response to a request for the list of domain controllers.

The logon process begins with negotiation of the SMB/CIFS protocols that are to be used; this is followed by an exchange of information that ultimately includes the client sending the credentials with which the user is attempting to logon. The logon server must now approve the further establishment of the connection, but that is a good point to halt for now. The priority here must center around identification of network infrastructure needs. A secondary fact we need to know is, what happens when local domain controllers fail or break?

Under most circumstances, the nearest domain controller responds to the netlogon mailslot broadcast. The exception to this norm occurs when the nearest domain controller is too busy or is out of service. Herein lies an important fact. This means it is important that every network segment should have at least two domain controllers. Since there can be only one PDC, all additional domain controllers are by definition BDCs.

The provision of sufficient servers that are BDCs is an important design factor. The second important design factor involves how each of the BDCs obtains user authentication data. That is the subject of the next section, which involves key decisions regarding Identity Management facilities.

6.2.1.3   Identity Management Needs

Network managers recognize that in large organizations users generally need to be given resource access based on needs, while being excluded from other resources for reasons of privacy. It is therefore essential that all users identify themselves at the point of network access. The network logon is the principal means by which user credentials are validated and filtered and appropriate rights and privileges are allocated.

Unfortunately, network resources tend to have their own Identity Management facilities, the quality and manageability of which varies from quite poor to exceptionally good. Corporations that use a mixture of systems soon discover that until recently, few systems were designed to interoperate. For example, UNIX systems each have an independent user database. Sun Microsystems developed a facility that was originally called `Yellow Pages`, and was renamed when a telephone company objected to the use of its trademark. What was once called `Yellow Pages` is today known as `Network Information System` (NIS).

NIS gained a strong following throughout the UNIX/VMS space in a short period of time and retained that appeal and use for over a decade. Security concerns and inherent limitations have caused it to enter its twilight. NIS did not gain widespread appeal outside of the UNIX world and was not universally adopted. Sun updated this to a more secure implementation called NIS+, but even it has fallen victim to changing demands as the demand for directory services that can be coupled with other information systems is catching on.

Nevertheless, both NIS and NIS+ continue to hold ground in business areas where UNIX still has major sway. Examples of organizations that remain firmly attached to the use of NIS and NIS+ include large government departments, education institutions, and large corporations that have a scientific or engineering focus.

Today's networking world needs a scalable, distributed Identity Management infrastructure, commonly called a directory. The most popular technologies today are Microsoft Active Directory service and a number of LDAP implementations.

The problem of managing multiple directories has become a focal point over the past decade, creating a large market for metadirectory products and services that allow organizations that have multiple directories and multiple management and control centers to provision information from one directory into another. The attendant benefit to end users is the promise of having to remember and deal with fewer login identities and passwords.

The challenge of every large network is to find the optimum balance of internal systems and facilities for Identity Management resources. How well the solution is chosen and implemented has potentially significant impact on network bandwidth and systems response needs.

In Chapter 5, "Making Happy Users", you implemented a single LDAP server for the entire network. This may work for smaller networks, but almost certainly fails to meet the needs of large and complex networks. The following section documents how you may implement a single master LDAP server with multiple slave servers.

What is the best method for implementing master/slave LDAP servers within the context of a distributed 2,000-user network is a question that remains to be answered.

One possibility that has great appeal is to create a single, large distributed domain. The practical implications of this design (see Figure 6.6) demands the placement of sufficient BDCs in each location. Additionally, network administrators must make sure that profiles are not transferred over the wide-area links, except as a totally unavoidable measure. Network design must balance the risk of loss of user productivity against the cost of network management and maintenance.

The network design in Figure 6.7 takes the approach that management of networks that are too remote to be managed effectively from New York ought to be given a certain degree of autonomy. With this rationale, the Los Angeles and London networks, though fully integrated with those on the East Coast, each have their own domain name space and can be independently managed and controlled. One of the key drawbacks of this design is that it flies in the face of the ability for network users to roam globally without some compromise in how they may access global resources.

Desk-bound users need not be negatively affected by this design, since the use of interdomain trusts can be used to satisfy the need for global data sharing.

When Samba-3 is configured to use an LDAP backend, it stores the domain account information in a directory entry. This account entry contains the domain SID. An unintended but exploitable side effect is that this makes it possible to operate with more than one PDC on a distributed network.

How might this peculiar feature be exploited? The answer is simple. It is imperative that each network segment have its own WINS server. Major servers on remote network segments can be given a static WINS entry in the `wins.dat` file on each WINS server. This allows all essential data to be visible from all locations. Each location would, however, function as if it is an independent domain, while all sharing the same domain SID. Since all domain account information can be stored in a single LDAP backend, users have unfettered ability to roam.

This concept has not been exhaustively validated, though we can see no reason why this should not work. The important facets are the following: The name of the domain must be identical in all locations. Each network segment must have its own WINS server. The name of the PDC must be the same in all locations; this necessitates the use of NetBIOS name aliases for each PDC so that they can be accessed globally using the alias and not the PDC's primary name. A single master LDAP server can be based in New York, with multiple LDAP slave servers located on every network segment. Finally, the BDCs should each use failover LDAP servers that are in fact slave LDAP servers on the local segments.

With a single master LDAP server, all network updates are effected on a single server. In the event that this should become excessively fragile or network bandwidth limiting, one could implement a delegated LDAP domain. This is also known as a partitioned (or multiple partition) LDAP database and as a distributed LDAP directory.

As the LDAP directory grows, it becomes increasingly important that its structure is implemented in a manner that mirrors organizational needs, so as to limit network update and referential traffic. It should be noted that all directory administrators must of necessity follow the same standard procedures for managing the directory, because retroactive correction of inconsistent directory information can be exceedingly difficult.

6.2.2   Political Issues

As organizations grow, the number of points of control increases also. In a large distributed organization, it is important that the Identity Management system be capable of being updated from many locations, and it is equally important that changes made should become usable in a reasonable period, typically minutes rather than days (the old limitation of highly manual systems).

6.3   Implementation

Samba-3 has the ability to use multiple password (authentication and identity resolution) backends. The diagram in Figure 6.1 demonstrates how Samba uses winbind, LDAP, and NIS, the traditional system password database. The diagram only documents the mechanisms for authentication and identity resolution (obtaining a UNIX UID/GID) using the specific systems shown.

Figure 6.1 Samba and Authentication Backend Search Pathways

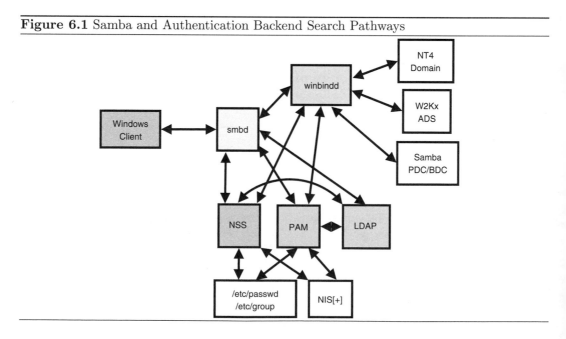

Samba is capable of using the `smbpasswd`, `tdbsam`, `xmlsam`, and `mysqlsam` authentication databases. The SMB passwords can, of course, also be stored in an LDAP ldapsam backend. LDAP is the preferred passdb backend for distributed network operations.

Additionally, it is possible to use multiple passdb backends concurrently as well as have multiple LDAP backends. As a result, you can specify a failover LDAP backend. The syntax for specifying a single LDAP backend in `smb.conf` is:

```
...
passdb backend = ldapsam:ldap://master.abmas.biz
...
```

This configuration tells Samba to use a single LDAP server, as shown in Figure 6.2.

Figure 6.2 Samba Configuration to Use a Single LDAP Server

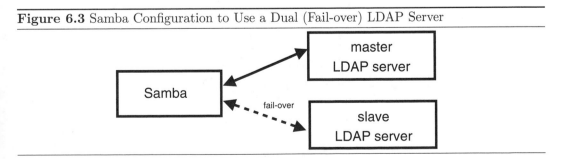

The addition of a failover LDAP server can simply be done by adding a second entry for the failover server to the single *ldapsam* entry, as shown here (note the particular use of the double quotes):

```
...
passdb backend = ldapsam:"ldap://master.abmas.biz \
                 ldap://slave.abmas.biz"
...
```

This configuration tells Samba to use a master LDAP server, with failover to a slave server if necessary, as shown in Figure 6.3.

Figure 6.3 Samba Configuration to Use a Dual (Fail-over) LDAP Server

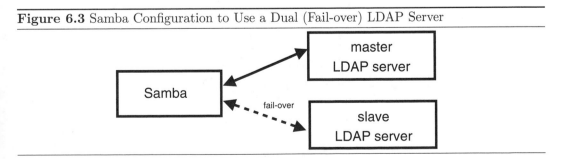

Some folks have tried to implement this without the use of double quotes. This is the type of entry they created:

```
...
passdb backend = ldapsam:ldap://master.abmas.biz \
                 ldapsam:ldap://slave.abmas.biz
...
```

The effect of this style of entry is that Samba lists the users that are in both LDAP databases. If both contain the same information, it results in each record being shown twice. This is, of course, not the solution desired for a failover implementation. The net effect of this configuration is shown in Figure 6.4

Figure 6.4 Samba Configuration to Use Dual LDAP Databases - Broken - Do Not Use!

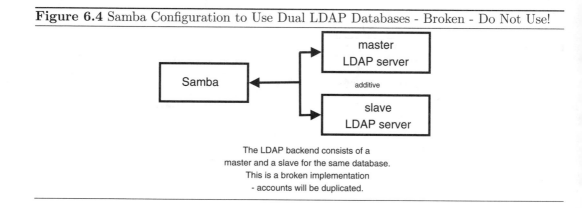

If, however, each LDAP database contains unique information, this may well be an advantageous way to effectively integrate multiple LDAP databases into one seemingly contiguous directory. Only the first database will be updated. An example of this configuration is shown in Figure 6.5.

Figure 6.5 Samba Configuration to Use Two LDAP Databases - The result is additive.

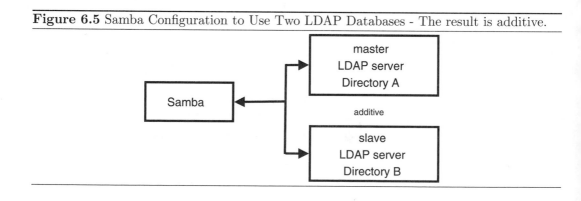

NOTE

When the use of ldapsam is specified twice, as shown here, it is imperative that the two LDAP directories must be disjoint. If the entries are for a master LDAP server as well as its own slave server, updates to the LDAP database may end up being lost or corrupted. You may safely use multiple LDAP backends only if both are entirely separate from each other.

It is assumed that the network you are working with follows in a pattern similar to what was covered in Chapter 5, "Making Happy Users". The following steps permit the operation of a master/slave OpenLDAP arrangement.

IMPLEMENTATION STEPS FOR AN LDAP SLAVE SERVER

1. Log onto the master LDAP server as `root`. You are about to change the configuration of the LDAP server, so it makes sense to temporarily halt it. Stop OpenLDAP from running on SUSE Linux by executing:

```
root#  rcldap stop
```

On Red Hat Linux, you can do this by executing:

```
root#  service ldap stop
```

2. Edit the `/etc/openldap/slapd.conf` file so it matches the content of Example 6.3.1.

3. Create a file called `admin-accts.ldif` with the following contents:

```
dn: cn=updateuser,dc=abmas,dc=biz
objectClass: person
cn: updateuser
sn: updateuser
userPassword: not24get

dn: cn=sambaadmin,dc=abmas,dc=biz
objectClass: person
cn: sambaadmin
sn: sambaadmin
userPassword: buttercup
```

4. Add an account called "updateuser" to the master LDAP server as shown here:

```
root#  slapadd -v -l admin-accts.ldif
```

5. Change directory to a suitable place to dump the contents of the LDAP server. The dump file (and LDIF file) is used to preload the slave LDAP server database. You can dump the database by executing:

```
root#  slapcat -v -l LDAP-transfer-LDIF.txt
```

   Each record is written to the file.

6. Copy the file LDAP-transfer-LDIF.txt to the intended slave LDAP server. A good location could be in the directory /etc/openldap/preload.

7. Log onto the slave LDAP server as root. You can now configure this server so the /etc/openldap/slapd.conf file matches the content of Example 6.3.2.

8. Change directory to the location in which you stored the LDAP-transfer-LDIF.txt file (/etc/openldap/preload). While in this directory, execute:

```
root#  slapadd -v -l LDAP-transfer-LDIF.txt
```

   If all goes well, the following output confirms that the data is being loaded as intended:

```
added: "dc=abmas,dc=biz" (00000001)
added: "cn=sambaadmin,dc=abmas,dc=biz" (00000002)
added: "cn=updateuser,dc=abmas,dc=biz" (00000003)
added: "ou=People,dc=abmas,dc=biz" (00000004)
added: "ou=Groups,dc=abmas,dc=biz" (00000005)
added: "ou=Computers,dc=abmas,dc=biz" (00000006)
added: "uid=Administrator,ou=People,dc=abmas,dc=biz" (00000007)
added: "uid=nobody,ou=People,dc=abmas,dc=biz" (00000008)
added: "cn=Domain Admins,ou=Groups,dc=abmas,dc=biz" (00000009)
added: "cn=Domain Users,ou=Groups,dc=abmas,dc=biz" (0000000a)
added: "cn=Domain Guests,ou=Groups,dc=abmas,dc=biz" (0000000b)
added: "uid=bobj,ou=People,dc=abmas,dc=biz" (0000000c)
added: "sambaDomainName=MEGANET2,dc=abmas,dc=biz" (0000000d)
added: "uid=stans,ou=People,dc=abmas,dc=biz" (0000000e)
added: "uid=chrisr,ou=People,dc=abmas,dc=biz" (0000000f)
added: "uid=maryv,ou=People,dc=abmas,dc=biz" (00000010)
added: "cn=Accounts,ou=Groups,dc=abmas,dc=biz" (00000011)
added: "cn=Finances,ou=Groups,dc=abmas,dc=biz" (00000012)
added: "cn=PIOps,ou=Groups,dc=abmas,dc=biz" (00000013)
```

9. Now start the LDAP server and set it to run automatically on system reboot by executing:

```
root#  rcldap start
root#  chkconfig ldap on
```

On Red Hat Linux, execute the following:

```
root#  service ldap start
root#  chkconfig ldap on
```

10. Go back to the master LDAP server. Execute the following to start LDAP as well as **slurpd**, the synchronization daemon, as shown here:

```
root#  rcldap start
root#  chkconfig ldap on
root#  rcslurpd start
root#  chkconfig slurpd on
```

On Red Hat Linux, check the equivalent command to start **slurpd**.

11. On the master LDAP server you may now add an account to validate that replication is working. Assuming the configuration shown in Chapter 5, "Making Happy Users", execute:

```
root#  /var/lib/samba/sbin/smbldap-useradd -a fruitloop
```

12. On the slave LDAP server, change to the directory **/var/lib/ldap**. There should now be a file called **replogfile**. If replication worked as expected, the content of this file should be:

```
time: 1072486403
dn: uid=fruitloop,ou=People,dc=abmas,dc=biz
changetype: modify
replace: sambaProfilePath
sambaProfilePath: \\MASSIVE\profiles\fruitloop
-
replace: sambaHomePath
sambaHomePath: \\MASSIVE\homes
-
replace: entryCSN
entryCSN: 2003122700:43:38Z#0x0005#0#0000
-
```

```
replace: modifiersName
modifiersName: cn=Manager,dc=abmas,dc=biz
-

replace: modifyTimestamp
modifyTimestamp: 20031227004338Z
-
```

13. Given that this first slave LDAP server is now working correctly, you may now implement additional slave LDAP servers as required.

14. On each machine (PDC and BDCs) after the respective `smb.conf` files have been created as shown in Example 6.3.3 and on BDCs the Example 6.3.6 execute the following:

```
root#  smbpasswd -w buttercup
```

This will install in the `secrets.tdb` file the password that Samba will need to manage (write to) the LDAP Master server to perform account updates.

6.3.1 Key Points Learned

- Where Samba-3 is used as a domain controller, the use of LDAP is an essential component to permit the use of BDCs.

- Replication of the LDAP master server to create a network of BDCs is an important mechanism for limiting WAN traffic.

- Network administration presents many complex challenges, most of which can be satisfied by good design but that also require sound communication and unification of management practices. This can be highly challenging in a large, globally distributed network.

- Roaming profiles must be contained to the local network segment. Any departure from this may clog wide-area arteries and slow legitimate network traffic to a crawl.

6.4 Questions and Answers

There is much rumor and misinformation regarding the use of MS Windows networking protocols. These questions are just a few of those frequently asked.

F.A.Q.

1. **Q:** *Is it true that DHCP uses lots of WAN bandwidth?*
A: It is a smart practice to localize DHCP servers on each network segment. As a rule, there should be two DHCP servers per network segment. This means that if one server fails, there is always another to service user needs. DHCP requests use only UDP broadcast

protocols. It is possible to run a DHCP Relay Agent on network routers. This makes it possible to run fewer DHCP servers.

A DHCP network address request and confirmation usually results in about six UDP packets. The packets are from 60 to 568 bytes in length. Let us consider a site that has 300 DHCP clients and that uses a 24-hour IP address lease. This means that all clients renew their IP address lease every 24 hours. If we assume an average packet length equal to the maximum (just to be on the safe side), and we have a 128 Kb/sec wide-area connection, how significant would the DHCP traffic be if all of it were to use DHCP Relay?

I must stress that this is a bad design, but here is the calculation:

```
Daily Network Capacity: 128,000 (Kbits/s) / 8 (bits/byte)
                        x 3600 (sec/hr) x 24 (hrs/day)= 2288 Mbytes/day.


DHCP traffic:           300 (clients) x 6 (packets)
                        x 512 (bytes/packet) = 0.9 Mbytes/day.
```

From this can be seen that the traffic impact would be minimal.

Even when DHCP is configured to do DNS update (dynamic DNS) over a wide-area link, the impact of the update is no more than the DHCP IP address renewal traffic and thus still insignificant for most practical purposes.

2. **Q:** *How much background communication takes place between a master LDAP server and its slave LDAP servers?*
A: The process that controls the replication of data from the master LDAP server to the slave LDAP servers is called **slurpd**. The **slurpd** remains nascent (quiet) until an update must be propagated. The propagation traffic per LDAP slave to update (add/modify/delete) two user accounts requires less than 10KB traffic.

3. **Q:** *LDAP has a database. Is LDAP not just a fancy database front end?*
A: LDAP does store its data in a database of sorts. In fact, the LDAP backend is an application-specific data storage system. This type of database is indexed so that records can be rapidly located, but the database is not generic and can be used only in particular pre-programmed ways. General external applications do not gain access to the data. This type of database is used also by SQL servers. Both an SQL server and an LDAP server provide ways to access the data. An SQL server has a transactional orientation and typically allows external programs to perform ad hoc queries, even across data tables. An LDAP front end is a purpose-built tool that has a search orientation that is designed around specific simple queries. The term `database` is heavily overloaded and thus much misunderstood.

4. **Q:** *Can Active Directory obtain account information from an OpenLDAP server?*
A: No, at least not directly. It is possible to provision Active Directory from and/or to an

OpenLDAP database through use of a metadirectory server. Microsoft MMS (now called MIIS) can interface to OpenLDAP using standard LDAP queries and updates.

5. **Q:** *What are the parts of a roaming profile? How large is each part?*
A: A roaming profile consists of

- Desktop folders such as `Desktop`, `My Documents`, `My Pictures`, `My Music`, `Internet Files`, `Cookies`, `Application Data`, `Local Settings`, and more. See Chapter 5, "Making Happy Users", Figure 5.3.

  Each of these can be anywhere from a few bytes to gigabytes in capacity. Fortunately, all such folders can be redirected to network drive resources. See Section 5.7.1 for more information regarding folder redirection.

- A static or rewritable portion that is typically only a few files (2-5 KB of information).

- The registry load file that modifies the `HKEY_LOCAL_USER` hive. This is the `NTUSER.DAT` file. It can be from 0.4 to 1.5 MB.

Microsoft Outlook PST files may be stored in the `Local Settings\Application Data` folder. It can be up to 2 GB in size per PST file.

6. **Q:** *Can the `My Documents` folder be stored on a network drive?*
A: Yes. More correctly, such folders can be redirected to network shares. No specific network drive connection is required. Registry settings permit this to be redirected directly to a UNC (Universal Naming Convention) resource, though it is possible to specify a network drive letter instead of a UNC name. See Section 5.7.1.

7. **Q:** *How much WAN bandwidth does WINS consume?*
A: MS Windows clients cache information obtained from WINS lookups in a local NetBIOS name cache. This keeps WINS lookups to a minimum. On a network with 3500 MS Windows clients and a central WINS server, the total bandwidth demand measured at the WINS server, averaged over an 8-hour working day, was less than 30 KB/sec. Analysis of network traffic over a 6-week period showed that the total of all background traffic consumed about 11 percent of available bandwidth over 64 Kb/sec links. Background traffic consisted of domain replication, WINS queries, DNS lookups, and authentication traffic. Each of 11 branch offices had a 64 Kb/sec wide-area link, with a 1.5 Mb/sec main connection that aggregated the branch office connections plus an Internet connection.

In conclusion, the total load afforded through WINS traffic is again marginal to total operational usage — as it should be.

8. **Q:** *How many BDCs should I have? What is the right number of Windows clients per server?*
A: It is recommended to have at least one BDC per network segment, including the segment

served by the PDC. Actual requirements vary depending on the working load on each of the BDCs and the load demand pattern of client usage. I have seen sites that function without problem with 200 clients served by one BDC, and yet other sites that had one BDC per 20 clients. In one particular company, there was a drafting office that had 30 CAD/CAM operators served by one server, a print server; and an application server. While all three were BDCs, typically only the print server would service network logon requests after the first 10 users had started to use the network. This was a reflection of the service load placed on both the application server and the data server.

As unsatisfactory as the answer might sound, it all depends on network and server load characteristics.

9. **Q:** *I've heard that you can store NIS accounts in LDAP. Is LDAP not just a smarter way to run an NIS server?*
A: The correct answer to both questions is yes. But do understand that an LDAP server has a configurable schema that can store far more information for many more purposes than just NIS.

10. **Q:** *Can I use NIS in place of LDAP?*
A: No. The NIS database does not have provision to store Microsoft encrypted passwords and does not deal with the types of data necessary for interoperability with Microsoft Windows networking. The use of LDAP with Samba requires the use of a number of schemas, one of which is the NIS schema, but also a Samba-specific schema extension.

Example 6.3.1 LDAP Master Server Configuration File — /etc/openldap/slapd.conf

```
include      /etc/openldap/schema/core.schema
include      /etc/openldap/schema/cosine.schema
include      /etc/openldap/schema/inetorgperson.schema
include      /etc/openldap/schema/nis.schema
include      /etc/openldap/schema/samba.schema

pidfile      /var/run/slapd/slapd.pid
argsfile     /var/run/slapd/slapd.args

database     bdb
suffix       "dc=abmas,dc=biz"
rootdn       "cn=Manager,dc=abmas,dc=biz"

# rootpw = not24get
rootpw       {SSHA}86kTavd9Dw3FAz6qzWTrCOKX/cOQe+UV

replica      host=lapdc.abmas.biz:389
             suffix="dc=abmas,dc=biz"
             binddn="cn=updateuser,dc=abmas,dc=biz"
             bindmethod=simple credentials=not24get

access to attrs=sambaLMPassword,sambaNTPassword
         by dn="cn=sambaadmin,dc=abmas,dc=biz" write
         by * none

replogfile  /var/lib/ldap/replogfile

directory   /var/lib/ldap

# Indices to maintain
index objectClass            eq
index cn                     pres,sub,eq
index sn                     pres,sub,eq
index uid                    pres,sub,eq
index displayName            pres,sub,eq
index uidNumber              eq
index gidNumber              eq
index memberUID              eq
index sambaSID               eq
index sambaPrimaryGroupSID   eq
index sambaDomainName        eq
index default                sub
```

Example 6.3.2 LDAP Slave Configuration File — /etc/openldap/slapd.conf

---

```
include      /etc/openldap/schema/core.schema
include      /etc/openldap/schema/cosine.schema
include      /etc/openldap/schema/inetorgperson.schema
include      /etc/openldap/schema/nis.schema
include      /etc/openldap/schema/samba.schema

pidfile      /var/run/slapd/slapd.pid
argsfile     /var/run/slapd/slapd.args

database     bdb
suffix       "dc=abmas,dc=biz"
rootdn       "cn=Manager,dc=abmas,dc=biz"

# rootpw = not24get
rootpw       {SSHA}86kTavd9Dw3FAz6qzWTrCOKX/c0Qe+UV

access to *
             by dn=cn=updateuser,dc=abmas,dc=biz write
             by * read

updatedn     cn=updateuser,dc=abmas,dc=biz
updateref    ldap://massive.abmas.biz

directory    /var/lib/ldap

# Indices to maintain
index objectClass           eq
index cn                    pres,sub,eq
index sn                    pres,sub,eq
index uid                   pres,sub,eq
index displayName           pres,sub,eq
index uidNumber             eq
index gidNumber             eq
index memberUID             eq
index sambaSID              eq
index sambaPrimaryGroupSID  eq
index sambaDomainName       eq
index default               sub
```

Example 6.3.3 Primary Domain Controller smb.conf File — Part A

```
# Global parameters
[global]
        unix charset = LOCALE
        workgroup = MEGANET2
        passdb backend = ldapsam:ldap://massive.abmas.biz
        username map = /etc/samba/smbusers
        log level = 1
        syslog = 0
        log file = /var/log/samba/%m
        max log size = 0
        smb ports = 139
        name resolve order = wins bcast hosts
        time server = Yes
        printcap name = CUPS
        add user script = /opt/IDEALX/sbin/smbldap-useradd -m '%u'
        delete user script = /opt/IDEALX/sbin/smbldap-userdel '%u'
        add group script = /opt/IDEALX/sbin/smbldap-groupadd -p '%g'
        delete group script = /opt/IDEALX/sbin/smbldap-groupdel '%g'
        add user to group script = /opt/IDEALX/sbin/smbldap-groupmod ←
                -m '%g' '%u'
        delete user from group script = /opt/IDEALX/sbin/smbldap- ←
                groupmod -x '%g' '%u'
        set primary group script = /opt/IDEALX/sbin/smbldap-usermod ←
                -g '%g' '%u'
        add machine script = /opt/IDEALX/sbin/smbldap-useradd -w '%u ←
                '
        shutdown script = /var/lib/samba/scripts/shutdown.sh
        abort shutdown script = /sbin/shutdown -c
        logon script = scripts\logon.bat
        logon path = \\%L\profiles\%U
        logon drive = X:
        domain logons = Yes
        domain master = Yes
        wins support = Yes
        ldap suffix = dc=abmas,dc=biz
        ldap machine suffix = ou=People
        ldap user suffix = ou=People
        ldap group suffix = ou=Groups
        ldap idmap suffix = ou=Idmap
        ldap admin dn = cn=sambaadmin,dc=abmas,dc=biz
        idmap backend = ldap://massive.abmas.biz
        idmap uid = 10000-20000
        idmap gid = 10000-20000
        printer admin = root
        printing = cups
```

Example 6.3.4 Primary Domain Controller smb.conf File — Part B

```
[IPC$]
        path = /tmp
[accounts]
        comment = Accounting Files
        path = /data/accounts
        read only = No
[service]
        comment = Financial Services Files
        path = /data/service
        read only = No
[pidata]
        comment = Property Insurance Files
        path = /data/pidata
        read only = No
[homes]
        comment = Home Directories
        valid users = %S
        read only = No
        browseable = No
[printers]
        comment = SMB Print Spool
        path = /var/spool/samba
        guest ok = Yes
        printable = Yes
        browseable = No
```

Example 6.3.5 Primary Domain Controller smb.conf File — Part C

```
[apps]
        comment = Application Files
        path = /apps
        admin users = bjones
        read only = No
[netlogon]
        comment = Network Logon Service
        path = /var/lib/samba/netlogon
        admin users = root, Administrator
        guest ok = Yes
        locking = No
[profiles]
        comment = Profile Share
        path = /var/lib/samba/profiles
        read only = No
        profile acls = Yes
[profdata]
        comment = Profile Data Share
        path = /var/lib/samba/profdata
        read only = No
        profile acls = Yes
[print$]
        comment = Printer Drivers
        path = /var/lib/samba/drivers
        write list = root
        admin users = root, Administrator
```

Example 6.3.6 Backup Domain Controller smb.conf File — Part A

```
# \# Global parameters
 [global]
        unix charset = LOCALE
        workgroup = MEGANET2
        netbios name = BLDG1
        passdb backend = ldapsam:ldap://lapdc.abmas.biz
        username map = /etc/samba/smbusers
        log level = 1
        syslog = 0
        log file = /var/log/samba/%m
        max log size = 50
        smb ports = 139
        name resolve order = wins bcast hosts
        printcap name = CUPS
        show add printer wizard = No
        logon script = scripts\logon.bat
        logon path = \\%L\profiles\%U
        logon drive = X:
        domain logons = Yes
        os level = 63
        domain master = No
        wins server = 192.168.2.1
        ldap suffix = dc=abmas,dc=biz
        ldap machine suffix = ou=People
        ldap user suffix = ou=People
        ldap group suffix = ou=Groups
        ldap idmap suffix = ou=Idmap
        ldap admin dn = cn=sambaadmin,dc=abmas,dc=biz
        utmp = Yes
        idmap backend = ldap://massive.abmas.biz
        idmap uid = 10000-20000
        idmap gid = 10000-20000
        printing = cups
 [accounts]
        comment = Accounting Files
        path = /data/accounts
        read only = No
 [service]
        comment = Financial Services Files
        path = /data/service
        read only = No
```

Example 6.3.7 Backup Domain Controller smb.conf File — Part B

```
[pidata]
        comment = Property Insurance Files
        path = /data/pidata
        read only = No
[homes]
        comment = Home Directories
        valid users = %S
        read only = No
        browseable = No
[printers]
        comment = SMB Print Spool
        path = /var/spool/samba
        guest ok = Yes
        printable = Yes
        browseable = No
[apps]
        comment = Application Files
        path = /apps
        admin users = bjones
        read only = No
[netlogon]
        comment = Network Logon Service
        path = /var/lib/samba/netlogon
        guest ok = Yes
        locking = No
[profiles]
        comment = Profile Share
        path = /var/lib/samba/profiles
        read only = No
        profile acls = Yes
[profdata]
        comment = Profile Data Share
        path = /var/lib/samba/profdata
        read only = No
        profile acls = Yes
```

Figure 6.6 Network Topology — 2000 User Complex Design A

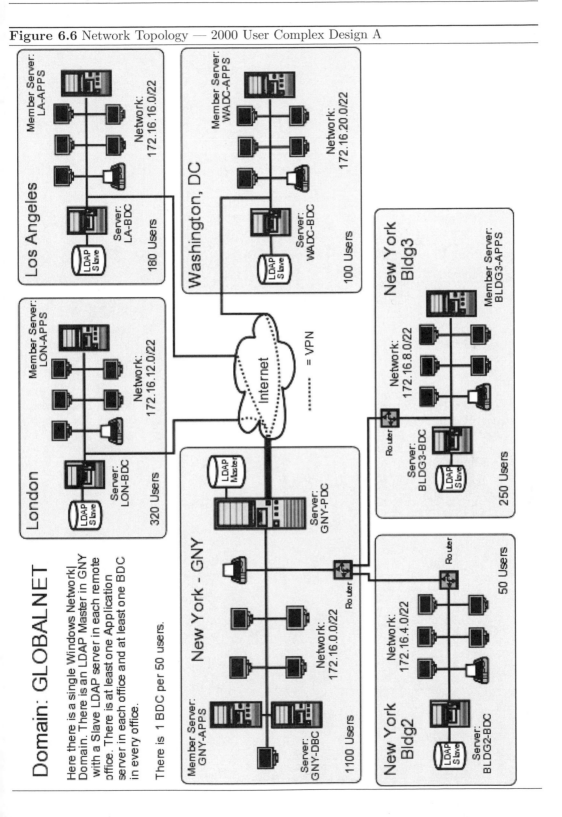

Figure 6.7 Network Topology — 2000 User Complex Design B

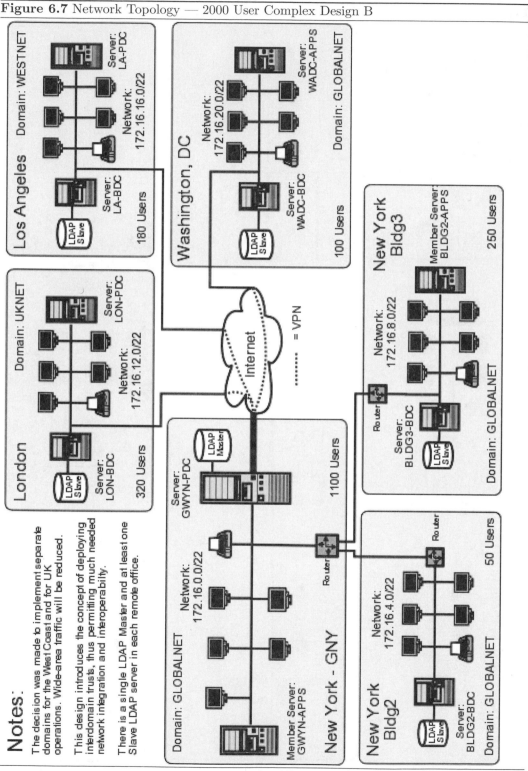

Notes:

The decision was made to implement separate domains for the West Coast and for UK operations. Wide-area traffic will be reduced.

This design introduces the concept of deploying interdomain trusts, thus permitting much needed network integration and interoperability.

There is a single LDAP Master and at least one Slave LDAP server in each remote office.

Part II

Domain Members, Updating Samba and Migration

This section *Samba-3 by Example* covers two main topics: How to add Samba Domain Member Servers and Samba Domain Member Clients to a Samba domain, the other subject is that of how to migrate from and NT4 Domain, a NetWare server, or from an earlier Samba version to environments that use the most recent Samba-3 release.

Those who are making use of the chapter on Adding UNIX clients and servers running Samba to a Samba or a Windows networking domain may also benefit by referring to the book *The Official Samba-3 HOWTO and Reference Guide.*

Chapter 7

ADDING DOMAIN MEMBER SERVERS AND CLIENTS

The most frequently discussed Samba subjects over the past 2 years have focused around domain control and printing. It is well known that Samba is a file and print server. A recent survey conducted by *Open Magazine* found that of all respondents, 97 percent use Samba for file and print services, and 68 percent use Samba for Domain Control. See the Open-Mag[1] Web site for current information. The survey results as found on January 14, 2004, are shown in Figure 7.1.

While domain control is an exciting subject, basic file and print sharing remains the staple bread-and-butter function that Samba provides. Yet this book may give the appearance of having focused too much on more exciting aspects of Samba deployment. This chapter directs your attention to provide important information on the addition of Samba servers into your present Windows network — whatever the controlling technology may be. So let's get back to our good friends at Abmas.

7.1 Introduction

Looking back over the achievements of the past year or two, daily events at Abmas are rather straightforward with not too many distractions or problems. Your team is doing well, but a number of employees are asking for Linux desktop systems. Your network has grown and demands additional domain member servers. Let's get on with this; Christine and Stan are ready to go.

Stan is firmly in control of the department of the future, while Christine is enjoying a stable and predictable network environment. It is time to add more servers and to add Linux desktops. It is time to meet the demands of future growth and endure trial by fire.

---

[1] <http://www.open-mag.com/cgi-bin/opencgi/surveys/survey.cgi?survey_name=samba>

Figure 7.1 Open Magazine Samba Survey

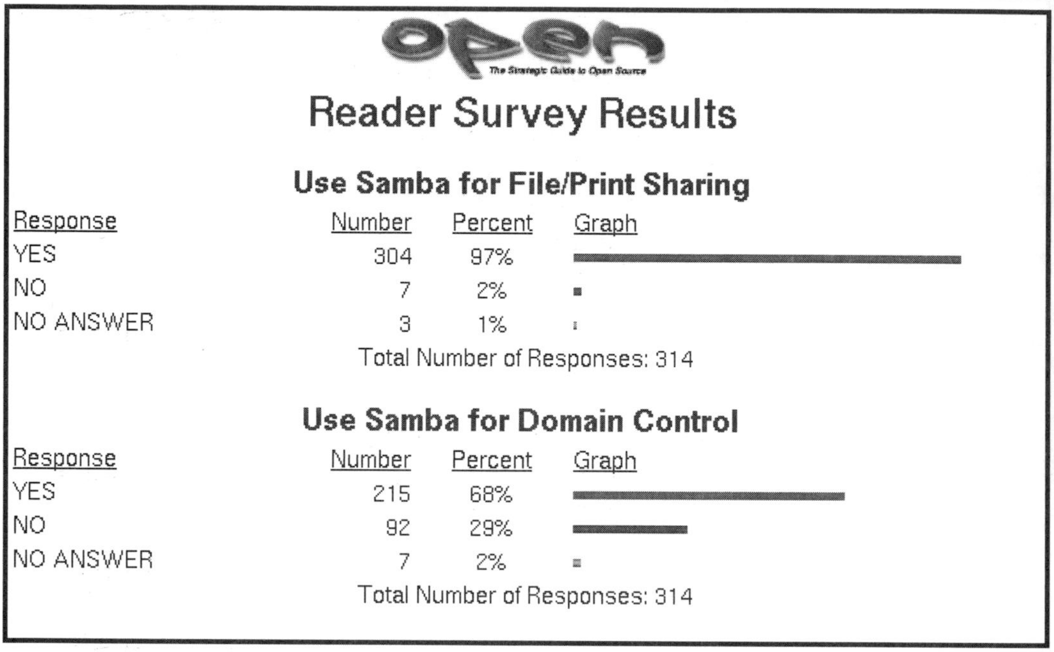

Reader Survey Results

Use Samba for File/Print Sharing

Response	Number	Percent	Graph
YES	304	97%	
NO	7	2%	
NO ANSWER	3	1%	

Total Number of Responses: 314

Use Samba for Domain Control

Response	Number	Percent	Graph
YES	215	68%	
NO	92	29%	
NO ANSWER	7	2%	

Total Number of Responses: 314

7.1.1   Assignment Tasks

You must now add UNIX/Linux domain member servers to your network. You have a friend who has a Windows 2003 Active Directory domain network who wants to add a Samba/Linux server and has asked Christine to help him out. Your real objective is to help Christine to see more of the way the Microsoft world lives and use her help to get validation that Samba really does live up to expectations.

Over the past 6 months, you have hired several new staff who want Linux on their desktops. You must integrate these systems to make sure that Abmas is not building islands of technology. You ask Christine to do likewise at Swodniw Biz NL (your friend's company) to help them to evaluate a Linux desktop. You want to make the right decision, don't you?

7.2   Dissection and Discussion

Recent Samba mailing-list activity is witness to how many sites are using winbind. Some have no trouble at all with it, yet to others the problems seem insurmountable. Periodically there are complaints concerning an inability to achieve identical user and group IDs between Windows and UNIX environments.

You provide step-by-step implementations of the various tools that can be used for identity resolution. You also provide working examples of solutions for integrated authentication for both UNIX/Linux and Windows environments.

7.2.1 Technical Issues

One of the great challenges we face when people ask us, "What is the best way to solve this problem?" is to get beyond the facts so we not only can clearly comprehend the immediate technical problem, but also can understand how needs may change.

There are a few facts we should note when dealing with the question of how best to integrate UNIX/Linux clients and servers into a Windows networking environment:

- A domain controller (PDC or BDC) is always authoritative for all accounts in its domain. This means that a BDC must (of necessity) be able to resolve all account UIDs and GIDs to the same values that the PDC resolved them to.

- A domain member can be authoritative for local accounts, but is never authoritative for domain accounts. If a user is accessing a domain member server and that user's account is not known locally, the domain member server must resolve the identity of that user from the domain in which that user's account resides. It must then map that ID to a UID/GID pair that it can use locally. This is handled by **winbindd**.

- Samba, when running on a domain member server, can resolve user identities from a number of sources:

  - By executing a system **getpwnam()** or **getgrnam()** call. On systems that support it, this utilizes the name service switch (NSS) facility to resolve names according to the configuration of the `/etc/nsswitch.conf` file. NSS can be configured to use LDAP, winbind, NIS, or local files.

  - Performing, via NSS, a direct LDAP search (where an LDAP passdb backend has been configured). This requires the use of the PADL nss_ldap tool (or equivalent).

  - Directly by querying **winbindd**. The **winbindd** contacts a domain controller to attempt to resolve the identity of the user or group. It receives the Windows networking security identifier (SID) for that appropriate account and then allocates a local UID or GID from the range of available IDs and creates an entry in its `winbindd_idmap.tdb` and `winbindd_cache.tdb` files.

    If the parameter *idmap backend* = ldap:ldap://myserver.domain was specified and the LDAP server has been configured with a container in which it may store the IDMAP entries, all domain members may share a common mapping.

  Irrespective of how `smb.conf` is configured, winbind creates and caches a local copy of the ID mapping database. It uses the `winbindd_idmap.tdb` and `winbindd_cache.tdb` files to do this.

  Which of the resolver methods is chosen is determined by the way that Samba is configured in the `smb.conf` file. Some of the configuration options are rather less than obvious to the casual user.

- If you wish to make use of accounts (users and/or groups) that are local to (i.e., capable of being resolved using) the NSS facility, it is possible to use the *winbind trusted domains only* = Yes in the `smb.conf` file. This parameter specifically applies to domain controllers, and to domain member servers.

For many administrators, it should be plain that the use of an LDAP-based repository for all network accounts (both for POSIX accounts and for Samba accounts) provides the most elegant and controllable facility. You eventually appreciate the decision to use LDAP.

If your network account information resides in an LDAP repository, you should use it ahead of any alternative method. This means that if it is humanly possible to use the **nss_ldap** tools to resolve UNIX account UIDs/GIDs via LDAP, this is the preferred solution, because it provides a more readily controllable method for asserting the exact same user and group identifiers throughout the network.

In the situation where UNIX accounts are held on the domain member server itself, the only effective way to use them involves the `smb.conf` entry *winbind trusted domains only* = Yes. This forces Samba (**smbd**) to perform a **getpwnam()** system call that can then be controlled via `/etc/nsswitch.conf` file settings. The use of this parameter disables the use of Samba with trusted domains (i.e., external domains).

Winbind can be used to create an appliance mode domain member server. In this capacity, **winbindd** is configured to automatically allocate UIDs/GIDs from numeric ranges set in the `smb.conf` file. The allocation is made for all accounts that connect to that domain member server, whether within its own domain or from trusted domains. If not stored in an LDAP backend, each domain member maintains its own unique mapping database. This means that it is almost certain that a given user who accesses two domain member servers does not have the same UID/GID on both servers — however, this is transparent to the Windows network user. This data is stored in the `winbindd_idmap.tdb` and `winbindd_cache.tdb` files.

The use of an LDAP backend for the Winbind IDMAP facility permits Windows domain SIDs mappings to UIDs/GIDs to be stored centrally. The result is a consistent mapping across all domain member servers so configured. This solves one of the major headaches for network administrators who need to copy files between or across network file servers.

7.2.2 Political Issues

One of the most fierce conflicts recently being waged is resistance to the adoption of LDAP, in particular OpenLDAP, as a replacement for UNIX NIS (previously called Yellow Pages). Let's face it, LDAP is different and requires a new approach to the need for a better identity management solution. The more you work with LDAP, the more its power and flexibility emerges from its dark, cavernous chasm.

LDAP is a most suitable solution for heterogenous environments. If you need crypto, add Kerberos. The reason these are preferable is because they are heterogenous. Windows solutions of this sort are *not* heterogenous by design. This is fundamental — it isn't religious or political. This also doesn't say that you can't use Windows Active Directory in a heterogenous environment — it can be done, it just requires commercial integration products. But it's not what Active Directory was designed for.

A number of long-term UNIX devotees have recently commented in various communications that the Samba Team is the first application group to almost force network administrators to use LDAP. It should be pointed out that we resisted this for as long as we could. It is not out of laziness or malice that LDAP has finally emerged as the preferred identity management backend for Samba. We recommend LDAP for your total organizational directory needs.

7.3 Implementation

The domain member server and the domain member client are at the center of focus in this chapter. Configuration of Samba-3 domain controller is covered in earlier chapters, so if your interest is in domain controller configuration, you will not find that here. You will find good oil that helps you to add domain member servers and clients.

In practice, domain member servers and domain member workstations are very different entities, but in terms of technology they share similar core infrastructure. A technologist would argue that servers and workstations are identical. Many users would argue otherwise, given that in a well-disciplined environment a workstation (client) is a device from which a user creates documents and files that are located on servers. A workstation is frequently viewed as a disposable (easy to replace) item, but a server is viewed as a core component of the business.

We can look at this another way. If a workstation breaks down, one user is affected, but if a server breaks down, hundreds of users may not be able to work. The services that a workstation must provide are document- and file-production oriented; a server provides information storage and is distribution oriented.

Why is this important? For starters, we must identify what components of the operating system and its environment must be configured. Also, it is necessary to recognize where the interdependencies between the various services to be used are. In particular, it is important to understand the operation of each critical part of the authentication process, the logon process, and how user identities get resolved and applied within the operating system and applications (like Samba) that depend on this and may actually contribute to it.

So, in this chapter we demonstrate how to implement the technology. It is done within a context of what type of service need must be fulfilled.

7.3.1 Samba Domain with Samba Domain Member Server — Using NSS LDAP

In this example, it is assumed that you have Samba PDC/BDC servers. This means you are using an LDAP ldapsam backend. We are adding to the LDAP backend database (directory) containers for use by the IDMAP facility. This makes it possible to have globally consistent mapping of SIDs to and from UIDs and GIDs. This means that it is necessary to run **winbindd** as part of your configuration. The primary purpose of running **winbindd** (within this operational context) is to permit mapping of foreign SIDs (those not originating from the the local Samba server). Foreign SIDs can come from any domain member client or server, or from Windows clients that do not belong to a domain. Another way to explain the necessity to run **winbindd** is that Samba can locally resolve only accounts that belong to the security context of its own machine SID. Winbind handles all non-local SIDs and maps them to a local UID/GID value. The UID and GID are allocated from the parameter values set in the smb.conf file for the *idmap uid* and *idmap gid* ranges. Where LDAP is used, the mappings can be stored in LDAP so that all domain member servers can use a consistent mapping.

If your installation is accessed only from clients that are members of your own domain, and all user accounts are present in a local passdb backend then it is not necessary to run **winbindd**. The local passdb backend can be in smbpasswd, tdbsam, or in ldapsam.

It is possible to use a local passdb backend with any convenient means of resolving the POSIX user and group account information. The POSIX information is usually obtained using the **getpwnam()** system call. On NSS-enabled systems, the actual POSIX account source can be provided from

- Accounts in /etc/passwd or in /etc/group.

- Resolution via NSS. On NSS-enabled systems, there is usually a facility to resolve IDs via multiple methods. The methods typically include **files**, **compat**, **db**, **ldap**, **nis**, **nisplus**, **hesiod.** When correctly installed, Samba adds to this list the **winbindd** facility. The ldap facility is frequently the nss_ldap tool provided by PADL Software.

NOTE

To advoid confusion the use of the term local passdb backend means that the user account backend is not shared by any other Samba server — instead, it is used only locally on the Samba domain member server under discussion.

The diagram in Figure 7.2 demonstrates the relationship of Samba and system components that are involved in the identity resolution process where Samba is used as a domain member server within a Samba domain control network.

In this example configuration, Samba will directly search the LDAP-based passwd backend ldapsam to obtain authentication and user identity information. The IDMAP information is stored in the LDAP backend so that it can be shared by all domain member servers so that every user will have a consistent UID and GID across all of them. The IDMAP facility will be used for all foreign (i.e., not having the same SID as the domain it is a member of) domains. The configuration of NSS will ensure that all UNIX processes will obtain a consistent UID/GID.

The instructions given here apply to the Samba environment shown in Chapter 5, "Making Happy Users" and Chapter 6, "A Distributed 2000-User Network". If the network does not have an LDAP slave server (i.e., Chapter 5, "Making Happy Users" configuration), change the target LDAP server from lapdc to massive.

Figure 7.2 Samba Domain: Samba Member Server

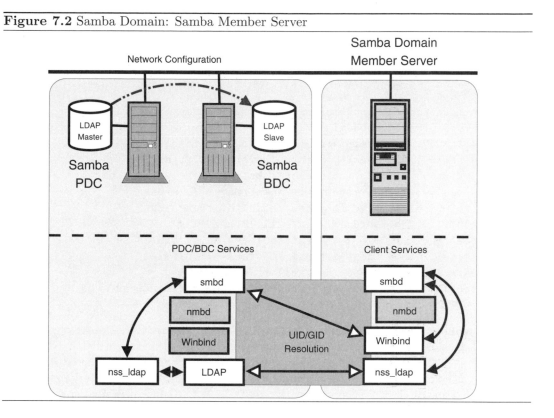

CONFIGURATION OF NSS_LDAP-BASED IDENTITY RESOLUTION

1. Create the `smb.conf` file as shown in Example 7.3.1. Locate this file in the directory `/etc/samba`.

2. Configure the file that will be used by `nss_ldap` to locate and communicate with the LDAP server. This file is called `ldap.conf`. If your implementation of `nss_ldap` is consistent with the defaults suggested by PADL (the authors), it will be located in the `/etc` directory. On some systems, the default location is the `/etc/openldap` directory, however this file is intended for use by the OpenLDAP utilities and should not really be used by the nss_ldap utility since its content and structure serves the specific purpose of enabling the resolution of user and group IDs via NSS. Change the parameters inside the file that is located on your OS so it matches Example 7.3.3. To find the correct location of this file, you can obtain this from the library that will be used by executing the following:

```
root#  strings /lib/libnss_ldap* | grep ldap.conf
/etc/ldap.conf
```

3. Configure the NSS control file so it matches the one shown in Example 7.3.4.

4. Before proceeding to configure Samba, validate the operation of the NSS identity resolution via LDAP by executing:

```
root#  getent passwd
...
root:x:0:512:Netbios Domain Administrator:/root:/bin/false
nobody:x:999:514:nobody:/dev/null:/bin/false
bobj:x:1000:513:Robert Jordan:/home/bobj:/bin/bash
stans:x:1001:513:Stanley Soroka:/home/stans:/bin/bash
chrisr:x:1002:513:Christine Roberson:/home/chrisr:/bin/bash
maryv:x:1003:513:Mary Vortexis:/home/maryv:/bin/bash
jht:x:1004:513:John H Terpstra:/home/jht:/bin/bash
bldg1$:x:1006:553:bldg1$:/dev/null:/bin/false
temptation$:x:1009:553:temptation$:/dev/null:/bin/false
vaioboss$:x:1005:553:vaioboss$:/dev/null:/bin/false
fran$:x:1008:553:fran$:/dev/null:/bin/false
josephj:x:1007:513:Joseph James:/home/josephj:/bin/bash
```

You should notice the location of the users' home directories. First, make certain that the home directories exist on the domain member server; otherwise, the home directory share is not available. The home directories could be mounted off a domain controller using NFS or by any other suitable means. Second, the absence of the domain name in the home directory path is indicative that identity resolution is not being done via winbind.

```
root#  getent group
...
Domain Admins:x:512:root,jht
Domain Users:x:513:bobj,stans,chrisr,maryv,jht,josephj
Domain Guests:x:514:
Accounts:x:1000:
Finances:x:1001:
PIOps:x:1002:
sammy:x:4321:
```

This shows that all is working as it should be. Notice that in the LDAP database the users' primary and secondary group memberships are identical. It is not necessary to add secondary group memberships (in the group database) if the user is already a member via primary group membership in the password database. When using winbind, it is in fact undesirable to do this because it results in doubling up of group memberships and may cause problems with winbind under certain conditions. It is intended that these limitations with winbind will be resolved soon after Samba-3.0.20 has been released.

5. The LDAP directory must have a container object for IDMAP data. There are several

ways you can check that your LDAP database is able to receive IDMAP information. One of the simplest is to execute:

```
root#  slapcat | grep -i idmap
dn: ou=Idmap,dc=abmas,dc=biz
ou: idmap
```

If the execution of this command does not return IDMAP entries, you need to create an LDIF template file (see Example 7.3.2). You can add the required entries using the following command:

```
root#  ldapadd -x -D "cn=Manager,dc=abmas,dc=biz" \
       -w not24get < /etc/openldap/idmap.LDIF
```

6. Samba automatically populates the LDAP directory container when it needs to. To permit Samba write access to the LDAP directory it is necessary to set the LDAP administrative password in the **secrets.tdb** file as shown here:

```
root#  smbpasswd -w not24get
```

7. The system is ready to join the domain. Execute the following:

```
root#  net rpc join -U root%not24get
Joined domain MEGANET2.
```

This indicates that the domain join succeeded. Failure to join the domain could be caused by any number of variables. The most common causes of failure to join are:

- Broken resolution of NetBIOS names to the respective IP address.

- Incorrect username and password credentials.

- The NT4 *restrict anonymous* is set to exclude anonymous connections.

The connection setup can be diagnosed by executing:

```
root#  net rpc join -S 'pdc-name' -U administrator%password -d 5
```

Note: Use "root" for UNIX/Linux and Samba, use "Administrator" for Windows NT4/200X. If the cause of the failure appears to be related to a rejected or failed NT_SESSION_SETUP* or an error message that says NT_STATUS_ACCESS_DENIED immediately check the Windows registry setting that controls the **restrict anonymous** setting. Set this to the value 0 so that an anonymous connection can be sustained, then try again. It is possible (perhaps even recommended) to use the following to validate the ability to connect to an NT4 PDC/BDC:

```
root#  net rpc info -S 'pdc-name' -U Administrator%not24get
Domain Name: MEGANET2
Domain SID: S-1-5-21-422319763-4138913805-7168186429
Sequence number: 1519909596
Num users: 7003
Num domain groups: 821
Num local groups: 8

root#  net rpc testjoin -S 'pdc-name' -U Administrator%not24get
Join to 'MEGANET2' is OK
```

If for any reason the following response is obtained to the last command above, it is time to call in the Networking Super-Snooper task force (i.e., start debugging):

```
NT_STATUS_ACCESS_DENIED
Join to 'MEGANET2' failed.
```

8. Just joining the domain is not quite enough; you must now provide a privileged set of credentials through which **winbindd** can interact with the domain servers. Execute the following to implant the necessary credentials:

```
root#  wbinfo --set-auth-user=Administrator%not24get
```

The configuration is now ready to obtain the Samba domain user and group information.

9. You may now start Samba in the usual manner, and your Samba domain member server is ready for use. Just add shares as required.

7.3.2   NT4/Samba Domain with Samba Domain Member Server: Using NSS and Winbind

You need to use this method for creating a Samba domain member server if any of the following conditions prevail:

- LDAP support (client) is not installed on the system.

- There are mitigating circumstances forcing a decision not to use LDAP.

- The Samba domain member server must be part of a Windows NT4 Domain, or a Samba Domain.

Later in the chapter, you can see how to configure a Samba domain member server for a Windows ADS domain. Right now your objective is to configure a Samba server that can be a member of a Windows NT4-style domain and/or does not use LDAP.

NOTE

> If you use **winbind** for identity resolution, make sure that there are no duplicate accounts.
>
> For example, do not have more than one account that has UID=0 in the password database. If there is an account called root in the /etc/passwd database, it is okay to have an account called root in the LDAP ldapsam or in the tdbsam. But if there are two accounts in the passdb backend that have the same UID, winbind will break. This means that the Administrator account must be called root.
>
> Winbind will break if there is an account in /etc/passwd that has the same UID as an account that is in LDAP ldapsam (or in tdbsam) but that differs in name only.

The following configuration uses CIFS/SMB protocols alone to obtain user and group credentials. The winbind information is locally cached in the winbindd_cache.tdb winbindd_idmap.tdb files. This provides considerable performance benefits compared with the LDAP solution, particularly where the LDAP lookups must traverse WAN links. You may examine the contents of these files using the tool **tdbdump**, though you may have to build this from the Samba source code if it has not been supplied as part of a binary package distribution that you may be using.

CONFIGURATION OF WINBIND-BASED IDENTITY RESOLUTION

1. Using your favorite text editor, create the smb.conf file so it has the contents shown in Example 7.3.5.

2. Edit the /etc/nsswitch.conf so it has the entries shown in Example 7.3.4.

3. The system is ready to join the domain. Execute the following:

```
net rpc join -U root%not2g4et
Joined domain MEGANET2.
```

This indicates that the domain join succeed.

4. Validate operation of **winbind** using the **wbinfo** tool as follows:

```
root#  wbinfo -u
```

```
MEGANET2+root
MEGANET2+nobody
MEGANET2+jht
MEGANET2+maryv
MEGANET2+billr
MEGANET2+jelliott
MEGANET2+dbrady
MEGANET2+joeg
MEGANET2+balap
```

This shows that domain users have been listed correctly.

```
root#  wbinfo -g
MEGANET2+Domain Admins
MEGANET2+Domain Users
MEGANET2+Domain Guests
MEGANET2+Accounts
MEGANET2+Finances
MEGANET2+PIOps
```

This shows that domain groups have been correctly obtained also.

5. The next step verifies that NSS is able to obtain this information correctly from **winbind** also.

```
root#  getent passwd
...
MEGANET2+root:x:10000:10001:NetBIOS Domain Admin:
                        /home/MEGANET2/root:/bin/bash
MEGANET2+nobody:x:10001:10001:nobody:
                        /home/MEGANET2/nobody:/bin/bash
MEGANET2+jht:x:10002:10001:John H Terpstra:
                        /home/MEGANET2/jht:/bin/bash
MEGANET2+maryv:x:10003:10001:Mary Vortexis:
                        /home/MEGANET2/maryv:/bin/bash
MEGANET2+billr:x:10004:10001:William Randalph:
                        /home/MEGANET2/billr:/bin/bash
MEGANET2+jelliott:x:10005:10001:John G Elliott:
                        /home/MEGANET2/jelliott:/bin/bash
MEGANET2+dbrady:x:10006:10001:Darren Brady:
                        /home/MEGANET2/dbrady:/bin/bash
MEGANET2+joeg:x:10007:10001:Joe Green:
                        /home/MEGANET2/joeg:/bin/bash
MEGANET2+balap:x:10008:10001:Bala Pillay:
```

```
/home/MEGANET2/balap:/bin/bash
```

The user account information has been correctly obtained. This information has been merged with the winbind template information configured in the `smb.conf` file.

```
root# # getent group
...
MEGANET2+Domain Admins:x:10000:MEGANET2+root,MEGANET2+jht
MEGANET2+Domain Users:x:10001:MEGANET2+jht,MEGANET2+maryv,\
        MEGANET2+billr,MEGANET2+jelliott,MEGANET2+dbrady,\
        MEGANET2+joeg,MEGANET2+balap
MEGANET2+Domain Guests:x:10002:MEGANET2+nobody
MEGANET2+Accounts:x:10003:
MEGANET2+Finances:x:10004:
MEGANET2+PIOps:x:10005:
```

6. The Samba member server of a Windows NT4 domain is ready for use.

7.3.3 NT4/Samba Domain with Samba Domain Member Server without NSS Support

No matter how many UNIX/Linux administrators there may be who believe that a UNIX operating system that does not have NSS and PAM support to be outdated, the fact is there are still many such systems in use today. Samba can be used without NSS support, but this does limit it to the use of local user and group accounts only.

The following steps may be followed to implement Samba with support for local accounts. In this configuration Samba is made a domain member server. All incoming connections to the Samba server will cause the look-up of the incoming username. If the account is found, it is used. If the account is not found, one will be automatically created on the local machine so that it can then be used for all access controls.

CONFIGURATION USING LOCAL ACCOUNTS ONLY

1. Using your favorite text editor, create the `smb.conf` file so it has the contents shown in Example 7.3.6.

2. The system is ready to join the domain. Execute the following:

```
net rpc join -U root%not24get
Joined domain MEGANET2.
```

This indicates that the domain join succeed.

3. Be sure to run all three Samba daemons: **smbd**, **nmbd**, **winbindd**.

4. The Samba member server of a Windows NT4 domain is ready for use.

7.3.4   Active Directory Domain with Samba Domain Member Server

One of the much-sought-after features new to Samba-3 is the ability to join an Active Directory domain using Kerberos protocols. This makes it possible to operate an entire Windows network without the need to run NetBIOS over TCP/IP and permits more secure networking in general. An exhaustively complete discussion of the protocols is not possible in this book; perhaps a later book may explore the intricacies of the NetBIOS-less operation that Samba-3 can participate in. For now, we simply focus on how a Samba-3 server can be made a domain member server.

The diagram in Figure 7.3 demonstrates how Samba-3 interfaces with Microsoft Active Directory components. It should be noted that if Microsoft Windows Services for UNIX (SFU) has been installed and correctly configured, it is possible to use client LDAP for identity resolution just as can be done with Samba-3 when using an LDAP passdb backend. The UNIX tool that you need for this, as in the case of LDAP on UNIX/Linux, is the PADL Software nss_ldap tool-set. Compared with use of winbind and Kerberos, the use of LDAP-based identity resolution is a little less secure. In view of the fact that this solution requires additional software to be installed on the Windows 200x ADS domain controllers, and that means more management overhead, it is likely that most Samba-3 ADS client sites may elect to use winbind.

Do not attempt to use this procedure if you are not 100 percent certain that the build of Samba-3 you are using has been compiled and linked with all the tools necessary for this to work. Given the importance of this step, you must first validate that the Samba-3 message block daemon (**smbd**) has the necessary features.

The hypothetical domain you are using in this example assumes that the Abmas London office decided to take its own lead (some would say this is a typical behavior in a global corporate world; besides, a little divergence and conflict makes for an interesting life). The Windows Server 2003 ADS domain is called `london.abmas.biz` and the name of the server is `W2K3S`. In ADS realm terms, the domain controller is known as `w2k3s.london.abmas.biz`. In NetBIOS nomenclature, the domain name is `LONDON` and the server name is `W2K3S`.

JOINING A SAMBA SERVER AS AN ADS DOMAIN MEMBER

1. Before you try to use Samba-3, you want to know for certain that your executables have support for Kerberos and for LDAP. Execute the following to identify whether or not this build is perhaps suitable for use:

```
root#  cd /usr/sbin
root#  smbd -b | grep KRB
   HAVE_KRB5_H
   HAVE_ADDR_TYPE_IN_KRB5_ADDRESS
   HAVE_KRB5
   HAVE_KRB5_AUTH_CON_SETKEY
   HAVE_KRB5_GET_DEFAULT_IN_TKT_ETYPES
   HAVE_KRB5_GET_PW_SALT
   HAVE_KRB5_KEYBLOCK_KEYVALUE
   HAVE_KRB5_KEYTAB_ENTRY_KEYBLOCK
```

Figure 7.3 Active Directory Domain: Samba Member Server

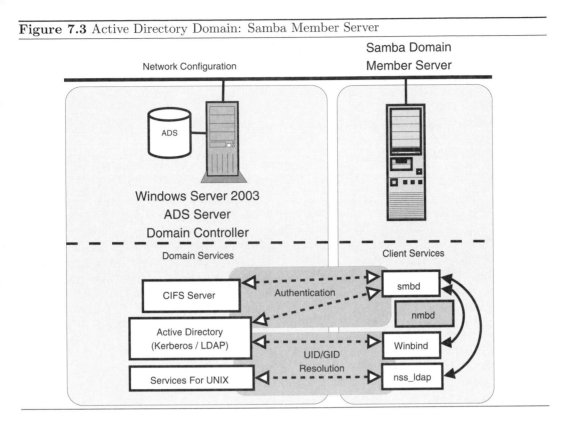

```
HAVE_KRB5_MK_REQ_EXTENDED
HAVE_KRB5_PRINCIPAL_GET_COMP_STRING
HAVE_KRB5_SET_DEFAULT_IN_TKT_ETYPES
HAVE_KRB5_STRING_TO_KEY
HAVE_KRB5_STRING_TO_KEY_SALT
HAVE_LIBKRB5
```

This output was obtained on a SUSE Linux system and shows the output for Samba that has been compiled and linked with the Heimdal Kerberos libraries. The following is a typical output that will be found on a Red Hat Linux system that has been linked with the MIT Kerberos libraries:

```
root#  cd /usr/sbin
root#  smbd -b | grep KRB
   HAVE_KRB5_H
   HAVE_ADDRTYPE_IN_KRB5_ADDRESS
   HAVE_KRB5
   HAVE_KRB5_AUTH_CON_SETUSERUSERKEY
   HAVE_KRB5_ENCRYPT_DATA
   HAVE_KRB5_FREE_DATA_CONTENTS
```

```
HAVE_KRB5_FREE_KTYPES
HAVE_KRB5_GET_PERMITTED_ENCTYPES
HAVE_KRB5_KEYTAB_ENTRY_KEY
HAVE_KRB5_LOCATE_KDC
HAVE_KRB5_MK_REQ_EXTENDED
HAVE_KRB5_PRINCIPAL2SALT
HAVE_KRB5_PRINC_COMPONENT
HAVE_KRB5_SET_DEFAULT_TGS_KTYPES
HAVE_KRB5_SET_REAL_TIME
HAVE_KRB5_STRING_TO_KEY
HAVE_KRB5_TKT_ENC_PART2
HAVE_KRB5_USE_ENCTYPE
HAVE_LIBGSSAPI_KRB5
HAVE_LIBKRB5
```

You can validate that Samba has been compiled and linked with LDAP support by executing:

```
root#  smbd -b | grep LDAP
massive:/usr/sbin # smbd -b | grep LDAP
   HAVE_LDAP_H
   HAVE_LDAP
   HAVE_LDAP_DOMAIN2HOSTLIST
   HAVE_LDAP_INIT
   HAVE_LDAP_INITIALIZE
   HAVE_LDAP_SET_REBIND_PROC
   HAVE_LIBLDAP
   LDAP_SET_REBIND_PROC_ARGS
```

This does look promising; **smbd** has been built with Kerberos and LDAP support. You are relieved to know that it is safe to progress.

2. The next step is to identify which version of the Kerberos libraries have been used. In order to permit Samba-3 to interoperate with Windows 2003 Active Directory, it is essential that it has been linked with either MIT Kerberos version 1.3.1 or later, or that it has been linked with Heimdal Kerberos 0.6 plus specific patches. You may identify what version of the MIT Kerberos libraries are installed on your system by executing (on Red Hat Linux):

```
root#  rpm -q krb5
```

Or on SUSE Linux, execute:

```
root#  rpm -q heimdal
```

Please note that the RPMs provided by the Samba-Team are known to be working
and have been validated. Red Hat Linux RPMs may be obtained from the Samba
FTP sites. SUSE Linux RPMs may be obtained from Sernet[2] in Germany. From
this point on, you are certain that the Samba-3 build you are using has the necessary
capabilities. You can now configure Samba-3 and the NSS.

3. Using you favorite editor, configure the `smb.conf` file that is located in the `/etc/`
   `samba` directory so that it has the contents shown in Example 7.3.7.

4. Edit or create the NSS control file so it has the contents shown in Example 7.3.4.

5. Delete the file `/etc/samba/secrets.tdb` if it exists. Of course, you do keep a backup,
   don't you?

6. Delete the tdb files that cache Samba information. You keep a backup of the old files,
   of course. You also remove all files to ensure that nothing can pollute your nice, new
   configuration. Execute the following (example is for SUSE Linux):

```
root#  rm /var/lib/samba/*tdb
```

7. Validate your `smb.conf` file using **testparm** (as you have done previously). Correct
   all errors reported before proceeding. The command you execute is:

```
root#  testparm -s | less
```

Now that you are satisfied that your Samba server is ready to join the Windows ADS
domain, let's move on.

8. This is a good time to double-check everything and then execute the following command when everything you have done has checked out okay:

```
root#  net ads join -UAdministrator%not24get
Using short domain name -- LONDON
Joined 'FRAN' to realm 'LONDON.ABMAS.BIZ'
```

You have successfully made your Samba-3 server a member of the ADS domain using
Kerberos protocols. In the event that you receive no output messages, a silent return
means that the domain join failed. You should use **ethereal** to identify what may be
failing. Common causes of a failed join include:

- Defective or misconfigured DNS name resolution.

---

[2]<ftp://ftp.sernet.de>

- Restrictive security settings on the Windows 200x ADS domain controller preventing needed communications protocols. You can check this by searching the Windows Server 200x Event Viewer.

- Incorrectly configured smb.conf file settings.

- Lack of support of necessary Kerberos protocols because the version of MIT Kerberos (or Heimdal) in use is not up to date enough to support the necessary functionality.

In any case, never execute the **net rpc join** command in an attempt to join the Samba server to the domain, unless you wish not to use the Kerberos security protocols. Use of the older RPC-based domain join facility requires that Windows Server 200x ADS has been configured appropriately for mixed mode operation.

9. If the **tdbdump** is installed on your system (not essential), you can look inside the /etc/samba/secrets.tdb file. If you wish to do this, execute:

```
root#  tdbdump secrets.tdb
{
key = "SECRETS/SID/LONDON"
data = "\01\04\00\00\00\00\00\05\15\00\00\00\EBw\86\F1\ED\BD\
   F6{\5C6\E5W\00\00\00\00\00\00\00\00\00\00\00\00\00\00\00\00\
   00\00\00\00\00\00\00\00\00\00\00\00\00\00\00\00\00\00\00\00\
   00\00\00\00\00\00\00\00"
}
{
key = "SECRETS/MACHINE_PASSWORD/LONDON"
data = "le3Q5FPnN5.ueC\00"
}
{
key = "SECRETS/MACHINE_SEC_CHANNEL_TYPE/LONDON"
data = "\02\00\00\00"
}
{
key = "SECRETS/MACHINE_LAST_CHANGE_TIME/LONDON"
data = "E\89\F6?"
}
```

This is given to demonstrate to the skeptics that this process truly does work.

10. It is now time to start Samba in the usual way (as has been done many time before in this book).

11. This is a good time to verify that everything is working. First, check that winbind is able to obtain the list of users and groups from the ADS domain controller. Execute the following:

```
root#  wbinfo -u
LONDON+Administrator
LONDON+Guest
LONDON+SUPPORT_388945a0
LONDON+krbtgt
LONDON+jht
```

Good, the list of users was obtained. Now do likewise for group accounts:

```
root#  wbinfo -g
LONDON+Domain Computers
LONDON+Domain Controllers
LONDON+Schema Admins
LONDON+Enterprise Admins
LONDON+Domain Admins
LONDON+Domain Users
LONDON+Domain Guests
LONDON+Group Policy Creator Owners
LONDON+DnsUpdateProxy
```

Excellent. That worked also, as expected.

12. Now repeat this via NSS to validate that full identity resolution is functional as required. Execute:

```
root#  getent passwd
...
LONDON+Administrator:x:10000:10000:Administrator:
            /home/LONDON/administrator:/bin/bash
LONDON+Guest:x:10001:10001:Guest:
            /home/LONDON/guest:/bin/bash
LONDON+SUPPORT_388945a0:x:10002:10000:SUPPORT_388945a0:
            /home/LONDON/support_388945a0:/bin/bash
LONDON+krbtgt:x:10003:10000:krbtgt:
            /home/LONDON/krbtgt:/bin/bash
LONDON+jht:x:10004:10000:John H. Terpstra:
            /home/LONDON/jht:/bin/bash
```

Okay, ADS user accounts are being resolved. Now you try group resolution:

```
root#  getent group
...
LONDON+Domain Computers:x:10002:
```

```
LONDON+Domain Controllers:x:10003:
LONDON+Schema Admins:x:10004:LONDON+Administrator
LONDON+Enterprise Admins:x:10005:LONDON+Administrator
LONDON+Domain Admins:x:10006:LONDON+jht,LONDON+Administrator
LONDON+Domain Users:x:10000:
LONDON+Domain Guests:x:10001:
LONDON+Group Policy Creator Owners:x:10007:LONDON+Administrator
LONDON+DnsUpdateProxy:x:10008:
```

This is very pleasing. Everything works as expected.

13. You may now perform final verification that communications between Samba-3 win-bind and the Active Directory server is using Kerberos protocols. Execute the following:

```
root#  net ads info
LDAP server: 192.168.2.123
LDAP server name: w2k3s
Realm: LONDON.ABMAS.BIZ
Bind Path: dc=LONDON,dc=ABMAS,dc=BIZ
LDAP port: 389
Server time: Sat, 03 Jan 2004 02:44:44 GMT
KDC server: 192.168.2.123
Server time offset: 2
```

It should be noted that Kerberos protocols are time-clock critical. You should keep all server time clocks synchronized using the network time protocol (NTP). In any case, the output we obtained confirms that all systems are operational.

14. There is one more action you elect to take, just because you are paranoid and disbelieving, so you execute the following command:

```
root#  net ads status -UAdministrator%not24get
objectClass: top
objectClass: person
objectClass: organizationalPerson
objectClass: user
objectClass: computer
cn: fran
distinguishedName: CN=fran,CN=Computers,DC=london,DC=abmas,DC=biz
instanceType: 4
whenCreated: 20040103092006.0Z
whenChanged: 20040103092006.0Z
uSNCreated: 28713
uSNChanged: 28717
name: fran
```

```
objectGUID: 58f89519-c467-49b9-acb0-f099d73696e
userAccountControl: 69632
badPwdCount: 0
codePage: 0
countryCode: 0
badPasswordTime: 0
lastLogoff: 0
lastLogon: 127175965783327936
localPolicyFlags: 0
pwdLastSet: 127175952062598496
primaryGroupID: 515
objectSid: S-1-5-21-4052121579-2079768045-1474639452-1109
accountExpires: 9223372036854775807
logonCount: 13
sAMAccountName: fran$
sAMAccountType: 805306369
operatingSystem: Samba
operatingSystemVersion: 3.0.20-SUSE
dNSHostName: fran
userPrincipalName: HOST/fran@LONDON.ABMAS.BIZ
servicePrincipalName: CIFS/fran.london.abmas.biz
servicePrincipalName: CIFS/fran
servicePrincipalName: HOST/fran.london.abmas.biz
servicePrincipalName: HOST/fran
objectCategory: CN=Computer,CN=Schema,CN=Configuration,
                           DC=london,DC=abmas,DC=biz
isCriticalSystemObject: FALSE
-------------- Security Descriptor (revision: 1, type: 0x8c14)
owner SID: S-1-5-21-4052121579-2079768045-1474639452-512
group SID: S-1-5-21-4052121579-2079768045-1474639452-513
------- (system) ACL (revision: 4, size: 120, number of ACEs: 2)
------- ACE (type: 0x07, flags: 0x5a, size: 0x38,
            mask: 0x20, object flags: 0x3)
access SID:  S-1-1-0
access type: AUDIT OBJECT
Permissions:
       [Write All Properties]
------- ACE (type: 0x07, flags: 0x5a, size: 0x38,
            mask: 0x20, object flags: 0x3)
access SID:  S-1-1-0
access type: AUDIT OBJECT
Permissions:
       [Write All Properties]
------- (user) ACL (revision: 4, size: 1944, number of ACEs: 40)
------- ACE (type: 0x00, flags: 0x00, size: 0x24, mask: 0xf01ff)
access SID:  S-1-5-21-4052121579-2079768045-1474639452-512
access type: ALLOWED
```

```
Permissions: [Full Control]
------- ACE (type: 0x00, flags: 0x00, size: 0x18, mask: 0xf01ff)
access SID:  S-1-5-32-548
...
------- ACE (type: 0x05, flags: 0x12, size: 0x38,
                mask: 0x10, object flags: 0x3)
access SID:  S-1-5-9
access type: ALLOWED OBJECT
Permissions:
        [Read All Properties]
-------------- End Of Security Descriptor
```

And now you have conclusive proof that your Samba-3 ADS domain member server
called FRAN is able to communicate fully with the ADS domain controllers.

Your Samba-3 ADS domain member server is ready for use. During training sessions, you
may be asked what is inside the `winbindd_cache.tdb` and `winbindd_idmap.tdb` files. Since
curiosity just took hold of you, execute the following:

```
root#  tdbdump /var/lib/samba/winbindd_idmap.tdb
{
key = "S-1-5-21-4052121579-2079768045-1474639452-501\00"
data = "UID 10001\00"
}
{
key = "UID 10005\00"
data = "S-1-5-21-4052121579-2079768045-1474639452-1111\00"
}
{
key = "GID 10004\00"
data = "S-1-5-21-4052121579-2079768045-1474639452-518\00"
}
{
key = "S-1-5-21-4052121579-2079768045-1474639452-502\00"
data = "UID 10003\00"
}
...

root#  tdbdump /var/lib/samba/winbindd_cache.tdb
{
key = "UL/LONDON"
data = "\00\00\00\00bp\00\00\06\00\00\00\0DAdministrator\0D
    Administrator-S-1-5-21-4052121579-2079768045-1474639452-500-
    S-1-5-21-4052121579-2079768045-1474639452-513\05Guest\05
    Guest-S-1-5-21-4052121579-2079768045-1474639452-501-
    S-1-5-21-4052121579-2079768045-1474639452-514\10
```

```
    SUPPORT_388945a0\10SUPPORT_388945a0.
    S-1-5-21-4052121579-2079768045-1474639452-1001-
    S-1-5-21-4052121579-2079768045-1474639452-513\06krbtgt\06
    krbtgt-S-1-5-21-4052121579-2079768045-1474639452-502-
    S-1-5-21-4052121579-2079768045-1474639452-513\03jht\10
    John H. Terpstra.S-1-5-21-4052121579-2079768045-1474639452-1110-
    S-1-5-21-4052121579-2079768045-1474639452-513"
}
{
key = "GM/S-1-5-21-4052121579-2079768045-1474639452-512"
data = "\00\00\00\00bp\00\00\02\00\00\00.
    S-1-5-21-4052121579-2079768045-1474639452-1110\03
    jht\01\00\00\00-S-1-5-21-4052121579-2079768045-1474639452-500\0D
    Administrator\01\00\00\00"
}
{
key = "SN/S-1-5-21-4052121579-2079768045-1474639452-513"
data = "\00\00\00\00xp\00\00\02\00\00\00\0CDomain Users"
}
{
key = "GM/S-1-5-21-4052121579-2079768045-1474639452-518"
data = "\00\00\00\00bp\00\00\01\00\00\00-
    S-1-5-21-4052121579-2079768045-1474639452-500\0D
    Administrator\01\00\00\00"
}
{
key = "SEQNUM/LONDON\00"
data = "xp\00\00C\92\F6?"
}
{
key = "U/S-1-5-21-4052121579-2079768045-1474639452-1110"
data = "\00\00\00\00xp\00\00\03jht\10John H. Terpstra.
    S-1-5-21-4052121579-2079768045-1474639452-1110-
    S-1-5-21-4052121579-2079768045-1474639452-513"
}
{
key = "NS/S-1-5-21-4052121579-2079768045-1474639452-502"
data = "\00\00\00\00bp\00\00-
    S-1-5-21-4052121579-2079768045-1474639452-502"
}
{
key = "SN/S-1-5-21-4052121579-2079768045-1474639452-1001"
data = "\00\00\00\00bp\00\00\01\00\00\00\10SUPPORT_388945a0"
}
{
key = "SN/S-1-5-21-4052121579-2079768045-1474639452-500"
data = "\00\00\00\00bp\00\00\01\00\00\00\0DAdministrator"
```

```
}
{
key = "U/S-1-5-21-4052121579-2079768045-1474639452-502"
data = "\00\00\00\00bp\00\00\06krbtgt\06krbtgt-
    S-1-5-21-4052121579-2079768045-1474639452-502-
    S-1-5-21-4052121579-2079768045-1474639452-513"
}
. . . .
```

Now all is revealed. Your curiosity, as well as that of your team, has been put at ease. May this server serve well all who happen upon it.

7.3.4.1   IDMAP_RID with Winbind

The **idmap_rid** facility is a new tool that, unlike native winbind, creates a predictable mapping of MS Windows SIDs to UNIX UIDs and GIDs. The key benefit of this method of implementing the Samba IDMAP facility is that it eliminates the need to store the IDMAP data in a central place. The downside is that it can be used only within a single ADS domain and is not compatible with trusted domain implementations.

This alternate method of SID to UID/GID mapping can be achieved with the idmap_rid plug-in. This plug-in uses the RID of the user SID to derive the UID and GID by adding the RID to a base value specified. This utility requires that the parameter "allow trusted domains = No" must be specified, as it is not compatible with multiple domain environments. The *idmap uid* and *idmap gid* ranges must be specified.

The idmap_rid facility can be used both for NT4/Samba-style domains as well as with Active Directory. To use this with an NT4 domain, the `realm` is not used. Additionally the method used to join the domain uses the `net rpc join` process.

An example `smb.conf` file for an ADS domain environment is shown in Example 7.3.8.

In a large domain with many users, it is imperative to disable enumeration of users and groups. For example, at a site that has 22,000 users in Active Directory the winbind-based user and group resolution is unavailable for nearly 12 minutes following first start-up of **winbind**. Disabling of such enumeration results in instantaneous response. The disabling of user and group enumeration means that it will not be possible to list users or groups using the **getent passwd** and **getent group** commands. It will be possible to perform the lookup for individual users, as shown in the procedure below.

The use of this tool requires configuration of NSS as per the native use of winbind. Edit the `/etc/nsswitch.conf` so it has the following parameters:

```
...
passwd: files winbind
shadow: files winbind
group:  files winbind
...
```

```
hosts:  files wins
...
```

The following procedure can be used to utilize the idmap_rid facility:

1. Create or install and `smb.conf` file with the above configuration.

2. Edit the `/etc/nsswitch.conf` file as shown above.

3. Execute:

   ```
   root#  net ads join -UAdministrator%password
   Using short domain name -- KPAK
   Joined 'BIGJOE' to realm 'CORP.KPAK.COM'
   ```

   An invalid or failed join can be detected by executing:

   ```
   root#  net ads testjoin
   BIGJOE$@'s password:
   [2004/11/05 16:53:03, 0] utils/net_ads.c:ads_startup(186)
     ads_connect: No results returned
   Join to domain is not valid
   ```

   The specific error message may differ from the above because it depends on the type of failure that may have occurred. Increase the *log level* to 10, repeat the above test, and then examine the log files produced to identify the nature of the failure.

4. Start the **nmbd**, **winbind,** and **smbd** daemons in the order shown.

5. Validate the operation of this configuration by executing:

   ```
   root#  getent passwd administrator
   administrator:x:1000:1013:Administrator:/home/BE/administrator:/bin/bash
   ```

7.3.4.2 IDMAP Storage in LDAP using Winbind

The storage of IDMAP information in LDAP can be used with both NT4/Samba-3-style domains as well as with ADS domains. OpenLDAP is a commonly used LDAP server for this purpose, although any standards-compliant LDAP server can be used. It is therefore possible to deploy this IDMAP configuration using the Sun iPlanet LDAP server, Novell eDirectory, Microsoft ADS plus ADAM, and so on.

The example in Example 7.3.9 is for an ADS-style domain.

In the case of an NT4 or Samba-3-style domain the *realm* is not used, and the command used to join the domain is **net rpc join**. The above example also demonstrates advanced error reporting techniques that are documented in the chapter called "Reporting Bugs" in "The Official Samba-3 HOWTO and Reference Guide, Second Edition" (TOSHARG2).

Where MIT kerberos is installed (version 1.3.4 or later), edit the `/etc/krb5.conf` file so it has the following contents:

```
[logging]
 default = FILE:/var/log/krb5libs.log
 kdc = FILE:/var/log/krb5kdc.log
 admin_server = FILE:/var/log/kadmind.log

[libdefaults]
 default_realm = SNOWSHOW.COM
 dns_lookup_realm = false
 dns_lookup_kdc = true

[appdefaults]
 pam = {
   debug = false
   ticket_lifetime = 36000
   renew_lifetime = 36000
   forwardable = true
   krb4_convert = false
 }
```

Where Heimdal kerberos is installed, edit the `/etc/krb5.conf` file so it is either empty (i.e., no contents) or it has the following contents:

```
[libdefaults]
        default_realm = SNOWSHOW.COM
        clockskew = 300

[realms]
        SNOWSHOW.COM = {
                kdc = ADSDC.SHOWSHOW.COM
        }

[domain_realm]
        .snowshow.com = SNOWSHOW.COM
```

NOTE

Samba cannot use the Heimdal libraries if there is no `/etc/krb5.conf`
file. So long as there is an empty file, the Heimdal kerberos libraries
will be usable. There is no need to specify any settings because Samba,
using the Heimdal libraries, can figure this out automatically.

Edit the NSS control file `/etc/nsswitch.conf` so it has the following entries:

```
...
passwd: files ldap
shadow: files ldap
group:  files ldap
...
hosts:  files wins
...
```

You will need the PADL[3] **nss_ldap** tool set for this solution. Configure the `/etc/ldap.conf` file so it has the information needed. The following is an example of a working file:

```
host    192.168.2.1
base    dc=snowshow,dc=com
binddn  cn=Manager,dc=snowshow,dc=com
bindpw  not24get

pam_password exop

nss_base_passwd ou=People,dc=snowshow,dc=com?one
nss_base_shadow ou=People,dc=snowshow,dc=com?one
nss_base_group  ou=Groups,dc=snowshow,dc=com?one
ssl     no
```

The following procedure may be followed to affect a working configuration:

1. Configure the `smb.conf` file as shown above.

2. Create the `/etc/krb5.conf` file following the indications above.

3. Configure the `/etc/nsswitch.conf` file as shown above.

4. Download, build, and install the PADL nss_ldap tool set. Configure the `/etc/ldap.conf` file as shown above.

---

[3]<http://www.padl.com>

5. Configure an LDAP server and initialize the directory with the top-level entries needed by IDMAP as shown in the following LDIF file:

```
dn: dc=snowshow,dc=com
objectClass: dcObject
objectClass: organization
dc: snowshow
o: The Greatest Snow Show in Singapore.
description: Posix and Samba LDAP Identity Database

dn: cn=Manager,dc=snowshow,dc=com
objectClass: organizationalRole
cn: Manager
description: Directory Manager

dn: ou=Idmap,dc=snowshow,dc=com
objectClass: organizationalUnit
ou: idmap
```

6. Execute the command to join the Samba domain member server to the ADS domain as shown here:

```
root#  net ads testjoin
Using short domain name -- SNOWSHOW
Joined 'GOODELF' to realm 'SNOWSHOW.COM'
```

7. Store the LDAP server access password in the Samba `secrets.tdb` file as follows:

```
root#  smbpasswd -w not24get
```

8. Start the **nmbd, winbind,** and **smbd** daemons in the order shown.

Follow the diagnostic procedures shown earlier in this chapter to identify success or failure of the join. In many cases a failure is indicated by a silent return to the command prompt with no indication of the reason for failure.

7.3.4.3 IDMAP and NSS Using LDAP from ADS with RFC2307bis Schema Extension

The use of this method is messy. The information provided in this section is for guidance only and is very definitely not complete. This method does work; it is used in a number of large sites and has an acceptable level of performance.

An example `smb.conf` file is shown in Example 7.3.10.

The DMS must be joined to the domain using the usual procedure. Additionally, it is necessary to build and install the PADL nss_ldap tool set. Be sure to build this tool set with the following:

```
./configure --enable-rfc2307bis --enable-schema-mapping
make install
```

The following /etc/nsswitch.conf file contents are required:

```
...
passwd: files ldap
shadow: files ldap
group:  files ldap
...
hosts:  files wins
...
```

The /etc/ldap.conf file must be configured also. Refer to the PADL documentation and source code for nss_ldap instructions.

The next step involves preparation on the ADS schema. This is briefly discussed in the remaining part of this chapter.

IDMAP, Active Directory, and MS Services for UNIX 3.5   The Microsoft Windows Service for UNIX version 3.5 is available for free download[4] from the Microsoft Web site. You will need to download this tool and install it following Microsoft instructions.

IDMAP, Active Directory, and AD4UNIX   Instructions for obtaining and installing the AD4UNIX tool set can be found from the Geekcomix[5] Web site.

7.3.5   UNIX/Linux Client Domain Member

So far this chapter has been mainly concerned with the provision of file and print services for domain member servers. However, an increasing number of UNIX/Linux workstations are being installed that do not act as file or print servers to anyone other than a single desktop user. The key demand for desktop systems is to be able to log onto any UNIX/Linux or Windows desktop using the same network user credentials.

The ability to use a common set of user credential across a variety of network systems is generally regarded as a single sign-on (SSO) solution. SSO systems are sold by a large number of vendors and include a range of technologies such as:

- Proxy sign-on

---

[4] <http://www.microsoft.com/windows/sfu/>

[5] <http://www.geekcomix.com/cgi-bin/classnotes/wiki.pl?LDAP01/An_Alternative_Approach>

- Federated directory provisioning

- Metadirectory server solutions

- Replacement authentication systems

There are really only three solutions that provide integrated authentication and user identity management facilities:

- Samba winbind (free)

- PADL[6] PAM and LDAP tools (free)

- Vintela[7] Authentication Services (commercial)

The following guidelines are pertinent to the deployment of winbind-based authentication and identity resolution with the express purpose of allowing users to log on to UNIX/Linux desktops using Windows network domain user credentials (username and password).

You should note that it is possible to use LDAP-based PAM and NSS tools to permit distributed systems logons (SSO), providing user and group accounts are stored in an LDAP directory. This provides logon services for UNIX/Linux users, while Windows users obtain their sign-on support via Samba-3.

On the other hand, if the authentication and identity resolution backend must be provided by a Windows NT4-style domain or from an Active Directory Domain that does not have the Microsoft Windows Services for UNIX installed, winbind is your best friend. Specific guidance for these situations now follows.

To permit users to log on to a Linux system using Windows network credentials, you need to configure identity resolution (NSS) and PAM. This means that the basic steps include those outlined above with the addition of PAM configuration. Given that most workstations (desktop/client) usually do not need to provide file and print services to a group of users, the configuration of shares and printers is generally less important. Often this allows the share specifications to be entirely removed from the `smb.conf` file. That is obviously an administrator decision.

7.3.5.1　NT4 Domain Member

The following steps provide a Linux system that users can log onto using Windows NT4 (or Samba-3) domain network credentials:

1. Follow the steps outlined in Section 7.3.2 and ensure that all validation tests function as shown.

2. Identify what services users must log on to. On Red Hat Linux, if it is intended that the user shall be given access to all services, it may be most expeditious to simply configure the file `/etc/pam.d/system-auth`.

---

[6]<http://www.padl.com>
[7]<http://www.vintela.com>

3. Carefully make a backup copy of all PAM configuration files before you begin making changes. If you break the PAM configuration, please note that you may need to use an emergency boot process to recover your Linux system. It is possible to break the ability to log into the system if PAM files are incorrectly configured. The entire directory /etc/pam.d should be backed up to a safe location.

4. If you require only console login support, edit the /etc/pam.d/login so it matches Example 7.3.11.

5. To provide the ability to log onto the graphical desktop interface, you must edit the files gdm and xdm in the /etc/pam.d directory.

6. Edit only one file at a time. Carefully validate its operation before attempting to reboot the machine.

7.3.5.2   ADS Domain Member

This procedure should be followed to permit a Linux network client (workstation/desktop) to permit users to log on using Microsoft Active Directory-based user credentials.

1. Follow the steps outlined in Section 7.3.4 and ensure that all validation tests function as shown.

2. Identify what services users must log on to. On Red Hat Linux, if it is intended that the user shall be given access to all services, it may be most expeditious to simply configure the file /etc/pam.d/system-auth as shown in Example 7.3.13.

3. Carefully make a backup copy of all PAM configuration files before you begin making changes. If you break the PAM configuration, please note that you may need to use an emergency boot process to recover your Linux system. It is possible to break the ability to log into the system if PAM files are incorrectly configured. The entire directory /etc/pam.d should be backed up to a safe location.

4. If you require only console login support, edit the /etc/pam.d/login so it matches Example 7.3.11.

5. To provide the ability to log onto the graphical desktop interface, you must edit the files gdm and xdm in the /etc/pam.d directory.

6. Edit only one file at a time. Carefully validate its operation before attempting to reboot the machine.

7.3.6   Key Points Learned

The addition of UNIX/Linux Samba servers and clients is a common requirement. In this chapter, you learned how to integrate such servers so that the UID/GID mappings they use can be consistent across all domain member servers. You also discovered how to implement the ability to use Samba or Windows domain account credentials to log on to a UNIX/Linux client.

The following are key points made in this chapter:

- Domain controllers are always authoritative for the domain.

- Domain members may have local accounts and must be able to resolve the identity of domain user accounts. Domain user account identity must map to a local UID/GID. That local UID/GID can be stored in LDAP. This way, it is possible to share the IDMAP data across all domain member machines.

- Resolution of user and group identities on domain member machines may be implemented using direct LDAP services or using winbind.

- On NSS/PAM enabled UNIX/Linux systems, NSS is responsible for identity management and PAM is responsible for authentication of logon credentials (username and password).

7.4   Questions and Answers

The following questions were obtained from the mailing list and also from private discussions with Windows network administrators.

F.A.Q.

1. Q: *We use NIS for all UNIX accounts. Why do we need winbind?*
A: You can use NIS for your UNIX accounts. NIS does not store the Windows encrypted passwords that need to be stored in one of the acceptable passdb backends. Your choice of backend is limited to *smbpasswd* or *tdbsam*. Winbind is needed to handle the resolution of SIDs from trusted domains to local UID/GID values.

On a domain member server, you effectively map Windows domain users to local users that are in your NIS database by specifying the *winbind trusted domains only*. This causes user and group account lookups to be routed via the **getpwnam()** family of systems calls. On an NIS-enabled client, this pushes the resolution of users and groups out through NIS.

As a general rule, it is always a good idea to run winbind on all Samba servers.

2. Q: *Our IT management people do not like LDAP but are looking at Microsoft Active Directory. Which is better?*
A: Microsoft Active Directory is an LDAP server that is intricately tied to a Kerberos infrastructure. Most IT managers who object to LDAP do so because an LDAP server is most often supplied as a raw tool that needs to be configured and for which the administrator must create the schema, create the administration tools, and devise the backup and recovery facilities in a site-dependent manner. LDAP servers in general are seen as a high-energy, high-risk facility.

Microsoft Active Directory by comparison is easy to install and configure and is supplied with all tools necessary to implement and manage the directory. For sites that lack a lot of technical competence, Active Directory is a good choice. For sites that have the technical competence to handle Active Directory well, LDAP is a good alternative. The real issue is, What type of solution does the site want? If management wants a choice to use an alternative, they may want to consider the options. On the other hand, if management just wants a solution that works, Microsoft Active Directory is a good solution.

3. **Q:** *We want to implement a Samba PDC, four Samba BDCs, and 10 Samba servers. Is it possible to use NIS in place of LDAP?*
A: Yes, it is possible to use NIS in place of LDAP, but there may be problems with keeping the Windows (SMB) encrypted passwords database correctly synchronized across the entire network. Workstations (Windows client machines) periodically change their domain membership secure account password. How can you keep changes that are on remote BDCs synchronized on the PDC?

LDAP is a more elegant solution because it permits centralized storage and management of all network identities (user, group, and machine accounts) together with all information Samba needs to provide to network clients and their users.

4. **Q:** *Are you suggesting that users should not log on to a domain member server? If so, why?*
A: Many UNIX administrators mock the model that the personal computer industry has adopted as normative since the early days of Novell NetWare. The old perception of the necessity to keep users off file and print servers was a result of fears concerning the security and integrity of data. It was a simple and generally effective measure to keep users away from servers, except through mapped drives.

UNIX administrators are fully correct in asserting that UNIX servers and workstations are identical in terms of the software that is installed. They correctly assert that in a well-secured environment it is safe to store files on a system that has hundreds of users. But all network administrators must factor into the decision to allow or reject general user logins to a UNIX system that is principally a file and print server the risk to operations through simple user errors. Only then can one begin to appraise the best strategy and adopt a site-specific policy that best protects the needs of users and of the organization alike.

From experience, it is my recommendation to keep general system-level logins to a practical minimum and to eliminate them if possible. This should not be taken as a hard rule, though. The better question is, what works best for the site?

5. **Q:** *In my* `smb.conf` *file, I enabled the parameter* `winbind enable local accounts` *on all domain member servers, but it does not work. The accounts I put in* `/etc/passwd` *do not show up in the options list when I try to set an ACL on a share. What have I done wrong?*
A: The manual page for this `smb.conf` file parameter clearly says, "This parameter controls whether or not winbindd will act as a stand-in replacement for the various account management hooks in smb.conf (for example, add user script). If enabled, winbindd will support the creation of local users and groups as another source of UNIX account informa-

tion available via getpwnam() or getgrgid(), etc...." By default this parameter is already enabled; therefore, the action you are seeing is a result of a failure of identity resolution in the domain.

These are the accounts that are available for Windows network domain logons. Providing identity resolution has been correctly configured on the domain controllers as well as on domain member servers. The domain user and group identities automatically map to a valid local UID and GID pair.

6. **Q:** *We want to ensure that only users from our own domain plus from trusted domains can use our Samba servers. In the* smb.conf *file on all servers, we have enabled the* winbind trusted domains only *parameter. We now find that users from trusted domains cannot access our servers, and users from Windows clients that are not domain members can also access our servers. Is this a Samba bug?*
A: The manual page for this *winbind trusted domains only* parameter says, "This parameter is designed to allow Samba servers that are members of a Samba-controlled domain to use UNIX accounts distributed vi NIS, rsync, or LDAP as the UIDs for winbindd users in the hosts primary domain. Therefore, the user SAMBA\user1 would be mapped to the account user1 in /etc/passwd instead of allocating a new UID for him or her." This clearly suggests that you are trying to use this parameter inappropriately.

A far better solution is to use the *valid users* by specifying precisely the domain users and groups that should be permitted access to the shares. You could, for example, set the following parameters:

```
[demoshare]
    path = /export/demodata
    valid users = @"Domain Users", @"OTHERDOMAIN\Domain Users"
```

7. **Q:** *What are the benefits of using LDAP for my domain member servers?*
A: The key benefit of using LDAP is that the UID of all users and the GID of all groups are globally consistent on domain controllers as well as on domain member servers. This means that it is possible to copy/replicate files across servers without loss of identity.

When use is made of account identity resolution via winbind, even when an IDMAP backend is stored in LDAP, the UID/GID on domain member servers is consistent, but differs from the ID that the user/group has on domain controllers. The winbind allocated UID/GID that is stored in LDAP (or locally) will be in the numeric range specified in the *idmap uid/gid* in the smb.conf file. On domain controllers, the UID/GID is that of the POSIX value assigned in the LDAP directory as part of the POSIX account information.

8. **Q:** *Is proper DNS operation necessary for Samba-3 plus LDAP? If so, what must I put into my DNS configuration?*

A: Samba depends on correctly functioning resolution of hostnames to their IP address. Samba makes no direct DNS lookup calls, but rather redirects all name-to-address calls via the **getXXXbyXXX()** function calls. The configuration of the **hosts** entry in the NSS / etc/nsswitch.conf file determines how the underlying resolution process is implemented. If the **hosts** entry in your NSS control file says:

```
hosts: files dns wins
```

this means that a hostname lookup first tries the **/etc/hosts**. If this fails to resolve, it attempts a DNS lookup, and if that fails, it tries a WINS lookup.

The addition of the WINS-based name lookup makes sense only if NetBIOS over TCP/IP has been enabled on all Windows clients. Where NetBIOS over TCP/IP has been disabled, DNS is the preferred name resolution technology. This usually makes most sense when Samba is a client of an Active Directory domain, where NetBIOS use has been disabled. In this case, the Windows 200x autoregisters all locator records it needs with its own DNS server or servers.

9. **Q:** *Our Windows 2003 Server Active Directory domain runs with NetBIOS disabled. Can we use Samba-3 with that configuration?*
A: Yes.

10. **Q:**   *When I tried to execute net ads join, I got no output. It did not work, so I think that it failed. I then executed net rpc join and that worked fine. That is okay, isn't it?*
A: No. This is not okay. It means that your Samba-3 client has joined the ADS domain as a Windows NT4 client, and Samba-3 will not be using Kerberos-based authentication.

Example 7.3.1 Samba Domain Member in Samba Domain Using LDAP — smb.conf File

```
# Global parameters
[global]
        unix charset = LOCALE
        workgroup = MEGANET2
        security = DOMAIN
        username map = /etc/samba/smbusers
        log level = 10
        syslog = 0
        log file = /var/log/samba/%m
        max log size = 50
        smb ports = 139
        name resolve order = wins bcast hosts
        printcap name = CUPS
        wins server = 192.168.2.1
        ldap suffix = dc=abmas,dc=biz
        ldap machine suffix = ou=People
        ldap user suffix = ou=People
        ldap group suffix = ou=Groups
        ldap idmap suffix = ou=Idmap
        ldap admin dn = cn=Manager,dc=abmas,dc=biz
        idmap backend = ldap:ldap://lapdc.abmas.biz
        idmap uid = 10000-20000
        idmap gid = 10000-20000
        winbind trusted domains only = Yes
        printer admin = root
        printing = cups
[homes]
        comment = Home Directories
        valid users = %S
        read only = No
        browseable = No
[printers]
        comment = SMB Print Spool
        path = /var/spool/samba
        guest ok = Yes
        printable = Yes
        browseable = No
[print$]
        comment = Printer Drivers
        path = /var/lib/samba/drivers
        admin users = root, Administrator
        write list = root
```

Example 7.3.2 LDIF IDMAP Add-On Load File — File: /etc/openldap/idmap.LDIF

```
dn: ou=Idmap,dc=abmas,dc=biz
objectClass: organizationalUnit
ou: idmap
structuralObjectClass: organizationalUnit
```

Example 7.3.3 Configuration File for NSS LDAP Support — /etc/ldap.conf

---

```
URI     ldap://massive.abmas.biz ldap://massive.abmas.biz:636
host    192.168.2.1
base    dc=abmas,dc=biz
binddn  cn=Manager,dc=abmas,dc=biz
bindpw  not24get

pam_password exop

nss_base_passwd ou=People,dc=abmas,dc=biz?one
nss_base_shadow ou=People,dc=abmas,dc=biz?one
nss_base_group  ou=Groups,dc=abmas,dc=biz?one
ssl     no
```

Example 7.3.4 NSS using LDAP for Identity Resolution — File: /etc/nsswitch.conf

---

```
passwd:         files ldap
shadow:         files ldap
group:          files ldap

hosts:          files dns wins
networks:       files dns

services:       files
protocols:      files
rpc:            files
ethers:         files
netmasks:       files
netgroup:       files
publickey:      files

bootparams:     files
automount:      files
aliases:        files
```

Example 7.3.5 Samba Domain Member Server Using Winbind smb.conf File for NT4 Domain

```
# Global parameters
[global]
        unix charset = LOCALE
        workgroup = MEGANET2
        security = DOMAIN
        username map = /etc/samba/smbusers
        log level = 1
        syslog = 0
        log file = /var/log/samba/%m
        max log size = 0
        smb ports = 139
        name resolve order = wins bcast hosts
        printcap name = CUPS
        wins server = 192.168.2.1
        idmap uid = 10000-20000
        idmap gid = 10000-20000
        template primary group = "Domain Users"
        template shell = /bin/bash
        winbind separator = +
        printer admin = root
        hosts allow = 192.168.2., 192.168.3., 127.
        printing = cups
[homes]
        comment = Home Directories
        valid users = %S
        read only = No
        browseable = No
[printers]
        comment = SMB Print Spool
        path = /var/spool/samba
        guest ok = Yes
        printable = Yes
        browseable = No
[print$]
        comment = Printer Drivers
        path = /var/lib/samba/drivers
        admin users = root, Administrator
        write list = root
```

Example 7.3.6 Samba Domain Member Server Using Local Accounts smb.conf File for NT4 Domain

```
# Global parameters
 [global]
          unix charset = LOCALE
          workgroup = MEGANET3
          netbios name = BSDBOX
          security = DOMAIN
          username map = /etc/samba/smbusers
          log level = 1
          syslog = 0
          add user script = /usr/sbin/useradd -m '%u'
          add machine script = /usr/sbin/useradd -M '%u'
          add group script = /usr/sbin/groupadd '%g'
          winbind enable local accounts = Yes
          log file = /var/log/samba/%m
          max log size = 0
          smb ports = 139
          name resolve order = wins bcast hosts
          printcap name = CUPS
          wins server = 192.168.2.1
          printer admin = root
          hosts allow = 192.168.2., 192.168.3., 127.
          printing = cups
 [homes]
          comment = Home Directories
          valid users = %S
          read only = No
          browseable = No
 [printers]
          comment = SMB Print Spool
          path = /var/spool/samba
          guest ok = Yes
          printable = Yes
          browseable = No
 [print$]
          comment = Printer Drivers
          path = /var/lib/samba/drivers
          admin users = root, Administrator
          write list = root
```

Example 7.3.7 Samba Domain Member smb.conf File for Active Directory Membership

```
# Global parameters
[global]
        unix charset = LOCALE
        workgroup = LONDON
        realm = LONDON.ABMAS.BIZ
        server string = Samba 3.0.20
        security = ADS
        username map = /etc/samba/smbusers
        log level = 1
        syslog = 0
        log file = /var/log/samba/%m
        max log size = 50
        printcap name = CUPS
        ldap ssl = no
        idmap uid = 10000-20000
        idmap gid = 10000-20000
        template primary group = "Domain Users"
        template shell = /bin/bash
        winbind separator = +
        printing = cups
[homes]
        comment = Home Directories
        valid users = %S
        read only = No
        browseable = No
[printers]
        comment = SMB Print Spool
        path = /var/spool/samba
        guest ok = Yes
        printable = Yes
        browseable = No
[print$]
        comment = Printer Drivers
        path = /var/lib/samba/drivers
        admin users = root, Administrator
        write list = root
```

Example 7.3.8 Example smb.conf File Using idmap_rid

```
# Global parameters
 [global]
         workgroup = KPAK
         netbios name = BIGJOE
         realm = CORP.KPAK.COM
         server string = Office Server
         security = ADS
         allow trusted domains = No
         idmap backend = idmap_rid :KPAK=500-100000000
         idmap uid = 500-100000000
         idmap gid = 500-100000000
         template shell = /bin/bash
         winbind use default domain = Yes
         winbind enum users = No
         winbind enum groups = No
         winbind nested groups = Yes
         printer admin = "KPAK\Domain Admins"
```

Example 7.3.9 Typical ADS Style Domain smb.conf File

```
# Global parameters
 [global]
         workgroup = SNOWSHOW
         netbios name = GOODELF
         realm = SNOWSHOW.COM
         server string = Samba Server
         security = ADS
         log level = 1 ads:10 auth:10 sam:10 rpc:10
         ldap admin dn = cn=Manager , dc=SNOWSHOW, dc=COM
         ldap idmap suffix = ou=Idmap
         ldap suffix = dc=SNOWSHOW, dc=COM
         idmap backend = ldap:ldap://ldap.snowshow.com
         idmap uid = 150000-550000
         idmap gid = 150000-550000
         template shell = /bin/bash
         winbind use default domain = Yes
```

Example 7.3.10 ADS Membership Using RFC2307bis Identity Resolution smb.conf File

```
# Global parameters
 [global]
        workgroup = BUBBAH
        netbios name = MADMAX
        realm = BUBBAH.COM
        server string = Samba Server
        security = ADS
        idmap uid = 150000-550000
        idmap gid = 150000-550000
        template shell = /bin/bash
        winbind use default domain = Yes
        winbind trusted domains only = Yes
        winbind nested groups = Yes
```

Example 7.3.11 SUSE: PAM login Module Using Winbind

```
# /etc/pam.d/login

#%PAM-1.0
auth sufficient pam_unix2.so     nullok
auth sufficient pam_winbind.so use_first_pass use_authtok
auth required   pam_securetty.so
auth required   pam_nologin.so
auth required   pam_env.so
auth required   pam_mail.so
account sufficient      pam_unix2.so
account sufficient      pam_winbind.so user_first_pass use_authtok
password required       pam_pwcheck.so   nullok
password sufficient     pam_unix2.so     nullok use_first_pass use_authtok
password sufficient     pam_winbind.so   use_first_pass use_authtok
session sufficient      pam_unix2.so     none
session sufficient      pam_winbind.so   use_first_pass use_authtok
session required        pam_limits.so
```

Example 7.3.12 SUSE: PAM xdm Module Using Winbind

```
# /etc/pam.d/gdm (/etc/pam.d/xdm)

#%PAM-1.0
auth      sufficient    pam_unix2.so      nullok
auth      sufficient    pam_winbind.so    use_first_pass use_authtok
account   sufficient    pam_unix2.so
account   sufficient    pam_winbind.so    use_first_pass use_authtok
password  sufficient    pam_unix2.so
password  sufficient    pam_winbind.so    use_first_pass use_authtok
session   sufficient    pam_unix2.so
session   sufficient    pam_winbind.so    use_first_pass use_authtok
session   required      pam_dev perm.so
session   required      pam_resmgr.so
```

Example 7.3.13 Red Hat 9: PAM System Authentication File: /etc/pam.d/system-auth
Module Using Winbind

```
#%PAM-1.0
auth       required      /lib/security/$ISA/pam_env.so
auth       sufficient    /lib/security/$ISA/pam_unix.so likeauth nullok
auth       sufficient    /lib/security/$ISA/pam_winbind.so use_first_pass
auth       required      /lib/security/$ISA/pam_deny.so

account    required      /lib/security/$ISA/pam_unix.so
account    sufficient    /lib/security/$ISA/pam_winbind.so use_first_pass

password   required      /lib/security/$ISA/pam_cracklib.so retry=3 type=
# Note: The above line is complete. There is nothing following the '='
password   sufficient    /lib/security/$ISA/pam_unix.so \
                                     nullok use_authtok md5 shadow
password   sufficient    /lib/security/$ISA/pam_winbind.so use_first_pass
password   required      /lib/security/$ISA/pam_deny.so

session    required      /lib/security/$ISA/pam_limits.so
session    sufficient    /lib/security/$ISA/pam_unix.so
session    sufficient    /lib/security/$ISA/pam_winbind.so use_first_pass
```

Chapter 8

UPDATING SAMBA-3

It was a little difficult to select an appropriate title for this chapter. From email messages on the Samba mailing lists it is clear that many people consider the updating and upgrading of Samba to be a migration matter. Others talk about migrating Samba servers when in fact the issue at hand is one of installing a new Samba server to replace an older existing Samba server.

There has also been much talk about migration of Samba-3 from an smbpasswd passdb backend to the use of the tdbsam or ldapsam facilities that are new to Samba-3.

Clearly, there is not a great deal of clarity in the terminology that various people apply to these modes by which Samba servers are updated. This is further highlighted by an email posting that included the following neat remark:

> I like the "net rpc vampire" on NT4, but that to my surprise does not seem to work against a Samba PDC and, if addressed in the Samba to Samba context in either book, I could not find it.

So in response to the significant request for these situations to be better documented, this chapter has now been added. User contributions and documentation of real-world experiences are a most welcome addition to this chapter.

8.1 Introduction

A Windows network administrator explained in an email what changes he was planning to make and followed with the question: "Anyone done this before?" Many of us have upgraded and updated Samba without incident. Others have experienced much pain and user frustration. So it is to be hoped that the notes in this chapter will make a positive difference by assuring that someone will be saved a lot of discomfort.

Before anyone commences an upgrade or an update of Samba, the one cardinal rule that must be observed is: Backup all Samba configuration files in case it is necessary to revert to the old version. Even if you do not like this precautionary step, users will punish an administrator who fails to take adequate steps to avoid situations that may inflict lost productivity on them.

WARNING

Samba makes it possible to upgrade and update configuration files, but it is not possible to downgrade the configuration files. Please ensure that all configuration and control files are backed up to permit a downgrade in the rare event that this may be necessary.

It is prudent also to backup all data files on the server before attempting to perform a major upgrade. Many administrators have experienced the consequences of failure to take adequate precautions. So what is adequate? That is simple! If data is lost during an upgrade or update and it can not be restored, the precautions taken were inadequate. If a backup was not needed, but was available, caution was on the side of the victor.

8.1.1   Cautions and Notes

Someone once said, "It is good to be sorry, but better never to need to be!" These are wise words of advice to those contemplating a Samba upgrade or update.

This is as good a time as any to define the terms `upgrade` and `update`. The term `upgrade` refers to the installation of a version of Samba that is a whole generation or more ahead of that which is installed. Generations are indicated by the first digit of the version number. So far Samba has been released in generations 1.x, 2.x, 3.x, and currently 4.0 is in development.

The term `update` refers to a minor version number installation in place of one of the same generation. For example, updating from Samba 3.0.10 to 3.0.14 is an update. The move from Samba 2.0.7 to 3.0.14 is an upgrade.

While the use of these terms is an exercise in semantics, what needs to be realized is that there are major functional differences between a Samba 2.x release and a Samba 3.0.x release. Such differences may require a significantly different approach to solving the same networking challenge and generally require careful review of the latest documentation to identify precisely how the new installation may need to be modified to preserve prior functionality.

There is an old axiom that says, "The greater the volume of the documentation, the greater the risk that noone will read it, but where there is no documentation, noone can read it!" While true, some documentation is an evil necessity. It is hoped that this update to the documentation will avoid both extremes.

8.1.1.1   Security Identifiers (SIDs)

Before the days of Windows NT and OS/2, every Windows and DOS networking client that used the SMB protocols was an entirely autonomous entity. There was no concept of a security identifier for a machine or a user outside of the username, the machine name, and the workgroup name. In actual fact, these were not security identifiers in the same context as the way that the SID is used since the development of Windows NT 3.10.

Versions of Samba prior to 1.9 did not make use of a SID. Instead they make exclusive use of the username that is embedded in the SessionSetUpAndX component of the connection setup process between a Windows client and an SMB/CIFS server.

Around November 1997 support was added to Samba-1.9 to handle the Windows security RPC-based protocols that implemented support for Samba to store a machine SID. This information was stored in a file called `MACHINE.SID`.

Within the lifetime of the early Samba 2.x series, the machine SID information was relocated into a tdb file called `secrets.tdb`, which is where it is still located in Samba 3.0.x along with other information that pertains to the local machine and its role within a domain security context.

There are two types of SID, those pertaining to the machine itself and the domain to which it may belong, and those pertaining to users and groups within the security context of the local machine, in the case of standalone servers (SAS) and domain member servers (DMS).

When the Samba **smbd** daemon is first started, if the `secrets.tdb` file does not exist, it is created at the first client connection attempt. If this file does exist, **smbd** checks that there is a machine SID (if it is a domain controller, it searches for the domain SID). If **smbd** does not find one for the current name of the machine or for the current name of the workgroup, a new SID will be generated and then written to the `secrets.tdb` file. The SID is generated in a nondeterminative manner. This means that each time it is generated for a particular combination of machine name (hostname) and domain name (workgroup), it will be different.

The SID is the key used by MS Windows networking for all networking operations. This means that when the machine or domain SID changes, all security-encoded objects such as profiles and ACLs may become unusable.

NOTE

 It is of paramount importance that the machine and domain SID be backed up so that in the event of a change of hostname (machine name) or domain name (workgroup) the SID can be restored to its previous value.

In Samba-3 on a domain controller (PDC or BDC), the domain name controls the domain SID. On all prior versions the hostname (computer name, or NetBIOS name) controlled the SID. On a standalone server the hostname still controls the SID.

The local machine SID can be backed up using this procedure (Samba-3):

```
root#  net getlocalsid > /etc/samba/my-local-SID
```

The contents of the file /etc/samba/my-local-SID will be:

```
SID for domain FRODO is: S-1-5-21-726309263-4128913605-1168186429
```

This SID can be restored by executing:

```
root#  net setlocalsid S-1-5-21-726309263-4128913605-1168186429
```

Samba 1.9.x stored the machine SID in the the file /etc/MACHINE.SID from which it could be recovered and stored into the secrets.tdb file using the procedure shown above.

Where the secrets.tdb file exists and a version of Samba 2.x or later has been used, there is no specific need to go through this update process. Samba-3 has the ability to read the older tdb file and to perform an in-situ update to the latest tdb format. This is not a reversible process — it is a one-way upgrade.

In the course of the Samba 2.0.x series the **smbpasswd** was modified to permit the domain SID to be captured to the secrets.tdb file by executing:

```
root#  smbpasswd -S PDC -Uadministrator%password
```

The release of the Samba 2.2.x series permitted the SID to be obtained by executing:

```
root#  smbpasswd -S PDC -Uadministrator%password
```

from which the SID could be copied to a file and then written to the Samba-2.2.x secrets.tdb file by executing:

```
root#  smbpasswd -W S-1-5-21-726309263-4128913605-1168186429
```

Domain security information, which includes the domain SID, can be obtained from Samba-2.2.x systems by executing:

```
root#  rpcclient hostname lsaquery -Uroot%password
```

This can also be done with Samba-3 by executing:

```
root#  net rpc info -Uroot%password
```

```
Domain Name: MIDEARTH
Domain SID: S-1-5-21-726309263-4128913605-1168186429
Sequence number: 1113415916
Num users: 4237
Num domain groups: 86
Num local groups: 0
```

It is a very good practice to store this SID information in a safely kept file, just in case it is ever needed at a later date.

Take note that the domain SID is used extensively in Samba. Where LDAP is used for the *passdb backend*, all user, group, and trust accounts are encoded with the domain SID. This means that if the domain SID changes for any reason, the entire Samba environment can become broken and require extensive corrective action if the original SID cannot be restored. Fortunately, it can be recovered from a dump of the LDAP database. A dump of the LDAP directory database can be obtained by executing:

```
root#  slapcat -v -l filename.ldif
```

When the domain SID has changed, roaming profiles cease to be functional. The recovery of roaming profiles necessitates resetting of the domain portion of the user SID that owns the profile. This is encoded in the NTUser.DAT and can be updated using the Samba **profiles** utility. Please be aware that not all Linux distributions of the Samba RPMs include this essential utility. Please do not complain to the Samba Team if this utility is missing; that issue that must be addressed to the creator of the RPM package. The Samba Team do their best to make available all the tools needed to manage a Samba-based Windows networking environment.

8.1.1.2   Change of hostname

Samba uses two methods by which the primary NetBIOS machine name (also known as a computer name or the hostname) may be determined: If the smb.conf file contains a *netbios name* entry, its value will be used directly. In the absence of such an entry, the UNIX system hostname will be used.

Many sites have become victims of lost Samba functionality because the UNIX system hostname was changed for one reason or another. Such a change will cause a new machine SID to be generated. If this happens on a domain controller, it will also change the domain SID. These SIDs can be updated (restored) using the procedure outlined previously.

> NOTE
>
>
> Do NOT change the hostname or the *netbios name*. If this is changed, be sure to reset the machine SID to the original setting. Otherwise there may be serious interoperability and/or operational problems.

8.1.1.3   Change of Workgroup (Domain) Name

The domain name of a Samba server is identical to the workgroup name and is set in the smb.conf file using the *workgroup* parameter. This has been consistent throughout the history of Samba and across all versions.

Be aware that when the workgroup name is changed, a new SID will be generated. The old domain SID can be reset using the procedure outlined earlier in this chapter.

8.1.1.4   Location of config files

The Samba-Team has maintained a constant default location for all Samba control files throughout the life of the project. People who have produced binary packages of Samba have varied the location of the Samba control files. This has led to some confusion for network administrators.

The Samba 1.9.x smb.conf file may be found either in the /etc directory or in /usr/local/samba/lib.

During the life of the Samba 2.x release, the smb.conf file was relocated on Linux systems to the /etc/samba directory where it remains located also for Samba 3.0.x installations.

Samba 2.x introduced the secrets.tdb file that is also stored in the /etc/samba directory, or in the /usr/local/samba/lib directory subsystem.

The location at which **smbd** expects to find all configuration and control files is determined at the time of compilation of Samba. For versions of Samba prior to 3.0, one way to find the expected location of these files is to execute:

```
root#   strings /usr/sbin/smbd | grep conf
root#   strings /usr/sbin/smbd | grep secret
root#   strings /usr/sbin/smbd | grep smbpasswd
```

Note: The **smbd** executable may be located in the path /usr/local/samba/sbin.

Samba-3 provides a neat new way to track the location of all control files as well as to find the compile-time options used as the Samba package was built. Here is how the dark secrets of the internals of the location of control files within Samba executables can be uncovered:

```
root#  smbd -b | less
Build environment:
   Built by:    root@frodo
   Built on:    Mon Apr 11 20:23:27 MDT 2005
   Built using: gcc
   Build host:  Linux frodo 2.6...
   SRCDIR:      /usr/src/packages/BUILD/samba-3.0.20/source
   BUILDDIR:    /usr/src/packages/BUILD/samba-3.0.20/source

Paths:
   SBINDIR: /usr/sbin
   BINDIR: /usr/bin
   SWATDIR: /usr/share/samba/swat
   CONFIGFILE: /etc/samba/smb.conf
   LOGFILEBASE: /var/log/samba
   LMHOSTSFILE: /etc/samba/lmhosts
   LIBDIR: /usr/lib/samba
   SHLIBEXT: so
   LOCKDIR: /var/lib/samba
   PIDDIR: /var/run/samba
   SMB_PASSWD_FILE: /etc/samba/smbpasswd
   PRIVATE_DIR: /etc/samba
   ...
```

It is important that both the `smb.conf` file and the `secrets.tdb` be backed up before attempting any upgrade. The `secrets.tdb` file is version-encoded, and therefore a newer version may not work with an older version of Samba. A backup means that it is always possible to revert a failed or problematic upgrade.

8.1.1.5   International Language Support

Samba-2.x had no support for Unicode; instead, all national language character-set support in file names was done using particular locale codepage mapping techniques. Samba-3 supports Unicode in file names, thus providing true internationalization support.

Non-English users whose national language character set has special characters and who upgrade naively will find that many files that have the special characters in the file name will see them garbled and jumbled up. This typically happens with umlauts and accents because these characters were particular to the codepage that was in use with Samba-2.x using an 8-bit encoding scheme.

Files that are created with Samba-3 will use UTF-8 encoding. Should the file system ever end up with a mix of codepage (unix charset)-encoded file names and UTF-8-encoded file names, the mess will take some effort to set straight.

A very helpful tool is available from Bjorn Jacke's convmv[1] work. Convmv is a tool that can be used to convert file and directory names from one encoding method to another. The most common use for this tool is to convert locale-encoded files to UTF-8 Unicode encoding.

8.1.1.6   Updates and Changes in Idealx smbldap-tools

The smbldap-tools have been maturing rapidly over the past year. With maturation comes change. The location of the `smbldap.conf` and the `smbldap_bind.conf` configuration files have been moved from the directory `/etc/smbldap-tools` to the new location of `/etc/opt/IDEALX/smblda-tools` directory.

The smbldap-tools maintains an entry in the LDAP directory in which it stores the next values that should be used for UID and GID allocation for POSIX accounts that are created using this tool. The DIT location of these values has changed recently. The original `sambaUnixIdPooldn` object entity was stored in a directory entry (DIT object) called `NextFreeUnixId`, this has been changed to the DIT object `sambaDomainName`. Anyone who updates from an older version to the current release should note that the information stored under `NextFreeUnixId` must now be relocated to the DIT object `sambaDomainName`.

8.2   Upgrading from Samba 1.x and 2.x to Samba-3

Sites that are being upgraded from Samba-2 (or earlier versions) to Samba-3 may experience little difficulty or may require a lot of effort, depending on the complexity of the configuration. Samba-1.9.x upgrades to Samba-3 will generally be simple and straightforward, although no upgrade should be attempted without proper planning and preparation.

There are two basic modes of use of Samba versions prior to Samba-3. The first does not use LDAP, the other does. Samba-1.9.x did not provide LDAP support. Samba-2.x could be compiled with LDAP support.

8.2.1   Samba 1.9.x and 2.x Versions Without LDAP

Where it is necessary to upgrade an old Samba installation to Samba-3, the following procedure can be followed:

UPGRADING FROM A PRE-SAMBA-3 VERSION

1. Stop Samba. This can be done using the appropriate system tool that is particular for each operating system or by executing the **kill** command on **smbd**, **nmbd**, and **winbindd**.

2. Find the location of the Samba `smb.conf` file and back it up to a safe location.

3. Find the location of the `smbpasswd` file and back it up to a safe location.

4. Find the location of the `secrets.tdb` file and back it up to a safe location.

---

[1]`<http://j3e.de/linux/convmv/>`

5. Find the location of the lock directory. This is the directory in which Samba stores all its tdb control files. The default location used by the Samba Team is in `/usr/local/samba/var/locks` directory, but on Linux systems the old location was under the `/var/cache/samba` directory. However, the Linux Standards Base specified location is now under the `/var/lib/samba` directory. Copy all the tdb files to a safe location.

6. It is now safe to upgrade the Samba installation. On Linux systems it is not necessary to remove the Samba RPMs because a simple upgrade installation will automatically remove the old files. On systems that do not support a reliable package management system it is advisable either to delete the Samba old installation or to move it out of the way by renaming the directories that contain the Samba binary files.

7. When the Samba upgrade has been installed, the first step that should be completed is to identify the new target locations for the control files. Follow the steps shown in Section 8.1.1.4 to locate the correct directories to which each control file must be moved.

8. Do not change the hostname.

9. Do not change the workgroup name.

10. Execute the **testparm** to validate the `smb.conf` file. This process will flag any parameters that are no longer supported. It will also flag configuration settings that may be in conflict. One solution that may be used to clean up and to update the `smb.conf` file involves renaming it to `smb.conf.master` and then executing the following:

```
root#  cd /etc/samba
root#  testparm -s smb.conf.master > smb.conf
```

The resulting `smb.conf` file will be stripped of all comments and of all nonconforming configuration settings.

11. It is now safe to start Samba using the appropriate system tool. Alternately, it is possible to just execute **nmbd**, **smbd**, and **winbindd** for the command line while logged in as the root user.

8.2.2   Applicable to All Samba 2.x to Samba-3 Upgrades

Samba 2.x servers that were running as a domain controller (PDC) require changes to the configuration of the scripting interface tools that Samba uses to perform OS updates for users, groups, and trust accounts (machines and interdomain).

The following parameters are new to Samba-3 and should be correctly configured. Please refer to Chapter 3, "Secure Office Networking" through Chapter 6, "A Distributed 2000-User Network" in this book for examples of use of the new parameters shown here:

add group script
add machine script
add user to group script
delete group script
delete user from group script
passdb backend
set primary group script

The *add machine script* functionality was previously handled by the *add user script*, which in Samba-3 is used exclusively to add user accounts.

Where the *passdb backend* used is either smbpasswd (the default) or the new tdbsam, the system interface scripts are typically used. These involve use of OS tools such as **useradd**, **usermod**, **userdel**, **groupadd**, **groupmod**, **groupdel**, and so on.

Where the *passdb backend* makes use of an LDAP directory, it is necessary either to use the smbldap-tools provided by Idealx or to use an alternate toolset provided by a third party or else home-crafted to manage the LDAP directory accounts.

8.2.3   Samba-2.x with LDAP Support

Samba version 2.x could be compiled for use either with or without LDAP. The LDAP control settings in the smb.conf file in this old version are completely different (and less complete) than they are with Samba-3. This means that after migrating the control files, it is necessary to reconfigure the LDAP settings entirely.

Follow the procedure outlined in Section 8.2.1 to affect a migration of all files to the correct locations.

The Samba SAM schema required for Samba-3 is significantly different from that used with Samba 2.x. This means that the LDAP directory must be updated using the procedure outlined in the Samba WHATSNEW.txt file that accompanies all releases of Samba-3. This information is repeated here directly from this file:

```
This is an extract from the Samba-3.0.x WHATSNEW.txt file:
============================================================
Changes in Behavior
-------------------


The following issues are known changes in behavior between Samba 2.2 and
Samba 3.0 that may affect certain installations of Samba.

  1)   When operating as a member of a Windows domain, Samba 2.2 would
       map any users authenticated by the remote DC to the 'guest account'
       if a uid could not be obtained via the getpwnam() call.  Samba 3.0
       rejects the connection as NT_STATUS_LOGON_FAILURE.  There is no
       current work around to re-establish the 2.2 behavior.
```

2) When adding machines to a Samba 2.2 controlled domain, the
    'add user script' was used to create the UNIX identity of the
    machine trust account. Samba 3.0 introduces a new 'add machine
    script' that must be specified for this purpose. Samba 3.0 will
    not fall back to using the 'add user script' in the absence of
    an 'add machine script'

```
################################################################
Passdb Backends and Authentication
################################
```

There have been a few new changes that Samba administrators should be
aware of when moving to Samba 3.0.

1) encrypted passwords have been enabled by default in order to
   inter-operate better with out-of-the-box Windows client
   installations. This does mean that either (a) a samba account
   must be created for each user, or (b) 'encrypt passwords = no'
   must be explicitly defined in smb.conf.

2) Inclusion of new 'security = ads' option for integration
   with an Active Directory domain using the native Windows
   Kerberos 5 and LDAP protocols.

   MIT kerberos 1.3.1 supports the ARCFOUR-HMAC-MD5 encryption
   type which is necessary for servers on which the
   administrator password has not been changed, or kerberos-enabled
   SMB connections to servers that require Kerberos SMB signing.
   Besides this one difference, either MIT or Heimdal Kerberos
   distributions are usable by Samba 3.0.

Samba 3.0 also includes the possibility of setting up chains
of authentication methods (auth methods) and account storage
backends (passdb backend). Please refer to the smb.conf(5)
man page for details. While both parameters assume sane default
values, it is likely that you will need to understand what the
values actually mean in order to ensure Samba operates correctly.

The recommended passdb backends at this time are

  * smbpasswd - 2.2 compatible flat file format
  * tdbsam - attribute rich database intended as an smbpasswd
    replacement for stand alone servers
  * ldapsam - attribute rich account storage and retrieval
    backend utilizing an LDAP directory.
  * ldapsam_compat - a 2.2 backward compatible LDAP account

```
backend
```

Certain functions of the smbpasswd(8) tool have been split between the
new smbpasswd(8) utility, the net(8) tool, and the new pdbedit(8)
utility. See the respective man pages for details.

```
#########################################################################
LDAP
####
```

This section outlines the new features affecting Samba / LDAP
integration.

New Schema

A new object class (sambaSamAccount) has been introduced to replace
the old sambaAccount. This change aids us in the renaming of
attributes to prevent clashes with attributes from other vendors.
There is a conversion script (examples/LDAP/convertSambaAccount) to
modify and LDIF file to the new schema.

Example:

```
$ ldapsearch .... -b "ou=people,dc=..." > sambaAcct.ldif
$ convertSambaAccount --sid=<Domain SID> \
  --input=sambaAcct.ldif --output=sambaSamAcct.ldif \
  --changetype=[modify|add]
```

The <DOM SID> can be obtained by running 'net getlocalsid
<DOMAINNAME>' on the Samba PDC as root. The changetype determines
the format of the generated LDIF output--either create new entries
or modify existing entries.

The old sambaAccount schema may still be used by specifying the
"ldapsam_compat" passdb backend. However, the sambaAccount and
associated attributes have been moved to the historical section of
the schema file and must be uncommented before use if needed.
The 2.2 object class declaration for a sambaAccount has not changed
in the 3.0 samba.schema file.

Other new object classes and their uses include:

* sambaDomain - domain information used to allocate rids
  for users and groups as necessary. The attributes are added
  in 'ldap suffix' directory entry automatically if
  an idmap uid/gid range has been set and the 'ldapsam'

passdb backend has been selected.

* sambaGroupMapping - an object representing the
  relationship between a posixGroup and a Windows
  group/SID. These entries are stored in the 'ldap
  group suffix' and managed by the 'net groupmap' command.

* sambaUnixIdPool - created in the 'ldap idmap suffix' entry
  automatically and contains the next available 'idmap uid' and
  'idmap gid'

* sambaIdmapEntry - object storing a mapping between a
  SID and a UNIX uid/gid. These objects are created by the
  idmap_ldap module as needed.

* sambaSidEntry - object representing a SID alone, as a Structural
  class on which to build the sambaIdmapEntry.

New Suffix for Searching

The following new smb.conf parameters have been added to aid in directing
certain LDAP queries when 'passdb backend = ldapsam://...' has been
specified.

* ldap suffix   - used to search for user and computer accounts
* ldap user suffix   - used to store user accounts
* ldap machine suffix - used to store machine trust accounts
* ldap group suffix   - location of posixGroup/sambaGroupMapping entries
* ldap idmap suffix   - location of sambaIdmapEntry objects

If an 'ldap suffix' is defined, it will be appended to all of the
remaining sub-suffix parameters. In this case, the order of the suffix
listings in smb.conf is important. Always place the 'ldap suffix' first
in the list.

Due to a limitation in Samba's smb.conf parsing, you should not surround
the DN's with quotation marks.

8.3   Updating a Samba-3 Installation

The key concern in this section is to deal with the changes that have been affected in Samba-
3 between the Samba-3.0.0 release and the current update. Network administrators have
expressed concerns over the steps that should be taken to update Samba-3 versions.

The information in Section 8.1.1.4 would not be necessary if every person who has ever produced Samba executable (binary) files could agree on the preferred location of the `smb.conf` file and other Samba control files. Clearly, such agreement is further away than a pipedream.

Vendors and packagers who produce Samba binary installable packages do not, as a rule, use the default paths used by the Samba-Team for the location of the binary files, the `smb.conf` file, and the Samba control files (tdb's as well as files such as `secrets.tdb`). This means that the network or UNIX administrator who sets out to build the Samba executable files from the Samba tarball must take particular care. Failure to take care will result in both the original vendor's version of Samba remaining installed and the new version being installed in the default location used by the Samba-Team. This can lead to confusion and to much lost time as the uninformed administrator deals with apparent failure of the update to take effect.

The best advice for those lacking in code compilation experience is to use only vendor (or Samba-Team) provided binary packages. The Samba packages that are provided by the Samba-Team are generally built to use file paths that are compatible with the original OS vendor's practices.

If you are not sure whether a binary package complies with the OS vendor's practices, it is better to ask the package maintainer via email than to waste much time dealing with the nuances. Alternately, just diagnose the paths specified by the binary files following the procedure outlined above.

8.3.1 Samba-3 to Samba-3 Updates on the Same Server

The guidance in this section deals with updates to an existing Samba-3 server installation.

8.3.1.1 Updating from Samba Versions Earlier than 3.0.5

With the provision that the binary Samba-3 package has been built with the same path and feature settings as the existing Samba-3 package that is being updated, an update of Samba-3 versions 3.0.0 through 3.0.4 can be updated to 3.0.5 without loss of functionality and without need to change either the `smb.conf` file or, where used, the LDAP schema.

8.3.1.2 Updating from Samba Versions between 3.0.6 and 3.0.10

When updating versions of Samba-3 prior to 3.0.6 to 3.0.6 through 3.0.10, it is necessary only to update the LDAP schema (where LDAP is used). Always use the LDAP schema file that is shipped with the latest Samba-3 update.

Samba-3.0.6 introduced the ability to remember the last n number of passwords a user has used. This information will work only with the `tdbsam` and `ldapsam` *passdb backend* facilities.

After updating the LDAP schema, do not forget to re-index the LDAP database.

8.3.1.3   Updating from Samba Versions after 3.0.6 to a Current Release

Samba-3.0.8 introduced changes in how the *username map* behaves. It also included a change in behavior of **winbindd**. Please refer to the man page for smb.conf before implementing any update from versions prior to 3.0.8 to a current version.

In Samba-3.0.11 a new privileges interface was implemented. Please refer to Section 5.3.1.1 for information regarding this new feature. It is not necessary to implement the privileges interface, but it is one that has been requested for several years and thus may be of interest at your site.

In Samba-3.0.11 there were some functional changes to the *ldap user suffix* and to the *ldap machine suffix* behaviors. The following information has been extracted from the WHATSNEW.txt file from this release:

```
============
LDAP Changes
============


If "ldap user suffix" or "ldap machine suffix" are defined in
smb.conf, all user-accounts must reside below the user suffix,
and all machine and inter-domain trust-accounts must be located
below the machine suffix.  Previous Samba releases would fall
back to searching the 'ldap suffix' in some cases.
```

8.3.2   Migrating Samba-3 to a New Server

The two most likely candidates for replacement of a server are domain member servers and domain controllers. Each needs to be handled slightly differently.

8.3.2.1   Replacing a Domain Member Server

Replacement of a domain member server should be done using the same procedure as outlined in Chapter 7, "Adding Domain Member Servers and Clients".

Usually the new server will be introduced with a temporary name. After the old server data has been migrated to the new server, it is customary that the new server be renamed to that of the old server. This will change its SID and will necessitate rejoining to the domain.

Following a change of hostname (NetBIOS name) it is a good idea on all servers to shut down the Samba **smbd**, **nmbd**, and **winbindd** services, delete the wins.dat and browse.dat files, then restart Samba. This will ensure that the old name and IP address information is no longer able to interfere with name to IP address resolution. If this is not done, there can be temporary name resolution problems. These problems usually clear within 45 minutes of a name change, but can persist for a longer period of time.

If the old domain member server had local accounts, it is necessary to create on the new domain member server the same accounts with the same UID and GID for each account. Where the *passdb backend* database is stored in the smbpasswd or in the tdbsam format, the user and group account information for UNIX accounts that match the Samba accounts will reside in the system /etc/passwd, /etc/shadow, and /etc/group files. In this case, be sure to copy these account entries to the new target server.

Where the user accounts for both UNIX and Samba are stored in LDAP, the new target server must be configured to use the **nss_ldap** tool set. This will automatically ensure that the appropriate user entities are available on the new server.

8.3.2.2 Replacing a Domain Controller

In the past, people who replaced a Windows NT4 domain controller typically installed a new server, created printers and file shares on it, then migrate across all data that was destined to reside on it. The same can of course be done with Samba.

From recent mailing list postings it would seem that some administrators have the intent to just replace the old Samba server with a new one with the same name as the old one. In this case, simply follow the same process as for upgrading a Samba 2.x system and do the following:

- Where UNIX (POSIX) user and group accounts are stored in the system /etc/passwd, /etc/shadow, and /etc/group files, be sure to add the same accounts with identical UID and GID values for each user.

  Where LDAP is used, if the new system is intended to be the LDAP server, migrate it across by configuring the LDAP server (/etc/openldap/slapd.conf). The directory can be populated either initially by setting this LDAP server up as a slave or by dumping the data from the old LDAP server using the **slapcat** command and then reloading the same data into the new LDAP server using the **slapadd** command. Do not forget to install and configure the **nss_ldap** tool and the /etc/nsswitch.conf (as shown in Chapter 5, "Making Happy Users").

- Copy the smb.conf file from the old server to the new server into the correct location as indicated previously in this chapter.

- Copy the secrets.tdb file, the smbpasswd file (if it is used), the /etc/samba/passdb. tdb file (only used by the tdbsam backend), and all the tdb control files from the old system to the correct location on the new system.

- Before starting the Samba daemons, verify that the hostname of the new server is identical to that of the old one. Note: The IP address can be different from that of the old server.

- Copy all files from the old server to the new server, taking precaution to preserve all file ownership and permissions as well as any POSIX ACLs that may have been created on the old server.

When replacing a Samba domain controller (PDC or BDC) that uses LDAP, the new server need simply be configured to use the LDAP directory, and for the rest it should just work.

The domain SID is obtained from the LDAP directory as part of the first connect to the LDAP directory server.

All Samba servers, other than one that uses LDAP, depend on the tdb files, and particularly on the `secrets.tdb` file. So long as the tdb files are all in place, the `smb.conf` file is preserved, and either the hostname is identical or the *netbios name* is set to the original server name, Samba should correctly pick up the original SID and preserve all other settings. It is sound advice to validate this before turning the system over to users.

8.3.3   Migration of Samba Accounts to Active Directory

Yes, it works. The Windows ADMT tool can be used to migrate Samba accounts to MS Active Directory. There are a few pitfalls to be aware of:

MIGRATION TO ACTIVE DIRECTORY

1. Administrator password must be THE SAME on the Samba server, the 2003 ADS, and the local Administrator account on the workstations. Perhaps this goes without saying, but there needs to be an account called `Administrator` in your Samba domain, with full administrative (root) rights to that domain.

2. In the Advanced/DNS section of the TCP/IP settings on your Windows workstations, make sure the *DNS suffix for this connection* field is blank.

3. Because you are migrating from Samba, user passwords cannot be migrated. You'll have to reset everyone's passwords. (If you were migrating from NT4 to ADS, you could migrate passwords as well.) To date this has not been attempted with roaming profile support; it has been documented as working with local profiles.

4. Disable the Windows Firewall on all workstations. Otherwise, workstations won't be migrated to the new domain.

5. When migrating machines, always test first (using ADMT's test mode) and satisfy all errors before committing the migration. Note that the test will always fail, because the machine will not have been actually migrated. You'll need to interpret the errors to know whether the failure was due to a problem or simply to the fact that it was just a test.

There are some significant benefits of using the ADMT, besides just migrating user accounts. ADMT can be found on the Windows 2003 CD.

- You can migrate workstations remotely. You can specify that SIDs be simply added instead of replaced, giving you the option of joining a workstation back to the old domain if something goes awry. The workstations will be joined to the new domain.

- Not only are user accounts migrated from the old domain to the new domain, but ACLs on the workstations are migrated as well. Like SIDs, ACLs can be added instead of replaced.

- Locally stored user profiles on workstations are migrated as well, presenting almost no disruption to the user. Saved passwords will be lost, just as when you administratively reset the password in Windows ADS.

- The ADMT lets you test all operations before actually performing the migration. Accounts and workstations can be migrated individually or in batches. User accounts can be safely migrated all at once (since no changes are made on the original domain). It is recommended to migrate only one or two workstations as a test before committing them all.

Chapter 9

MIGRATING NT4 DOMAIN TO SAMBA-3

Ever since Microsoft announced that it was discontinuing support for Windows NT4, Samba users started to ask for detailed instructions on how to migrate from NT4 to Samba-3. This chapter provides background information that should meet these needs.

One wonders how many NT4 systems will be left in service by the time you read this book though.

9.1 Introduction

Network administrators who want to migrate off a Windows NT4 environment know one thing with certainty. They feel that NT4 has been abandoned, and they want to update. The desire to get off NT4 and to not adopt Windows 200x and Active Directory is driven by a mixture of concerns over complexity, cost, fear of failure, and much more.

The migration from NT4 to Samba-3 can involve a number of factors, including migration of data to another server, migration of network environment controls such as group policies, and migration of the users, groups, and machine accounts.

It should be pointed out now that it is possible to migrate some systems from a Windows NT4 domain environment to a Samba-3 domain environment. This is certainly not possible in every case. It is possible to just migrate the domain accounts to Samba-3 and then to switch machines, but as a hands-off transition, this is more the exception than the rule. Most systems require some tweaking after migration before an environment that is acceptable for immediate use is obtained.

9.1.1 Assignment Tasks

You are about to migrate an MS Windows NT4 domain accounts database to a Samba-3 server. The Samba-3 server is using a *passdb backend* based on LDAP. The ldapsam is ideal because an LDAP backend can be distributed for use with BDCs — generally essential for larger networks.

Your objective is to document the process of migrating user and group accounts from several NT4 domains into a single Samba-3 LDAP backend database.

9.2 Dissection and Discussion

The migration process takes a snapshot of information that is stored in the Windows NT4 registry-based accounts database. That information resides in the Security Account Manager (SAM) portion of the NT4 registry under keys called `SAM` and `SECURITY`.

WARNING

The Windows NT4 registry keys called `SAM` and `SECURITY` are protected so that you cannot view the contents. If you change the security setting to reveal the contents under these hive keys, your Windows NT4 domain is crippled. Do not do this unless you are willing to render your domain controller inoperative.

Before commencing an NT4 to Samba-3 migration, you should consider what your objectives are. While in some cases it is possible simply to migrate an NT4 domain to a single Samba-3 server, that may not be a good idea from an administration perspective. Since the process involves going through a certain amount of disruptive activity anyhow, why not take this opportunity to review the structure of the network, how Windows clients are controlled and how they interact with the network environment.

MS Windows NT4 was introduced some time around 1996. Many environments in which NT4 was deployed have done little to keep the NT4 server environment up to date with more recent Windows releases, particularly Windows XP Professional. The migration provides opportunity to revise and update roaming profile deployment as well as folder redirection. Given that you must port the greater network configuration of this from the old NT4 server to the new Samba-3 server. Do not forget to validate the security descriptors in the profiles share as well as network logon scripts. Feedback from sites that are migrating to Samba-3 suggests that many are using this as a good time to update desktop systems also. In all, the extra effort should constitute no real disruption to users, but rather, with due diligence and care, should make their network experience a much happier one.

9.2.1 Technical Issues

Migration of an NT4 domain user and group database to Samba-3 involves a certain strategic element. Many sites have asked for instructions regarding merging of multiple NT4 domains into one Samba-3 LDAP database. It seems that this is viewed as a significant added value compared with the alternative of migration to Windows Server 200x and Active Directory.

The diagram in Figure 9.1 illustrates the effect of migration from a Windows NT4 domain to a Samba domain.

Figure 9.1 Schematic Explaining the net rpc vampire Process

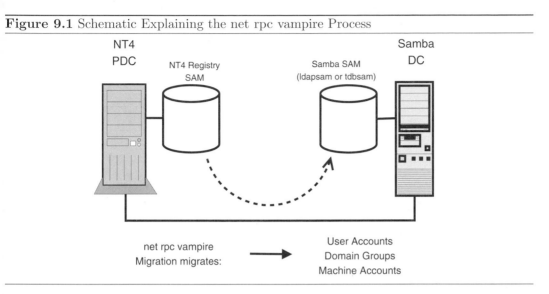

If you want to merge multiple NT4 domain account databases into one Samba domain, you must now dump the contents of the first migration and edit it as appropriate. Now clean out (remove) the tdbsam backend file (**passdb.tdb**) or the LDAP database files. You must start each migration with a new database into which you merge your NT4 domains.

At this point, you are ready to perform the second migration, following the same steps as for the first. In other words, dump the database, edit it, and then you may merge the dump for the first and second migrations.

You must be careful. If you choose to migrate to an LDAP backend, your dump file now contains the full account information, including the domain SID. The domain SID for each of the two NT4 domains will be different. You must choose one and change the domain portion of the account SIDs so that all are the same.

If you choose to use a tdbsam (**passdb.tdb**) backend file, your best choice is to use **pdbedit** to export the contents of the tdbsam file into an smbpasswd data file. This automatically strips out all domain-specific information, such as logon hours, logon machines, logon script, profile path, as well as the domain SID. The resulting file can be easily merged with other migration attempts (each of which must start with a clean file). It should also be noted that all users who end up in the merged smbpasswd file must have an account in **/etc/passwd**. The resulting smbpasswd file may be exported or imported into either a tdbsam (**passdb. tdb**) or an LDAP backend.

9.2.2   Political Issues

The merging of multiple Windows NT4-style domains into a single LDAP-backend-based Samba-3 domain may be seen by those who had power over them as a loss of prestige or

Figure 9.2 View of Accounts in NT4 Domain User Manager

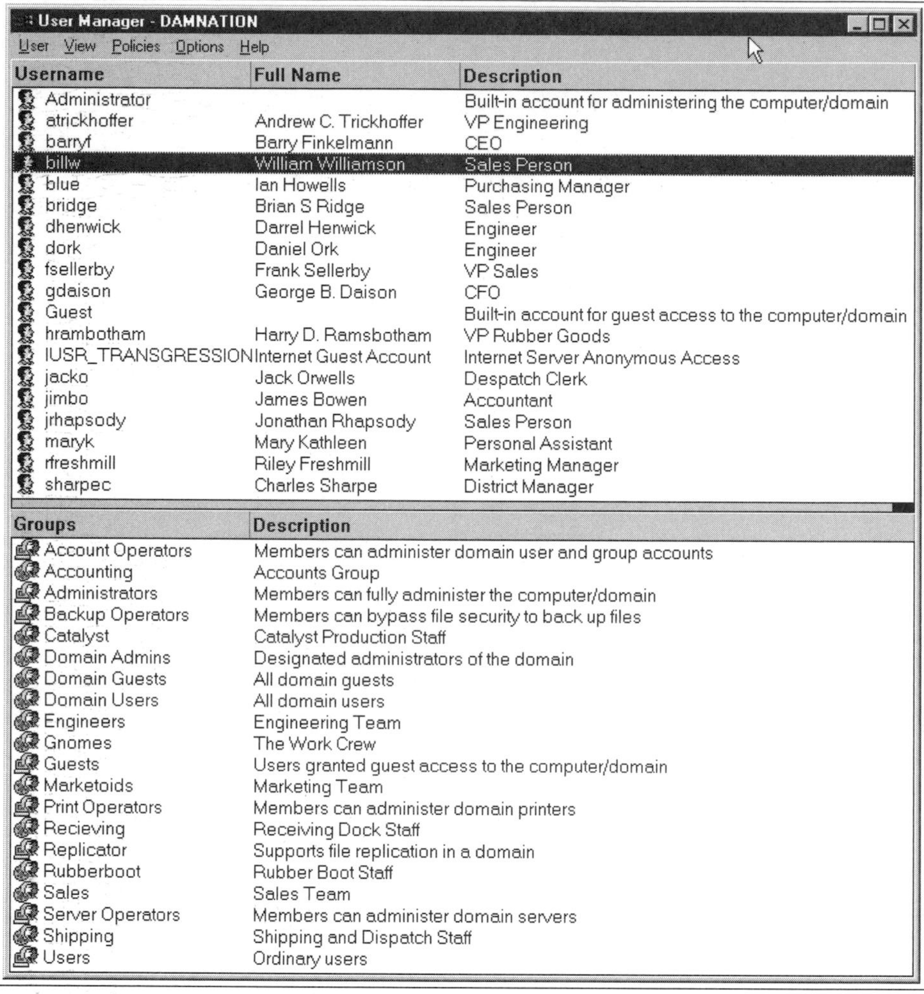

a loss of power. The imposition of a single domain may even be seen as a threat. So in migrating and merging account databases, be consciously aware of the political fall-out in which you may find yourself entangled when key staff feel a loss of prestige.

The best advice that can be given to those who set out to merge NT4 domains into a single Samba-3 domain is to promote (sell) the action as one that reduces costs and delivers greater network interoperability and manageability.

9.3   Implementation

From feedback on the Samba mailing lists, it seems that most Windows NT4 migrations to Samba-3 are being performed using a new server or a new installation of a Linux or UNIX server. If you contemplate doing this, please note that the steps that follow in this chapter assume familiarity with the information that has been previously covered in this book. You are particularly encouraged to be familiar with Chapter 3, "Secure Office Networking", Chapter 4, "The 500-User Office" and Chapter 5, "Making Happy Users".

We present here the steps and example output for two NT4 to Samba-3 domain migrations. The first uses an LDAP-based backend, and the second uses a tdbsam backend. In each case the scripts you specify in the `smb.conf` file for the *add user script* collection of parameters are used to effect the addition of accounts into the passdb backend.

Before proceeding to NT4 migration using either a tdbsam or ldapsam, it is most strongly recommended to review Section 4.3.1 for DNS and DHCP configuration. The importance of correctly functioning name resolution must be recognized. This applies equally for both hostname and NetBIOS names (machine names, computer names, domain names, workgroup names — ALL names!).

The migration process involves the following steps:

- Prepare the target Samba-3 server. This involves configuring Samba-3 for migration to either a tdbsam or an ldapsam backend.

- Clean up the source NT4 PDC. Delete all accounts that need not be migrated. Delete all files that should not be migrated. Where possible, change NT group names so there are no spaces or uppercase characters. This is important if the target UNIX host insists on POSIX-compliant all lowercase user and group names.

- Step through the migration process.

- Remove the NT4 PDC from the network.

- Upgrade the Samba-3 server from a BDC to a PDC, and validate all account information.

It may help to use the above outline as a pre-migration checklist.

9.3.1   NT4 Migration Using LDAP Backend

In this example, the migration is of an NT4 PDC to a Samba-3 PDC with an LDAP backend. The accounts about to be migrated are shown in Figure 9.2. In this example use is made of the smbldap-tools scripts to add the accounts that are migrated into the ldapsam passdb backend. Four scripts are essential to the migration process. Other scripts will be required for daily management, but these are not critical to migration. The critical scripts are dependant on which passdb backend is being used. Refer to Table 9.1 to see which scripts must be provided so that the migration process can complete.

Verify that you have correctly specified in the `smb.conf` file the scripts and arguments that should be passed to them before attempting to perform the account migration. Note also that the deletion scripts must be commented out during migration. These should be uncommented following successful migration of the NT4 Domain accounts.

WARNING

Under absolutely no circumstances should the Samba daemons be started until instructed to do so. Delete the /etc/samba/secrets. tdb file and all Samba control tdb files before commencing the following configuration steps.

Table 9.1 Samba smb.conf Scripts Essential to Samba Operation

Entity	ldapsam Script	tdbsam Script
Add User Accounts	smbldap-useradd	useradd
Delete User Accounts	smbldap-userdel	userdel
Add Group Accounts	smbldap-groupadd	groupadd
Delete Group Accounts	smbldap-groupdel	groupdel
Add User to Group	smbldap-groupmod	usermod (See Note)
Add Machine Accounts	smbldap-useradd	useradd

NOTE

The UNIX/Linux **usermod** utility does not permit simple user addition to (or deletion of users from) groups. This is a feature provided by the smbldap-tools scripts. If you want this capability, you must create your own tool to do this. Alternately, you can search the Web to locate a utility called **groupmem** (by George Kraft) that provides this functionality. The **groupmem** utility was contributed to the shadow package but has not surfaced in the formal commands provided by Linux distributions (March 2004).

NOTE

The **tdbdump** utility is a utility that you can build from the Samba source-code tree. Not all Linux binary distributions include this tool. If it is missing from your Linux distribution, you will need to build this yourself or else forgo its use.

Before starting the migration, all dead accounts were removed from the NT4 domain using the User Manager for Domains.

USER MIGRATION STEPS

1. Configure the Samba smb.conf file to create a BDC. An example configuration is given in Example 9.3.1. The delete scripts are commented out so that during the process of migration no account information can be deleted.

2. Configure OpenLDAP in preparation for the migration. An example sladp.conf file is shown in Example 9.3.3. The rootpw value is an encrypted password string that can be obtained by executing the **slappasswd** command.

3. Install the PADL **nss_ldap** tool set, then configure the /etc/ldap.conf as shown in Example 9.3.5.

4. Edit the /etc/nsswitch.conf file so it has the entries shown in Example 9.3.6. Note that the LDAP entries have been commented out. This is deliberate. If these entries are active (not commented out), and the /etc/ldap.conf file has been configured, when the LDAP server is started, the process of starting the LDAP server will cause LDAP lookups. This causes the LDAP server **slapd** to hang because it finds port 389 open and therefore cannot gain exclusive control of it. By commenting these entries out, it is possible to avoid this gridlock situation and thus the overall installation and configuration will progress more smoothly.

5. Validate the the target NT4 PDC name is being correctly resolved to its IP address by executing the following:

```
root#  ping transgression
PING transgression.terpstra-world.org (192.168.1.5) 56(84) bytes of data.
64 bytes from (192.168.1.5): icmp_seq=1 ttl=128 time=0.159 ms
64 bytes from (192.168.1.5): icmp_seq=2 ttl=128 time=0.192 ms
64 bytes from (192.168.1.5): icmp_seq=3 ttl=128 time=0.141 ms

--- transgression.terpstra-world.org ping statistics ---
3 packets transmitted, 3 received, 0% packet loss, time 2000ms
rtt min/avg/max/mdev = 0.141/0.164/0.192/0.021 ms
```

Do not proceed to the next step if this step fails. It is imperative that the name of the PDC can be resolved to its IP address. If this is broken, fix it.

6. Pull the domain SID from the NT4 domain that is being migrated as follows:

```
root#  net rpc getsid -S TRANGRESSION -U Administrator%not24get
Storing SID S-1-5-21-1385457007-882775198-1210191635 \
                    for Domain DAMNATION in secrets.tdb
```

Another way to obtain the domain SID from the target NT4 domain that is being migrated to Samba-3 is by executing the following:

```
root#  net rpc info -S TRANSGRESSION
```

If this method is used, do not forget to store the SID obtained into the `secrets.tdb` file. This can be done by executing:

```
root#  net setlocalsid S-1-5-21-1385457007-882775198-1210191635
```

7. Install the Idealx **smbldap-tools** software package, following the instructions given in Section 5.4.4. The resulting perl scripts should be located in the `/opt/IDEALX/sbin` directory. Change into that location, or wherever the scripts have been installed. Execute the `configure.pl` script to configure the Idealx package for use. Note: Use the domain SID obtained from the step above. The following is an example configuration session:

```
root#  ./configure.pl
-=-=-=-=-=-=-=-=-=-=-=-=-=-=-=-=-=-=-=-=-=-=-=-=-=-=-=-=-=-=-=-=-=
         smbldap-tools script configuration
         -=-=-=-=-=-=-=-=-=-=-=-=-=-=-=
Before starting, check
  . if your samba controller is up and running.
  . if the domain SID is defined
                           (you can get it with the 'net getlocalsid')

  . you can leave the configuration using the Crtl-c key combination
  . empty value can be set with the "." character
-=-=-=-=-=-=-=-=-=-=-=-=-=-=-=-=-=-=-=-=-=-=-=-=-=-=-=-=-=-=-=-=-=
Looking for configuration files...

Samba Config File Location [/etc/samba/smb.conf] >
smbldap Config file Location (global parameters)
            [/etc/smbldap-tools/smbldap.conf] >
smbldap Config file Location (bind parameters)
        [/etc/smbldap-tools/smbldap_bind.conf] >
-=-=-=-=-=-=-=-=-=-=-=-=-=-=-=-=-=-=-=-=-=-=-=-=-=-=-=-=-=-=-=-=-=
Let's start configuring the smbldap-tools scripts ...

  . workgroup name: name of the domain Samba act as a PDC
    workgroup name [DAMNATION] >
  . netbios name: netbios name of the samba controller
    netbios name [MERLIN] >
  . logon drive: local path to which the home directory
            will be connected (for NT Workstations). Ex: 'H:'
    logon drive [X:] > H:
  . logon home: home directory location (for Win95/98 or NT Workstation)
```

```
     (use %U as username) Ex:'\\MERLIN\home\%U'
     logon home (leave blank if you don't want homeDirectory)
                                        [\\MERLIN\home\%U] > \\%L\%U
 . logon path: directory where roaming profiles are stored.
                                        Ex:'\\MERLIN\profiles\%U'
     logon path (leave blank if you don't want roaming profile)
                              [\\MERLIN\profiles\%U] > \\%L\profiles\%U
 . home directory prefix (use %U as username) [/home/%U] >
                                                        /home/users/%U
 . default user netlogon script (use %U as username)
                              [%U.cmd] > scripts\logon.cmd
     default password validation time (time in days) [45] > 180
 . ldap suffix [dc=terpstra-world,dc=org] >
 . ldap group suffix [ou=Groups] >
 . ldap user suffix [ou=People] >
 . ldap machine suffix [ou=People] >
 . Idmap suffix [ou=Idmap] >
 . sambaUnixIdPooldn: object where you want to store the next uidNumber
     and gidNumber available for new users and groups
     sambaUnixIdPooldn object (relative to ${suffix})
                              [sambaDomainName=DAMNATION] >
 . ldap master server:
               IP address or DNS name of the master (writable) ldap server
     ldap master server [] > 127.0.0.1
 . ldap master port [389] >
 . ldap master bind dn [cn=Manager,dc=terpstra-world,dc=org] >
 . ldap master bind password [] >
 . ldap slave server: IP address or DNS name of the slave ldap server:
                                        can also be the master one
     ldap slave server [] > 127.0.0.1
 . ldap slave port [389] >
 . ldap slave bind dn [cn=Manager,dc=terpstra-world,dc=org] >
 . ldap slave bind password [] >
 . ldap tls support (1/0) [0] >
 . SID for domain DAMNATION: SID of the domain
                         (can be obtained with 'net getlocalsid MERLIN')
     SID for domain DAMNATION []
          > S-1-5-21-1385457007-882775198-1210191635
 . unix password encryption: encryption used for unix passwords
 unix password encryption (CRYPT, MD5, SMD5, SSHA, SHA) [SSHA] > MD5
 . default user gidNumber [513] >
 . default computer gidNumber [515] >
 . default login shell [/bin/bash] >
 . default domain name to append to mail address [] >
                                                  terpstra-world.org
 -=-=-=-=-=-=-=-=-=-=-=-=-=-=-=-=-=-=-=-=-=-=-=-=-=-=-=-=-=-=-=-=
 backup old configuration files:
```

```
/etc/smbldap-tools/smbldap.conf->
                            /etc/smbldap-tools/smbldap.conf.old
/etc/smbldap-tools/smbldap_bind.conf->
                            /etc/smbldap-tools/smbldap_bind.conf.old
writing new configuration file:
  /etc/smbldap-tools/smbldap.conf done.
  /etc/smbldap-tools/smbldap_bind.conf done.
```

Note that the NT4 domain SID that was previously obtained was entered above. Also, the sambaUnixIdPooldn object was specified as sambaDomainName=DAMNATION. This is the location into which the Idealx smbldap-tools store the next available UID/GID information. It is also where Samba stores domain specific information such as the next RID, the SID, and so on. In older version of the smbldap-tools this information was stored in the sambaUnixIdPooldn DIT location cn=NextFreeUnixId. Where smbldap-tools are being upgraded to version 0.9.1 it is appropriate to update this to the new location only if the directory information is also relocated.

8. Start the LDAP server using the system interface script. On Novell SLES9 this is done as shown here:

```
root#  rcldap start
```

9. Edit the /etc/nsswitch.conf file so it has the entries shown in Example 9.3.7. Note that the LDAP entries have now been uncommented.

10. The LDAP management password must be installed into the secrets.tdb file as follows:

```
root#  smbpasswd -w not24get
Setting stored password for
            "cn=Manager,dc=terpstra-world,dc=org" in secrets.tdb
```

11. Populate the LDAP directory as shown here:

```
root#  /opt/IDEALX/sbin/smbldap-populate -a root -k 0 -m 0
Using workgroup name from sambaUnixIdPooldn (smbldap.conf):
                        sambaDomainName=DAMNATION
Using builtin directory structure
adding new entry: dc=terpstra-world,dc=org
adding new entry: ou=People,dc=terpstra-world,dc=org
adding new entry: ou=Groups,dc=terpstra-world,dc=org
entry ou=People,dc=terpstra-world,dc=org already exist.
adding new entry: ou=Idmap,dc=terpstra-world,dc=org
adding new entry: sambaDomainName=DAMNATION,dc=terpstra-world,dc=org
adding new entry: uid=root,ou=People,dc=terpstra-world,dc=org
```

```
adding new entry: uid=nobody,ou=People,dc=terpstra-world,dc=org
adding new entry: cn=Domain Admins,ou=Groups,dc=terpstra-world,dc=org
adding new entry: cn=Domain Users,ou=Groups,dc=terpstra-world,dc=org
adding new entry: cn=Domain Guests,ou=Groups,dc=terpstra-world,dc=org
adding new entry: cn=Domain Computers,ou=Groups,dc=terpstra-world,dc=org
adding new entry: cn=Administrators,ou=Groups,dc=terpstra-world,dc=org
adding new entry: cn=Print Operators,ou=Groups,dc=terpstra-world,dc=org
adding new entry: cn=Backup Operators,ou=Groups,dc=terpstra-world,dc=org
adding new entry: cn=Replicators,ou=Groups,dc=terpstra-world,dc=org
```

The script tries to add the ou=People container twice, hence the error message. This is expected behavior.

12. Restart the LDAP server following initialization of the LDAP directory. Execute the system control script provided on your system. The following steps can be used on Novell SUSE SLES 9:

```
root#  rcldap restart
root#  chkconfig ldap on
```

13. Verify that the new user accounts that have been added to the LDAP directory can be resolved as follows:

```
root#  getent passwd
...
nobody:x:65534:65533:nobody:/var/lib/nobody:/bin/bash
man:x:13:62:Manual pages viewer:/var/cache/man:/bin/bash
news:x:9:13:News system:/etc/news:/bin/bash
uucp:x:10:14:Unix-to-Unix CoPy system:/etc/uucp:/bin/bash
+::0:0:::
root:x:0:0:Netbios Domain Administrator:/home/users/root:/bin/false
nobody:x:999:514:nobody:/dev/null:/bin/false
```

Now repeat this for the group accounts as shown here:

```
root#  getent group
...
nobody:x:65533:
nogroup:x:65534:nobody
users:x:100:
+::0:
Domain Admins:x:512:root
Domain Users:x:513:
Domain Guests:x:514:
```

```
Domain Computers:x:515:
Administrators:x:544:
Print Operators:x:550:
Backup Operators:x:551:
Replicators:x:552:
```

In both cases the LDAP accounts follow the "+::0:" entry.

14. Now it is time to join the Samba BDC to the target NT4 domain that is being migrated
    to Samba-3 by executing the following:

```
root#  net rpc join -S TRANSGRESSION -U Administrator%not24get
merlin:/opt/IDEALX/sbin # net rpc join -S TRANSGRESSION \
                         -U Administrator%not24get
Joined domain DAMNATION.
```

15. Set the new domain administrator (root) password for both UNIX and Windows as
    shown here:

```
root#  /opt/IDEALX/sbin/smbldap-passwd root
Changing password for root
New password : ********
Retype new password : ********
```

Note: During account migration, the Windows Administrator account will not be
migrated to the Samba server.

16. Now validate that these accounts can be resolved using Samba's tools as shown here
    for user accounts:

```
root#  pdbedit -Lw
root:0:84B0D8E14D158FF8417EAF50CFAC29C3:
        AF6DD3FD4E2EA8BDE1695A3F05EFBF52:[U          ]:LCT-425F6467:
nobody:65534:NO PASSWORDXXXXXXXXXXXXXXXXXXXXX:
        NO PASSWORDXXXXXXXXXXXXXXXXXXXXXX:[NU         ]:LCT-00000000:
```

Now complete the following step to validate that group account mappings have been
correctly set:

```
root#  net groupmap list
Domain Admins (S-1-5-21-1385457007-882775198-1210191635-512)
                                        -> Domain Admins
Domain Users (S-1-5-21-1385457007-882775198-1210191635-513)
                                        -> Domain Users
```

```
Domain Guests (S-1-5-21-1385457007-882775198-1210191635-514)
                                              -> Domain Guests
Domain Computers (S-1-5-21-1385457007-882775198-1210191635-515)
                                              -> Domain Computers
Administrators (S-1-5-32-544) -> Administrators
Print Operators (S-1-5-32-550) -> Print Operators
Backup Operators (S-1-5-32-551) -> Backup Operators
Replicators (S-1-5-32-552) -> Replicators
```

These are the expected results for a correctly configured system.

17. Commence migration as shown here:

```
root#  net rpc vampire -S TRANSGRESSION \
       -U Administrator%not24get > /tmp/vampire.log 2>1
```

Check the vampire log to confirm that only expected errors have been reported. See Section 9.3.1.1.

18. The migration of user accounts can be quickly validated as follows:

```
root#  pdbedit -Lw
root:0:84B0D8E14D158FF8417EAF50CFAC29C3:...
nobody:65534:NO PASSWORDXXXXXXXXXXXXXXXXXXXXX:...
Administrator:0:84B0D8E14D158FF8417EAF50CFAC29C3:...
Guest:1:XXXXXXXXXXXXXXXXXXXXXXXXXXXXXXXX:...
TRANSGRESSION$:2:CC044B748CEE294CE76B6B0D1B86C1A8:...
IUSR_TRANSGRESSION:3:64046AC81B056C375F9537FC409085F8:...
MIDEARTH$:4:E93186E5819706D2AAD3B435B51404EE:...
atrickhoffer:5:DC08CFE0C12B2867352502E32A407F23:...
barryf:6:B829BCDE01FF24376E45D5F10408CFBD:...
fsellerby:7:6A97CBEBE8F9826B417EAF50CFAC29C3:...
gdaison:8:48F6A8C8A900024351DA8C2061C5F1D3:...
hrambotham:9:7330D9EA0964465EAAD3B435B51404EE:...
jrhapsody:10:ACBA7D207E2BA35D9BD41A26B01626BD:...
maryk:11:293B5A4CA41F6CA1A7D80430B8342B73:...
jacko:12:8E8982D86BD037C364BBD09A598E07AD:...
bridge:13:0D2CA7D2BE67FE2193BE3A377C968336:...
sharpec:14:8841A75CAC19D2855D8B73B1F4D430F8:...
jimbo:15:6E8BDC904FD9EC5C17306D272A9441BB:...
dhenwick:16:D1694A03C33584BDAAD3B435B51404EE:...
dork:17:69E2D19E69A593D5AAD3B435B51404EE:...
blue:18:E355EBF9559979FEAAD3B435B51404EE:...
billw:19:EE35C3481CF7F7DB484448BC86A641A5:...
rfreshmill:20:7EC033B58661B60CAAD3B435B51404EE:...
MAGGOT$:21:A3B9334765AD30F7AAD3B435B51404EE:...
```

```
TRENTWARE$:22:1D92C8DD5E7F0DDF93BE3A377C968336:...
MORTON$:23:89342E69DCA9D3F8AAD3B435B51404EE:...
NARM$:24:2B93E2D1D25448BDAAD3B435B51404EE:...
LAPDOG$:25:14AA535885120943AAD3B435B51404EE:...
SCAVENGER$:26:B6288EB6D147B56F8963805A19B0ED49:...
merlin$:27:820C50523F368C54AB9D85AE603AD09D:...
```

19. The mapping of UNIX and Windows groups can be validated as show here:

```
root#  net groupmap list
Domain Admins (S-1-5-21-1385457007-882775198-1210191635-512)
                                          -> Domain Admins
Domain Users (S-1-5-21-1385457007-882775198-1210191635-513)
                                          -> Domain Users
Domain Guests (S-1-5-21-1385457007-882775198-1210191635-514)
                                          -> Domain Guests
Domain Computers (S-1-5-21-1385457007-882775198-1210191635-515)
                                          -> Domain Computers
Administrators (S-1-5-32-544) -> Administrators
Print Operators (S-1-5-32-550) -> Print Operators
Backup Operators (S-1-5-32-551) -> Backup Operators
Replicator (S-1-5-32-552) -> Replicators
Engineers (S-1-5-21-1385457007-882775198-1210191635-1020) -> Engineers
Marketoids (S-1-5-21-1385457007-882775198-1210191635-1022) -> Marketoids
Gnomes (S-1-5-21-1385457007-882775198-1210191635-1023) -> Gnomes
Catalyst (S-1-5-21-1385457007-882775198-1210191635-1024) -> Catalyst
Recieving (S-1-5-21-1385457007-882775198-1210191635-1025) -> Recieving
Rubberboot (S-1-5-21-1385457007-882775198-1210191635-1026) -> Rubberboot
Sales (S-1-5-21-1385457007-882775198-1210191635-1027) -> Sales
Accounting (S-1-5-21-1385457007-882775198-1210191635-1028) -> Accounting
Shipping (S-1-5-21-1385457007-882775198-1210191635-1029) -> Shipping
Account Operators (S-1-5-32-548) -> Account Operators
Guests (S-1-5-32-546) -> Guests
Server Operators (S-1-5-32-549) -> Server Operators
Users (S-1-5-32-545) -> Users
```

It is of vital importance that the domain SID portions of all group accounts are identical.

20. The final responsibility in the migration process is to create identical shares and printing resources on the new Samba-3 server, copy all data across, set up privileges, and set share and file/directory access controls.

21. Edit the **smb.conf** file to reset the parameter *domain master* = Yes so that the Samba server functions as a PDC for the purpose of migration. Also, uncomment the deletion scripts so they will now be fully functional, enable the *wins support = yes* parameter

and comment out the *wins server*. Validate the configuration with the **testparm**
utility as shown here:

```
root#  testparm
Load smb config files from /etc/samba/smb.conf
Processing section "[apps]"
Processing section "[media]"
Processing section "[homes]"
Processing section "[printers]"
Processing section "[netlogon]"
Processing section "[profiles]"
Processing section "[profdata]"
Processing section "[print$]"
Loaded services file OK.
Server role: ROLE_DOMAIN_PDC
Press enter to see a dump of your service definitions
```

22. Now shut down the old NT4 PDC. Only when the old NT4 PDC and all NT4 BDCs
    have been shut down can the Samba-3 PDC be started.

23. All workstations should function as they did with the old NT4 PDC. All interdomain
    trust accounts should remain in place and fully functional. All machine accounts and
    user logon accounts should also function correctly.

24. The configuration of Samba-3 BDC servers can be accomplished now or at any con-
    venient time in the future. Please refer to the carefully detailed process for doing so
    is outlined in Section 5.5.

9.3.1.1 Migration Log Validation

The following `vampire.log` file is typical of a valid migration.

```
adding user Administrator to group Domain Admins
adding user atrickhoffer to group Engineers
adding user dhenwick to group Engineers
adding user dork to group Engineers
adding user rfreshmill to group Marketoids
adding user jacko to group Gnomes
adding user jimbo to group Gnomes
adding user maryk to group Gnomes
adding user gdaison to group Gnomes
adding user dhenwick to group Catalyst
adding user jacko to group Catalyst
adding user jacko to group Recieving
adding user blue to group Recieving
adding user hrambotham to group Rubberboot
```

```
adding user billw to group Sales
adding user bridge to group Sales
adding user jrhapsody to group Sales
adding user maryk to group Sales
adding user rfreshmill to group Sales
adding user fsellerby to group Sales
adding user sharpec to group Sales
adding user jimbo to group Accounting
adding user gdaison to group Accounting
adding user jacko to group Shipping
adding user blue to group Shipping
Fetching DOMAIN database
Creating unix group: 'Engineers'
Creating unix group: 'Marketoids'
Creating unix group: 'Gnomes'
Creating unix group: 'Catalyst'
Creating unix group: 'Recieving'
Creating unix group: 'Rubberboot'
Creating unix group: 'Sales'
Creating unix group: 'Accounting'
Creating unix group: 'Shipping'
Creating account: Administrator
Creating account: Guest
Creating account: TRANSGRESSION$
Creating account: IUSR_TRANSGRESSION
Creating account: MIDEARTH$
Creating account: atrickhoffer
Creating account: barryf
Creating account: fsellerby
Creating account: gdaison
Creating account: hrambotham
Creating account: jrhapsody
Creating account: maryk
Creating account: jacko
Creating account: bridge
Creating account: sharpec
Creating account: jimbo
Creating account: dhenwick
Creating account: dork
Creating account: blue
Creating account: billw
Creating account: rfreshmill
Creating account: MAGGOT$
Creating account: TRENTWARE$
Creating account: MORTON$
Creating account: NARM$
Creating account: LAPDOG$
```

```
Creating account: SCAVENGER$
Creating account: merlin$
Group members of Domain Admins: Administrator,
Group members of Domain Users: Administrator(primary),
TRANSGRESSION$(primary),IUSR_TRANSGRESSION(primary),
MIDEARTH$(primary),atrickhoffer(primary),barryf(primary),
fsellerby(primary),gdaison(primary),hrambotham(primary),
jrhapsody(primary),maryk(primary),jacko(primary),bridge(primary),
sharpec(primary),jimbo(primary),dhenwick(primary),dork(primary),
blue(primary),billw(primary),rfreshmill(primary),MAGGOT$(primary),
TRENTWARE$(primary),MORTON$(primary),NARM$(primary),
LAPDOG$(primary),SCAVENGER$(primary),merlin$(primary),
Group members of Domain Guests: Guest(primary),
Group members of Engineers: atrickhoffer,dhenwick,dork,
Group members of Marketoids: rfreshmill,
Group members of Gnomes: jacko,jimbo,maryk,gdaison,
Group members of Catalyst: dhenwick,jacko,
Group members of Recieving: jacko,blue,
Group members of Rubberboot: hrambotham,
Group members of Sales: billw,bridge,jrhapsody,maryk,
rfreshmill,fsellerby,sharpec,
Group members of Accounting: jimbo,gdaison,
Group members of Shipping: jacko,blue,
Fetching BUILTIN database
skipping SAM_DOMAIN_INFO delta for 'Builtin' (is not my domain)
Creating unix group: 'Account Operators'
Creating unix group: 'Guests'
Creating unix group: 'Server Operators'
Creating unix group: 'Users'
```

9.3.2   NT4 Migration Using tdbsam Backend

In this example, we change the domain name of the NT4 server from DRUGPREP to MEGANET prior to the use of the vampire (migration) tool. This migration process makes use of Linux system tools (like **useradd**) to add the accounts that are migrated into the UNIX/Linux /etc/passwd and /etc/group databases. These entries must therefore be present, and correct options specified, in your smb.conf file, or else the migration does not work as it should.

MIGRATION STEPS USING TDBSAM

1. Prepare a Samba-3 server precisely per the instructions shown in Chapter 4, "The 500-User Office". Set the workgroup name to MEGANET.

2. Edit the smb.conf file to temporarily change the parameter *domain master* = No so the Samba server functions as a BDC for the purpose of migration.

3. Start Samba as you have done previously.

4. Join the NT4 Domain as a BDC, as shown here:

```
root#  net rpc join -S oldnt4pdc -W MEGANET -UAdministrator%not24get
Joined domain MEGANET.
```

5. You may vampire the accounts from the NT4 PDC by executing the command, as shown here:

```
root#  net rpc vampire -S oldnt4pdc -U Administrator%not24get
Fetching DOMAIN database
SAM_DELTA_DOMAIN_INFO not handled
Creating unix group: 'Domain Admins'
Creating unix group: 'Domain Users'
Creating unix group: 'Domain Guests'
Creating unix group: 'Engineers'
Creating unix group: 'Marketoids'
Creating unix group: 'Account Operators'
Creating unix group: 'Administrators'
Creating unix group: 'Backup Operators'
Creating unix group: 'Guests'
Creating unix group: 'Print Operators'
Creating unix group: 'Replicator'
Creating unix group: 'Server Operators'
Creating unix group: 'Users'
Creating account: Administrator
Creating account: Guest
Creating account: oldnt4pdc$
Creating account: jacko
Creating account: maryk
Creating account: bridge
Creating account: sharpec
Creating account: jimbo
Creating account: dhenwick
Creating account: dork
Creating account: blue
Creating account: billw
Creating account: massive$
Group members of Engineers: Administrator,
                sharpec(primary),bridge,billw(primary),dhenwick
Group members of Marketoids: Administrator,jacko(primary),
                maryk(primary),jimbo,blue(primary),dork(primary)
Creating unix group: 'Gnomes'
Fetching BUILTIN database
```

```
SAM_DELTA_DOMAIN_INFO not handled
```

6. At this point, we can validate our migration. Let's look at the accounts in the form
   in which they are seen in a smbpasswd file. This achieves that:

```
root#  pdbedit -Lw
Administrator:505:84B0D8E14D158FF8417EAF50CFAC29C3:
        AF6DD3FD4E2EA8BDE1695A3F05EFBF52:[UX         ]:LCT-3DF7AA9F:
jimbo:512:6E9A2A51F64A1BD5C187B8085FE1D9DF:
        CDF7E305E639966E489A0CEFB95EE5E0:[UX         ]:LCT-3E9362BC:
sharpec:511:E4301A7CD8FDD1EC6BBF9BC19CDF8151:
        7000255938831D5B948C95C1931534C5:[UX         ]:LCT-3E8B42C4:
dhenwick:513:DCD8886141E3F892AAD3B435B51404EE:
        2DB36465949CB938DD98C312EFDC2639:[UX         ]:LCT-3E939F41:
bridge:510:3FE6873A43101B46417EAF50CFAC29C3:
        891741F481AF111B4CAA09A94016BD01:[UX         ]:LCT-3E8B4291:
blue:515:256D41D2559BB3D2AAD3B435B51404EE:
        9CCADDA4F7D281DD0FAD321478C6F971:[UX         ]:LCT-3E939FDC:
diamond$:517:6C8E7B64EDCDBC4218B6345447A4454B:
        3323AC63C666CFAACB60C13F65D54E9A:[S          ]:LCT-00000000:
oldnt4pdc$:507:3E39430CDCABB5B09ED320D0448AE568:
        95DBAF885854A919C7C7E671060478B9:[S          ]:LCT-3DF7AA9F:
Guest:506:XXXXXXXXXXXXXXXXXXXXXXXXXXXXXXXX:
        XXXXXXXXXXXXXXXXXXXXXXXXXXXXXXXX:[DUX        ]:LCT-3E93A008:
billw:516:85380CA7C21B6EBE168C8150662AF11B:
        5D7478508293709937E55FB5FBA14C17:[UX         ]:LCT-3FED7CA1:
dork:514:78C70DDEC35A35B5AAD3B435B51404EE:
        0AD886E015AC595EC0AF40E6C9689E1A:[UX         ]:LCT-3E939F9A:
jacko:508:BC472F3BF9A0A5F63832C92FC614B7D1:
        0C6822AAF85E86600A40DC73E40D06D5:[UX         ]:LCT-3E8B4242:
maryk:509:3636AB7E12EBE79AB79AE2610DD89D4C:
        CF271B744F7A55AFDA277FF88D80C527:[UX         ]:LCT-3E8B4270:
```

7. An expanded view of a user account entry shows more of what was obtained from the
   NT4 PDC:

```
sleeth:~ # pdbedit -Lv maryk
Unix username:          maryk
NT username:            maryk
Account Flags:          [UX        ]
User SID:               S-1-5-21-1988699175-926296742-1295600288-1003
Primary Group SID:      S-1-5-21-1988699175-926296742-1295600288-1007
Full Name:              Mary Kathleen
Home Directory:         \\diamond\maryk
HomeDir Drive:          X:
```

```
Logon Script:            scripts\logon.bat
Profile Path:            \\diamond\profiles\maryk
Domain:                  MEGANET
Account desc:            Peace Maker
Workstations:
Munged dial:
Logon time:              0
Logoff time:             Mon, 18 Jan 2038 20:14:07 GMT
Kickoff time:            Mon, 18 Jan 2038 20:14:07 GMT
Password last set:       Wed, 02 Apr 2003 13:05:04 GMT
Password can change:     0
Password must change:    Mon, 18 Jan 2038 20:14:07 GMT
```

8. The following command lists the long names of the groups that have been imported (vampired) from the NT4 PDC:

```
root#  net group -l -Uroot%not24get -Smassive

Group name              Comment
-----------------------------
Engineers               Snake Oil Engineers
Marketoids              Untrustworthy Hype Vendors
Gnomes                  Plain Vanilla Garden Gnomes
Replicator              Supports file replication in a domain
Guests                  Users granted guest access to the computer/domain
Administrators          Members can fully administer the computer/domain
Users                   Ordinary users
```

Everything looks well and in order.

9. Edit the `smb.conf` file to reset the parameter *domain master* = Yes so the Samba server functions as a PDC for the purpose of migration.

9.3.3   Key Points Learned

Migration of an NT4 PDC database to a Samba-3 PDC is possible.

- An LDAP backend is a suitable vehicle for NT4 migrations.

- A tdbsam backend can be used to perform a migration.

- Multiple NT4 domains can be merged into a single Samba-3 domain.

- The net Samba-3 domain most likely requires some administration and updating before going live.

9.4 Questions and Answers

F.A.Q.

1. **Q:** *Why must I start each migration with a clean database?*
A: This is a recommendation that permits the data from each NT4 domain to be kept separate until you are ready to merge them. Also, if you do not start with a clean database, you may find errors due to users or groups from multiple domains having the same name but different SIDs. It is better to permit each migration to complete without undue errors and then to handle the merging of vampired data under proper supervision.

2. **Q:** *Is it possible to set my domain SID to anything I like?*
A: Yes, so long as the SID you create has the same structure as an autogenerated SID. The typical SID looks like this: S-1-5-21-XXXXXXXXXX-XXXXXXXXXX-XXXXXXXXXX, where the XXXXXXXXXX can be any number with from 6 to 10 digits. On the other hand, why would you really want to create your own SID? I cannot think of a good reason. You may want to set the SID to one that is already in use somewhere on your network, but that is a little different from straight out creating your own domain SID.

3. **Q:** *When using a tdbsam passdb backend, why must I have all domain user and group accounts in /etc/passwd and /etc/group?*
A: Samba-3 must be able to tie all user and group account SIDs to a UNIX UID or GID. Samba does not fabricate the UNIX IDs from thin air, but rather requires them to be located in a suitable place.

When migrating a `smbpasswd` file to an LDAP backend, the UID of each account is taken together with the account information in the `/etc/passwd`, and both sets of data are used to create the account entry in the LDAP database.

If you elect to create the POSIX account also, the entire UNIX account is copied to the LDAP backend. The same occurs with NT groups and UNIX groups. At the conclusion of migration to the LDAP database, the accounts may be removed from the UNIX database files. In short then, all UNIX and Windows networking accounts, both in tdbsam as well as in LDAP, require UIDs/GIDs.

4. **Q:** *Why did you validate connectivity before attempting migration?*
A: Access validation before attempting to migrate NT4 domain accounts helps to pinpoint potential problems that may otherwise affect or impede account migration. I am always mindful of the 4 P's of migration: Planning Prevents Poor Performance.

5. **Q:** *How would you merge 10 tdbsam-based domains into an LDAP database?*
A: If you have 10 tdbsam Samba domains, there is considerable risk that there are a

number of accounts that have the same UNIX identifier (UID/GID). This means that you almost certainly have to edit a lot of data. It would be easiest to dump each database in smbpasswd file format and then manually edit all records to ensure that each has a unique UID. Each file can then be imported a number of ways. You can use the **pdbedit** tool to affect a transfer from the smbpasswd file to LDAP, or you can migrate them en masse to tdbsam and then to LDAP. The final choice is yours. Just remember to verify all accounts that you have migrated before handing over access to a user. After all, too many users with a bad migration experience may threaten your career.

6. **Q:** *I want to change my domain name after I migrate all accounts from an NT4 domain to a Samba-3 domain. Does it make any sense to migrate the machine accounts in that case?*

A: I would recommend not to migrate the machine account. The machine accounts should still work, but there are registry entries on each Windows NT4 and upward client that have a tattoo of the old domain name. If you unjoin the domain and then rejoin the newly renamed Samba-3 domain, you can be certain to avoid this tattooing effect.

7. **Q:** *After merging multiple NT4 domains into a Samba-3 domain, I lost all multiple group mappings. Why?*

A: Samba-3 currently does not implement multiple group membership internally. If you use the Windows NT4 Domain User Manager to manage accounts and you have an LDAP backend, the multiple group membership is stored in the POSIX groups area. If you use either tdbsam or smbpasswd backend, then multiple group membership is handled through the UNIX groups file. When you dump the user accounts, no group account information is provided. When you edit (change) UIDs and GIDs in each file to which you migrated the NT4 Domain data, do not forget to edit the UNIX /etc/passwd and /etc/group information also. That is where the multiple group information is most closely at your fingertips.

8. **Q:** *How can I reset group membership after loading the account information into the LDAP database?*

A: You can use the NT4 Domain User Manager that can be downloaded from the Microsoft Web site. The installation file is called SRVTOOLS.EXE.

9. **Q:** *What are the limits or constraints that apply to group names?*

A: A Windows 200x group name can be up to 254 characters long, while in Windows NT4 the group name is limited to 20 characters. Most UNIX systems limit this to 32 characters. Windows groups can contain upper- and lowercase characters, as well as spaces. Many UNIX system do not permit the use of uppercase characters, and some do not permit the space character either. A number of systems (i.e., Linux) work fine with both uppercase and space characters in group names, but the shadow-utils package that provides the group control functions (**groupadd**, **groupmod**, **groupdel**, and so on) do not permit them. Also, a number of UNIX systems management tools enforce their own particular interpretation of the POSIX standards and likewise do not permit uppercase or space characters in group or user account names. You have to experiment with your system to find what its peculiarities are.

10. **Q:** *My Windows NT4 PDC has 323,000 user accounts. How long will it take to migrate them to a Samba-3 LDAP backend system using the vampire process?*

A: UNIX UIDs and GIDs on most UNIX systems use an unsigned short or an unsigned integer. Recent Linux kernels support at least a much larger number. On systems that have a 16-bit constraint on UID/GIDs, you would not be able to migrate 323,000 accounts because this number cannot fit into a 16-bit unsigned integer. UNIX/Linux systems that have a 32-bit UID/GID can easily handle this number of accounts. Please check this carefully before you attempt to effect a migration using the vampire process.

Migration speed depends much on the processor speed, the network speed, disk I/O capability, and LDAP update overheads. On a dual processor AMD MP1600+ with 1 GB memory that was mirroring LDAP to a second identical system over 1 Gb Ethernet, I was able to migrate around 180 user accounts per minute. Migration would obviously go much faster if LDAP mirroring were turned off during the migration.

Example 9.3.1 NT4 Migration Samba-3 Server smb.conf — Part: A

```
[global]
        workgroup = DAMNATION
        netbios name = MERLIN
        passdb backend = ldapsam:ldap://localhost
        log level = 1
        syslog = 0
        log file = /var/log/samba/%m
        max log size = 0
        smb ports = 139 445
        name resolve order = wins bcast hosts
        add user script = /opt/IDEALX/sbin/smbldap−useradd −m '%u'
        #delete user script = /opt/IDEALX/sbin/smbldap−userdel '%u'
        add group script = /opt/IDEALX/sbin/smbldap−groupadd '%g'
        #delete group script = /opt/IDEALX/sbin/smbldap−groupdel '%g ↩
        '
        add user to group script = /opt/IDEALX/sbin/ smbldap− ↩
        groupmod −m '%u' '%g'
        #delete user from group script = /opt/IDEALX/sbin/smbldap− ↩
        groupmod −x '%u' '%g'
        set primary group script = /opt/IDEALX/sbin/smbldap−usermod ↩
        −g '%g' '%u'
        add machine script = /opt/IDEALX/sbin/smbldap−useradd −w '%u ↩
        '
        logon script = scripts\logon.cmd
        logon path = \\%L\profiles\%U
        logon home = \\%L\%U
        logon drive = X:
        domain logons = Yes
        domain master = No
        #wins support = Yes
        wins server = 192.168.123.124
        ldap admin dn = cn=Manager,dc=terpstra−world,dc=org
        ldap group suffix = ou=Groups
        ldap idmap suffix = ou=Idmap
        ldap machine suffix = ou=People
        ldap passwd sync = Yes
        ldap suffix = dc=terpstra−world,dc=org
        ldap ssl = no
        ldap timeout = 20
        ldap user suffix = ou=People
        idmap backend = ldap:ldap://localhost
        idmap uid = 15000−20000
        idmap gid = 15000−20000
        winbind nested groups = Yes
        ea support = Yes
        map acl inherit = Yes
```

Example 9.3.2 NT4 Migration Samba-3 Server smb.conf — Part: B

```
[apps]
        comment = Application Data
        path = /data/home/apps
        read only = No
[homes]
        comment = Home Directories
        path = /home/users/%U/Documents
        valid users = %S
        read only = No
        browseable = No
[printers]
        comment = SMB Print Spool
        path = /var/spool/samba
        guest ok = Yes
        printable = Yes
        use client driver = No
        browseable = No
[netlogon]
        comment = Network Logon Service
        path = /var/lib/samba/netlogon
        guest ok = Yes
        locking = No
[profiles]
        comment = Profile Share
        path = /var/lib/samba/profiles
        read only = No
        profile acls = Yes
[profdata]
        comment = Profile Data Share
        path = /var/lib/samba/profdata
        read only = No
        profile acls = Yes
[print$]
        comment = Printer Drivers
        path = /var/lib/samba/drivers
```

Example 9.3.3 NT4 Migration LDAP Server Configuration File: /etc/openldap/slapd. conf — Part A

```
include          /etc/openldap/schema/core.schema
include          /etc/openldap/schema/cosine.schema
include          /etc/openldap/schema/inetorgperson.schema
include          /etc/openldap/schema/nis.schema
include          /etc/openldap/schema/samba3.schema

pidfile          /var/run/slapd/slapd.pid
argsfile         /var/run/slapd/slapd.args

access to dn.base=""
                 by self write
                 by * auth

access to attr=userPassword
                 by self write
                 by * auth

access to attr=shadowLastChange
                 by self write
                 by * read

access to *
                 by * read
                 by anonymous auth
```

Example 9.3.4 NT4 Migration LDAP Server Configuration File: /etc/openldap/slapd.
conf — Part B

```
#loglevel        256

#schemacheck     on
idletimeout      30
#backend          bdb
database         bdb
checkpoint       1024 5
cachesize        10000

suffix           "dc=terpstra-world,dc=org"
rootdn           "cn=Manager,dc=terpstra-world,dc=org"

# rootpw = not24get
rootpw           {SSHA}86kTavd9Dw3FAz6qzWTrCOKX/c0Qe+UV

directory        /var/lib/ldap

# Indices to maintain
index objectClass            eq
index cn                     pres,sub,eq
index sn                     pres,sub,eq
index uid                    pres,sub,eq
index displayName            pres,sub,eq
index uidNumber              eq
index gidNumber              eq
index memberUID              eq
index sambaSID               eq
index sambaPrimaryGroupSID   eq
index sambaDomainName        eq
index default                sub
```

Example 9.3.5 NT4 Migration NSS LDAP File: /etc/ldap.conf

```
host     127.0.0.1

base     dc=terpstra-world,dc=org

ldap_version     3

binddn cn=Manager,dc=terpstra-world,dc=org
bindpw not24get

pam_password exop

nss_base_passwd          ou=People,dc=terpstra-world,dc=org?one
nss_base_shadow          ou=People,dc=terpstra-world,dc=org?one
nss_base_group           ou=Groups,dc=terpstra-world,dc=org?one

ssl off
```

Example 9.3.6 NT4 Migration NSS Control File: /etc/nsswitch.conf (Stage:1)

```
passwd:          files #ldap
shadow:          files #ldap
group:           files #ldap

hosts:           files dns wins
networks:        files dns

services:        files
protocols:       files
rpc:             files
ethers:          files
netmasks:        files
netgroup:        files
publickey:       files

bootparams:      files
automount:       files nis
aliases:         files
#passwd_compat:  ldap        #Not needed.
#group_compat:   ldap        #Not needed.
```

Example 9.3.7 NT4 Migration NSS Control File: /etc/nsswitch.conf (Stage:2)

```
passwd:         files ldap
shadow:         files ldap
group:          files ldap

hosts:          files dns wins
networks:       files dns

services:       files
protocols:      files
rpc:            files
ethers:         files
netmasks:       files
netgroup:       files
publickey:      files

bootparams:     files
automount:      files nis
aliases:        files
#passwd_compat: ldap        #Not needed.
#group_compat:  ldap        #Not needed.
```

Chapter 10

MIGRATING NETWARE SERVER TO SAMBA-3

Novell is a company any seasoned IT manager has to admire. It has become increasingly Linux-friendly and is emerging out of a deep regression that almost saw the company disappear into obscurity. Novell's SUSE Linux hosts the NetWare server and it is the platform of choice to which many older NetWare servers are being migrated. It will be interesting to see what becomes of NetWare over time. Meanwhile, there can be no denying that Novell is a Linux company.

Whatever flavor of Linux is preferred in your environment, whether Red Hat, Debian, Gentoo, Mandrake, or SUSE (Novell), the information in this chapter should be read with the knowledge that file locations may vary a little; even so, the information in this chapter should provide something of value.

Contributions to this chapter were made by Misty Stanley-Jones, a UNIX administrator of many years who surfaced on the Samba mailing list with a barrage of questions and who regularly helps other administrators to solve thorny Samba migration questions.

One wonders how many NetWare servers remain in active service. Many are being migrated to Samba on Linux. Red Hat Linux, SUSE Linux 9.x, and SUSE Linux Enterprise Server 9 are ideal target platforms to which a NetWare server may be migrated. The migration method of choice is much dependent on the tools that the administrator finds most natural to use. The old-hand NetWare guru will likely want to use tools like the NetWare NLM for **rsync** to migrate files from the NetWare server to the Samba server. The UNIX administrator might prefer tools that are part of the Mars_NWE (Martin Stovers' NetWare Emulator) open source package. The MS Windows network administrator will likely make use of the NWConv utility that is a part of Windows NT4 Server. Whatever your tool of choice, migration will be filled with joyous and challenging moments — though probably not concurrently.

The priority that Misty faced was one of migration of the data files off the NetWare 4.11 server and onto a Samba-based Windows file and print server. This chapter does not pretend to document all the different methods that could be used to migrate user and group accounts off a NetWare server. Its focus is on migration of data files.

This chapter tells its own story, so ride along. Maybe the information presented here will help to smooth over a similar migration challenge in your favorite networking environment.

File paths have been modified to permit use of RPM packages provided by Novell. In the original documentation contributed by Misty, the Courier-IMAP package had been built directly from the original source tarball.

10.1   Introduction

Misty Stanley-Jones was recruited by Abmas to administer a network that had not received much attention for some years and was much in need of a makeover. As a brand-new sysadmin to this company, she inherited a very old Novell file server and came with a determination to change things for the better.

A site survey turned up the following details for the old NetWare server:

200 MHz MMX processor
512K RAM
24 GB disk space in RAID1
Novell 4.11 patched to service pack 7
60+ users
7 network-attached printers

The company had outgrown this server several years before and was dealing with severe growing pains. Some of the problems experienced were:

- Very slow performance

- Available storage hovering around the 5% range

    - Extremely slow print spooling.

    - Users storing information on their local hard drives, causing backup integrity problems

At one point disk space had filled up to 100 percent, causing the payroll database to become corrupt. This caused the accounting department to be down for over a week and necessitated deployment of another file server. The replacement server was created with very poor security and design considerations from a discarded desktop PC.

10.1.1   Assignment Tasks

Misty has provided this summary of her migration experience in the hope that it will help someone to avoid the challenges she faced. Perhaps her configuration files and background will accelerate your learning as you grapple with a similar migration challenge. Let there be no confusion, the information presented in this chapter is provided to demonstrate how Misty dealt with a particular NetWare migration requirement, and it provides an overall approach to the implementation of a Samba-3 environment that is significantly divergent from that presented in Chapter 5, "Making Happy Users".

The complete removal of all site-specific information in order to produce a generic migration solution would rob this chapter of its character. It should be recognized, therefore, that the examples given require significant adaptation to suit local needs and thus there are some gaps in the example files. That is not Misty's fault;it is the result of treatment given to her files in an attempt to make the overall information more useful to you.

After management reviewed a cost-benefit report as well as an estimated time-to-completion, approval was given proceed with the solution proposed. The server was built from purchased components. The total project cost was $3,000. A brief description of the configuration follows:

3.0 GHz P4 Processor
1 GB RAM
120 GB SATA operating system drive
4 x 80 GB SATA data drives (RAID5 240 GB capacity)
2 x 80 GB SATA removable drives for online backup
A DLT drive for asynchronous offline backup
SUSE Linux Professional 9.1

The new system has operated for 6 months without problems. Over the past months much attention has been focused on cleaning up desktops and user profiles.

10.2   Dissection and Discussion

A decision to use LDAP was made even though I knew nothing about LDAP except that I had been reading the book "LDAP System Administration," by Gerald Carter. LDAP seemed to provide some of the functionality of Novell's e-Directory Services and would provide centralized authentication and identity management.

Building the LDAP database took a while and a lot of trial and error. Following the guidance I obtained from "LDAP System Administration," I installed OpenLDAP (from RPM; later I compiled a more current version from source) and built my initial LDAP tree.

10.2.1   Technical Issues

The first challenge was to create a company white pages, followed by manually entering everything from the printed company directory. This used only the inetOrgPerson object class from the OpenLDAP schemas. The next step was to write a shell script that would look at the `/etc/passwd` and `/etc/shadow` files on our mail server and create an LDIF file from which the information could be imported into LDAP. This would allow use of LDAP for Linux authentication, IMAP, POP3, and SMTP.

Because a decision was made to use Courier-IMAP the schema "authldap.schema" from the Courier-IMAP source, tarball is necessary to resolve Courier-specific LDAP directory needs. Where the Courier-IMAP file provided by SUSE is used, this file is named **courier.schema**.

Looking back, it would have been much easier to populate the LDAP directory using a convenient tool such as **phpLDAPAdmin** from the outset. An excessive amount of time was spent trying to generate LDIF files that could be parsed using the **ldapmodify** so that necessary changes could be written to the directory. This was a learning experience!

An attempt was made to use the PADL POSIX account migration scripts, but I gave up trying to make them work. Instead, even though it is most inelegant, I wrote a simple script that did what I needed. It is enclosed as a simple example to demonstrate that you do not need to be a guru to make light of otherwise painful repetition. This file is listed in Example 10.2.1.

Example 10.2.1 A Rough Tool to Create an LDIF File from the System Account Files

```
#!/bin/bash

cat /etc/passwd | while read l; do
  uid=`echo $l | cut -d : -f 1`
  uidNumber=`echo $l | cut -d : -f 3`
  gidNumber=`echo $l | cut -d : -f 4`
  gecos=`echo $l | cut -d : -f 5`
  homeDirectory=`echo $l | cut -d : -f 6`
  loginShell=`echo $l | cut -d : -f 6`
  userPassword=`cat /etc/shadow | grep $uid | cut -d : -f 2`

  echo "dn: cn=$gecos,ou=people,dc=mycompany,dc=com"
  echo "objectClass: account"
  echo "objectClass: posixAccount"
  echo "cn: $gecos"
  echo "uid: $uid"
  echo "uidNumber: $uidNumber"
  echo "gidNumber: $gidNumber"
  echo "homeDirectory: $homeDirectory"
  echo "loginShell: $loginShell"
  echo "userPassword: $userPassword"
done
```

NOTE

The PADL MigrationTools are recommended for migration of the UNIX account information into the LDAP directory. The tools consist of a set of Perl scripts for migration of users, groups, aliases, hosts, netgroups, networks, protocols, PRCs, and services from the existing ASCII text files (or from a name service such as NIS). This too set can be obtained from the PADL Web site[a].

---

[a]<http://www.padl.com>

10.3   Implementation

10.3.1   NetWare Migration Using LDAP Backend

The following software must be installed on the SUSE Linux Enterprise Server to perform this migration:

courier-imap
courier-imap-ldap
nss_ldap
openldap2-client
openldap2-devel (only for Samba compilation)
openldap2
pam_ldap
samba-3.0.20 or later
samba-client-3.0.20 or later
samba-winbind-3.0.20 or later
smbldap-tools Version 0.9.1

Each software application must be carefully configured in preparation for migration. The configuration files used at Abmas are provided as a guide and should be modified to meet needs at your site.

10.3.1.1   LDAP Server Configuration

The /etc/openldap/slapd.conf file Misty used is shown here:

```
#/etc/openldap/slapd.conf
#
# See slapd.conf(5) for details on configuration options.
# This file should NOT be world readable.
#
include    /etc/openldap/schema/core.schema
include    /etc/openldap/schema/cosine.schema
include    /etc/openldap/schema/inetorgperson.schema
include    /etc/openldap/schema/nis.schema
include    /etc/openldap/schema/samba3.schema
include    /etc/openldap/schema/dhcp.schema
include    /etc/openldap/schema/misc.schema
include    /etc/openldap/schema/idpool.schema
include    /etc/openldap/schema/eduperson.schema
include    /etc/openldap/schema/commURI.schema
include    /etc/openldap/schema/local.schema
include    /etc/openldap/schema/courier.schema

pidfile    /var/run/slapd/run/slapd.pid
argsfile   /var/run/slapd/run/slapd.args
```

```
replogfile  /data/ldap/log/slapd.replog

# Load dynamic backend modules:
modulepath  /usr/lib/openldap/modules

######################################################################
# Logging parameters
######################################################################
loglevel 256


######################################################################
# SASL and TLS options
######################################################################
sasl-host      ldap.corp.abmas.org
sasl-realm     DIGEST-MD5
sasl-secprops   none
TLSCipherSuite HIGH:MEDIUM:+SSLV2
TLSCertificateFile    /etc/ssl/certs/private/abmas-cert.pem
TLSCertificateKeyFile /etc/ssl/certs/private/abmas-key.pem
password-hash   {SSHA}
defaultsearchbase "dc=abmas,dc=biz"


######################################################################
# bdb database definitions
######################################################################
database        bdb
suffix          "dc=abmas,dc=biz"
rootdn          "cn=manager,dc=abmas,dc=biz"
rootpw          {SSHA}gdo/dUvoT4ZJmULz3rUt6A3H/hBEduJ5
directory       /data/ldap
mode    0600
# The following is for BDB to make it flush its data to disk every
# 500 seconds or 5kb of data
checkpoint 500 5

## For running slapindex
#readonly on

## Indexes for often-requested attributes
index   objectClass             eq
index   cn                      eq,sub
index   sn                      eq,sub
index   uid                     eq,sub
index   uidNumber               eq
index   gidNumber               eq
index   sambaSID                eq
```

```
index    sambaPrimaryGroupSID    eq
index    sambaDomainName         eq
index    default                 sub
cachesize 2000

replica          host=baa.corp.abmas.org:389
                 suffix="dc=abmas,dc=biz"
                 binddn="cn=replica,dc=abmas,dc=biz"
                 credentials=verysecret
                 bindmethod=simple
                 tls=yes
replica          host=ns.abmas.org:389
                 suffix="dc=abmas,dc=biz"
                 binddn="cn=replica,dc=abmas,dc=biz"
                 credentials=verysecret
                 bindmethod=simple
                 tls=yes

###########################################################################
# ACL section
###########################################################################
## MOST RESTRICTIVE RULES MUST GO FIRST!
# Admins get access to everything. This way I do not have to rename.
access to *
  by group/groupOfUniqueNames/uniqueMember="cn=LDAP
Administrators,ou=groups,dc=abmas,dc=biz" write
  by * break

## Users can change their own passwords.
access to
attrs=userPassword,sambaNTPassword,sambaLMPassword,sambaPwdLastSet,
sambaPwdMustChange,sambaPwdCanChange
  by self write
  by * auth

## Home contact info restricted to the logged-in user and the HR dept
access to attrs=hometelephoneNumber,homePostalAddress,
mobileTelephoneNumber,pagerTelephoneNumber
  by group/groupOfUniqueNames/uniqueMember="cn=hr_admin,
ou=groups,dc=abmas,dc=biz"
write
  by self write
  by * none

## Everyone can read email aliases
access to dn.sub="ou=Email Aliases,dc=abmas,dc=biz"
  by * read
```

```
## Only admins can manage email aliases
## If someone is the role occupant of an alias they can change it -- this
## is accomplished by the "organizationalRole" objectclass and is
## pretty cool -- like a groupOfUniqueNames but for individual
## users.
access to dn.children="ou=Email Aliases,dc=abmas,dc=biz"
  by dnattr=roleOccupant write
  by * read

## Admins and HR can add and delete users
access to dn.sub="ou=people,dc=abmas,dc=biz"
  by group/groupOfUniqueNames/uniqueMember="cn=hr_admin,
ou=groups,dc=abmas,dc=biz"
write
  by * read

## Admins and HR can add and delete bizputers
access to dn.sub="ou=bizputers,dc=abmas,dc=biz"
  by group/groupOfUniqueNames/uniqueMember="cn=hr_admin,
ou=groups,dc=abmas,dc=biz"
write
  by * read

## Admins and HR can add and delete groups
access to dn.sub="ou=groups,dc=abmas,dc=biz"
  by group/groupOfUniqueNames/uniqueMember="cn=hr_admin,
ou=groups,dc=abmas,dc=biz"
write
  by * read

## This is used to quickly deactivate any LDAP object only
##  Admins have access.
access to dn.sub="ou=inactive,dc=abmas,dc=biz"
  by * none

## This is for programs like Windows Address Book that can
## detect the default search base.
access to attrs=namingcontexts,supportedControl
  by anonymous =cs
  by * read

## Default to read-only access
access to *
  by dn.base="cn=replica,ou=people,dc=abmas,dc=biz" write
  by * read
```

The /etc/ldap.conf file used is listed in Example 10.3.1.

Example 10.3.1 NSS LDAP Control File — /etc/ldap.conf

```
# /etc/ldap.conf
# This file is present on every *NIX client that authenticates to LDAP.
# For me, most of the defaults are fine. There is an amazing amount of
# customization that can be done see the man page for info.

# Your LDAP server. Must be resolvable without using LDAP. The following
# is for the LDAP server all others use the FQDN of the server
URI ldap://127.0.0.1

# The distinguished name of the search base.
base ou=corp,dc=abmas,dc=biz

# The LDAP version to use (defaults to 3 if supported by client library)
ldap_version 3

# The distinguished name to bind to the server with if the effective
# user ID is root. Password is stored in /etc/ldap.secret (mode 600)
rootbinddn cn=Manager,dc=abmas,dc=biz

# Filter to AND with uid=%s
pam_filter objectclass=posixAccount

# The user ID attribute (defaults to uid)
pam_login_attribute uid

# Group member attribute
pam_member_attribute memberUID

# Use the OpenLDAP password change
# extended operation to update the password.
pam_password exop

# OpenLDAP SSL mechanism
# start_tls mechanism uses the normal LDAP port, LDAPS typically 636
ssl start_tls

tls_cacertfile /etc/ssl/certs/private/abmas-cert.pem
...
```

The NSS control file /etc/nsswitch.conf has the following contents:

```
# /etc/nsswitch.conf
```

```
# This file controls the resolve order for system databases.

# the following two lines obviate the "+" entry in /etc/passwd and /etc/group
passwd:    compat ldap
group:     compat ldap
# The above are all that I store in LDAP at this point. There are
# possibilities to store hosts, services, ethers, and lots of other things.
```

In my setup, users authenticate via PAM and NSS using LDAP-based accounts. The configuration file that controls the behavior of the PAM **pam_unix2** module is shown in Example 10.3.2 file. This works out of the box with the configuration files in this chapter. It enables you to have no local accounts for users (it is highly advisable to have a local account for the root user). Traps for the unwary include the following:

- If your LDAP database goes down, nobody can authenticate except for root.

- If failover is configured incorrectly, weird behavior can occur. For example, DNS can fail to resolve.

I do have two LDAP slave servers configured. That subject is beyond the scope of this document, and steps for implementing it are well documented.

The following services authenticate using LDAP:

UNIX login/ssh
Postfix (SMTP)
Courier-IMAP/IMAPS/POP3/POP3S

Companywide white pages can be searched using an LDAP client such as the one in the Windows Address Book.

Having gained a solid understanding of LDAP and a relatively workable LDAP tree thus far, it was time to configure Samba. I compiled the latest stable Samba and also installed the latest **smbldap-tools** from Idealx[1].

The Samba `smb.conf` file was configured as shown in Example 10.3.3.

Most of these shares are only used by one company group, but they are required because of some ancient Qbasic and Rbase applications were that written expecting their own drive letters.

Note: During the process of building the new server, I kept data files up to date with the Novell server via use of **rsync**. On a separate system (my workstation in fact), which could be rebooted whenever necessary, I set up a mount point to the Novell server via **ncpmount**. I then created a `rsyncd.conf` to share that mount point out to my new server, and synchronized once an hour. The script I used to synchronize is shown in Example 10.3.8. The files exclusion list I used is shown in Example 10.3.9. The reason I had to have the **rsync** daemon running on a system that could be rebooted frequently is because **ncpfs** (part of the MARS NetWare Emulation package) has a nasty habit of creating stale mount points that cannot be recovered without a reboot. The reason for hourly synchronization is

---

[1]<http://idealx.com>

Example 10.3.2 The PAM Control File /etc/security/pam_unix2.conf

---

```
# pam_unix2 config file
#
# This file contains options for the pam_unix2.so module.
# It contains a list of options for every type of management group,
# which will be used for authentication, account management and
# password management. Not all options will be used from all types of
# management groups.
#
# At first, pam_unix2 will read this file and then uses the local
# options. Not all options can be set her global.
#
# Allowed options are:
#
# debug                 (account, auth, password, session)
# nullok                (auth)
# md5                   (password / overwrites /etc/default/passwd)
# bigcrypt              (password / overwrites /etc/default/passwd)
# blowfish              (password / overwrites /etc/default/passwd)
# crypt_rounds=XX
# none                  (session)
# trace                 (session)
# call_modules=x,y,z    (account, auth, password)
#
#   Example:
#   auth:        nullok
#   account:
#   password:    nullok blowfish crypt_rounds=8
#   session:     none
#
auth: use_ldap
account: use_ldap
password: use_ldap
session: none
```

---

because some part of the chain was very slow and performance-heavy (whether **rsync** itself, the network, or the Novell server, I am not sure, but it was probably the Novell server).

After Samba was configured, I initialized the LDAP database. The first thing I had to do was store the LDAP password in the Samba configuration by issuing the command (as root):

```
root#   smbpasswd -w verysecret
```

where "verysecret" is replaced by the LDAP bind password.

Example 10.3.3 Samba Configuration File — smb.conf Part A

```
# Global parameters
[global]
        workgroup = MEGANET2
        netbios name = MASSIVE
        server string = Corp File Server
        passdb backend = ldapsam:ldap://localhost
        pam password change = Yes
        username map = /etc/samba/smbusers
        log level = 1
        log file = /data/samba/log/%m.log
        name resolve order = wins host bcast
        time server = Yes
        printcap name = cups
        show add printer wizard = No
        cups options = Raw
        add user script = /opt/IDEALX/sbin/smbldap-useradd -m "%u"
        add group script = /opt/IDEALX/sbin/smbldap-groupadd -p "%g"
        add user to group script = /opt/IDEALX/sbin/smbldap-groupmod ↩
            -m "%u" "%g"
        delete user from group script = /opt/IDEALX/sbin/smbldap- ↩
            groupmod -x "%u" "%g"
        set primary group script = /opt/IDEALX/sbin/smbldap-usermod ↩
            -g "%g" "%u"
        add machine script = /usr/local/sbin/smbldap-useradd -w "%m"
        logon script = logon.bat
        logon path = \\%L\profiles\%U\%a
        logon drive = H:
        logon home = \\%L\%U
        domain logons = Yes
        wins support = Yes
        ldap admin dn = cn=Manager,dc=abmas,dc=biz
        ldap group suffix = ou=Groups
        ldap idmap suffix = ou=People
        ldap machine suffix = ou=People
        ldap passwd sync = Yes
        ldap suffix = ou=MEGANET2,dc=abmas,dc=biz
        ldap ssl = no
        ldap user suffix = ou=People
        admin users = root, "@Domain Admins"
        printer admin = "@Domain Admins"
        force printername = Yes
```

Example 10.3.4 Samba Configuration File — smb.conf Part B

```
[netlogon]
        comment = Network logon service
        path = /data/samba/netlogon
        write list = "@Domain Admins"
        guest ok = Yes
[profiles]
        comment = Roaming Profile Share
        path = /data/samba/profiles/
        read only = No
        profile acls = Yes
        veto files = desktop.ini
        browseable = No
[homes]
        comment = Home Directories
        valid users = %S
        read only = No
        create mask = 0770
        veto files = desktop.ini
        hide files = desktop.ini
        browseable = No
[software]
        comment = Software for %a computers
        path = /data/samba/shares/software/%a
        guest ok = Yes
[public]
        comment = Public Files
        path = /data/samba/shares/public
        read only = No
        guest ok = Yes
[PDF]
        comment = Location of documents printed to PDFCreator  ←
            printer
        path = /data/samba/shares/pdf
        guest ok = Yes
```

NOTE

The Idealx smbldap-tools package can be configured using a script called **configure.pl** that is provided as part of the tool. See Chapter 5, "Making Happy Users" for an example of its use. Many administrators, like Misty, choose to do this manually so as to maintain greater awareness of how the tool-chain works and possibly to avoid undesirable actions from occurring unnoticed.

Example 10.3.5 Samba Configuration File — smb.conf Part C

```
[EVERYTHING]
        comment = All shares
        path = /data/samba
        valid users = "@Domain Admins"
        read only = No
[CDROM]
        comment = CD-ROM on MASSIVE
        path = /mnt
        guest ok = Yes
[print$]
        comment = Printer Drivers Share
        path = /data/samba/drivers
        write list = root
        browseable = No
[printers]
        comment = All Printers
        path = /data/samba/spool
        create mask = 0644
        printable = Yes
        browseable = No
[acct_hp8500]
        comment = "Accounting Color Laser Printer"
        path = /data/samba/spool/private
        valid users = @acct, @acct_admin, @hr, "@Domain Admins", ↩
            @Receptionist, dwayne, terri, danae, jerry
        create mask = 0644
        printable = Yes
        copy = printers
[plotter]
        comment = Engineering Plotter
        path = /data/samba/spool
        create mask = 0644
        printable = Yes
        use client driver = Yes
        copy = printers
```

Now Samba was ready for use and it was time to configure the smbldap-tools. There are two relevant files, which are usually put into the directory /etc/smbldap-tools. The main file, smbldap.conf is shown in Example 10.3.10.

Note: I chose not to take advantage of the TLS capability of this. Eventually I may go back and tweak it. Also, I chose not to take advantage of the master/slave configuration as I heard horror stories that it was unstable. My slave servers are replicas only.

The /etc/smbldap-tools/smbldap_bind.conf file is shown here:

```
# smbldap_bind.conf
```

Example 10.3.6 Samba Configuration File — smb.conf Part D

```
[APPS]
        path = /data/samba/shares/Apps
        force group = "Domain Users"
        read only = No
 [ACCT]
        path = /data/samba/shares/Accounting
        valid users = @acct, "@Domain Admins"
        force group = acct
        read only = No
        create mask = 0660
        directory mask = 0770
 [ACCT_ADMIN]
        path = /data/samba/shares/Acct_Admin
        valid users = @â acct_adminâ
        force group = acct_admin
 [HR_PR]
        path = /data/samba/shares/HR_PR
        valid users = @hr, @acct_admin
        force group = hr
 [ENGR]
        path = /data/samba/shares/Engr
        valid users = @engr, @receptionist, @truss, "@Domain Admins ↩
            ", cheri
        force group = engr
        read only = No
        create mask = 0770
 [DATA]
        path = /data/samba/shares/DATA
        valid users = @engr, @receptionist, @truss, "@Domain Admins ↩
            ", cheri
        force group = engr
        read only = No
        create mask = 0770
        copy = engr
```

```
#
# This file simply tells smbldap-tools how to bind to your LDAP server.
# It has to be a DN with full write access to the Samba portion of
# the database.

##############################
# Credential Configuration #
##############################
# Notes: you can specify two different configurations if you use a
# master ldap for writing access and a slave ldap server for reading access
# By default, we will use the same DN (so it will work for standard Samba
```

Example 10.3.7 Samba Configuration File — smb.conf Part E

```
[X]
        path = /data/samba/shares/X
        valid users = @engr, @acct
        force group = engr
        read only = No
        create mask = 0770
        copy = engr
[NETWORK]
        path = /data/samba/shares/network
        valid users = "@Domain Users"
        read only = No
        create mask = 0770
        guest ok = Yes
[UTILS]
        path = /data/samba/shares/Utils
        write list = "@Domain Admins"
[SYS]
        path = /data/samba/shares/SYS
        valid users = chad
        read only = No
        browseable = No
```

```
# release)
slaveDN="cn=Manager,dc=abmas,dc=biz"
slavePw="verysecret"
masterDN="cn=Manager,dc=abmas,dc=biz"
masterPw="verysecret"
```

The next step was to run the **smbldap-populate** command, which populates the LDAP tree with the appropriate default users, groups, and UID and GID pools. It creates a user called Administrator with UID=0 and GID=0 matching the Domain Admins group. This is fine because you can still log on as root to a Windows system, but it will break cached credentials if you need to log on as the administrator to a system that is not on the network.

After the LDAP database has been preloaded, it is prudent to validate that the information needed is in the LDAP directory. This can be done done by restarting the LDAP server, then performing an LDAP search by executing:

```
root#  ldapsearch -W -x -b "dc=abmas,dc=biz"\
    -D "cn=Manager,dc=abmas,dc=biz" \
  "(Objectclass=*)"
Enter LDAP Password:
# extended LDIF
#
```

Example 10.3.8 Rsync Script

```
#!/bin/bash
# Part 1 - rsync the Novell directories to the new server
echo "###########################################"
echo "New sync operation starting at `date`"
if ! pgrep -fl '^rsync\> ; then
        echo "Good, no rsync is running!"
  echo "Synchronizing oink to BHPRO"
        rsync -av --exclude-from=/root/excludes.txt
baa.corp:/BHPRO/SYS1/ /data/samba/shares/SYS1
        retval=$?
        [ ${retval} = 0 ] && echo "Sync operation completed at `date`"
        echo "Fixing permissions"
        # I had a whole lot more permission-fixing stuff here.  It got
        # pared down as groups got moved over.  The problem
        # was that the way I was mounting the directory, everything
        # was owned by the Novell administrator which translated to
        # Root.  This is also why I could only do one-way sync because
        # I could not fix the ACLs on the Novell side.
        find /data/samba/shares/Engr/ -perm +770 -exec chmod 770 {} \;
        find /data/samba/shares/Engr/ ! -group engr -exec chgrp engr {} \;
else
        # This rsync took ages and ages -- I had it set to run every hour but
        # I needed a way to prevent it running into itself.
        echo "Oh no, rsync is already running!"
echo "###########################################"
fi
```

```
# LDAPv3
# base <dc=abmas,dc=biz> with scope sub
# filter: (ObjectClass=*)
# requesting: ALL
#

# abmas.biz
dn: dc=abmas,dc=biz
objectClass: dcObject
objectClass: organization
o: abmas
dc: abmas

# People, abmas.biz
dn: ou=People,dc=abmas,dc=biz
objectClass: organizationalUnit
```

Example 10.3.9 Rsync Files Exclusion List — /root/excludes.txt

```
/Acct/
/Apps/
/DATA/
/Engr/*.pc3
/Engr/plotter
/Engr/APPOLO/
/Engr/LIBRARY/
/Home/Accounting/
/Home/Angie/
/Home/AngieY/
/Home/Brandon/
/Home/Carl/
```

```
ou: People

# Groups, abmas.biz
dn: ou=Groups,dc=abmas,dc=biz
objectClass: organizationalUnit
ou: Groups

# Idmap, abmas.biz
dn: ou=Idmap,dc=abmas,dc=biz
objectClass: organizationalUnit
ou: Idmap
...
```

With the LDAP directory now initialized, it was time to create the Windows and POSIX (UNIX) group accounts as well as the mappings from Windows groups to UNIX groups. The easiest way to do this was to use **smbldap-groupadd** command. It creates the group with the posixGroup and sambaGroupMapping attributes, a unique GID, and an automatically determined RID. I learned the hard way not to try to do this by hand.

After I had my group mappings in place, I added users to the groups (the users don't really have to exist yet). I used the **smbldap-groupmod** command to accomplish this. It can also be done manually by adding memberUID attributes to the group entries in LDAP.

The most monumental task of all was adding the sambaSamAccount information to each already existent posixAccount entry. I did it one at a time as I moved people onto the new server, by issuing the command:

```
root#  smbldap-usermod -a -P username
```

I completed that step for every user after asking the person what his or her current NetWare password was. The wiser way to have done it would probably have been to dump the entire database to an LDIF file. This can be done by executing:

```
root#  slapcat > somefile.ldif
```

Then update the LDIF file created by using a Perl script to parse and add the appropriate attributes and objectClasses to each entry, followed by re-importing the entire database into the LDAP directory.

Rebuilding of the LDAP directory can be done as follows:

```
root#  rcldap stop
root#  cd /data/ldap
root#  rm *bdb _* log*
root#  su - ldap -c "slapadd -l somefile.ldif"
root#  rcldap start
```

This can be done at any time and for any reason, with no harm to the database.

I first added a test user, of course. The LDIF for this test user looks like this, to give you an idea:

```
# Entry 1: cn=Test User,ou=people,ou=corp,dc=abmas,dc=biz
dn:cn=Test User,ou=people,ou=corp,dc=abmas,dc=biz
cn: Test User
gecos: Test User
gidNumber: 513
givenName: Test
homeDirectory: /home/test.user
homePhone: 555
l: Somewhere
l: ST
mail: test.user
o: Corp
objectClass: top
objectClass: inetOrgPerson
objectClass: posixAccount
objectClass: sambaSamAccount
postalCode: 12345
sn: User
street: 10 Some St.
uid: test.user
uidNumber: 1074
sambaLogonTime: 0
```

```
sambaLogoffTime: 2147483647
sambaKickoffTime: 2147483647
sambaPwdCanChange: 0
displayName: Samba User
sambaSID: S-1-5-21-725326080-1709766072-2910717368-3148
sambaLMPassword: 9D29C287C58448F9AAD3B435B51404EE
sambaAcctFlags: [U]
sambaNTPassword: D062088E99C95E37D7702287BB35E770
sambaPwdLastSet: 1102537694
sambaPwdMustChange: 1106425694
userPassword: {SSHA}UzFZ2VxRGdwUueLnTGtsTBtnsvMO1oj8
loginShell: /bin/false
```

Then I went over to a spare Windows NT machine and joined it to the MEGANET2 domain.
It worked, and the machine's account entry under ou=Computers looks like this:

```
dn:uid=w2kengrspare$,ou=Computers,ou=MEGANET2,dc=abmas,dc=biz
objectClass: top
objectClass: inetOrgPerson
objectClass: posixAccount
objectClass: sambaSamAccount
cn: w2kengrspare$
sn: w2kengrspare$
uid: w2kengrspare$
uidNumber: 1104
gidNumber: 515
homeDirectory: /dev/null
loginShell: /bin/false
description: Computer
gecos: Computer
sambaSID: S-1-5-21-725326080-1709766072-2910717368-3208
sambaPrimaryGroupSID: S-1-5-21-725326080-1709766072-2910717368-2031
displayName: W2KENGRSPARE$
sambaPwdCanChange: 1103149236
sambaPwdMustChange: 2147483647
sambaNTPassword: CA199C45CB6737035DB6D9D9F6CD1834
sambaPwdLastSet: 1103149236
sambaAcctFlags: [W          ]
```

So now I could log on with a test user from the machine w2kengrspare. It was all well and
good, but that user was in no groups yet and so had pretty boring access. I fixed that by
writing the login script! To write the login script, I used Kixtart[2] because it will work with
every architecture of Windows, has an active and helpful user base, and was both easier to

---

[2] <http://www.kixtart.org>

learn and more powerful than the standard netlogon scripts I have seen. I also did not have
to do a logon script per user or per group.

I downloaded Kixtart and put the following files in my netlogon share:

```
KIX32.EXE
KX32.dll
KX95.dll  <-- Not needed unless you are running Win9x clients.
kx16.dll  <-- Probably not needed unless you are running DOS clients.
kxrpc.exe <-- Probably useless as it has to run on the server and can
              only be run on NT.  It's for Windows 95 to become group-aware.
              We can get around the need.
```

I then wrote the `logon.kix` file that is shown in Example 10.3.14. I chose to keep it all in
one file, but it can be split up and linked via include directives.

As you can see in the script, I redirected the My Documents to the user's home share if
he or she were not in the Laptop group. I also added printers on a group-by-group basis,
and if applicable I set the group printer. For this to be effective, the print drivers must be
installed on the Samba server in the **[print$]** share. Ample documentation exists about
how to do that, so it is not covered here.

I call this script via the logon.bat script in the [netlogon] directory:

```
\\corpsrv\netlogon\kix32 \\corpsrv\netlogon\logon.kix /f
```

I only had to fully qualify the paths for Windows 9x, as Windows NT and greater automatically add [NETLOGON] to the path.

Also of note for Win9x is that the drive mappings and printer setup will not work because
they rely on RPC. You merely have to put the appropriate settings into the `c:\autoexec.`
`bat` file or map the drives manually. One option is to check the OS as part of the Kixtart
script, and if it is Win9x and is the first login, copy a premade `autoexec.bat` to the `C:`
drive. I have only three such machines, and one is going away in the very near future, so it
was easier to do it by hand.

At this point I was able to add the users. This is the part that really falls into upgrade.
I moved the users over one group at a time, starting with the people who used the least
amount of resources on the network. With each group that I moved, I first logged on as a
standard user in that group and took careful note of the environment, mainly the printers
he or she used, the PATH, and what network resources he or she had access to (most
importantly, which ones the user actually needed access to).

I then added the user's SambaSamAccount information as mentioned earlier, and join the
computer to the domain. The very first thing I had to do was to copy the user's profile to
the new server. This was very important, and I really struggled with the most effective way
to do it. Here is the method that worked for every one of my users on Windows NT, 2000,
and XP:

1. Log in as the user on the domain. This creates the local copy of the user's profile and copies it to the server as he or she logs out.

2. Reboot the computer and log in as the local machine administrator.

3. Right-click My Computer, click Properties, and navigate to the user profiles tab (varies per version of Windows).

4. Select the user's local profile (`COMPUTERNAME\username`), and click the **Copy To** button.

5. In the next dialog, copy it directly to the profiles share on the Samba server (in my case \\PDCname\profiles\user\<architecture>. You will have had to make a connection to the share as that user (e.g., Windows Explorer type \\PDCname\profiles\username).

6. When the copy is complete (it can take a while) log out, and log back in as the user. All of his or her settings and all contents of My Documents, Favorites, and the registry should have been copied successfully.

7. If it doesn't look right (the dead giveaway is the desktop background), shut down the computer without logging out (power cycle) and try logging in as the user again. If it still doesn't work, repeat the steps above. I only had to ever repeat it once.

Words to the Wise:

- If the user was anything other than a standard user on his or her system before, you will save yourself some headaches by giving him or her identical permissions (on the local machine) as his or her domain account *before* copying the profile over. Do this through the User Administrator in the Control Panel, after joining the computer to the domain and before logging on as that user for the first time. Otherwise the user will have trouble with permissions on his or her registry keys.

- If any application was installed for the user only, rather than for the entire system, it will probably not work without being reinstalled.

After all these steps are accomplished, only cleanup details are left. Make sure user's shortcuts and Network Places point to the appropriate place on the new server, check the important applications to be sure they work as expected and troubleshoot any problems that might arise, and check to be sure the user's printers are present and working. By the way, if there are any network printers installed as system printers (the Novell way), you will need to log in as a local administrator and delete them.

For my non-laptop systems, I would then log in and out a couple times as the user to be sure that his or her registry settings were modified, and then I was finished.

Some compatibility issues that cropped up included the following:

Blackberry client: It did not like having its registry settings moved around and so had to be reinstalled. Also, it needed write permissions to a portion of the hard drive, and I had to give it those manually on the one system where this was an issue.

CAMedia: Digital camera software for Canon cameras caused all kinds of trouble with the registry. I had to use the Run as service to open the registry of the local user while logged in as the domain user, and give the domain user the appropriate permissions to some registry keys, then export that portion of the registry to a file. Then, as the domain user, I had to import that file into the registry.

Crystal Reports version 7: More registry problems that were solved by recopying the user's profile.

Printing from legacy applications: I found out that Novell sends its jobs to the printer in a raw format. CUPS sends them in PostScript by default. I had to make a second printer definition for one printer and tell CUPS specifically to send raw data to the printer, then assign this printer to the LPT port with Kixtart's version of the net use command.

These were all eventually solved by elbow grease, queries to the Samba mailing list and others, and diligence. The complete migration took about 5 weeks. My userbase is relatively small but includes multiple versions of Windows, multiple Linux member servers, a mechanized saw, a pen plotter, and legacy applications written in Qbasic and R:Base, just to name a few. I actually ended up making some of these applications work better (or work again, as some of them had stopped functioning on the old server) because as part of the process I had to find out how things were supposed to work.

The one thing I have not been able to get working is a very old database that we had around for reference purposes; it uses Novell's Btrieve engine.

As the resources compare, I went from 95 percent disk usage to just around 10 percent. I went from a very high load on the server to an average load of between one and two runnable processes on the server. I have improved the security and robustness of the system. I have also implemented ClamAV[3] antivirus software, which scans the entire Samba server for viruses every 2 hours and quarantines them. I have found it much less problematic than our ancient version of Norton Antivirus Corporate Edition, and much more up-to-date.

In short, my users are much happier now that the new server is running, and that is what is important to me.

---

[3] <http://www.clamav.net>

Example 10.3.10 Idealx smbldap-tools Control File — Part A

```
#########
#
# located in /etc/smbldap-tools/smbldap.conf
#
##############################################################################
#
# General Configuration
#
##############################################################################

# Put your own SID
# to obtain this number do: net getlocalsid
SID="S-1-5-21-725326080-1709766072-2910717368"


##############################################################################
#
# LDAP Configuration
#
##############################################################################

# Notes: to use to dual ldap servers backend for Samba, you must patch
# Samba with the dual-head patch from IDEALX. If not using this patch
# just use the same server for slaveLDAP and masterLDAP.
# Those two servers declarations can also be used when you have
# . one master LDAP server where all writing operations must be done
# . one slave LDAP server where all reading operations must be done
#   (typically a replication directory)

# Ex: slaveLDAP=127.0.0.1
slaveLDAP="127.0.0.1"
slavePort="389"

# Master LDAP : needed for write operations
# Ex: masterLDAP=127.0.0.1
masterLDAP="127.0.0.1"
masterPort="389"

# Use TLS for LDAP
# If set to 1, this option will use start_tls for connection
# (you should also used the port 389)
ldapTLS="0"

# How to verify the server's certificate (none, optional or require)
# see "man Net::LDAP" in start_tls section for more details
verify=""
```

Example 10.3.11 Idealx smbldap-tools Control File — Part B

```
# CA certificate
# see "man Net::LDAP" in start_tls section for more details
cafile=""
 certificate to use to connect to the ldap server
# see "man Net::LDAP" in start_tls section for more details
clientcert=""

# key certificate to use to connect to the ldap server
# see "man Net::LDAP" in start_tls section for more details
clientkey=""

# LDAP Suffix
# Ex: suffix=dc=IDEALX,dc=ORG
suffix="ou=MEGANET2,dc=abmas,dc=biz"

# Where are stored Users
# Ex: usersdn="ou=Users,dc=IDEALX,dc=ORG"
usersdn="ou=People,${suffix}"

# Where are stored Computers
# Ex: computersdn="ou=Computers,dc=IDEALX,dc=ORG"
computersdn="ou=People,${suffix}"

# Where are stored Groups
# Ex groupsdn="ou=Groups,dc=IDEALX,dc=ORG"
groupsdn="ou=Groups,${suffix}"

# Where are stored Idmap entries
# (used if samba is a domain member server)
# Ex groupsdn="ou=Idmap,dc=IDEALX,dc=ORG"
idmapdn="ou=Idmap,${suffix}"

# Where to store next uidNumber and gidNumber available
sambaUnixIdPooldn="sambaDomainName=MEGANET2,${suffix}"

# Default scope Used
scope="sub"
```

Example 10.3.12 Idealx smbldap-tools Control File — Part C

```
# Unix password encryption (CRYPT, MD5, SMD5, SSHA, SHA)
hash_encrypt="MD5"

# if hash_encrypt is set to CRYPT, you may set a salt format.
# default is "%s", but many systems will generate MD5 hashed
# passwords if you use "$1$%.8s". This parameter is optional!
crypt_salt_format="%s"


#####################################################################
#
# Unix Accounts Configuration
#
#####################################################################

# Login defs
# Default Login Shell
# Ex: userLoginShell="/bin/bash"
userLoginShell="/bin/false"

# Home directory
# Ex: userHome="/home/%U"
userHome="/home/%U"

# Gecos
userGecos="Samba User"

# Default User (POSIX and Samba) GID
defaultUserGid="513"

# Default Computer (Samba) GID
defaultComputerGid="515"

# Skel dir
skeletonDir="/etc/skel"

# Default password validation time (time in days) Comment the next
# line if you don't want password to be enable for
# defaultMaxPasswordAge days (be careful to the sambaPwdMustChange
# attribute's value)
defaultMaxPasswordAge="45"
```

Example 10.3.13 Idealx smbldap-tools Control File — Part D

```
##########################################################################
#
# SAMBA Configuration
#
##########################################################################


# The UNC path to home drives location (%U username substitution)
# Ex: \\My-PDC-netbios-name\homes\%U
# Just set it to a null string if you want to use the smb.conf
# 'logon home' directive and/or disable roaming profiles
userSmbHome=""

# The UNC path to profiles locations (%U username substitution)
# Ex: \\My-PDC-netbios-name\profiles\%U
# Just set it to a null string if you want to use the smb.conf
# 'logon path' directive and/or disable roaming profiles
userProfile=""

# The default Home Drive Letter mapping
# (will be automatically mapped at logon time if home directory exist)
# Ex: H: for H:
userHomeDrive=""

# The default user netlogon script name (%U username substitution)
# if not used, will be automatically username.cmd
# make sure script file is edited under DOS
# Ex: %U.cmd
# userScript="startup.cmd" # make sure script file is edited under DOS
userScript=""

# Domain appended to the users "mail"-attribute
# when smbldap-useradd -M is used
mailDomain="abmas.org"


##########################################################################
#
# SMBLDAP-TOOLS Configuration (default are ok for a RedHat)
#
##########################################################################
# Allows not to use smbpasswd
# (if with_smbpasswd == 0 in smbldap_conf.pm) but
# prefer Crypt::SmbHash library
with_smbpasswd="0"
smbpasswd="/usr/bin/smbpasswd"
```

Example 10.3.14 Kixtart Control File — File: logon.kix

```
; This script just calls the other scripts.

; First we want to get things done for everyone.

; Second, we do first-time login stuff.

; Third, we go through the group-oriented scripts one at a time.


; We want to check for group membership here to avoid the overhead of running
; scripts which don't apply.
call "\\massive\netlogon\scripts\main.kix"
call "\\massive\netlogon\scripts\setup.kix"
IF INGROUP("MEGANET2\ACCT")
  call "scripts\acct.kix"
ENDIF
IF INGROUP("MEGANET2\ENGR","MEGANET2\RECEPTIONIST")
call "\\massive\netlogon\scripts\engr.kix"
ENDIF
IF INGROUP("MEGANET2\FURN")
  call "\\massive\netlogon\scripts\furn.kix"
ENDIF
IF INGROUP("MEGANET2\TRUSS")
  call "\\massive\netlogon\scripts\truss.kix"
ENDIF
```

Example 10.3.15 Kixtart Control File — File: main.kix

```
break on

; Choose whether to hide the login window or not
IF INGROUP("MEGANET2\Domain Admins")
  USE Z: \\massive\everything
  SETCONSOLE("show")
ELSE
  ; Nobody cares about seeing the login script except admins
  SETCONSOLE("hide")
ENDIF

; Delete all previously connected shares
USE * /delete

SETTITLE("Logging on @USERID to @LDOMAIN at @TIME")

; Set the time on the workstation
$Timeserver = "\\massive"
Settime $TimeServer

; Map the home directory
USE H: @HOMESHR ; connect to user's home share
IF @ERROR = 0

  H:
  CD @HOMEDIR ; change directory to user's home directory
ENDIF

; Everyone gets the N drive
USE N: \\massive\network
```

Example 10.3.16 Kixtart Control File — File: setup.kix, Part A

```
; My setup.kix is where all of the redirection stuff happens.  Note that with
; the use of registry keys, this only happens the first time they log in. or  if
; I delete the pertinent registry keys which triggers it to happen again:

; Check to see if we have written the abmas sub-key before
$RETURNCODE = EXISTKEY("HKEY_CURRENT_USER\abmas")
IF NOT $RETURNCODE = 0
; Add key for abmas-specific things on the first login
  ADDKEY("HKEY_CURRENT_USER\abmas")
  ; The following key gets deleted at the end of the first login
  ADDKEY("HKEY_CURRENT_USER\abmas\FIRST_LOGIN")
ENDIF


; People with laptops need My Documents to be in their profile.  People with
; desktops can have My Documents redirected to their home directory to avoid
; long delays with logging out and out-of-sync files.

; Check to see if this is the first login -- doesn't make sense to do this
; at the very first login

$RETURNCODE = EXISTKEY("HKEY_CURRENT_USER\abmas\FIRST_LOGIN")
IF NOT $RETURNCODE = 0

; We don't want to do this stuff for people with laptops or people in the FURN
; group.  (They store their profiles in a different server)

  IF NOT INGROUP("MASSIVE\Laptop","MASSIVE\FURN")
    $RETURNCODE=EXISTKEY("HKEY_CURRENT_USER\abmas\profile_copied")

; A  crude way to tell what OS our profile is for and copy the "My Documents"
; to the redirected folder on the server.  It works because the profiles
; are stored as \\server\profiles\user\architecture
    IF NOT $RETURNCODE = 0
      IF EXIST("\\massive\profiles\@userID\WinXP")
        copy "\\massive\profiles\@userID\WinXP\My Documents\*"
"\\massive\@userID\"
      ENDIF
      IF EXIST("\\massive\profiles\@userID\Win2K")
        copy "\\massive\profiles\@userID\Win2K\My Documents\*"
"\\massive\@userID\"
      ENDIF
      IF EXIST("\\massive\profiles\@userID\WinNT")
        copy "\\massive\profiles\@userID\WinNT\My Documents\*"
"\\massive\@userID\"
      ENDIF
```

Example 10.3.17 Kixtart Control File — File: setup.kix, Part B

```
; Now we will write the registry values to redirect the locations of "My
Documents"
; and other folders.
     ADDKEY("HKEY_CURRENT_USER\abmas\profile_copied")
     WRITEVALUE("HKEY_CURRENT_USER\Software\Microsoft\
Windows\CurrentVersion\Explorer\User
Shell Folders", "Personal","\\massive\@userID","REG_SZ")
     WRITEVALUE("HKEY_CURRENT_USER\Software\Microsoft\
Windows\CurrentVersion\Explorer\User
Shell Folders", "My Pictures", "\\massive\@userID\My Pictures", "REG_SZ")
     IF @PRODUCTTYPE="Windows 2000 Professional" or @PRODUCTTYPE="Windows XP
Professional"
     WRITEVALUE("HKEY_CURRENT_USER\Software\Microsoft\
Windows\CurrentVersion\Explorer\User
Shell Folders", "My Videos", "\\massive\@userID\My Videos", "REG_SZ")
     WRITEVALUE("HKEY_CURRENT_USER\Software\Microsoft\
Windows\CurrentVersion\Explorer\User
Shell Folders", "My Music", "\\massive\@userID\My Music", "REG_SZ")
     WRITEVALUE("HKEY_CURRENT_USER\Software\Microsoft\
Windows\CurrentVersion\Explorer\User
Shell Folders", "My eBooks", "\\massive\@userID\My eBooks", "REG_SZ")
     ENDIF
   ENDIF
 ENDIF

; Now we will delete the FIRST_LOGIN sub-key that we made before.
; Note - to run this script again you will want to delete the HKCU\abmas
; sub-key, log out, and log back in.
$RETURNVALUE = EXISTKEY("HKEY_CURRENT_USER\abmas\FIRST_LOGIN")
IF $RETURNVALUE = 0
  DELKEY("HKEY_CURRENT_USER\abmas\FIRST_LOGIN")
ENDIF
```

Example 10.3.18 Kixtart Control File — File: acct.kix

```
; And here is one group-oriented script to show what can be
; done that way: acct.kix:

IF INGROUP("MASSIVE\Acct_Admin","MASSIVE\HR")
  USE I: \\MEGANET2\HR_PR
ENDIF

; Set up printer
$RETURNVALUE = existkey("HKEY_CURRENT_USER\Printers\,,massive,acct_hp8500")
IF NOT $RETURNVALUE = 0
  ADDPRINTERCONNECTION("\\massive\acct_hp8500")
  SETDEFAULTPRINTER("\\massive\acct_hp8500")
ENDIF
; Set up drive mappings
  USE M: \\massive\ACCT
  IF INGROUP("MEGANET2\ABRA")
    USE T: \\trussrv\abra
  ENDIF
```

Part III

Reference Section

This section *Samba-3 by Example* provides important reference material that may help you to solve network performance issues, to answer some of the critiques published regarding Samba, or just to gain a more broad understanding of how Samba can play in a Windows networking world.

Chapter 11

ACTIVE DIRECTORY, KERBEROS, AND SECURITY

By this point in the book, you have been exposed to many Samba-3 features and capabilities. More importantly, if you have implemented the examples given, you are well on your way to becoming a Samba-3 networking guru who knows a lot about Microsoft Windows. If you have taken the time to practice, you likely have thought of improvements and scenarios with which you can experiment. You are rather well plugged in to the many flexible ways Samba can be used.

This is a book about Samba-3. Understandably, its intent is to present it in a positive light. The casual observer might conclude that this book is one-eyed about Samba. It is — what would you expect? This chapter exposes some criticisms that have been raised concerning the use of Samba. For each criticism, there are good answers and appropriate solutions.

Some criticism always comes from deep inside ranks that one would expect to be supportive of a particular decision. Criticism can be expected from the outside. Let's see how the interesting dynamic of criticism develops with respect to Abmas.

This chapter provides a shameless self-promotion of Samba-3. The objections raised were not pulled out of thin air. They were drawn from comments made by Samba users and from criticism during discussions with Windows network administrators. The tone of the objections reflects as closely as possible that of the original. The case presented is a straw-man example that is designed to permit each objection to be answered as it might occur in real life.

11.1 Introduction

Abmas is continuing its meteoric growth with yet further acquisitions. The investment community took note of the spectacular projection of Abmas onto the global business stage. Abmas is building an interesting portfolio of companies that includes accounting services, financial advice, investment portfolio management, property insurance, risk assessment, and the recent addition of a a video rental business. The pieces do not always appear to fit together, but Mr. Meany is certainly executing an interesting business growth and development plan. Abmas Video Rentals was recently acquired. During the time that the acquisition was closing, the Video Rentals business upgraded its Windows NT4-based network to Windows 2003 Server and Active Directory.

You have accepted the fact that Abmas Video Rentals will use Microsoft Active Directory. The IT team, led by Stan Soroka, is committed to Samba-3 and to maintaining a uniform technology platform. Stan Soroka's team voiced its disapproval over the decision to permit this business to continue to operate with a solution that is viewed by Christine and her group as "an island of broken technologies." This comment was made by one of Christine's staff as they were installing a new Samba-3 server at the new business.

Abmas Video Rentals' head of IT heard of this criticism. He was offended that a junior engineer should make such a comment. He felt that he had to prepare in case he might be criticized for his decision to use Active Directory. He decided he would defend his decision by hiring the services of an outside security systems consultant to report[1] on his unit's operations and to investigate the role of Samba at his site. Here are key extracts from this hypothetical report:

> ... the implementation of Microsoft Active Directory at the Abmas Video Rentals, Bamingsham site, has been examined. We find no evidence to support a notion that vulnerabilities exist at your site. ... we took additional steps to validate the integrity of the installation and operation of Active Directory and are pleased that your staff are following sound practices.
>
> ...
>
> User and group accounts, and respective privileges, have been well thought out. File system shares are appropriately secured. Backup and disaster recovery plans are well managed and validated regularly, and effective off-site storage practices are considered to exceed industry norms.
>
> Your staff are justifiably concerned that the use of Samba may compromise their good efforts to maintain a secure network.
>
> The recently installed Linux file and application server uses a tool called **winbind** that is indiscriminate about security. All user accounts in Active Directory can be used to access data stored on the Linux system. We are alarmed that secure information is accessible to staff who should not even be aware that it exists. We share the concerns of your network management staff who have gone to great lengths to set fine-grained controls that limit information access to those who need access. It seems incongruous to us that Samba winbind should be permitted to be used considering that it voids this fine work.
>
> Graham Judd [head of network administration] has locked down the security of all systems and is following the latest Microsoft guidelines. ... null session connections have been disabled ... the internal network is isolated from the outside world, the [product name removed] firewall is under current contract maintenance support from [the manufacturer]. ... our attempts to penetrate security of your systems failed to find problems common to Windows networking

---

[1]This report is entirely fictitious. Any resemblance to a factual report is purely coincidental.

sites. We commend your staff on their attention to detail and for following Microsoft recommended best practices.

...

Regarding the use of Samba, we offer the following comments: Samba is in use in nearly half of all sites we have surveyed. ... It is our opinion that Samba offers no better security than Microsoft ... what worries us regarding Samba is the need to disable essential Windows security features such as secure channel support, digital sign'n'scal on all communication traffic, and running Active Directory in mixed mode so that Samba clients and servers can authenticate all of it. Additionally, we are concerned that Samba is not at the full capabilities of Microsoft Windows NT4 server. Microsoft has moved well beyond that with trusted computing initiatives that the Samba developers do not participate in.

One wonders about the integrity of an open source program that is developed by a team of hackers who cannot be held accountable for the flaws in their code. The sheer number of updates and bug fixes they have released should ring alarm bells in any business.

Another factor that should be considered is that buying Microsoft products and services helps to provide employment in the IT industry. Samba and Open Source software place those jobs at risk.

This is also a challenge to rise above the trouble spot. You call Stan's team together for a simple discussion, but it gets further out of hand. When you return to your office, you find the following email in your in-box:

Good afternoon,

I apologize for the leak of internal discussions to the new business. It reflects poorly on our professionalism and has put you in an unpleasant position. I regret the incident.

I also wish to advise that two of the recent recruits want to implement Kerberos authentication across all systems. I concur with the desire to improve security. One of the new guys who is championing the move to Kerberos was responsible for the comment that caused the embarrassment.

I am experiencing difficulty in handling the sharp push for Kerberos. He claims that Kerberos, OpenLDAP, plus Samba-3 will seamlessly replace Microsoft Active Directory. I am a little out of my depth with respect to the feasibility of such a move, but have taken steps to pull both of them into line. With your consent, I would like to hire the services of a well-known Samba consultant to set the record straight.

I intend to use this report to answer the criticism raised and would like to establish a policy that we will approve the use of Microsoft Windows Servers (and Active Directory) subject to all costs being covered out of the budget of the division that wishes to go its own way. I propose that dissenters will still remain responsible to meet the budgeted contribution to IT operations as a whole. I believe we should not coerce use of any centrally proposed standards, but make all noncompliance the financial responsibility of the out-of-step division. Hopefully, this will encourage all divisions to walk with us and not alone.

—Stan

11.1.1   Assignment Tasks

You agreed with Stan's recommendations and hired a consultant to help defuse the powder keg. The consultant's task is to provide a tractable answer to each of the issues raised. The consultant must be able to support his or her claims, keep emotions to the side, and answer technically.

11.2   Dissection and Discussion

Samba-3 is a tool. No one is pounding your door to make you use Samba. That is a choice that you are free to make or reject. It is likely that your decision to use Samba can greatly benefit your company. The Samba Team obviously believes that the Samba software is a worthy choice. If you hire a consultant to assist with the installation and/or deployment of Samba, or if you hire someone to help manage your Samba installation, you can create income and employment. Alternately, money saved by not spending in the IT area can be spent elsewhere in the business. All money saved or spent creates employment.

In the long term, the use of Samba must be economically sustainable. In some situations, Samba is adopted purely to provide file and print service interoperability on platforms that otherwise cannot provide access to data and to printers for Microsoft Windows clients. Samba is used by some businesses to effect a reduction in the cost of providing IT services. Obviously, it is also used by some as an alternative to the use of a Microsoft file and print serving platforms with no consideration of costs.

It would be foolish to adopt a technology that might put any data or users at risk. Security affects everyone. The Samba-Team is fully cognizant of the responsibility they have to their users. The Samba documentation clearly reveals that full responsibility is accepted to fix anything that is broken.

There is a mistaken perception in the IT industry that commercial software providers are fully accountable for the defects in products. Open Source software comes with no warranty, so it is often assumed that its use confers a higher degree of risk. Everyone should read commercial software End User License Agreements (EULAs). You should determine what real warranty is offered and the extent of liability that is accepted. Doing so soon dispels the popular notion that commercial software vendors are willingly accountable for product defects. In many cases, the commercial vendor accepts liability only to reimburse the price paid for the software.

The real issues that a consumer (like you) needs answered are What is the way of escape from technical problems, and how long will it take? The average problem turnaround time in the Open Source community is approximately 48 hours. What does the EULA offer? What is the track record in the commercial software industry? What happens when your commercial vendor decides to cease providing support?

Open Source software at least puts you in possession of the source code. This means that when all else fails, you can hire a programmer to solve the problem.

11.2.1   Technical Issues

Each issue is now discussed and, where appropriate, example implementation steps are provided.

Winbind and Security   Windows network administrators may be dismayed to find that **winbind** exposes all domain users so that they may use their domain account credentials to log on to a UNIX/Linux system. The fact that all users in the domain can see the UNIX/Linux server in their Network Neighborhood and can browse the shares on the server seems to excite them further.

winbind provides for the UNIX/Linux domain member server or client, the same as one would obtain by adding a Microsoft Windows server or client to the domain. The real objection is the fact that Samba is not MS Windows and therefore requires handling a little differently from the familiar Windows systems. One must recognize fear of the unknown.

Windows network administrators need to recognize that **winbind** does not, and cannot, override account controls set using the Active Directory management tools. The control is the same. Have no fear.

Where Samba and the ADS domain account information obtained through the use of **winbind** permits access, by browsing or by the drive mapping to a share, to data that should be better protected. This can only happen when security controls have not been properly implemented. Samba permits access controls to be set on:

- Shares themselves (i.e., the logical share itself)

- The share definition in `smb.conf`

- The shared directories and files using UNIX permissions

- Using Windows 2000 ACLs — if the file system is POSIX enabled

Examples of each are given in Section 11.3.

User and Group Controls   User and group management facilities as known in the Windows ADS environment may be used to provide equivalent access control constraints or to provide equivalent permissions and privileges on Samba servers. Samba offers greater flexibility in the use of user and group controls because it has additional layers of control compared to Windows 200x/XP. For example, access controls on a Samba server may be set within the share definition in a manner for which Windows has no equivalent.

In any serious analysis of system security, it is important to examine the safeguards that remain when all other protective measures fail. An administrator may inadvertently set excessive permissions on the file system of a shared resource, or he may set excessive privileges on the share itself. If that were to happen in a Windows 2003 Server environment, the data would indeed be laid bare to abuse. Yet, within a Samba share definition, it is possible to guard against that by enforcing controls on the share definition itself. You see a practical example of this a little later in this chapter.

The report that is critical of Samba really ought to have exercised greater due diligence: the real weakness is on the side of a Microsoft Windows environment.

Security Overall Samba is designed in such a manner that weaknesses inherent in the design of Microsoft Windows networking ought not to expose the underlying UNIX/Linux file system in any way. All software has potential defects, and Samba is no exception. What matters more is how defects that are discovered get dealt with.

The Samba Team totally agrees with the necessity to observe and fully implement every security facility to provide a level of protection and security that is necessary and that the end user (or network administrator) needs. Never would the Samba Team recommend a compromise to system security, nor would deliberate defoliation of security be publicly condoned; yet this is the practice by many Windows network administrators just to make happy users who have no notion of consequential risk.

The report condemns Samba for releasing updates and security fixes, yet Microsoft online updates need to be applied almost weekly. The answer to the criticism lies in the fact that Samba development is continuing, documentation is improving, user needs are being increasingly met or exceeded, and security updates are issued with a short turnaround time.

The release of Samba-4 is expected around late 2004 to early 2005 and involves a near complete rewrite to permit extensive modularization and to prepare Samba for new functionality planned for addition during the next-generation series. The Samba Team is responsible and can be depended upon; the history to date suggests a high degree of dependability and on charter development consistent with published roadmap projections.

Not well published is the fact that Microsoft was a foundation member of the Common Internet File System (CIFS) initiative, together with the participation of the network attached storage (NAS) industry. Unfortunately, for the past few years, Microsoft has been absent from active involvement at CIFS conferences and has not exercised the leadership expected of a major force in the networking technology space. The Samba Team has maintained consistent presence and leadership at all CIFS conferences and at the interoperability laboratories run concurrently with them.

Cryptographic Controls (schannel, sign'n'seal) The report correctly mentions that Samba did not support the most recent `schannel` and `digital sign'n'seal` features of Microsoft Windows NT/200x/XPPro products. This is one of the key features of the Samba-3 release. Market research reports take so long to generate that they are seldom a reflection of current practice, and in many respects reports are like a pathology report — they reflect accurately (at best) status at a snapshot in time. Meanwhile, the world moves on.

It should be pointed out that had clear public specifications for the protocols been published, it would have been much easier to implement these features and would have taken less time to do. The sole mechanism used to find an algorithm that is compatible with the methods used by Microsoft has been based on observation of network traffic and trial-and-error implementation of potential techniques. The real value of public and defensible standards is obvious to all and would have enabled more secure networking for everyone.

Critics of Samba often ignore fundamental problems that may plague (or may have plagued) the users of Microsoft's products also. Those who are first to criticize Samba for not rushing into release of `digital sign'n'seal` support often dismiss the problems that Microsoft has acknowledged[2] and for which a fix was provided. In fact, Tangent Systems[3] have documented a significant problem with delays writes that can be connected with the implementation of sign'n'seal. They provide a work-around that is not trivial for many Windows networking sites. From notes such as this it is clear that there are benefits from not rushing new technology out of the door too soon.

One final comment is warranted. If companies want more secure networking protocols, the most effective method by which this can be achieved is by users seeking and working together to help define open and publicly refereed standards. The development of closed source, proprietary methods that are developed in a clandestine framework of secrecy, under claims of digital rights protection, does not favor the diffusion of safe networking protocols and certainly does not help the consumer to make a better choice.

Active Directory Replacement with Kerberos, LDAP, and Samba

The Microsoft networking protocols extensively make use of remote procedure call (RPC) technology. Active Directory is not a simple mixture of LDAP and Kerberos together with file and print services, but rather is a complex, intertwined implementation of them that uses RPCs that are not supported by any of these component technologies and yet by which they are made to interoperate in ways that the components do not support.

In order to make the popular request for Samba to be an Active Directory Server a reality, it is necessary to add to OpenLDAP, Kerberos, as well as Samba, RPC calls that are not presently supported. The Samba Team has not been able to gain critical overall support for all project maintainers to work together on the complex challenge of developing and integrating the necessary technologies. Therefore, if the Samba Team does not make it a priority to absorb Kerberos and LDAP functionality into the Samba project, this dream request cannot become a reality.

At this time, the integration of LDAP, Kerberos, and the missing RPCs is not on the Samba development roadmap. If it is not on the published roadmap, it cannot be delivered anytime soon. Ergo, ADS server support is not a current goal for Samba development. The Samba Team is most committed to permitting Samba to be a full

---

[2]<http://support.microsoft.com/default.aspx?kbid=321733>
[3]<http://www.tangent-systems.com/support/delayedwrite.html>

ADS domain member that is increasingly capable of being managed using Microsoft
Windows MMC tools.

11.2.1.1 Kerberos Exposed

Kerberos is a network authentication protocol that provides secure authentication for client-
server applications by using secret-key cryptography. Firewalls are an insufficient barrier
mechanism in today's networking world; at best they only restrict incoming network traffic
but cannot prevent network traffic that comes from authorized locations from performing
unauthorized activities.

Kerberos was created by MIT as a solution to network security problems. The Kerberos
protocol uses strong cryptography so that a client can prove its identity to a server (and vice
versa) across an insecure network connection. After a client and server has used Kerberos
to prove their identity, they can also encrypt all of their communications to assure privacy
and data integrity as they go about their business.

Kerberos is a trusted third-party service. That means that there is a third party (the
kerberos server) that is trusted by all the entities on the network (users and services, usually
called principals). All principals share a secret password (or key) with the kerberos server
and this enables principals to verify that the messages from the kerberos server are authentic.
Therefore, trusting the kerberos server, users and services can authenticate each other.

Kerberos was, until recently, a technology that was restricted from being exported from
the United States. For many years that hindered global adoption of more secure networking technologies both within the United States and abroad. A free and unencumbered
implementation of MIT Kerberos has been produced in Europe and is available from the
University of Paderborn, Sweden. It is known as the Heimdal Kerberos project. In recent
times the U.S. government has removed sanctions affecting the global distribution of MIT
Kerberos. It is likely that there will be a significant surge forward in the development of
Kerberos-enabled applications and in the general deployment and use of Kerberos across
the spectrum of the information technology industry.

A storm has broken out concerning interoperability between MIT Kerberos and Microsofts'
implementation of it. For example, a 2002 IDG[4] report[5] by states:

> A Microsoft Corp. executive testified at the software giant's remedy hearing that
> the company goes to great lengths to disclose interfaces and protocols that allow
> third-party software products to interact with Windows. But a lawyer with the
> states suing Microsoft pointed out that when it comes to the company's use of
> the Kerberos authentication specification, not everyone agrees.
>
> Robert Short, vice president of Windows core technology at Microsoft, wrote in
> his direct testimony prepared before his appearance that non-Microsoft operating
> systems can disregard the portion of the Kerberos version 5 specification that
> Windows clients use for proprietary purposes and still achieve interoperability

---

[4] <http://www.idg.com.sg/idgwww.nsf/0/5DDA8D153A7505A748256BAB000D992A?OpenDocument>

[5] Note: This link is no longer active. The same article is still available from ITWorld.com <http:
//199.105.191.226/Man/2699/020430msdoj/> (July 5, 2005)

with the Microsoft OS. Microsoft takes advantage of unspecified fields in the Kerberos specification for storing Windows-specific authorization data, Short wrote. The designers of Kerberos left these fields undefined so that software developers could add their own authorization information, he said.

It so happens that Microsoft Windows clients depend on and expect the contents of the *unspecified fields* in the Kerberos 5 communications data stream for their Windows interoperability, particularly when Samba is expected to emulate a Windows Server 200x domain controller. But the interoperability issue goes far deeper than this. In the domain control protocols that are used by MS Windows XP Professional, there is a tight interdependency between the Kerberos protocols and the Microsoft distributed computing environment (DCE) RPCs that themselves are an integral part of the SMB/CIFS protocols as used by Microsoft.

Microsoft makes the following comment in a reference in a technet[6] article:

> The DCE Security Services are also layered on the Kerberos protocol. DCE authentication services use RPC representation of Kerberos protocol messages. In addition, DCE uses the authorization data field in Kerberos tickets to convey Privilege Attribute Certificates (PACs) that define user identity and group membership. The DCE PAC is used in a similar manner as Windows NT Security IDs for user authorization and access control. Windows NT services will not be able to translate DCE PACs into Windows NT user and group identifiers. This is not an issue with Kerberos interoperability, but rather an issue of interoperability between DCE and Windows NT access control information.

11.3   Implementation

The following procedures outline the implementation of the security measures discussed so far.

11.3.1   Share Access Controls

Access control entries placed on the share itself act as a filter at the time a when CIFS/SMB client (such as Windows XP Pro) attempts to make a connection to the Samba server.

CREATE/EDIT/DELETE SHARE ACLS

1. From a Windows 200x/XP Professional workstation, log on to the domain using the Domain Administrator account (on Samba domains, this is usually the account called root).

2. Click **Start** → **Settings** → **Control Panel** → **Administrative Tools** → **Computer Management**.

3. In the left panel, **[Right mouse menu item] Computer Management (Local)** → **Connect to another computer ...** → **Browse...** → **Advanced** → **Find Now**. In the lower panel, click on the name of the server you wish to administer. Click **OK** → **OK**

---

[6]<http://www.microsoft.com/technet/itsolutions/interop/mgmt/kerberos.asp>

→ **OK**. In the left panel, the entry **Computer Management (Local)** should now reflect the change made. For example, if the server you are administering is called FRODO, the Computer Management entry should now say **Computer Management (FRODO)**.

4. In the left panel, click **Computer Management (FRODO)** → **[+] Shared Folders** → **Shares**.

5. In the right panel, double-click on the share on which you wish to set/edit ACLs. This will bring up the Properties panel. Click the **Share Permissions** tab.

6. You may now edit/add/remove access control settings. Be very careful. Many problems have been created by people who decided that everyone should be rejected but one particular group should have full control. This is a catch-22 situation because members of that particular group also belong to the group Everyone, which therefore overrules any permissions set for the permitted group.

7. When you are done with editing, close all panels by clicking through the **OK** buttons.

11.3.2 Share Definition Controls

Share-definition-based access controls can be used like a checkpoint or like a pile-driver. Just as a checkpoint can be used to require someone who wants to get through to meet certain requirements, so it is possible to require the user (or group the user belongs to) to meet specified credential-related objectives. It can be likened to a pile-driver by overriding default controls in that having met the credential-related objectives, the user can be granted powers and privileges that would not normally be available under default settings.

It must be emphasized that the controls discussed here can act as a filter or give rights of passage that act as a superstructure over normal directory and file access controls. However, share-level ACLs act at a higher level than do share definition controls because the user must filter through the share-level controls to get to the share-definition controls. The proper hierarchy of controls implemented by Samba and Windows networking consists of:

1. Share-level ACLs

2. Share-definition controls

3. Directory and file permissions

4. Directory and file POSIX ACLs

11.3.2.1 Checkpoint Controls

Consider the following extract from a `smb.conf` file defining the share called Apps:

```
[Apps]
   comment = Application Share
   path = /data/apps
   read only = Yes
```

```
valid users = @Employees
```

This definition permits only those who are members of the group called `Employees` to access the share.

NOTE

On domain member servers and clients, even when the *winbind use default domain* has been specified, the use of domain accounts in security controls requires fully qualified domain specification, for example, *valid users* = @"MEGANET\Northern Engineers". Note the necessity to use the double quotes to avoid having the space in the Windows group name interpreted as a delimiter.

If there is an ACL on the share itself to permit read/write access for all `Employees` as well as read/write for the group `Doctors`, both groups are permitted through to the share. However, at the moment an attempt is made to set up a connection to the share, a member of the group `Doctors`, who is not also a member of the group `Employees`, would immediately fail to validate.

Consider another example. In this case, you want to permit all members of the group `Employees` except the user `patrickj` to access the `Apps` share. This can be easily achieved by setting a share-level ACL permitting only `Employees` to access the share, and then in the share definition controls excluding just `patrickj`. Here is how that might be done:

```
[Apps]
        comment = Application Share
        path = /data/apps
        read only = Yes
        invalid users = patrickj
```

Let us assume that you want to permit the user **gbshaw** to manage any file in the UNIX/Linux file system directory **/data/apps**, but you do not want to grant any write permissions beyond that directory tree. Here is one way this can be done:

```
[Apps]
        comment = Application Share
        path = /data/apps
        read only = Yes
        invalid users = patrickj
        admin users = gbshaw
```

Now we have a set of controls that permits only **Employees** who are also members of the group **Doctors**, excluding the user **patrickj**, to have read-only privilege, but the user **gbshaw** is granted administrative rights. The administrative rights conferred upon the user **gbshaw** permit operation as if that user has logged in as the user **root** on the UNIX/Linux system and thus, for access to the directory tree that has been shared (exported), permit the user to override controls that apply to all other users on that resource.

There are additional checkpoint controls that may be used. For example, if for the same share we now want to provide the user **peters** with the ability to write to one directory to which he has write privilege in the UNIX file system, you can specifically permit that with the following settings:

```
[Apps]
        comment = Application Share
        path = /data/apps
        read only = Yes
        invalid users = patrickj
        admin users = gbshaw
        write list = peters
```

This is a particularly complex example at this point, but it begins to demonstrate the possibilities. You should refer to the online manual page for the `smb.conf` file for more information regarding the checkpoint controls that Samba implements.

11.3.2.2 Override Controls

Override controls implemented by Samba permit actions like the adoption of a different identity during file system operations, the forced overwriting of normal file and directory permissions, and so on. You should refer to the online manual page for the `smb.conf` file for more information regarding the override controls that Samba implements.

In the following example, you want to create a Windows networking share that any user can access. However, you want all read and write operations to be performed as if the user **billc** and member of the group **Mentors** read/write the files. Here is one way this can be done:

```
[someshare]
   comment = Some Files Everyone May Overwrite
   path = /data/somestuff
   read only = No
   force user = billc
   force group = Mentors
```

That is all there is to it. Well, it is almost that simple. The downside of this method is that users are logged onto the Windows client as themselves, and then immediately before accessing the file, Samba makes system calls to change the effective user and group to the forced settings specified, completes the file transaction, and then reverts to the actually logged-on identity. This imposes significant overhead on Samba. The alternative way to effectively achieve the same result (but with lower system CPU overheads) is described next.

The use of the *force user* or the *force group* may also have a severe impact on system (particularly on Windows client) performance. If opportunistic locking is enabled on the share (the default), it causes an `oplock break` to be sent to the client even if the client has not opened the file. On networks that have high traffic density, or on links that are routed to a remote network segment, `oplock breaks` can be lost. This results in possible retransmission of the request, or the client may time-out while waiting for the file system transaction (read or write) to complete. The result can be a profound apparent performance degradation as the client continually attempts to reconnect to overcome the effect of the lost `oplock break`, or time-out.

11.3.3   Share Point Directory and File Permissions

Samba has been designed and implemented so that it respects as far as is feasible the security and user privilege controls that are built into the UNIX/Linux operating system. Samba does nothing with respect to file system access that violates file system permission settings, unless it is explicitly instructed to do otherwise through share definition controls. Given that Samba obeys UNIX file system controls, this chapter does not document simple information that can be obtained from a basic UNIX training guide. Instead, one common example of a typical problem is used to demonstrate the most effective solution referred to in the immediately preceding paragraph.

One of the common issues that repeatedly pops up on the Samba mailing lists involves the saving of Microsoft Office files (Word and Excel) to a network drive. Here is the typical sequence:

1. A user opens a Work document from a network drive. The file was owned by user `janetp` and [users], and was set read/write-enabled for everyone.

2. File changes and edits are made.

3. The file is saved, and MS Word is closed.

4. The file is now owned by the user `billc` and group `doctors`, and is set read/write by `billc`, read-only by `doctors`, and no access by everyone.

5. The original owner cannot now access her own file and is "justifiably" upset.

There have been many postings over the years that report the same basic problem. Frequently Samba users want to know when this "bug" will be fixed. The fact is, this is not a bug in Samba at all. Here is the real sequence of what happens in this case.

When the user saves a file, MS Word creates a new (temporary) file. This file is naturally owned by the user who creates the file (`billc`) and has the permissions that follow that user's default settings within the operating system (UNIX/Linux). When MS Word has finished writing the file to disk, it then renames the new (temporary) file to the name of the old one. MS Word does not change the ownership or permissions to what they were on the original file. The file is thus a totally new file, and the old one has been deleted in the process.

Samba received a request to create a new file, and then to rename the file to a new name. The old file that has the same name is now automatically deleted. Samba has no way of knowing that the new file should perhaps have the same ownership and permissions as the old file. To Samba, these are entirely independent operations.

The question is, "How can we solve the problem?"

The solution is simple. Use UNIX file system permissions and controls to your advantage. Follow these simple steps to create a share in which all files will consistently be owned by the same user and the same group:

USING DIRECTORY PERMISSIONS TO FORCE FILE USER AND GROUP OWNERSHIP

1. Change your share definition so that it matches this pattern:

```
[finance]
        path = /usr/data/finance
        browseable = Yes
        read only = No
```

2. Set consistent user and group permissions recursively down the directory tree as shown here:

```
root#  chown -R janetp.users /usr/data/finance
```

3. Set the files and directory permissions to be read/write for owner and group, and not accessible to others (everyone), using the following command:

```
root#  chmod ug+rwx,o-rwx /usr/data/finance
```

4. Set the SGID (supergroup) bit on all directories from the top down. This means all files can be created with the permissions of the group set on the directory. It means all users who are members of the group **finance** can read and write all files in the directory. The directory is not readable or writable by anyone who is not in the **finance** group. Simply follow this example:

```
root#  find /usr/data/finance -type d -exec chmod ug+s {}\;
```

5. Make sure all users that must have read/write access to the directory have **finance** group membership as their primary group, for example, the group they belong to in /etc/passwd.

11.3.4   Managing Windows 200x ACLs

Samba must translate Windows 2000 ACLs to UNIX POSIX ACLs. This has some interesting side effects because there is not a one-to-one equivalence between them. The as-close-as-possible ACLs match means that some transactions are not possible from MS Windows clients. One of these is to reset the ownership of directories and files. If you want to reset ownership, this must be done from a UNIX/Linux login.

There are two possible ways to set ACLs on UNIX/Linux file systems from a Windows network workstation, either via File Manager or via the Microsoft Management Console (MMC) Computer Management interface.

11.3.4.1   Using the MMC Computer Management Interface

1. From a Windows 200x/XP Professional workstation, log on to the domain using the Domain Administrator account (on Samba domains, this is usually the account called root).

2. Click **Start** → **Settings** → **Control Panel** → **Administrative Tools** → **Computer Management**.

3. In the left panel, **[Right mouse menu item] Computer Management (Local)** → **Connect to another computer ...** → **Browse...** → **Advanced** → **Find Now**. In the lower panel, click on the name of the server you wish to administer. Click **OK** → **OK** → **OK**. In the left panel, the entry **Computer Management (Local)** should now reflect the change made. For example, if the server you are administering is called FRODO, the Computer Management entry should now say: **Computer Management (FRODO)**.

4. In the left panel, click **Computer Management (FRODO)** → **[+] Shared Folders** → **Shares**.

5. In the right panel, double-click on the share on which you wish to set/edit ACLs. This brings up the Properties panel. Click the **Security** tab. It is best to edit ACLs using the Advanced editing features. Click the **Advanced** button. This opens a panel that has four tabs. Only the functionality under the Permissions tab can be utilized with respect to a Samba domain server.

6. You may now edit/add/remove access control settings. Be very careful. Many problems have been created by people who decided that everyone should be rejected but one particular group should have full control. This is a catch-22 situation because members of that particular group also belong to the group Everyone, which therefore overrules any permissions set for the permitted group.

7. When you are done with editing, close all panels by clicking through the **OK** buttons until the last panel closes.

11.3.4.2   Using MS Windows Explorer (File Manager)

The following alternative method may be used from a Windows workstation. In this example
we work with a domain called MEGANET, a server called MASSIVE, and a share called Apps.
The underlying UNIX/Linux share point for this share is /data/apps.

1. Click **Start → [right-click] My Computer → Explore → [left panel] [+] My Network
   Places → [+] Entire Network → [+] Microsoft Windows Network → [+] Meganet
   → [+] Massive → [right-click] Apps → Properties → Security → Advanced**. This
   opens a panel that has four tabs. Only the functionality under the Permissions tab
   can be utilized for a Samba domain server.

2. You may now edit/add/remove access control settings. Be very careful. Many problems have been created by people who decided that everyone should be rejected but
   one particular group should have full control. This is a catch-22 situation because
   members of that particular group also belong to the group Everyone, which therefore
   overrules any permissions set for the permitted group.

3. When you are done with editing, close all panels by clicking through the **OK** buttons
   until the last panel closes.

11.3.4.3   Setting Posix ACLs in UNIX/Linux

Yet another alternative method for setting desired security settings on the shared resource
files and directories can be achieved by logging into UNIX/Linux and setting POSIX ACLs
directly using command-line tools. Here is an example session on the same resource as in
the immediately preceding example on a SUSE 9 Linux system:

1. Log into the Linux system as the user root.

2. Change directory to the location of the exported (shared) Windows file share (Apps),
   which is in the directory /data. Execute the following:

   ```
   root#  cd /data
   ```

   Retrieve the existing POSIX ACLs entry by executing:

   ```
   root#  getfacl apps
   # file: apps
   # owner: root
   # group: root
   user::rwx
   group::rwx
   other::r-x
   ```

3. You want to add permission for AppsMgrs to enable them to manage the applications
   (apps) share. It is important to set the ACL recursively so that the AppsMgrs have

this capability throughout the directory tree that is being shared. This is done using the -R option as shown. Execute the following:

```
root#  setfacl -m -R group:AppsMgrs:rwx /data/apps
```

Because setting an ACL does not provide a response, you immediately validate the command executed as follows:

```
root#  getfacl /data/apps
# file: apps
# owner: root
# group: root
user::rwx
group::rwx
group:AppsMgrs:rwx
mask::rwx
other::r-x
```

This confirms that the change of POSIX ACL permissions has been effective.

4. It is highly recommended that you read the online manual page for the **setfacl** and **getfacl** commands. This provides information regarding how to set/read the default ACLs and how that may be propagated through the directory tree. In Windows ACLs terms, this is the equivalent of setting `inheritance` properties.

11.3.5   Key Points Learned

The mish-mash of issues were thrown together into one chapter because it seemed like a good idea. Looking back, this chapter could be broken into two, but it's too late now. It has been done. The highlights covered are as follows:

- Winbind honors and does not override account controls set in Active Directory. This means that password change, logon hours, and so on, are (or soon will be) enforced by Samba winbind. At this time, an out-of-hours login is denied and password change is enforced. At this time, if logon hours expire, the user is not forcibly logged off. That may be implemented at some later date.

- Sign'n'seal (plus schannel support) has been implemented in Samba-3. Beware of potential problems acknowledged by Microsoft as having been fixed but reported by some as still possibly an open issue.

- The combination of Kerberos 5, plus OpenLDAP, plus Samba, cannot replace Microsoft Active Directory. The possibility to do this is not planned in the current Samba-3 roadmap. Samba-3 does aim to provide further improvements in interoperability so that UNIX/Linux systems may be fully integrated into Active Directory domains.

- This chapter reviewed mechanisms by which Samba servers may be kept secure. Each of the four key methodologies was reviewed with specific reference to example deployment techniques.

11.4   Questions and Answers

F.A.Q.

1. **Q:** *Does Samba-3 require the* `Sign'n'seal` *registry hacks needed by Samba-2?*
A: No. Samba-3 fully supports `Sign'n'seal` as well as `schannel` operation. The registry change should not be applied when Samba-3 is used as a domain controller.

2. **Q:** *Does Samba-3 support Active Directory?*
A: Yes. Samba-3 can be a fully participating native mode Active Directory client. Samba-3 does not provide Active Directory services. It cannot be used to replace a Microsoft Active Directory server implementation. Samba-3 can function as an Active Directory client (workstation) toolkit, and it can function as an Active Directory domain member server.

3. **Q:** *When Samba-3 is used with Active Directory, is it necessary to run mixed-mode operation, as was necessary with Samba-2?*
A: No. Samba-3 can be used with NetBIOS over TCP/IP disabled, just as can be done with Windows 200x Server and 200x/XPPro client products. It is no longer necessary to run mixed-mode operation, because Samba-3 can join a native Windows 2003 Server ADS domain.

4. **Q:** *Is it safe to set share-level access controls in Samba?*
A: Yes. Share-level access controls have been supported since early versions of Samba-2. This is very mature technology. Not enough sites make use of this powerful capability, neither on Windows server or with Samba servers.

5. **Q:** *Is it mandatory to set share ACLs to get a secure Samba-3 server?*
A: No. Samba-3 honors UNIX/Linux file system security, supports Windows 200x ACLs, and provides means of securing shares through share definition controls in the `smb.conf` file. The additional support for share-level ACLs is like frosting on the cake. It adds to security but is not essential to it.

6. **Q:** *The* `valid users` *did not work on the* [homes]. *Has this functionality been restored yet?*
A: Yes. This was fixed in Samba-3.0.2. The use of this parameter is strongly recommended

as a safeguard on the *[homes]* meta-service. The correct way to specify this is: *valid users* = %S.

7. **Q:** *Is the bias against use of the* **force user** *and* **force group** *really warranted?*
A: There is no bias. There is a determination to recommend the right tool for the task at hand. After all, it is better than putting users through performance problems, isn't it?

8. **Q:** *The example given for file and directory access control forces all files to be owned by one particular user. I do not like that. Is there any way I can see who created the file?*
A: Sure. You do not have to set the SUID bit on the directory. Simply execute the following command to permit file ownership to be retained by the user who created it:

```
root#  find /usr/data/finance -type d -exec chmod g+s {}\;
```

Note that this required no more than removing the u argument so that the SUID bit is not set for the owner.

9. **Q:** *In the book, "The Official Samba-3 HOWTO and Reference Guide", you recommended use of the Windows NT4 Server Manager (part of the* **SRVTOOLS.EXE**) *utility. Why have you mentioned only the use of the Windows 200x/XP MMC Computer Management utility?*
A: Either tool can be used with equal effect. There is no benefit of one over the other, except that the MMC utility is present on all Windows 200x/XP systems and does not require additional software to be downloaded and installed. Note that if you want to manage user and group accounts in your Samba-controlled domain, the only tool that permits that is the NT4 Domain User Manager, which is provided as part of the **SRVTOOLS.EXE** utility.

10. **Q:** *I tried to set* **valid users = @Engineers**, *but it does not work. My Samba server is an Active Directory domain member server. Has this been fixed now?*
A: The use of this parameter has always required the full specification of the domain account, for example, **valid users = @"MEGANET2\Domain Admins"**.

Chapter 12

INTEGRATING ADDITIONAL SERVICES

You've come a long way now. You have pretty much mastered Samba-3 for most uses it can be put to. Up until now, you have cast Samba-3 in the leading role, and where authentication was required, you have used one or another of Samba's many authentication backends (from flat text files with smbpasswd to LDAP directory integration with ldapsam). Now you can design a solution for a new Abmas business. This business is running Windows Server 2003 and Active Directory, and these are to stay. It's time to master implementing Samba and Samba-supported services in a domain controlled by the latest Windows authentication technologies. Let's get started — this is leading edge.

12.1 Introduction

Abmas has continued its miraculous growth; indeed, nothing seems to be able to stop its diversification into multiple (and seemingly unrelated) fields. Its latest acquisition is Abmas Snack Foods, a big player in the snack-food business.

With this acquisition comes new challenges for you and your team. Abmas Snack Foods is a well-developed business with a huge and heterogeneous network. It already has Windows, NetWare, and Proprietary UNIX, but as yet no Samba or Linux. The network is mature and well-established, and there is no question of its chosen user authentication scheme being changed for now. You need to take a wise new approach.

You have decided to set the ball rolling by introducing Samba-3 into the network gradually, taking over key services and easing the way to a full migration and, therefore, integration into Abmas's existing business later.

12.1.1 Assignment Tasks

You've promised the skeptical Abmas Snack Foods management team that you can show them how Samba can ease itself and other Open Source technologies into their existing infrastructure and deliver sound business advantages. Cost cutting is high on their agenda (a major promise of the acquisition). You have chosen Web proxying and caching as your proving ground.

Abmas Snack Foods has several thousand users housed at its head office and multiple regional offices, plants, and warehouses. A high proportion of the business's work is done online, so Internet access for most of these users is essential. All Internet access, including for all regional offices, is funneled through the head office and is the job of the (now your) networking team. The bandwidth requirements were horrific (comparable to a small ISP), and the team soon discovered proxying and caching. In fact, they became one of the earliest commercial users of Microsoft ISA.

The team is not happy with ISA. Because it never lived up to its marketing promises, it underperformed and had reliability problems. You have pounced on the opportunity to show what Open Source can do. The one thing they do like, however, is ISA's integration with Active Directory. They like that their users, once logged on, are automatically authenticated against the proxy. If your alternative to ISA can operate completely seamlessly in their Active Directory domain, it will be approved.

This is a hands-on exercise. You build software applications so that you obtain the functionality Abmas needs.

12.2   Dissection and Discussion

The key requirements in this business example are straightforward. You are not required to do anything new, just to replicate an existing system, not lose any existing features, and improve performance. The key points are:

- Internet access for most employees

- Distributed system to accommodate load and geographical distribution of users

- Seamless and transparent interoperability with the existing Active Directory domain

12.2.1   Technical Issues

Functionally, the user's Internet Explorer requests a browsing session with the Squid proxy, for which it offers its AD authentication token. Squid hands off the authentication request to the Samba-3 authentication helper application called **ntlm_auth**. This helper is a hook into winbind, the Samba-3 NTLM authentication daemon. Winbind enables UNIX services to authenticate against Microsoft Windows domains, including Active Directory domains. As Active Directory authentication is a modified Kerberos authentication, winbind is assisted in this by local Kerberos 5 libraries configured to check passwords with the Active Directory server. Once the token has been checked, a browsing session is established. This process is entirely transparent and seamless to the user.

Enabling this consists of:

- Preparing the necessary environment using preconfigured packages

- Setting up raw Kerberos authentication against the Active Directory domain

- Configuring, compiling, and then installing the supporting Samba-3 components

- Tying it all together

12.2.2 Political Issues

You are a stranger in a strange land, and all eyes are upon you. Some would even like to see you fail. For you to gain the trust of your newly acquired IT people, it is essential that your solution does everything the old one did, but does it better in every way. Only then will the entrenched positions consider taking up your new way of doing things on a wider scale.

12.3 Implementation

First, your system needs to be prepared and in a known good state to proceed. This consists of making sure that everything the system depends on is present and that everything that could interfere or conflict with the system is removed. You will be configuring the Squid and Samba-3 packages and updating them if necessary. If conflicting packages of these programs are installed, they must be removed.

The following packages should be available on your Red Hat Linux system:

- krb5-libs

- krb5-devel

- krb5-workstation

- krb5-server

- pam_krb5

In the case of SUSE Linux, these packages are called:

- heimdal-lib

- heimdal-devel

- heimdal

- pam_krb5

If the required packages are not present on your system, you must install them from the vendor's installation media. Follow the administrative guide for your Linux system to ensure that the packages are correctly updated.

NOTE

If the requirement is for interoperation with MS Windows Server 2003, it will be necessary to ensure that you are using MIT Kerberos version 1.3.1 or later. Red Hat Linux 9 ships with MIT Kerberos 1.2.7 and thus requires updating.

Heimdal 0.6 or later is required in the case of SUSE Linux. SUSE Enterprise Linux Server 8 ships with Heimdal 0.4. SUSE 9 ships with the necessary version.

12.3.1   Removal of Pre-Existing Conflicting RPMs

If Samba and/or Squid RPMs are installed, they should be updated. You can build both from source.

Locating the packages to be un-installed can be achieved by running:

```
root#  rpm -qa | grep -i samba
root#  rpm -qa | grep -i squid
```

The identified packages may be removed using:

```
root#  rpm -e samba-common
```

12.3.2   Kerberos Configuration

The systems Kerberos installation must be configured to communicate with your primary Active Directory server (ADS KDC).

Strictly speaking, MIT Kerberos version 1.3.4 currently gives the best results, although the current default Red Hat MIT version 1.2.7 gives acceptable results unless you are using Windows 2003 servers.

Officially, neither MIT (1.3.4) nor Heimdal (0.63) Kerberos needs an /etc/krb5.conf file in order to work correctly. All ADS domains automatically create SRV records in the DNS zone Kerberos.REALM.NAME for each KDC in the realm. Since both MIT and Heimdal, KRB5 libraries default to checking for these records, so they automatically find the KDCs. In addition, krb5.conf allows specifying only a single KDC, even if there is more than one. Using the DNS lookup allows the KRB5 libraries to use whichever KDCs are available.

KERBEROS CONFIGURATION STEPS

1. If you find the need to manually configure the `krb5.conf`, you should edit it to have the contents shown in Example 12.3.1. The final fully qualified path for this file should be `/etc/krb5.conf`.

2. The following gotchas often catch people out. Kerberos is case sensitive. Your realm must be in UPPERCASE, or you will get an error: "Cannot find KDC for requested realm while getting initial credentials". Kerberos is picky about time synchronization. The time according to your participating servers must be within 5 minutes or you get an error: "kinit(v5): Clock skew too great while getting initial credentials". Clock skew limits are, in fact, configurable in the Kerberos protocols (the default is 5 minutes). A better solution is to implement NTP throughout your server network. Kerberos needs to be able to do a reverse DNS lookup on the IP address of your KDC. Also, the name that this reverse lookup maps to must either be the NetBIOS name of the KDC (i.e., the hostname with no domain attached) or the NetBIOS name followed by the realm. If all else fails, you can add a `/etc/hosts` entry mapping the IP address of your KDC to its NetBIOS name. If Kerberos cannot do this reverse lookup, you will get a local error when you try to join the realm.

3. You are now ready to test your installation by issuing the command:

```
root#  kinit [USERNAME@REALM]
```

You are asked for your password, which you should enter. The following is a typical console sequence:

```
root#  kinit ADMINISTRATOR@LONDON.ABMAS.BIZ
Password for ADMINISTRATOR@LONDON.ABMAS.BIZ:
```

Make sure that your password is accepted by the Active Directory KDC.

Example 12.3.1 Kerberos Configuration — File: /etc/krb5.conf

```
[libdefaults]
   default_realm = LONDON.ABMAS.BIZ

[realms]
   LONDON.ABMAS.BIZ = {
   kdc = w2k3s.london.abmas.biz
   }
```

The command

```
root#  klist -e
```

shows the Kerberos tickets cached by the system.

12.3.2.1   Samba Configuration

Samba must be configured to correctly use Active Directory. Samba-3 must be used, since it has the necessary components to interface with Active Directory.

SECURING SAMBA-3 WITH ADS SUPPORT STEPS

1. Download the latest stable Samba-3 for Red Hat Linux from the official Samba Team FTP site.[1] The official Samba Team RPMs for Red Hat Fedora Linux contain the **ntlm_auth** tool needed, and are linked against MIT KRB5 version 1.3.1 and therefore are ready for use. The necessary, validated RPM packages for SUSE Linux may be obtained from the SerNet[2] FTP site that is located in Germany. All SerNet RPMs are validated, have the necessary **ntlm_auth** tool, and are statically linked against suitably patched Heimdal 0.6 libraries.

2. Using your favorite editor, change the /etc/samba/smb.conf file so it has contents similar to the example shown in Example 12.3.2.

3. i Next you need to create a computer account in the Active Directory. This sets up the trust relationship needed for other clients to authenticate to the Samba server with an Active Directory Kerberos ticket. This is done with the "net ads join -U [Administrator%Password]" command, as follows:

    ```
    root#  net ads join -U administrator%vulcon
    ```

4. Your new Samba binaries must be started in the standard manner as is applicable to the platform you are running on. Alternatively, start your Active Directory-enabled Samba with the following commands:

    ```
    root#  smbd -D
    root#  nmbd -D
    root#  winbindd -B
    ```

5. We now need to test that Samba is communicating with the Active Directory domain; most specifically, we want to see whether winbind is enumerating users and groups. Issue the following commands:

    ```
    root#  wbinfo -t
    ```

---

[1] <http://ftp.samba.org>
[2] <ftp://ftp.sernet.de/pub/samba>

```
checking the trust secret via RPC calls succeeded
```

This tests whether we are authenticating against Active Directory:

```
root#  wbinfo -u
LONDON+Administrator
LONDON+Guest
LONDON+SUPPORT_388945a0
LONDON+krbtgt
LONDON+jht
LONDON+xjht
```

This enumerates all the users in your Active Directory tree:

```
root#  wbinfo -g
LONDON+Domain Computers
LONDON+Domain Controllers
LONDON+Schema Admins
LONDON+Enterprise Admins
LONDON+Domain Admins
LONDON+Domain Users
LONDON+Domain Guests
LONDON+Group Policy Creator Owners
LONDON+DnsUpdateProxy
```

This enumerates all the groups in your Active Directory tree.

6. Squid uses the **ntlm_auth** helper build with Samba-3. You may test **ntlm_auth** with the command:

```
root#  /usr/bin/ntlm_auth --username=jht
password: XXXXXXX
```

You are asked for your password, which you should enter. You are rewarded with:

```
root#  NT_STATUS_OK: Success (0x0)
```

7. The **ntlm_auth** helper, when run from a command line as the user "root", authenticates against your Active Directory domain (with the aid of winbind). It manages this by reading from the winbind privileged pipe. Squid is running with the permissions of user "squid" and group "squid" and is not able to do this unless we make a vital change. Squid cannot read from the winbind privilege pipe unless you change the

permissions of its directory. This is the single biggest cause of failure in the whole
process. Remember to issue the following command (for Red Hat Linux):

```
root#   chgrp squid /var/cache/samba/winbindd_privileged
root#   chmod 750 /var/cache/samba/winbindd_privileged
```

For SUSE Linux 9, execute the following:

```
root#   chgrp squid /var/lib/samba/winbindd_privileged
root#   chmod 750 /var/lib/samba/winbindd_privileged
```

12.3.2.2   NSS Configuration

For Squid to benefit from Samba-3, NSS must be updated to allow winbind as a valid route
to user authentication.

Edit your /etc/nsswitch.conf file so it has the parameters shown in Example 12.3.3.

Example 12.3.2 Samba Configuration — File: /etc/samba/smb.conf

```
[global]
        workgroup = LONDON
        netbios name = W2K3S
        realm = LONDON.ABMAS.BIZ
        security = ads
        encrypt passwords = yes
        password server = w2k3s.london.abmas.biz
# separate domain and username with '/', like DOMAIN/username
        winbind separator = /
# use UIDs from 10000 to 20000 for domain users
        idmap uid = 10000-20000
\# use GIDs from 10000 to 20000 for domain groups          idmap gid = ←↩
    10000-20000
# allow enumeration of winbind users and groups
        winbind enum users = yes
        winbind enum groups = yes
        winbind user default domain = yes
```

Example 12.3.3 NSS Configuration File Extract — File: /etc/nsswitch.conf

```
passwd: files winbind
shadow: files
group: files winbind
```

12.3.2.3 Squid Configuration

Squid must be configured correctly to interact with the Samba-3 components that handle Active Directory authentication.

12.3.3 Configuration

SQUID CONFIGURATION STEPS

1. If your Linux distribution is SUSE Linux 9, the version of Squid supplied is already enabled to use the winbind helper agent. You can therefore omit the steps that would build the Squid binary programs.

2. Squid, by default, runs as the user `nobody`. You need to add a system user `squid` and a system group `squid` if they are not set up already (if the default Red Hat squid rpms were installed, they will be). Set up a `squid` user in `/etc/passwd` and a `squid` group in `/etc/group` if these aren't there already.

3. You now need to change the permissions on Squid's `var` directory. Enter the following command:

    ```
    root#  chown -R squid /var/cache/squid
    ```

4. Squid must also have control over its logging. Enter the following commands:

    ```
    root#  chown -R chown squid:squid /var/log/squid
    root#  chmod 770 /var/log/squid
    ```

5. Finally, Squid must be able to write to its disk cache! Enter the following commands:

    ```
    root#  chown -R chown squid:squid /var/cache/squid
    root#  chmod 770 /var/cache/squid
    ```

6. The `/etc/squid/squid.conf` file must be edited to include the lines from Example 12.3.4 and Example 12.3.5.

7. You must create Squid's cache directories before it may be run. Enter the following command:

    ```
    root#  squid -z
    ```

8. Finally, start Squid and enjoy transparent Active Directory authentication. Enter the following command:

```
root#  squid
```

Example 12.3.4 Squid Configuration File Extract — /etc/squid.conf [ADMINISTRATIVE PARAMETERS Section]

```
cache_effective_user squid
cache_effective_group squid
```

Example 12.3.5 Squid Configuration File extract — File: /etc/squid.conf [AUTHENTI-CATION PARAMETERS Section]

```
auth_param ntlm program /usr/bin/ntlm_auth \
                        --helper-protocol=squid-2.5-ntlmssp
auth_param ntlm children 5
auth_param ntlm max_challenge_reuses 0
auth_param ntlm max_challenge_lifetime 2 minutes
auth_param basic program /usr/bin/ntlm_auth \
                        --helper-protocol=squid-2.5-basic
auth_param basic children 5
auth_param basic realm Squid proxy-caching web server
auth_param basic credentialsttl 2 hours
acl AuthorizedUsers proxy_auth REQUIRED
http_access allow all AuthorizedUsers
```

12.3.4   Key Points Learned

Microsoft Windows networking protocols permeate the spectrum of technologies that Microsoft Windows clients use, even when accessing traditional services such as Web browsers. Depending on whom you discuss this with, this is either good or bad. No matter how you might evaluate this, the use of NTLMSSP as the authentication protocol for Web proxy access has some advantages over the cookie-based authentication regime used by all competing browsers. It is Samba's implementation of NTLMSSP that makes it attractive to implement the solution that has been demonstrated in this chapter.

12.4   Questions and Answers

The development of the **ntlm_auth** module was first discussed in many Open Source circles in 2002. At the SambaXP conference in Goettingen, Germany, Mr. Francesco Chemolli demonstrated the use of **ntlm_auth** during one of the late developer meetings that took place. Since that time, the adoption of **ntlm_auth** has spread considerably.

The largest report from a site that uses Squid with **ntlm_auth**-based authentication support uses a dual processor server that has 2 GB of memory. It provides Web and FTP proxy services for 10,000 users. Approximately 2,000 of these users make heavy use of the proxy services. According to the source, who wishes to remain anonymous, the sustained transaction load on this server hovers around 140 hits/sec. The following comments were made with respect to questions regarding the performance of this installation:

> [In our] EXTREMELY optimized environment . . . [the] performance impact is almost [nothing]. The "almost" part is due to the brain damage of the ntlm-over-http protocol definition. Suffice to say that its worst-case scenario triples the number of hits needed to perform the same transactions versus basic or digest auth[entication].

You would be well-advised to recognize that all cache-intensive proxying solutions demand a lot of memory. Make certain that your Squid proxy server is equipped with sufficient memory to permit all proxy operations to run out of memory without invoking the overheads involved in the use of memory that has to be swapped to disk.

F.A.Q.

1. **Q:** *What does Samba have to do with Web proxy serving?*
A: To provide transparent interoperability between Windows clients and the network services that are used from them, Samba had to develop tools and facilities that deliver that feature. The benefit of Open Source software is that it can readily be reused. The current **ntlm_auth** module is basically a wrapper around authentication code from the core of the Samba project.

The **ntlm_auth** module supports basic plain-text authentication and NTLMSSP protocols. This module makes it possible for Web and FTP proxy requests to be authenticated without the user being interrupted via his or her Windows logon credentials. This facility is available with MS Windows Explorer and is one of the key benefits claimed for Microsoft Internet Information Server. There are a few open source initiatives to provide support for these protocols in the Apache Web server also.

The short answer is that by adding a wrapper around key authentication components of Samba, other projects (like Squid) can benefit from the labors expended in meeting user interoperability needs.

2. **Q:** *What other services does Samba provide?*
A: Samba-3 is a file and print server. The core components that provide this functionality are **smbd**, **nmbd**, and the identity resolver daemon, **winbindd**.

Samba-3 is an SMB/CIFS client. The core component that provides this is called **smbclient**.

Samba-3 includes a number of helper tools, plug-in modules, utilities, and test and validation facilities. Samba-3 includes glue modules that help provide interoperability between MS Windows clients and UNIX/Linux servers and clients. It includes Winbind agents that make it possible to authenticate UNIX/Linux access attempts as well as logins to an SMB/CIFS authentication server backend. Samba-3 includes name service switch (NSS) modules to permit identity resolution via SMB/CIFS servers (Windows NT4/200x, Samba, and a host of other commercial server products).

3. **Q:** *Does use of Samba (**ntlm_auth**) improve the performance of Squid?*
A: Not really. Samba's **ntlm_auth** module handles only authentication. It requires that Squid make an external call to **ntlm_auth** and therefore actually incurs a little more overhead. Compared with the benefit obtained, that overhead is well worth enduring. Since Squid is a proxy server, and proxy servers tend to require lots of memory, it is good advice to provide sufficient memory when using Squid. Just add a little more to accommodate **ntlm_auth**.

Chapter 13

PERFORMANCE, RELIABILITY, AND AVAILABILITY

Well, you have reached one of the last chapters of this book. It is customary to attempt to wrap up the theme and contents of a book in what is generally regarded as the chapter that should draw conclusions. This book is a suspense thriller, and since the plot of the stories told mostly lead you to bigger, better Samba-3 networking solutions, it is perhaps appropriate to close this book with a few pertinent comments regarding some of the things everyone can do to deliver a reliable Samba-3 network.

In a world so full of noise, how can the sparrow be heard?

—Anonymous

13.1 Introduction

The sparrow is a small bird whose sounds are drowned out by the noise of the busy world it lives in. Likewise, the simple steps that can be taken to improve the reliability and availability of a Samba network are often drowned out by the volume of discussions about grandiose Samba clustering designs. This is not intended to suggest that clustering is not important, because clearly it is. This chapter does not devote itself to discussion of clustering because each clustering methodology uses its own custom tools and methods. Only passing comments are offered concerning these methods.

A search[1] for "samba cluster" produced 71,600 hits. And a search for "highly available samba" and "highly available windows" produced an amazing number of references. It is clear from the resources on the Internet that Windows file and print services availability, reliability, and scalability are of vital interest to corporate network users.

So without further background, you can review a checklist of simple steps that can be taken to ensure acceptable network performance while keeping costs of ownership well under control.

---

[1] <http://www.google.com/search?hl=en&lr=&ie=ISO-8859-1&q=samba+cluster&btnG=Google+Search>

13.2   Dissection and Discussion

If it is your purpose to get the best mileage out of your Samba servers, there is one rule that must be obeyed. If you want the best, keep your implementation as simple as possible. You may well be forced to introduce some complexities, but you should do so only as a last resort.

Simple solutions are likely to be easier to get right than are complex ones. They certainly make life easier for your successor. Simple implementations can be more readily audited than can complex ones.

Problems reported by users fall into three categories: configurations that do not work, those that have broken behavior, and poor performance. The term *broken behavior* means that the function of a particular Samba component appears to work sometimes, but not at others. The resulting intermittent operation is clearly unacceptable. An example of *broken behavior* known to many Windows networking users occurs when the list of Windows machines in MS Explorer changes, sometimes listing machines that are running and at other times not listing them even though the machines are in use on the network.

A significant number of reports concern problems with the **smbfs** file system driver that is part of the Linux kernel, not part of Samba. Users continue to interpret that **smbfs** is part of Samba, simply because Samba includes the front-end tools that are used to manage **smbfs**-based file service connections. So, just for the record, the tools **smbmnt**, **smbmount**, **smbumount**, and **smbumnt** are front-end facilities to core drivers that are supplied as part of the Linux kernel. These tools share a common infrastructure with some Samba components, but they are not maintained as part of Samba and are really foreign to it.

The new project, **cifsfs**, is destined to replace **smbfs**. It, too, is not part of Samba, even though one of the Samba Team members is a prime mover in this project.

Table 13.1 lists typical causes of:

- Not Working (NW)

- Broken Behavior (BB)

- Poor Performance (PP)

Table 13.1 Effect of Common Problems

Problem	NW	BB	PP
File locking	-	X	-
Hardware problems	X	X	X
Incorrect authentication	X	X	-
Incorrect configuration	X	X	X
LDAP problems	X	X	-
Name resolution	X	X	X
Printing problems	X	X	-
Slow file transfer	-	-	X
Winbind problems	X	X	-

It is obvious to all that the first requirement (as a matter of network hygiene) is to eliminate problems that affect basic network operation. This book has provided sufficient working examples to help you to avoid all these problems.

13.3   Guidelines for Reliable Samba Operation

Your objective is to provide a network that works correctly, can grow at all times, is resilient at times of extreme demand, and can scale to meet future needs. The following subject areas provide pointers that can help you today.

13.3.1   Name Resolution

There are three basic current problem areas: bad hostnames, routed networks, and network collisions. These are covered in the following discussion.

13.3.1.1   Bad Hostnames

When configured as a DHCP client, a number of Linux distributions set the system hostname to `localhost`. If the parameter *netbios name* is not specified to something other than `localhost`, the Samba server appears in the Windows Explorer as `LOCALHOST`. Moreover, the entry in the `/etc/hosts` on the Linux server points to IP address `127.0.0.1`. This means that when the Windows client obtains the IP address of the Samba server called `LOCALHOST`, it obtains the IP address `127.0.0.1` and then proceeds to attempt to set up a NetBIOS over TCP/IP connection to it. This cannot work, because that IP address is the local Windows machine itself. Hostnames must be valid for Windows networking to function correctly.

A few sites have tried to name Windows clients and Samba servers with a name that begins with the digits 1-9. This does not work either because it may result in the client or server attempting to use that name as an IP address.

A Samba server called `FRED` in a NetBIOS domain called `COLLISION` in a network environment that is part of the fully-qualified Internet domain namespace known as `parrots.com`, results in DNS name lookups for `fred.parrots.com` and `collision.parrots.com`. It is therefore a mistake to name the domain (workgroup) `collision.parrots.com`, since this results in DNS lookup attempts to resolve `fred.parrots.com.parrots.com`, which most likely fails given that you probably do not have this in your DNS namespace.

NOTE

An Active Directory realm called collision.parrots.com is perfectly okay, although it too must be capable of being resolved via DNS, something that functions correctly if Windows 200x ADS has been properly installed and configured.

13.3.1.2   Routed Networks

NetBIOS networks (Windows networking with NetBIOS over TCP/IP enabled) makes extensive use of UDP-based broadcast traffic, as you saw during the exercises in Chapter 16, "Networking Primer".

UDP broadcast traffic is not forwarded by routers. This means that NetBIOS broadcast-based networking cannot function across routed networks (i.e., multi-subnet networks) unless special provisions are made:

- Either install on every Windows client an LMHOSTS file (located in the directory C:\windows\system32\drivers\etc). It is also necessary to add to the Samba server smb.conf file the parameters *remote announce* and *remote browse sync*. For more information, refer to the online manual page for the smb.conf file.

- Or configure Samba as a WINS server, and configure all network clients to use that WINS server in their TCP/IP configuration.

NOTE

The use of DNS is not an acceptable substitute for WINS. DNS does not store specific information regarding NetBIOS networking particulars that get stored in the WINS name resolution database and that Windows clients require and depend on.

13.3.1.3   Network Collisions

Excessive network activity causes NetBIOS network timeouts. Timeouts may result in blue screen of death (BSOD) experiences. High collision rates may be caused by excessive UDP broadcast activity, by defective networking hardware, or through excessive network loads (another way of saying that the network is poorly designed).

The use of WINS is highly recommended to reduce network broadcast traffic, as outlined in Chapter 16, "Networking Primer".

Under no circumstances should the facility be supported by many routers, known as **Net-BIOS forwarding**, unless you know exactly what you are doing. Inappropriate use of this facility can result in UDP broadcast storms. In one case in 1999, a university network became unusable due to NetBIOS forwarding being enabled on all routers. The problem was discovered during performance testing of a Samba server. The maximum throughput on a 100-Base-T (100 MB/sec) network was less than 15 KB/sec. After the NetBIOS forwarding was turned off, file transfer performance immediately returned to 11 MB/sec.

13.3.2   Samba Configuration

As a general rule, the contents of the `smb.conf` file should be kept as simple as possible. No parameter should be specified unless you know it is essential to operation.

Many UNIX administrators like to fully document the settings in the `smb.conf` file. This is a bad idea because it adds content to the file. The `smb.conf` file is re-read by every **smbd** process every time the file timestamp changes (or, on systems where this does not work, every 20 seconds or so).

As the size of the `smb.conf` file grows, the risk of introducing parsing errors also increases. It is recommended to keep a fully documented `smb.conf` file on hand, and then to operate Samba only with an optimized file.

The preferred way to maintain a documented file is to call it something like `smb.conf.master`. You can generate the optimized file by executing:

```
root#  testparm -s smb.conf.master > smb.conf
```

You should carefully observe all warnings issued. It is also a good practice to execute the following command to confirm correct interpretation of the `smb.conf` file contents:

```
root#  testparm
Load smb config files from /etc/samba/smb.conf
Can't find include file /etc/samba/machine.
Processing section "[homes]"
Processing section "[print$]"
Processing section "[netlogon]"
Processing section "[Profiles]"
Processing section "[printers]"
Processing section "[media]"
Processing section "[data]"
Processing section "[cdr]"
Processing section "[apps]"
Loaded services file OK.
'winbind separator = +' might cause problems with group membership.
Server role: ROLE_DOMAIN_PDC
```

```
Press enter to see a dump of your service definitions
```

You now, of course, press the enter key to complete the command, or else abort it by pressing Ctrl-C. The important thing to note is the noted Server role, as well as warning messages. Noted configuration conflicts must be remedied before proceeding. For example, the following error message represents a common fatal problem:

```
ERROR: both 'wins support = true' and 'wins server = <server list>'
cannot be set in the smb.conf file. nmbd will abort with this setting.
```

There are two parameters that can cause severe network performance degradation: *socket options* and *socket address*. The *socket options* parameter was often necessary when Samba was used with the Linux 2.2.x kernels. Later kernels are largely self-tuning and seldom benefit from this parameter being set. Do not use either parameter unless it has been proven necessary to use them.

Another `smb.conf` parameter that may cause severe network performance degradation is the *strict sync* parameter. Do not use this at all. There is no good reason to use this with any modern Windows client. The *strict sync* is often used with the *sync always* parameter. This, too, can severely degrade network performance, so do not set it; if you must, do so with caution.

Finally, many network administrators deliberately disable opportunistic locking support. While this does not degrade Samba performance, it significantly degrades Windows client performance because this disables local file caching on Windows clients and forces every file read and written to invoke a network read or write call. If for any reason you must disable oplocks (opportunistic locking) support, do so only on the share on which it is required. That way, all other shares can provide oplock support for operations that are tolerant of it. See Section 15.9 for more information.

13.3.3   Use and Location of BDCs

On a network segment where there is a PDC and a BDC, the BDC carries the bulk of the network logon processing. If the BDC is a heavily loaded server, the PDC carries a greater proportion of authentication and logon processing. When a sole BDC on a routed network segment gets heavily loaded, it is possible that network logon requests and authentication requests may be directed to a BDC on a distant network segment. This significantly hinders WAN operations and is undesirable.

As a general guide, instead of adding domain member servers to a network, you would be better advised to add BDCs until there are fewer than 30 Windows clients per BDC. Beyond that ratio, you should add domain member servers. This practice ensures that there are always sufficient domain controllers to handle logon requests and authentication traffic.

13.3.4   Use One Consistent Version of MS Windows Client

Every network client has its own peculiarities. From a management perspective, it is easier to deal with one version of MS Windows that is maintained to a consistent update level than it is to deal with a mixture of clients.

On a number of occasions, particular Microsoft service pack updates of a Windows server or client have necessitated special handling from the Samba server end. If you want to remain sane, keep you client workstation configurations consistent.

13.3.5   For Scalability, Use SAN-Based Storage on Samba Servers

Many SAN-based storage systems permit more than one server to share a common data store. Use of a shared SAN data store means that you do not need to use time- and resource-hungry data synchronization techniques.

The use of a collection of relatively low-cost front-end Samba servers that are coupled to a shared backend SAN data store permits load distribution while containing costs below that of installing and managing a complex clustering facility.

13.3.6   Distribute Network Load with MSDFS

Microsoft DFS (distributed file system) technology has been implemented in Samba. MS-DFS permits data to be accessed from a single share and yet to actually be distributed across multiple actual servers. Refer to *TOSHARG2*, Chapter 19, for information regarding implementation of an MSDFS installation.

The combination of multiple backend servers together with a front-end server and use of MSDFS can achieve almost the same as you would obtain with a clustered Samba server.

13.3.7   Replicate Data to Conserve Peak-Demand Wide-Area Bandwidth

Consider using **rsync** to replicate data across the WAN during times of low utilization. Users can then access the replicated data store rather than needing to do so across the WAN. This works best for read-only data, but with careful planning can be implemented so that modified files get replicated back to the point of origin. Be careful with your implementation if you choose to permit modification and return replication of the modified file; otherwise, you may inadvertently overwrite important data.

13.3.8   Hardware Problems

Networking hardware prices have fallen sharply over the past 5 years. A surprising number of Samba networking problems over this time have been traced to defective network interface cards (NICs) or defective HUBs, switches, and cables.

Not surprising is the fact that network administrators do not like to be shown to have made a bad decision. Money saved in buying low-cost hardware may result in high costs incurred in corrective action.

Defective NICs, HUBs, and switches may appear as intermittent network access problems, intermittent or persistent data corruption, slow network throughput, low performance, or even as BSOD problems with MS Windows clients. In one case, a company updated several workstations with newer, faster Windows client machines that triggered problems during logon as well as data integrity problems on an older PC that was unaffected so long as the new machines were kept shut down.

Defective hardware problems may take patience and persistence before the real cause can be discovered.

Networking hardware defects can significantly impact perceived Samba performance, but defective RAID controllers as well as SCSI and IDE hard disk controllers have also been known to impair Samba server operations. One business came to this realization only after replacing a Samba installation with MS Windows Server 2000 running on the same hardware. The root of the problem completely eluded the network administrator until the entire server was replaced. While you may well think that this would never happen to you, experience shows that given the right (unfortunate) circumstances, this can happen to anyone.

13.3.9   Large Directories

There exist applications that create or manage directories containing many thousands of files. Such applications typically generate many small files (less than 100 KB). At the best of times, under UNIX, listing of the files in a directory that contains many files is slow. By default, Windows NT, 200x, and XP Pro cause network file system directory lookups on a Samba server to be performed for both the case preserving file name as well as for the mangled (8.3) file name. This incurs a huge overhead on the Samba server that may slow down the system dramatically.

In an extreme case, the performance impact was dramatic. File transfer from the Samba server to a Windows XP Professional workstation over 1 Gigabit Ethernet for 250-500 KB files was measured at approximately 30 MB/sec. But when tranferring a directory containing 120,000 files, all from 50KB to 60KB in size, the transfer rate to the same workstation was measured at approximately 1.5 KB/sec. The net transfer was on the order of a factor of 20-fold slower.

The symptoms that will be observed on the Samba server when a large directory is accessed will be that aggregate I/O (typically blocks read) will be relatively low, yet the wait I/O times will be incredibly long while at the same time the read queue is large. Close observation will show that the hard drive that the file system is on will be thrashing wildly.

Samba-3.0.12 and later, includes new code that radically improves Samba perfomance. The secret to this is really in the *case sensitive* = True line. This tells smbd never to scan for case-insensitive versions of names. So if an application asks for a file called FOO, and it can not be found by a simple stat call, then smbd will return "file not found" immediately without scanning the containing directory for a version of a different case.

Canonicalize all the files in the directory to have one case, upper or lower - either will do. Then set up a new custom share for the application as follows:

```
[bigshare]
        path = /data/xrayfiles/neurosurgeons/
        read only = no
        case sensitive = True
        default case = upper
        preserve case = no
        short preserve case = no
```

All files and directories under the *path* directory must be in the same case as specified in the smb.conf stanza. This means that smbd will not be able to find lower case filenames with these settings. Note, this is done on a per-share basis.

13.4   Key Points Learned

This chapter has touched in broad sweeps on a number of simple steps that can be taken to ensure that your Samba network is resilient, scalable, and reliable, and that it performs well.

Always keep in mind that someone is responsible to maintain and manage your design. In the long term, that may not be you. Spare a thought for your successor and give him or her an even break.

Last, but not least, you should not only keep the network design simple, but also be sure it is well documented. This book may serve as your pattern for documenting every aspect of your design, its implementation, and particularly the objects and assumptions that underlie it.

Chapter 14

SAMBA SUPPORT

One of the most difficult to answer questions in the information technology industry is, "What is support?". That question irritates some folks, as much as common answers may annoy others.

The most aggravating situation pertaining to support is typified when, as a Linux user, a call is made to an Internet service provider who, instead of listening to the problem to find a solution, blandly replies: "Oh, Linux? We do not support Linux!". It has happened to me, and similar situations happen through-out the IT industry. Answers like that are designed to inform us that there are some customers that a business just does not want to deal with, and well may we feel the anguish of the rejection that is dished out.

One way to consider support is to view it as consisting of the right answer, in the right place, at the right time, no matter the situation. Support is all that it takes to take away pain, disruption, inconvenience, loss of productivity, disorientation, uncertainty, and real or perceived risk.

One of the forces that has become a driving force for the adoption of open source software is the fact that many IT businesses have provided services that have perhaps failed to deliver what the customer expected, or that have been found wanting for other reasons.

In recognition of the need for needs satisfaction as the primary experience an information technology user or consumer expects, the information provided in this chapter may help someone to avoid an unpleasant experience in respect of problem resolution.

In the open source software arena there are two support options: free support and paid-for (commercial) support.

14.1 Free Support

Free support may be obtained from friends, colleagues, user groups, mailing lists, and interactive help facilities. An example of an interactive dacility is the Internet relay chat (IRC) channels that host user supported mutual assistance.

The Samba project maintains a mailing list that is commonly used to discuss solutions to Samba deployments. Information regarding subscription to the Samba mailing list can be found on the Samba web[1] site. The public mailing list that can be used to obtain free, user contributed, support is called the **samba** list. The email address for this list is at **mail:samba@samba.org**. Information regarding the Samba IRC channels may be found on the Samba IRC[2] web page.

As a general rule, it is considered poor net behavior to contact a Samba Team member directly for free support. Most active members of the Samba Team work exceptionally long hours to assist users who have demonstrated a qualified problem. Some team members may respond to direct email or telephone contact, with requests for assistance, by requesting payment. A few of the Samba Team members actually provide professional paid-for Samba support and it is therefore wise to show appropriate discretion and reservation in all direct contact.

When you stumble across a Samba bug, often the quickest way to get it resolved is by posting a bug report[3]. All such reports are mailed to the responsible code maintainer for action. The better the report, and the more serious it is, the sooner it will be dealt with. On the other hand, if the responsible person can not duplicate the reported bug it is likely to be rejected. It is up to you to provide sufficient information that will permit the problem to be reproduced.

We all recognize that sometimes free support does not provide the answer that is sought within the time-frame required. At other times the problem is elusive and you may lack the experience necessary to isolate the problem and thus to resolve it. This is a situation where is may be prudent to purchase paid-for support.

14.2   Commercial Support

There are six basic support oriented services that are most commonly sought by Samba sites:

- Assistance with network design
- Staff Training
- Assistance with Samba network deployment and installation
- Priority telephone or email Samba configuration assistance
- Trouble-shooting and diagnostic assistance
- Provision of quality assured ready-to-install Samba binary packages

Information regarding companies that provide professional Samba support can be obtained by performing a Google search, as well as by reference to the Samba Support[4] web page. Companies who notify the Samba Team that they provide commercial support are given a free listing that is sorted by the country of origin. Multiple listings are permitted, however

---

[1] <https://lists.samba.org/mailman/>
[2] <http://www.samba.org/samba.irc.html>
[3] <https://bugzilla.samba.org/>
[4] <http://www.samba.org/samba/support.html>

no guarantee is offered. It is left to you to qualify a support provider and to satisfy yourself that both the company and its staff are able to deliver what is required of them.

The policy within the Samba Team is to treat all commercial support providers equally and to show no preference. As a result, Samba Team members who provide commercial support are lumped in with everyone else. You are encouraged to obtain the services needed from a company in your local area. The open source movement is pro-community; so do what you can to help a local business to prosper.

Open source software support can be found in any quality, at any price and in any place you can to obtain it. Over 180 companies around the world provide Samba support, there is no excuse for suffering in the mistaken belief that Samba is unsupported software — it is supported.

Chapter 15

A COLLECTION OF USEFUL TIDBITS

Information presented here is considered to be either basic or well-known material that is informative yet helpful. Over the years, I have observed an interesting behavior. There is an expectation that the process for joining a Windows client to a Samba-controlled Windows domain may somehow involve steps different from doing so with Windows NT4 or a Windows ADS domain. Be assured that the steps are identical, as shown in the example given below.

15.1 Joining a Domain: Windows 200x/XP Professional

Microsoft Windows NT/200x/XP Professional platforms can participate in Domain Security. This section steps through the process for making a Windows 200x/XP Professional machine a member of a Domain Security environment. It should be noted that this process is identical when joining a domain that is controlled by Windows NT4/200x as well as a Samba PDC.

STEPS TO JOIN A DOMAIN

1. Click **Start**.

2. Right-click **My Computer**, and then select **Properties**.

3. The opening panel is the same one that can be reached by clicking **System** on the Control Panel. See Figure 15.1.

4. Click the **Computer Name** tab. This panel shows the **Computer Description**, the **Full computer name**, and the **Workgroup** or **Domain name**. Clicking the **Network ID** button launches the configuration wizard. Do not use this with Samba-3. If you wish to change the computer name, or join or leave the domain, click the **Change** button. See Figure 15.2.

5. Click on **Change**. This panel shows that our example machine (TEMPTATION) is in a workgroup called WORKGROUP. We join the domain called MIDEARTH. See Figure 15.3.

Figure 15.1 The General Panel.

6. Enter the name **MIDEARTH** in the field below the Domain radio button. This panel shows that our example machine (TEMPTATION) is set to join the domain called MIDEARTH. See Figure 15.4.

7. Now click the **OK** button. A dialog box should appear to allow you to provide the credentials (username and password) of a domain administrative account that has the rights to add machines to the domain. Enter the name "root" and the root password from your Samba-3 server. See Figure 15.5.

8. Click **OK**. The "Welcome to the MIDEARTH domain" dialog box should appear. At this point, the machine must be rebooted. Joining the domain is now complete.

The screen capture shown in Figure 15.4 has a button labeled **More...**. This button opens a panel in which you can set (or change) the Primary DNS suffix of the computer. This is a parameter that mainly affects members of Microsoft Active Directory. Active Directory is heavily oriented around the DNS namespace.

Where NetBIOS technology uses WINS as well as UDP broadcast as key mechanisms for name resolution, Active Directory servers register their services with the Microsoft Dynamic DNS server. Windows clients must be able to query the correct DNS server to find the services (like which machines are domain controllers or which machines have the Netlogon service running).

The default setting of the Primary DNS suffix is the Active Directory domain name. When you change the Primary DNS suffix, this does not affect domain membership, but it can break network browsing and the ability to resolve your computer name to a valid IP address.

Figure 15.2 The Computer Name Panel.

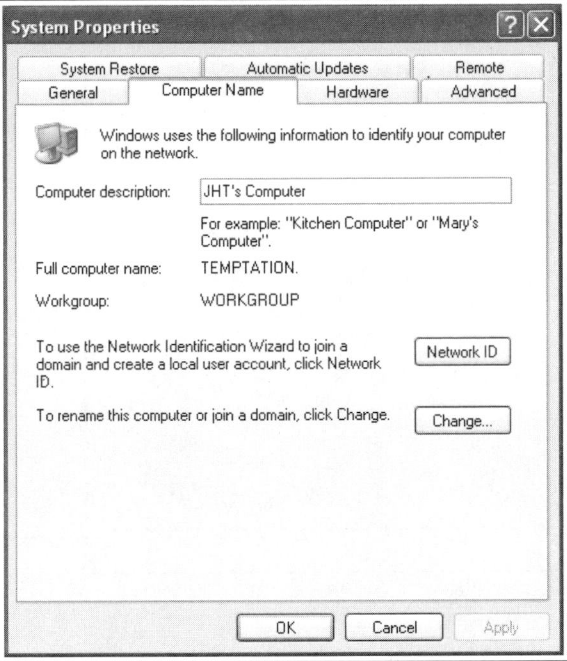

The Primary DNS suffix parameter principally affects MS Windows clients that are members of an Active Directory domain. Where the client is a member of a Samba domain, it is preferable to leave this field blank.

According to Microsoft documentation, "If this computer belongs to a group with **Group Policy** enabled on **Primary DNS suffice of this computer**, the string specified in the Group Policy is used as the primary DNS suffix and you might need to restart your computer to view the correct setting. The local setting is used only if Group Policy is disabled or unspecified."

15.2   Samba System File Location

One of the frustrations expressed by subscribers to the Samba mailing lists revolves around the choice of where the default Samba Team build and installation process locates its Samba files. The location, chosen in the early 1990s, for the default installation is in the `/usr/local/samba` directory. This is a perfectly reasonable location, particularly given all the other Open Source software that installs into the `/usr/local` subdirectories.

Several UNIX vendors, and Linux vendors in particular, elected to locate the Samba files in a location other than the Samba Team default.

Linux vendors, working in conjunction with the Free Standards Group (FSG), Linux Standards Base (LSB), and File Hierarchy System (FHS), have elected to locate the configuration files under the `/etc/samba` directory, common binary files (those used by users) in the `/usr/`

Figure 15.3 The Computer Name Changes Panel

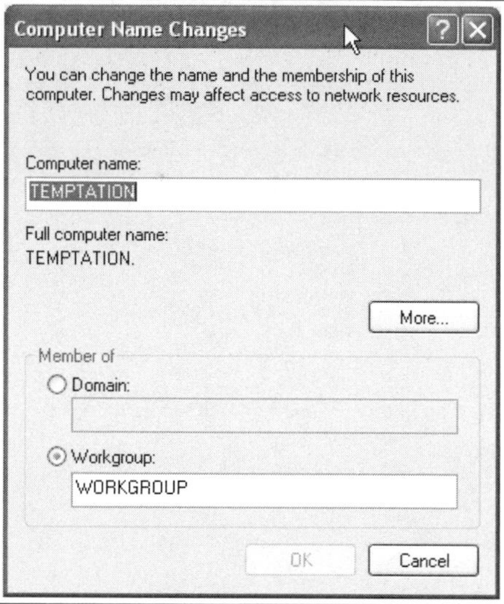

Figure 15.4 The Computer Name Changes Panel — Domain MIDEARTH

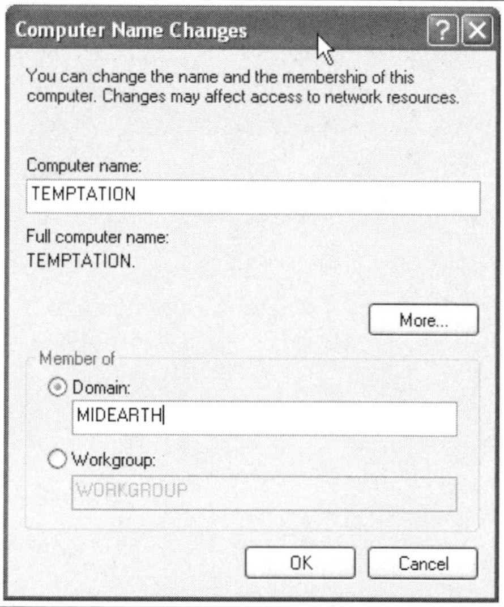

bin directory, and the administrative files (daemons) in the /usr/sbin directory. Support files for the Samba Web Admin Tool (SWAT) are located under the /usr/share directory, either in /usr/share/samba/swat or in /usr/share/swat. There are additional support files for **smbd** in the /usr/lib/samba directory tree. The files located there include the dynamically loadable modules for the passdb backend as well as for the VFS modules.

Samba creates runtime control files and generates log files. The runtime control files (tdb and dat files) are stored in the /var/lib/samba directory. Log files are created in /var/log/samba.

Figure 15.5 Computer Name Changes — User name and Password Panel

When Samba is built and installed using the default Samba Team process, all files are located under the `/usr/local/samba` directory tree. This makes it simple to find the files that Samba owns.

One way to find the Samba files that are installed on your UNIX/Linux system is to search for the location of all files called **smbd**. Here is an example:

```
root#  find / -name smbd -print
```

You can find the location of the configuration files by running:

```
root#  /path-to-binary-file/smbd -b | more
...
Paths:
   SBINDIR: /usr/sbin
   BINDIR: /usr/bin
   SWATDIR: /usr/share/samba/swat
   CONFIGFILE: /etc/samba/smb.conf
   LOGFILEBASE: /var/log/samba
   LMHOSTSFILE: /etc/samba/lmhosts
   LIBDIR: /usr/lib/samba
   SHLIBEXT: so
   LOCKDIR: /var/lib/samba
   PIDDIR: /var/run/samba
   SMB_PASSWD_FILE: /etc/samba/smbpasswd
   PRIVATE_DIR: /etc/samba
...
```

If you wish to locate the Samba version, just run:

```
root#  /path-to-binary-file/smbd -V
Version 3.0.20-SUSE
```

Many people have been caught by installation of Samba using the default Samba Team process when it was already installed by the platform vendor's method. If your platform uses RPM format packages, you can check to see if Samba is installed by executing:

```
root#  rpm -qa | grep samba
samba3-pdb-3.0.20-1
samba3-vscan-0.3.6-0
samba3-winbind-3.0.20-1
samba3-3.0.20-1
samba3-python-3.0.20-1
samba3-utils-3.0.20-1
samba3-doc-3.0.20-1
samba3-client-3.0.20-1
samba3-cifsmount-3.0.20-1
```

The package names, of course, vary according to how the vendor, or the binary package builder, prepared them.

15.3   Starting Samba

Samba essentially consists of two or three daemons. A daemon is a UNIX application that runs in the background and provides services. An example of a service is the Apache Web server for which the daemon is called **httpd**. In the case of Samba, there are three daemons, two of which are needed as a minimum.

The Samba server is made up of the following daemons:

nmbd This daemon handles all name registration and resolution requests. It is the primary vehicle involved in network browsing. It handles all UDP-based protocols. The **nmbd** daemon should be the first command started as part of the Samba startup process.

smbd This daemon handles all TCP/IP-based connection services for file- and print-based operations. It also manages local authentication. It should be started immediately following the startup of **nmbd**.

winbindd This daemon should be started when Samba is a member of a Windows NT4 or ADS domain. It is also needed when Samba has trust relationships with another domain. The **winbindd** daemon will check the `smb.conf` file for the presence of the *idmap uid* and *idmap gid* parameters. If they are not found, **winbindd** bails out and refuses to start.

Example 15.3.1 A Useful Samba Control Script for SUSE Linux

```
#!/bin/bash
#
# Script to start/stop samba
# Locate this in /sbin as a file called 'samba'

RCD=/etc/rc.d

if [ z$1 == 'z' ]; then
        echo $0 - No arguments given; must be start or stop.
        exit
fi

if [ $1 == 'start' ]; then
        ${RCD}/nmb start
        ${RCD}/smb start
        ${RCD}/winbind start

fi
if [ $1 == 'stop' ]; then
        ${RCD}/smb stop
        ${RCD}/winbind stop
        ${RCD}/nmb stop
fi
if [ $1 == 'restart' ]; then
        ${RCD}/smb stop
        ${RCD}/winbind stop
        ${RCD}/nmb stop
        sleep 5
        ${RCD}/nmb start
        ${RCD}/smb start
        ${RCD}/winbind start
fi
exit 0
```

When Samba has been packaged by an operating system vendor, the startup process is typically a custom feature of its integration into the platform as a whole. Please refer to your operating system platform administration manuals for specific information pertaining to correct management of Samba startup.

SUSE Linux implements individual control over each Samba daemon. A Samba control script that can be conveniently executed from the command line is shown in Example 15.3.1. This can be located in the directory /sbin in a file called samba. This type of control script should be owned by user root and group root, and set so that only root can execute it.

A sample startup script for a Red Hat Linux system is shown in Example 15.3.2. This file could be located in the directory /etc/rc.d and can be called samba. A similar startup script is required to control **winbind**. If you want to find more information regarding startup scripts please refer to the packaging section of the Samba source code distribution tarball. The packaging files for each platform include a startup control file.

15.4   DNS Configuration Files

The following files are common to all DNS server configurations. Rather than repeat them multiple times, they are presented here for general reference.

15.4.1   The Forward Zone File for the Loopback Adaptor

The forward zone file for the loopback address never changes. An example file is shown in Example 15.4.1. All traffic destined for an IP address that is hosted on a physical interface on the machine itself is routed to the loopback adaptor. This is a fundamental design feature of the TCP/IP protocol implementation. The loopback adaptor is called localhost.

15.4.2   The Reverse Zone File for the Loopback Adaptor

The reverse zone file for the loopback address as shown in Example 15.4.2 is necessary so that references to the address 127.0.0.1 can be resolved to the correct name of the interface.

15.4.3   DNS Root Server Hint File

The content of the root hints file as shown in Example 15.4.3 changes slowly over time. Periodically this file should be updated from the source shown. Because of its size, this file is located at the end of this chapter.

15.5   Alternative LDAP Database Initialization

The following procedure may be used as an alternative means of configuring the initial LDAP database. Many administrators prefer to have greater control over how system files get configured.

15.5.1   Initialization of the LDAP Database

The first step to get the LDAP server ready for action is to create the LDIF file from which the LDAP database will be preloaded. This is necessary to create the containers into which the user, group, and other accounts are written. It is also necessary to preload the well-known Windows NT Domain Groups, as they must have the correct SID so that they can be recognized as special NT Groups by the MS Windows clients.

LDAP DIRECTORY PRE-LOAD STEPS

1. Create a directory in which to store the files you use to generate the LDAP LDIF file for your system. Execute the following:

```
root#   mkdir /etc/openldap/SambaInit
root#   chown root:root /etc/openldap/SambaInit
root#   chmod 700 /etc/openldap/SambaInit
```

2. Install the files shown in Example 15.5.1, Example 15.5.2, and Example 15.5.3 into the directory /etc/openldap/SambaInit/SMBLDAP-ldif-preconfig.sh. These three files are, respectively, parts A, B, and C of the SMBLDAP-ldif-preconfig.sh file.

3. Install the files shown in Example 15.5.4 and Example 15.5.5 into the directory /etc/openldap/SambaInit/nit-ldif.pat. These two files are parts A and B, respectively, of the init-ldif.pat file.

4. Change to the /etc/openldap/SambaInit directory. Execute the following:

```
root#   ./SMBLDAP-ldif-preconfig.sh

How do you wish to refer to your organization?
Suggestions:
        Black Tire Company, Inc.
        Cat With Hat Ltd.
How would you like your organization name to appear?
Your organization name is: My Organization
Enter a new name is this is not what you want, press Enter to Continue.
Name [My Organization]: Abmas Inc.

Samba Config File Location [/etc/samba/smb.conf]:
Enter a new full path or press Enter to continue.
Samba Config File Location [/etc/samba/smb.conf]:
Domain Name: MEGANET2
Domain SID: S-1-5-21-3504140859-1010554828-2431957765

The name of your Internet domain is now needed in a special format
as follows, if your domain name is mydomain.org, what we need is
the information in the form of:
        Domain ID: mydomain
        Top level: org
If your fully qualified hostname is: snoopy.bazaar.garagesale.net
where "snoopy" is the name of the machine,
Then the information needed is:
        Domain ID: garagesale
        Top Level: net
```

```
Found the following domain name: abmas.biz
I think the bit we are looking for might be: abmas
Enter the domain name or press Enter to continue:

The top level organization name I will use is: biz
Enter the top level org name or press Enter to continue:
root#
```

This creates a file called `MEGANET2.ldif`.

5. It is now time to preload the LDAP database with the following command:

```
root#  slapadd -v -l MEGANET2.ldif
added: "dc=abmas,dc=biz" (00000001)
added: "cn=Manager,dc=abmas,dc=biz" (00000002)
added: "ou=People,dc=abmas,dc=biz" (00000003)
added: "ou=Computers,dc=abmas,dc=biz" (00000004)
added: "ou=Groups,dc=abmas,dc=biz" (00000005)
added: "ou=Domains,dc=abmas,dc=biz" (00000006)
added: "sambaDomainName=MEGANET2,ou=Domains,dc=abmas,dc=biz" (00000007)
added: "cn=domadmins,ou=Groups,dc=abmas,dc=biz" (00000008)
added: "cn=domguests,ou=Groups,dc=abmas,dc=biz" (00000009)
added: "cn=domusers,ou=Groups,dc=abmas,dc=biz" (0000000a)
```

You should verify that the account information was correctly loaded by executing:

```
root#  slapcat
dn: dc=abmas,dc=biz
objectClass: dcObject
objectClass: organization
dc: abmas
o: Abmas Inc.
description: Posix and Samba LDAP Identity Database
structuralObjectClass: organization
entryUUID: af552f8e-c4a1-1027-9002-9421e01bf474
creatorsName: cn=manager,dc=abmas,dc=biz
modifiersName: cn=manager,dc=abmas,dc=biz
createTimestamp: 20031217055747Z
modifyTimestamp: 20031217055747Z
entryCSN: 2003121705:57:47Z#0x0001#0#0000
...

dn: cn=domusers,ou=Groups,dc=abmas,dc=biz
objectClass: posixGroup
objectClass: sambaGroupMapping
```

```
gidNumber: 513
cn: domusers
sambaSID: S-1-5-21-3504140859-1010554828-2431957765-513
sambaGroupType: 2
displayName: Domain Users
description: Domain Users
structuralObjectClass: posixGroup
entryUUID: af7e98ba-c4a1-1027-900b-9421e01bf474
creatorsName: cn=manager,dc=abmas,dc=biz
modifiersName: cn=manager,dc=abmas,dc=biz
createTimestamp: 20031217055747Z
modifyTimestamp: 20031217055747Z
entryCSN: 2003121705:57:47Z#0x000a#0#0000
```

6. Your LDAP database is ready for testing. You can now start the LDAP server using the system tool for your Linux operating system. For SUSE Linux, you can do this as follows:

```
root#  rcldap start
```

7. It is now a good idea to validate that the LDAP server is running correctly. Execute the following:

```
root#  ldapsearch -x -b "dc=abmas,dc=biz" "(ObjectClass=*)"
# extended LDIF
#
# LDAPv3
# base <dc=abmas,dc=biz> with scope sub
# filter: (ObjectClass=*)
# requesting: ALL
#

# abmas.biz
dn: dc=abmas,dc=biz
objectClass: dcObject
objectClass: organization
dc: abmas
o: Abmas Inc.
description: Posix and Samba LDAP Identity Database
...
# domusers, Groups, abmas.biz
dn: cn=domusers,ou=Groups,dc=abmas,dc=biz
objectClass: posixGroup
objectClass: sambaGroupMapping
gidNumber: 513
```

```
cn: domusers
sambaSID: S-1-5-21-3504140859-1010554828-2431957765-513
sambaGroupType: 2
displayName: Domain Users
description: Domain Users

# search result
search: 2
result: 0 Success

# numResponses: 11
# numEntries: 10
```

Your LDAP server is ready for creation of additional accounts.

15.6   The LDAP Account Manager

The LDAP Account Manager (LAM) is an application suite that has been written in PHP. LAM can be used with any Web server that has PHP4 support. It connects to the LDAP server either using unencrypted connections or via SSL/TLS. LAM can be used to manage Posix accounts as well as SambaSAMAccounts for users, groups, and Windows machines (hosts).

LAM is available from the LAM[1] home page and from its mirror sites. LAM has been released under the GNU GPL version 2. The current version of LAM is 0.4.9. Release of version 0.5 is expected in the third quarter of 2005.

Requirements:

- A web server that will work with PHP4.

- PHP4 (available from the PHP[2] home page.)

- OpenLDAP 2.0 or later.

- A Web browser that supports CSS.

- Perl.

- The gettext package.

- mcrypt + mhash (optional).

- It is also a good idea to install SSL support.

LAM is a useful tool that provides a simple Web-based device that can be used to manage the contents of the LDAP directory to:

- Display user/group/host and Domain entries.

---

[1] <http://sourceforge.net/projects/lam/>
[2] <http://www.php.net/>

- Manage entries (Add/Delete/Edit).

- Filter and sort entries.

- Store and use multiple operating profiles.

- Edit organizational units (OUs).

- Upload accounts from a file.

- Is compatible with Samba-2.2.x and Samba-3.

When correctly configured, LAM allows convenient management of UNIX (Posix) and Samba user, group, and windows domain member machine accounts.

The default password is "lam." It is highly recommended that you use only an SSL connection to your Web server for all remote operations involving LAM. If you want secure connections, you must configure your Apache Web server to permit connections to LAM using only SSL.

APACHE CONFIGURATION STEPS FOR LAM

1. Extract the LAM package by untarring it as shown here:

```
root#  tar xzf ldap-account-manager_0.4.9.tar.gz
```

Alternatively, install the LAM DEB for your system using the following command:

```
root#  dpkg -i ldap-account-manager_0.4.9.all.deb
```

2. Copy the extracted files to the document root directory of your Web server. For example, on SUSE Linux Enterprise Server 9, copy to the /srv/www/htdocs directory.

3. Set file permissions using the following commands:

```
root#  chown -R wwwrun:www /srv/www/htdocs/lam
root#  chmod 755 /srv/www/htdocs/lam/sess
root#  chmod 755 /srv/www/htdocs/lam/tmp
root#  chmod 755 /srv/www/htdocs/lam/config
root#  chmod 755 /srv/www/htdocs/lam/lib/*pl
```

4. Using your favorite editor create the following config.cfg LAM configuration file:

```
root#  cd /srv/www/htdocs/lam/config
root#  cp config.cfg_sample config.cfg
root#  vi config.cfg
```

An example file is shown in Example 15.6.1. This is the minimum configuration that must be completed. The LAM profile file can be created using a convenient wizard that is part of the LAM configuration suite.

5. Start your Web server then, using your Web browser, connect to LAM[3] URL. Click on the the *Configuration Login* link then click on the Configuration Wizard link to begin creation of the default profile so that LAM can connect to your LDAP server. Alternately, copy the `lam.conf_sample` file to a file called `lam.conf` then, using your favorite editor, change the settings to match local site needs.

An example of a working file is shown here in Example 15.6.2. This file has been stripped of comments to keep the size small. The comments and help information provided in the profile file that the wizard creates is very useful and will help many administrators to avoid pitfalls. Your configuration file obviously reflects the configuration options that are preferred at your site.

It is important that your LDAP server is running at the time that LAM is being configured. This permits you to validate correct operation. An example of the LAM login screen is provided in Figure 15.6.

Figure 15.6 The LDAP Account Manager Login Screen

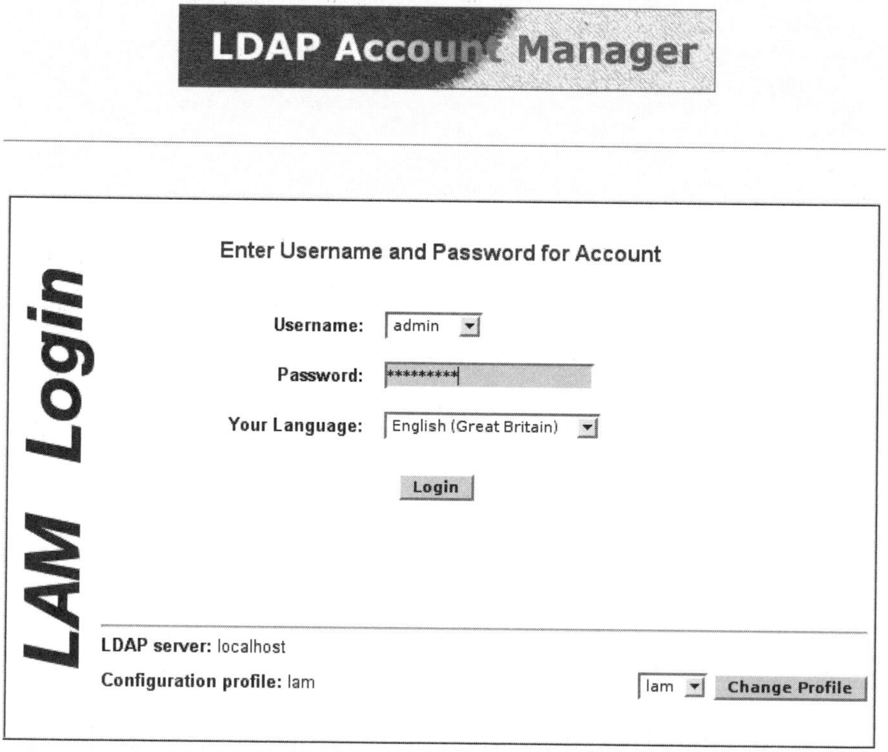

The LAM configuration editor has a number of options that must be managed correctly. An example of use of the LAM configuration editor is shown in Figure 15.7. It is important that you correctly set the minimum and maximum UID/GID values that are permitted for use at your site. The default values may not be compatible with a need to modify initial default account values for well-known Windows network users and groups. The best work-around is to temporarily set the minimum values to zero (0) to permit the initial settings to be made. Do not forget to reset these to sensible values before using LAM to add additional users and groups.

Figure 15.7 The LDAP Account Manager Configuration Screen

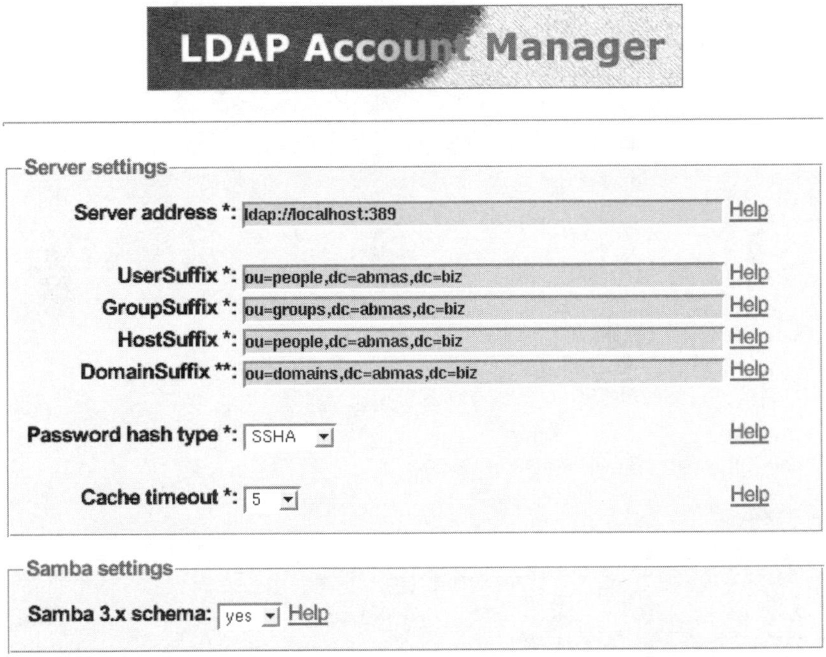

LAM has some nice, but unusual features. For example, one unexpected feature in most application screens permits the generation of a PDF file that lists configuration information. This is a well thought out facility. This option has been edited out of the following screen shots to conserve space.

When you log onto LAM the opening screen drops you right into the user manager as shown in Figure 15.8. This is a logical action as it permits the most-needed facility to be used immediately. The editing of an existing user, as with the addition of a new user, is easy to follow and very clear in both layout and intent. It is a simple matter to edit generic settings, UNIX specific parameters, and then Samba account requirements. Each step involves clicking a button that intuitively drives you through the process. When you have finished editing simply press the **Final** button.

The edit screen for groups is shown in Figure 15.9. As with the edit screen for user accounts, group accounts may be rapidly dealt with. Figure 15.10 shows a sub-screen from the group

Figure 15.8 The LDAP Account Manager User Edit Screen

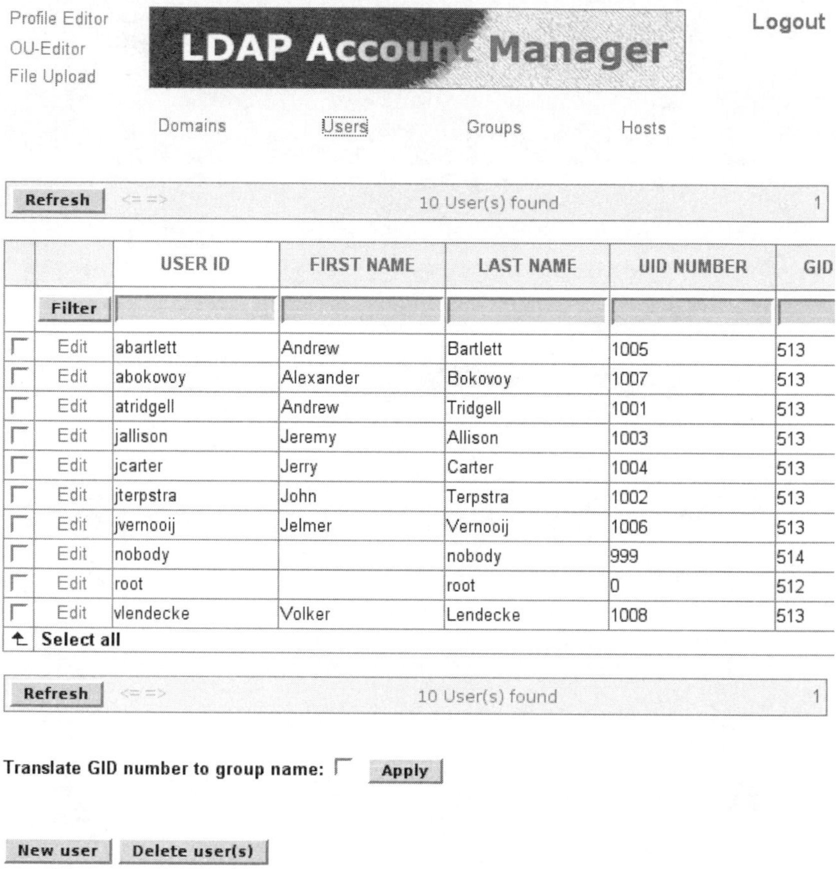

		USER ID	FIRST NAME	LAST NAME	UID NUMBER	GID
Filter						
□	Edit	abartlett	Andrew	Bartlett	1005	513
□	Edit	abokovoy	Alexander	Bokovoy	1007	513
□	Edit	atridgell	Andrew	Tridgell	1001	513
□	Edit	jallison	Jeremy	Allison	1003	513
□	Edit	jcarter	Jerry	Carter	1004	513
□	Edit	jterpstra	John	Terpstra	1002	513
□	Edit	jvernooij	Jelmer	Vernooij	1006	513
□	Edit	nobody		nobody	999	514
□	Edit	root		root	0	512
□	Edit	vlendecke	Volker	Lendecke	1008	513

Profile Editor OU-Editor File Upload   LDAP Account Manager   Logout

Domains   Users   Groups   Hosts

Refresh <= =>   10 User(s) found   1

Select all

Refresh <= =>   10 User(s) found   1

Translate GID number to group name: □ Apply

New user   Delete user(s)

editor that permits users to be assigned secondary group memberships.

The final screen presented here is one that you should not normally need to use. Host accounts will be automatically managed using the smbldap-tools scripts. This means that the screen Figure 15.11 will, in most cases, not be used.

One aspect of LAM that may annoy some users is the way it forces certain conventions on the administrator. For example, LAM does not permit the creation of Windows user and group accounts that contain spaces even though the underlying UNIX/Linux operating system may exhibit no problems with them. Given the propensity for using upper-case characters and spaces (particularly in the default Windows account names) this may cause some annoyance. For the rest, LAM is a very useful administrative tool.

The next major release, LAM 0.5, will have fewer restrictions and support the latest Samba features (e.g., logon hours). The new plugin-based architecture also allows management of much more different account types like plain UNIX accounts. The upload can now handle groups and hosts, too. Another important point is the tree view which allows browsing and

Figure 15.9 The LDAP Account Manager Group Edit Screen

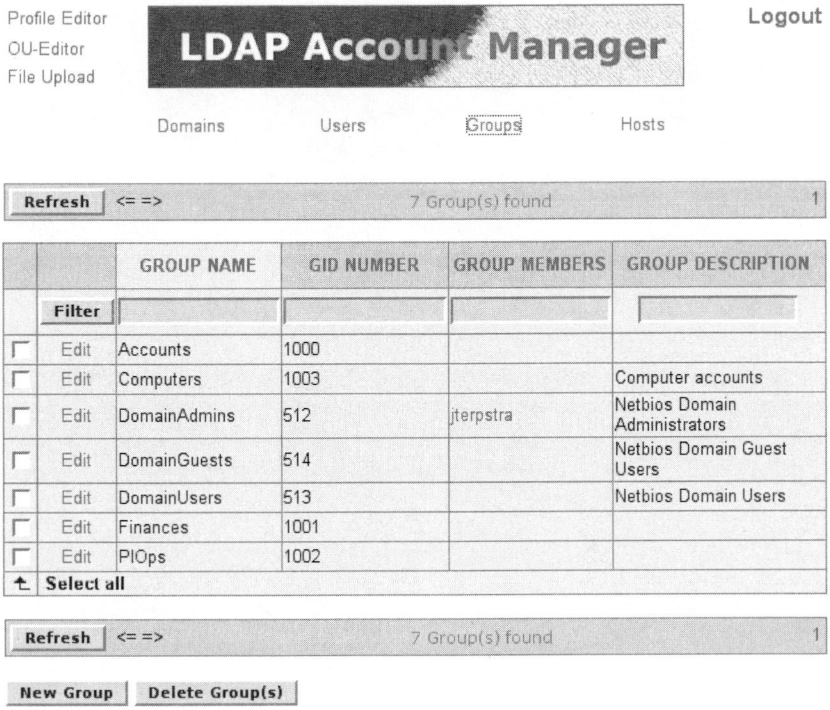

Profile Editor   Logout
OU-Editor
File Upload

LDAP Account Manager

Domains   Users   Groups   Hosts

| Refresh | <= => | | 7 Group(s) found | 1 |

		GROUP NAME	GID NUMBER	GROUP MEMBERS	GROUP DESCRIPTION
	Filter				
☐	Edit	Accounts	1000		
☐	Edit	Computers	1003		Computer accounts
☐	Edit	DomainAdmins	512	jterpstra	Netbios Domain Administrators
☐	Edit	DomainGuests	514		Netbios Domain Guest Users
☐	Edit	DomainUsers	513		Netbios Domain Users
☐	Edit	Finances	1001		
☐	Edit	PIOps	1002		
↥	Select all				

| Refresh | <= => | | 7 Group(s) found | 1 |

| New Group | Delete Group(s) |

editing LDAP objects directly.

15.7 IDEALX Management Console

IMC (the IDEALX Mamagement Console) is a tool that can be used as the basis for a comprehensive web-based management interface for UNIX and Linux systems.

The Samba toolset is the first console developped for IMC. It offers a simple and ergonomic interface for managing a Samba domain controler. The goal is to give Linux administrators who need to manage production Samba servers an effective, intuitive and consistent management experience. An IMC screenshot of the user management tool is shown in Figure 15.12.

IMC is built on a set of Perl modules. Most modules are standard CPAN modules. Some are bundled with IMC, but will soon to be hosted on the CPAN independently, like Struts4P, a port of Struts to the Perl language.

For further information regarding IMC refer to the web site.[4] Prebuilt RPM packages are also available.[5]

---

[4] <http://imc.sourceforge.net/>
[5] <http://imc.sourceforge.net/download.html>

Figure 15.10 The LDAP Account Manager Group Membership Edit Screen

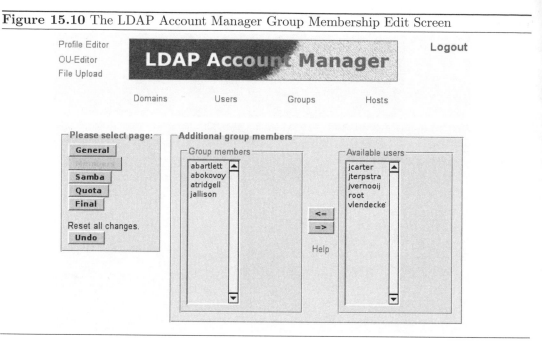

15.8   Effect of Setting File and Directory SUID/SGID Permissions Explained

The setting of the SUID/SGID bits on the file or directory permissions flag has particular consequences. If the file is executable and the SUID bit is set, it executes with the privilege of (with the UID of) the owner of the file. For example, if you are logged onto a system as a normal user (let's say as the user bobj), and you execute a file that is owned by the user root (uid = 0), and the file has the SUID bit set, then the file is executed as if you had logged in as the user root and then executed the file. The SUID bit effectively gives you (as bobj) administrative privilege for the use of that executable file.

The setting of the SGID bit does precisely the same as the effect of the SUID bit, except that it applies the privilege to the UNIX group setting. In other words, the file executes with the force of capability of the group.

When the SUID/SGID permissions are set on a directory, all files that are created within that directory are automatically given the ownership of the SUID user and the SGID group, as per the ownership of the directory in which the file is created. This means that the system level **create()** function executes with the SUID user and/or SGID group of the directory in which the file is created.

If you want to obtain the SUID behavior, simply execute the following command:

```
root#   chmod u+s file-or-directory
```

Figure 15.11 The LDAP Account Manager Host Edit Screen

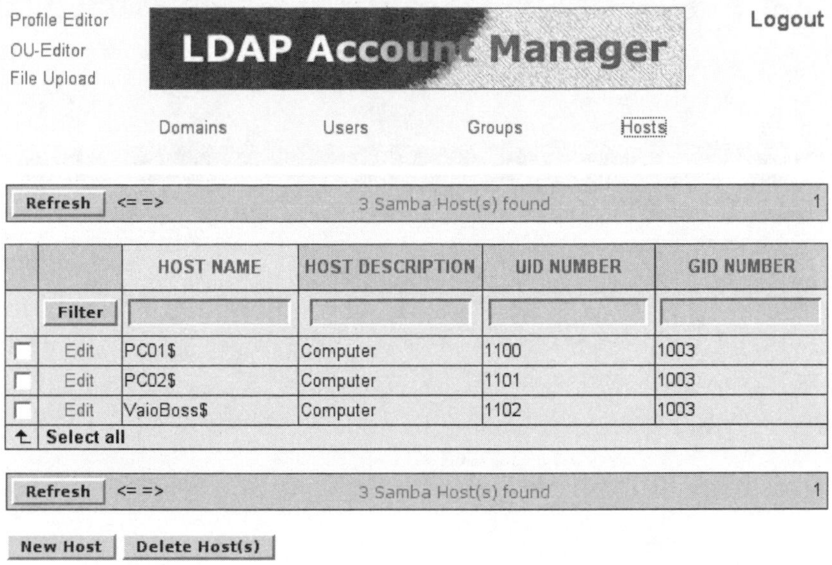

To set the SGID properties on a file or a directory, execute this command:

```
root#  chmod g+s file-or-directory
```

And to set both SUID and SGID properties, execute the following:

```
root#  chmod ug+s file-or-directory
```

Let's consider the example of a directory /data/accounts. The permissions on this directory before setting both SUID and SGID on this directory are:

```
root#  ls -al /data/accounts
total 1
drwxr-xr-x   10 root      root           232 Dec 18 17:08 .
drwxr-xr-x   21 root      root           600 Dec 17 23:15 ..
drwxrwxrwx    2 bobj      Domain Users    48 Dec 18 17:08 accounts/
drwx------    2 root      root            48 Jan 26  2002 lost+found
```

In this example, if the user maryv creates a file, it is owned by her. If maryv has the primary group of Accounts, the file is owned by the group Accounts, as shown in this listing:

```
root#  ls -al /data/accounts/maryvfile.txt
```

Figure 15.12 The IMC Samba User Account Screen

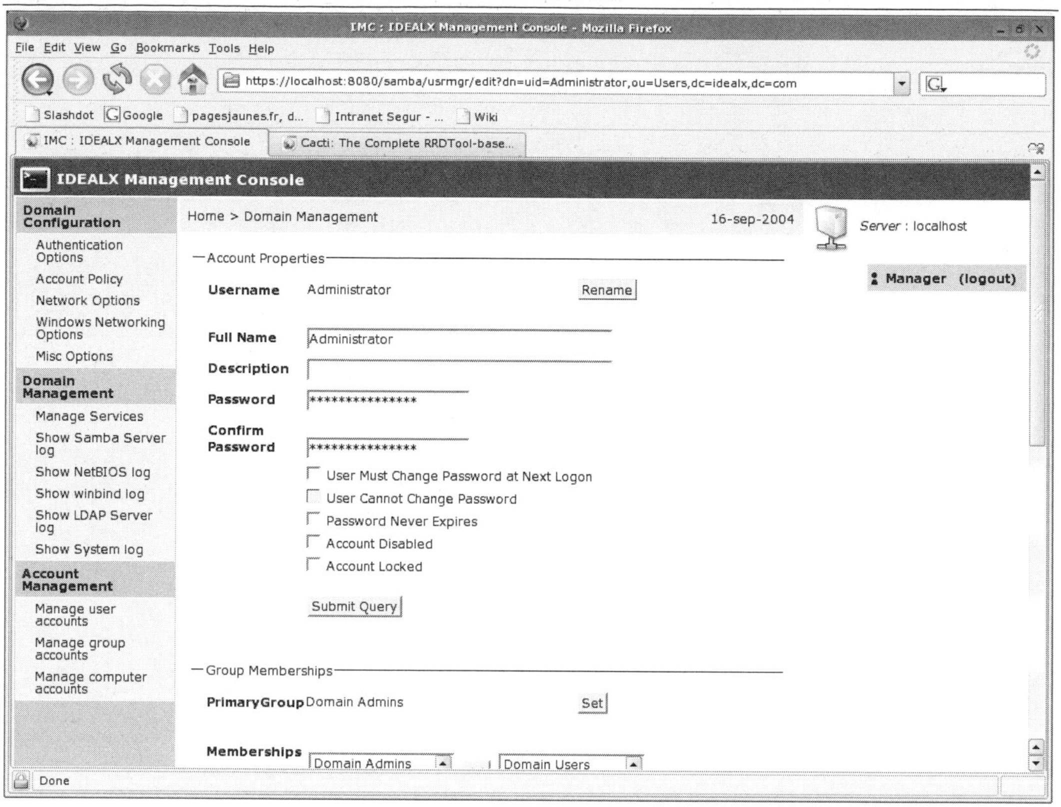

```
drw-rw-r--     2 maryv     Accounts     12346 Dec 18 17:53
```

Now you set the SUID and SGID and check the result as follows:

```
root#  chmod ug+s /data/accounts
root#  ls -al /data/accounts
total 1
drwxr-xr-x   10 root     root          232 Dec 18 17:08 .
drwxr-xr-x   21 root     root          600 Dec 17 23:15 ..
drwsrwsr-x    2 bobj     Domain Users   48 Dec 18 17:08 accounts
drwx------    2 root     root           48 Jan 26  2002 lost+found
```

If maryv creates a file in this directory after this change has been made, the file is owned by the user bobj, and the group is set to the group Domain Users, as shown here:

```
root#  chmod ug+s /data/accounts
```

```
root#  ls -al /data/accounts/maryvfile.txt
total 1
drw-rw-r--    2 bobj     Domain Users  12346 Dec 18 18:11 maryvfile.txt
```

15.9 Shared Data Integrity

The integrity of shared data is often viewed as a particularly emotional issue, especially where there are concurrent problems with multiuser data access. Contrary to the assertions of some who have experienced problems in either area, the cause has nothing to do with the phases of the moons of Jupiter.

The solution to concurrent multiuser data access problems must consider three separate areas from which the problem may stem:

- application-level locking controls

- client-side locking controls

- server-side locking controls

Many database applications use some form of application-level access control. An example of one well-known application that uses application-level locking is Microsoft Access. Detailed guidance is provided here because this is the most common application for which problems have been reported.

Common applications that are affected by client- and server-side locking controls include MS Excel and Act!. Important locking guidance is provided here.

15.9.1 Microsoft Access

The best advice that can be given is to carefully read the Microsoft knowledgebase articles that cover this area. Examples of relevant documents include:

- http://support.microsoft.com/default.aspx?scid=kb;en-us;208778

- http://support.microsoft.com/default.aspx?scid=kb;en-us;299373

Make sure that your MS Access database file is configured for multiuser access (not set for exclusive open). Open MS Access on each client workstation, then set the following: **(Menu bar) Tools+Options+[tab] General**. Set network path to Default database folder: \\server\share\folder.

You can configure MS Access file sharing behavior as follows: click **[tab] Advanced**. Set:

- Default open mode: Shared

- Default Record Locking: Edited Record

- Open databases using record_level locking

You must now commit the changes so that they will take effect. To do so, click **ApplyOk**. At this point, you should exit MS Access, restart it, and then validate that these settings have not changed.

15.9.2   Act! Database Sharing

Where the server sharing the ACT! database(s) is running Samba,or Windows NT, 200x, or XP, you must disable opportunistic locking on the server and all workstations. Failure to do so results in data corruption. This information is available from the Act! Web site knowledgebase articles 19982231629256[6] as well as from article 2001104850367[7].

These documents clearly state that opportunistic locking must be disabled on both the server (Samba in the case we are interested in here), as well as on every workstation from which the centrally shared Act! database will be accessed. Act! provides a tool called **Act!Diag** that may be used to disable all workstation registry settings that may otherwise interfere with the operation of Act! Registered Act! users may download this utility from the Act! Web site.[8]

15.9.3   Opportunistic Locking Controls

Third-party Windows applications may not be compatible with the use of opportunistic file and record locking. For applications that are known not to be compatible,[9] oplock support may need to be disabled both on the Samba server and on the Windows workstations.

Oplocks enable a Windows client to cache parts of a file that are being edited. Another windows client may then request to open the file with the ability to write to it. The server will then ask the original workstation that had the file open with a write lock to release its lock. Before doing so, that workstation must flush the file from cache memory to the disk or network drive.

Disabling of Oplocks usage may require server and client changes. Oplocks may be disabled by file, by file pattern, on the share, or on the Samba server.

The following are examples showing how Oplock support may be managed using Samba `smb.conf` file settings:

```
By file:       veto oplock files = myfile.mdb

By Pattern:    veto oplock files = /*.mdb/

On the Share:  oplocks = No
```

---

[6]<http://itdomino.saleslogix.com/act.nsf/docid/1998223162925>

[7]<http://itdomino.saleslogix.com/act.nsf/docid/200110485036>

[8]<http://www.act.com/support/updates/index.cfm>

[9]Refer to the application manufacturer's installation guidelines and knowledge base for specific information regarding compatibility. It is often safe to assume that if the software manufacturer does not specifically mention incompatibilities with opportunistic file and record locking, or with Windows client file caching, the application is probably compatible with Windows (as well as Samba) default settings.

```
                    level2 oplocks = No

On the server:
(in [global])    oplocks = No
                 level2 oplocks = No
```

The following registry entries on Microsoft Windows XP Professional, 2000 Professional, and Windows NT4 workstation clients must be configured as shown here:

```
REGEDIT4

[HKEY_LOCAL_MACHINE\SYSTEM\CurrentControlSet\
         Services\LanmanServer\Parameters]
    "EnableOplocks"=dword:00000000

[HKEY_LOCAL_MACHINE\SYSTEM\CurrentControlSet\
         Services\LanmanWorkstation\Parameters]
    "UseOpportunisticLocking"=dword:00000000
```

Comprehensive coverage of file and record-locking controls is provided in TOSHARG2, Chapter 13. The information in that chapter was obtained from a wide variety of sources.

Example 15.3.2 A Sample Samba Control Script for Red Hat Linux

```sh
#!/bin/sh
#
# chkconfig: 345 81 35
# description: Starts and stops the Samba smbd and nmbd daemons \
#              used to provide SMB network services.

# Source function library.
. /etc/rc.d/init.d/functions
# Source networking configuration.
. /etc/sysconfig/network
# Check that networking is up.
[ ${NETWORKING} = "no" ] && exit 0
CONFIG=/etc/samba/smb.conf
# Check that smb.conf exists.
[ -f $CONFIG ] || exit 0

# See how we were called.
case "$1" in
  start)
        echo -n "Starting SMB services: "
        daemon smbd -D; daemon nmbd -D; echo;
        touch /var/lock/subsys/smb
        ;;
  stop)
        echo -n "Shutting down SMB services: "
        smbdpids=`ps guax | grep smbd | grep -v grep | awk '{print $2}'`
        for pid in $smbdpids; do
                kill -TERM $pid
        done
        killproc nmbd -TERM; rm -f /var/lock/subsys/smb
        echo ""
        ;;
  status)
        status smbd; status nmbd;
        ;;
  restart)
        echo -n "Restarting SMB services: "
        $0 stop; $0 start;
        echo "done."
        ;;
  *)
        echo "Usage: smb {start|stop|restart|status}"
        exit 1
esac
```

Example 15.4.1 DNS Localhost Forward Zone File: /var/lib/named/localhost.zone

---

```
$TTL 1W
@      IN SOA   @   root (
              42     ; serial
              2D     ; refresh
              4H     ; retry
              6W     ; expiry
              1W )      ; minimum

       IN NS    @
       IN A     127.0.0.1
```

Example 15.4.2 DNS Localhost Reverse Zone File: /var/lib/named/127.0.0.zone

---

```
$TTL 1W
@      IN SOA      localhost.   root.localhost. (
              42     ; serial
              2D     ; refresh
              4H     ; retry
              6W     ; expiry
              1W )      ; minimum

       IN NS    localhost.
1      IN PTR      localhost.
```

Example 15.4.3 DNS Root Name Server Hint File: /var/lib/named/root.hint

```
; This file is made available by InterNIC under anonymous FTP as
;       file              /domain/named.root
;       on server         FTP.INTERNIC.NET
; last update: Nov 5, 2002. Related version of root zone: 2002110501
; formerly NS.INTERNIC.NET
.                          3600000  IN  NS   A.ROOT-SERVERS.NET.
A.ROOT-SERVERS.NET.        3600000      A    198.41.0.4
; formerly NS1.ISI.EDU
.                          3600000      NS   B.ROOT-SERVERS.NET.
B.ROOT-SERVERS.NET.        3600000      A    128.9.0.107
; formerly C.PSI.NET
.                          3600000      NS   C.ROOT-SERVERS.NET.
C.ROOT-SERVERS.NET.        3600000      A    192.33.4.12
; formerly TERP.UMD.EDU
.                          3600000      NS   D.ROOT-SERVERS.NET.
D.ROOT-SERVERS.NET.        3600000      A    128.8.10.90
; formerly NS.NASA.GOV
.                          3600000      NS   E.ROOT-SERVERS.NET.
E.ROOT-SERVERS.NET.        3600000      A    192.203.230.10
; formerly NS.ISC.ORG
.                          3600000      NS   F.ROOT-SERVERS.NET.
F.ROOT-SERVERS.NET.        3600000      A    192.5.5.241
; formerly NS.NIC.DDN.MIL
.                          3600000      NS   G.ROOT-SERVERS.NET.
G.ROOT-SERVERS.NET.        3600000      A    192.112.36.4
; formerly AOS.ARL.ARMY.MIL
.                          3600000      NS   H.ROOT-SERVERS.NET.
H.ROOT-SERVERS.NET.        3600000      A    128.63.2.53
; formerly NIC.NORDU.NET
.                          3600000      NS   I.ROOT-SERVERS.NET.
I.ROOT-SERVERS.NET.        3600000      A    192.36.148.17
; operated by VeriSign, Inc.
.                          3600000      NS   J.ROOT-SERVERS.NET.
J.ROOT-SERVERS.NET.        3600000      A    192.58.128.30
; housed in LINX, operated by RIPE NCC
.                          3600000      NS   K.ROOT-SERVERS.NET.
K.ROOT-SERVERS.NET.        3600000      A    193.0.14.129
; operated by IANA
.                          3600000      NS   L.ROOT-SERVERS.NET.
L.ROOT-SERVERS.NET.        3600000      A    198.32.64.12
; housed in Japan, operated by WIDE
.                          3600000      NS   M.ROOT-SERVERS.NET.
M.ROOT-SERVERS.NET.        3600000      A    202.12.27.33
; End of File
```

Example 15.5.1 LDAP Pre-configuration Script: SMBLDAP-ldif-preconfig.sh — Part A

```
#!/bin/bash
#
# This script prepares the ldif LDAP load file only
#

# Pattern File Name
file=init-ldif.pat

# The name of my organization
ORGNAME="My Organization"

# My Internet domain. ie: if my domain is: buckets.org, INETDOMAIN="buckets"
INETDOMAIN="my-domain"

# In the above case, md domain is: buckets.org, TLDORG="org"
TLDORG="org"

# This is the Samba Domain/Workgroup Name
DOMNAME="MYWORKGROUP"

#
# Here We Go ...
#

cat <<EOF

How do you wish to refer to your organization?

Suggestions:
   Black Tire Company, Inc.
   Cat With Hat Ltd.

How would you like your organization name to appear?

EOF

echo "Your organization name is: $ORGNAME"
echo
echo "Enter a new name or, press Enter to Continue."
echo
```

Example 15.5.2 LDAP Pre-configuration Script: SMBLDAP-ldif-preconfig.sh — Part B

```
echo -e -n "Name [$ORGNAME]: "
   read name

if [ ! -z "$name" ]; then
   ORGNAME=${name}
fi
echo
sed "s/ORGNAME/${ORGNAME}/g" < $file > $file.tmp1

# Try to find smb.conf

if [ -e /usr/local/samba/lib/smb.conf ]; then
   CONF=/usr/local/samba/lib/smb.conf
elif [ -e /etc/samba/smb.conf ]; then
   CONF=/etc/samba/smb.conf
fi

echo "Samba Config File Location [$CONF]: "
echo
echo "Enter a new full path or press Enter to continue."
echo
echo -n "Samba Config File Location [$CONF]: "
   read name
if [ ! -z "$name" ]; then
   CONF=$name
fi
echo

# Find the name of our Domain/Workgroup
DOMNAME=`grep -i workgroup ${CONF} | sed "s/ //g" | cut -f2 -d=`
echo Domain Name: $DOMNAME
echo

sed "s/DOMNAME/${DOMNAME}/g" < $file.tmp1 > $file.tmp2

DOMSID=`net getlocalsid ${DOMNAME} | cut -f2 -d: | sed "s/ //g"`
echo Domain SID: $DOMSID

sed "s/DOMSID/${DOMSID}/g" < $file.tmp2 > $file.tmp1
```

Example 15.5.3 LDAP Pre-configuration Script: SMBLDAP-ldif-preconfig.sh — Part C

```
cat >>EOL
The name of your Internet domain is now needed in a special format
as follows, if your domain name is mydomain.org, what we need is
the information in the form of:
    Domain ID: mydomain
    Top level: org

If your fully qualified hostname is: snoopy.bazaar.garagesale.net
where "snoopy" is the name of the machine,
Then the information needed is:
    Domain ID: garagesale
    Top Level: net

EOL
INETDOMAIN=`hostname -d | cut -f1 -d.`
echo Found the following domain name: `hostname -d`
echo "I think the bit we are looking for might be: $INETDOMAIN"
echo
echo -n "Enter the domain name or press Enter to continue: "
    read domnam
if [ ! -z $domnam ]; then
    INETDOMAIN=$domnam
fi
echo
sed "s/INETDOMAIN/${INETDOMAIN}/g" < $file.tmp1 > $file.tmp2
TLDORG=`hostname -d | sed "s/${INETDOMAIN}.//g"`
echo "The top level organization name I will use is: ${TLDORG}"
echo
echo -n "Enter the top level org name or press Enter to continue: "
    read domnam
if [ ! -z $domnam ]; then
        TLDORG=$domnam
fi
sed "s/TLDORG/${TLDORG}/g" < $file.tmp2 > $DOMNAME.ldif
rm $file.tmp*
exit 0
```

Example 15.5.4 LDIF Pattern File Used to Pre-configure LDAP — Part A

```
dn: dc=INETDOMAIN,dc=TLDORG
objectClass: dcObject
objectClass: organization
dc: INETDOMAIN
o: ORGNAME
description: Posix and Samba LDAP Identity Database

dn: cn=Manager,dc=INETDOMAIN,dc=TLDORG
objectClass: organizationalRole
cn: Manager
description: Directory Manager

dn: ou=People,dc=INETDOMAIN,dc=TLDORG
objectClass: top
objectClass: organizationalUnit
ou: People

dn: ou=Computers,dc=INETDOMAIN,dc=TLDORG
objectClass: top
objectClass: organizationalUnit
ou: Computers

dn: ou=Groups,dc=INETDOMAIN,dc=TLDORG
objectClass: top
objectClass: organizationalUnit
ou: Groups

dn: ou=Idmap,dc=INETDOMAIN,dc=TLDORG
objectClass: top
objectClass: organizationalUnit
ou: Idmap

dn: sambaDomainName=DOMNAME,ou=Domains,dc=INETDOMAIN,dc=TLDORG
objectClass: sambaDomain
sambaDomainName: DOMNAME
sambaSID: DOMSID
sambaAlgorithmicRidBase: 1000
structuralObjectClass: sambaDomain
```

Example 15.5.5 LDIF Pattern File Used to Pre-configure LDAP — Part B

```
dn: cn=domadmins,ou=Groups,dc=INETDOMAIN,dc=TLDORG
objectClass: posixGroup
objectClass: sambaGroupMapping
gidNumber: 512
cn: domadmins
sambaSID: DOMSID-512
sambaGroupType: 2
displayName: Domain Admins
description: Domain Administrators

dn: cn=domguests,ou=Groups,dc=INETDOMAIN,dc=TLDORG
objectClass: posixGroup
objectClass: sambaGroupMapping
gidNumber: 514
cn: domguests
sambaSID: DOMSID-514
sambaGroupType: 2
displayName: Domain Guests
description: Domain Guests Users

dn: cn=domusers,ou=Groups,dc=INETDOMAIN,dc=TLDORG
objectClass: posixGroup
objectClass: sambaGroupMapping
gidNumber: 513
cn: domusers
sambaSID: DOMSID-513
sambaGroupType: 2
displayName: Domain Users
description: Domain Users
```

Example 15.6.1 Example LAM Configuration File — config.cfg

```
# password to add/delete/rename configuration profiles
password: not24get

# default profile, without ".conf"
default: lam
```

Example 15.6.2 LAM Profile Control File — lam.conf

```
ServerURL: ldap://massive.abmas.org:389
Admins: cn=Manager,dc=abmas,dc=biz
Passwd: not24get
usersuffix: ou=People,dc=abmas,dc=biz
groupsuffix: ou=Groups,dc=abmas,dc=biz
hostsuffix: ou=Computers,dc=abmas,dc=biz
domainsuffix: ou=Domains,dc=abmas,dc=biz
MinUID: 0
MaxUID: 65535
MinGID: 0
MaxGID: 65535
MinMachine: 20000
MaxMachine: 25000
userlistAttributes: #uid;#givenName;#sn;#uidNumber;#gidNumber
grouplistAttributes: #cn;#gidNumber;#memberUID;#description
hostlistAttributes: #cn;#description;#uidNumber;#gidNumber
maxlistentries: 30
defaultLanguage: en_GB:ISO-8859-1:English (Great Britain)
scriptPath:
scriptServer:
samba3: yes
cachetimeout: 5
pwdhash: SSHA
```

Chapter 16

NETWORKING PRIMER

You are about to use the equivalent of a microscope to look at the information that runs through the veins of a Windows network. We do more to observe the information than to interrogate it. When you are done with this primer, you should have a good understanding of the types of information that flow over the network. Do not worry, this is not a biology lesson. We won't lose you in unnecessary detail. Think to yourself, "This is easy," then tackle each exercise without fear.

Samba can be configured with a minimum of complexity. Simplicity should be mastered before you get too deeply into complexities. Let's get moving: we have work to do.

16.1 Requirements and Notes

Successful completion of this primer requires two Microsoft Windows 9x/Me Workstations as well as two Microsoft Windows XP Professional Workstations, each equipped with an Ethernet card connected using a hub. Also required is one additional server (either Windows NT4 Server, Windows 2000 Server, or a Samba-3 on UNIX/Linux server) running a network sniffer and analysis application (ethereal is a good choice). All work should be undertaken on a quiet network where there is no other traffic. It is best to use a dedicated hub with only the machines under test connected at the time of the exercises.

Ethereal has become the network protocol analyzer of choice for many network administrators. You may find more information regarding this tool from the Ethereal[1] Web site. Ethereal installation files for Windows may be obtained from the Ethereal Web site. Ethereal is provided with SUSE and Red Hat Linux distributions, as well as with many other Linux distributions. It may not be installed on your system by default. If it is not installed, you may also need to install the **libpcap** software before you can install or use Ethereal. Please refer to the instructions for your operating system or to the Ethereal Web site for information regarding the installation and operation of Ethereal.

To obtain **ethereal** for your system, please visit the Ethereal download site[2].

---

[1] <http://www.ethereal.com>
[2] <http://www.ethereal.com/download.html#binaries>

 NOTE

The successful completion of this chapter requires that you capture network traffic using **Ethereal**. It is recommended that you use a hub, not an Ethernet switch. It is necessary for the device used to act as a repeater, not as a filter. Ethernet switches may filter out traffic that is not directed at the machine that is used to monitor traffic; this would not allow you to complete the projects.

Do not worry too much if you do not have access to all this equipment; network captures from the exercises are provided on the enclosed CD-ROM. This makes it possible to dive directly into the analytical part of the exercises if you so desire.

Please do not be alarmed at the use of a high-powered analysis tool (Ethereal) in this primer. We expose you only to a minimum of detail necessary to complete the exercises. If you choose to use any other network sniffer and protocol analysis tool, be advised that it may not allow you to examine the contents of recently added security protocols used by Windows 200x/XP.

You could just skim through the exercises and try to absorb the key points made. The exercises provide all the information necessary to convince the die-hard network engineer. You possibly do not require so much convincing and may just want to move on, in which case you should at least read Section 16.4.

Section 16.5 also provides useful information that may help you to avoid significantly time-consuming networking problems.

16.2   Introduction

The purpose of this chapter is to create familiarity with key aspects of Microsoft Windows network computing. If you want a solid technical grounding, do not gloss over these exercises. The points covered are recurrent issues on the Samba mailing lists.

You can see from these exercises that Windows networking involves quite a lot of network broadcast traffic. You can look into the contents of some packets, but only to see some particular information that the Windows client sends to a server in the course of establishing a network connection.

To many people, browsing is everything that happens when one uses Microsoft Internet Explorer. It is only when you start looking at network traffic and noting the protocols and types of information that are used that you can begin to appreciate the complexities of Windows networking and, more importantly, what needs to be configured so that it can work. Detailed information regarding browsing is provided in the recommended preparatory reading.

Recommended preparatory reading: *The Official Samba-3 HOWTO and Reference Guide, Second Edition* (TOSHARG2) Chapter 9, "Network Browsing," and Chapter 3, "Server Types and Security Modes."

16.2.1 Assignment Tasks

You are about to witness how Microsoft Windows computer networking functions. The exercises step through identification of how a client machine establishes a connection to a remote Windows server. You observe how Windows machines find each other (i.e., how browsing works) and how the two key types of user identification (share mode security and user mode security) are affected.

The networking protocols used by MS Windows networking when working with Samba use TCP/IP as the transport protocol. The protocols that are specific to Windows networking are encapsulated in TCP/IP. The network analyzer we use (Ethereal) is able to show you the contents of the TCP/IP packets (or messages).

DIAGNOSTIC TASKS

1. Examine network traces to witness SMB broadcasts, host announcements, and name resolution processes.

2. Examine network traces to witness how share mode security functions.

3. Examine network traces to witness the use of user mode security.

4. Review traces of network logons for a Windows 9x/Me client as well as a domain logon for a Windows XP Professional client.

16.3 Exercises

You are embarking on a course of discovery. The first part of the exercise requires two MS Windows 9x/Me systems. We called one machine `WINEPRESSME` and the other `MILGATE98`. Each needs an IP address; we used `10.1.1.10` and `10.1.1.11`. The test machines need to be networked via a *hub*. A UNIX/Linux machine is required to run **Ethereal** to enable the network activity to be captured. It is important that the machine from which network activity is captured must not interfere with the operation of the Windows workstations. It is helpful for this machine to be passive (does not send broadcast information) to the network.

For these exercises, our test environment consisted of a SUSE 9.2 Professional Linux Workstation running VMWare 4.5. The following VMWare images were prepared:

- Windows 98 — name: MILGATE98

- Windows Me — name: WINEPRESSME

- Windows XP Professional — name: LightrayXP

- Samba-3.0.20 running on a SUSE Enterprise Linux 9

Choose a workgroup name (MIDEARTH) for each exercise.

The network captures provided on the CD-ROM included with this book were captured using `Ethereal` version `0.10.6`. A later version suffices without problems, but an earlier version may not expose all the information needed. Each capture file has been decoded and listed as a trace file. A summary of all packets has also been included. This makes it possible for you to do all the studying you like without the need to perform the time-consuming equipment configuration and test work. This is a good time to point out that the value that can be derived from this book really does warrant your taking sufficient time to practice each exercise with care and attention to detail.

16.3.1   Single-Machine Broadcast Activity

In this section, we start a single Windows 9x/Me machine, then monitor network activity for 30 minutes.

MONITORING WINDOWS 9X STEPS

1. Start the machine from which network activity will be monitored (using **ethereal**). Launch **ethereal**, click **Capture** → **Start**. Click the following:

    (a) Update list of packets in real time

    (b) Automatic scrolling in live capture

    (c) Enable MAC name resolution

    (d) Enable network name resolution

    (e) Enable transport name resolution

    Click **OK**.

2. Start the Windows 9x/Me machine to be monitored. Let it run for a full 30 minutes. While monitoring, do not press any keyboard keys, do not click any on-screen icons or menus, and do not answer any dialog boxes.

3. At the conclusion of 30 minutes, stop the capture. Save the capture to a file so you can go back to it later. Leave this machine running in preparation for the task in Section 16.3.2.

4. Analyze the capture. Identify each discrete message type that was captured. Note what transport protocol was used. Identify the timing between messages of identical types.

16.3.1.1   Findings

The summary of the first 10 minutes of the packet capture should look like Figure 16.1. A screenshot of a later stage of the same capture is shown in Figure 16.2.

Broadcast messages observed are shown in Table 16.1. Actual observations vary a little, but not by much. Early in the startup process, the Windows Me machine broadcasts its name

Figure 16.1 Windows Me — Broadcasts — The First 10 Minutes

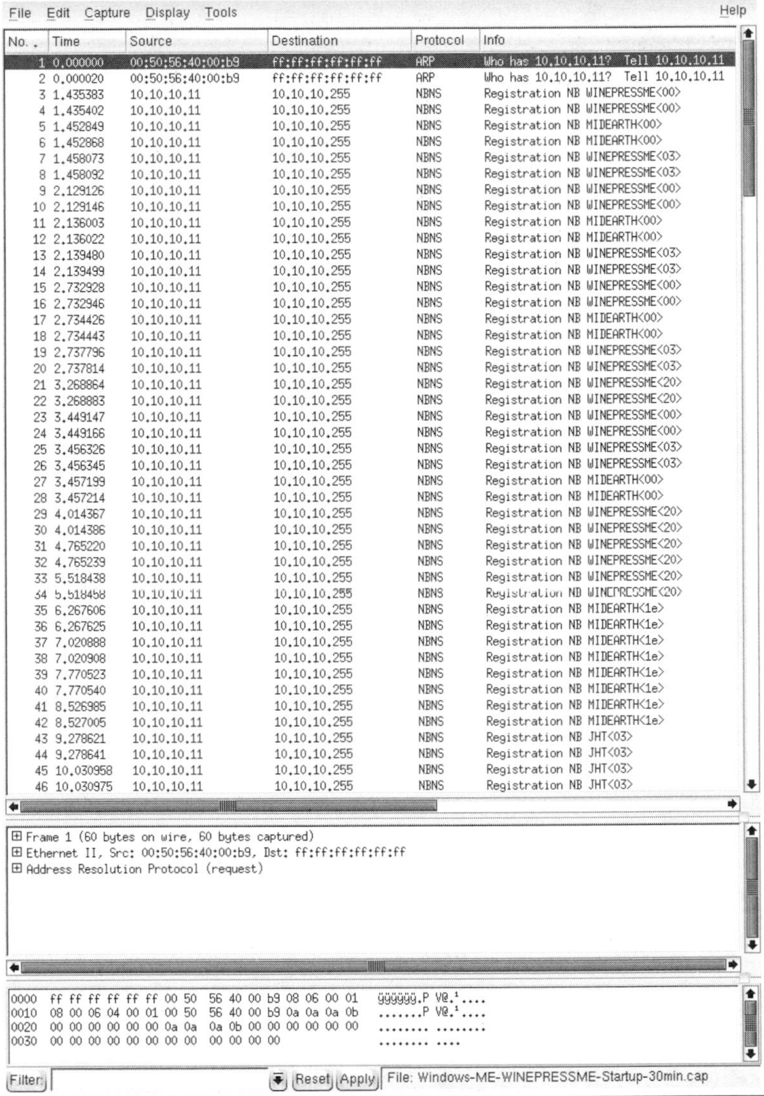

for two reasons: first to ensure that its name would not result in a name clash, and second to establish its presence with the Local Master Browser (LMB).

From the packet trace, it should be noted that no messages were propagated over TCP/IP; all messages employed UDP/IP. When steady-state operation has been achieved, there is a cycle of various announcements, re-election of a browse master, and name queries. These create the symphony of announcements by which network browsing is made possible.

For detailed information regarding the precise behavior of the CIFS/SMB protocols, refer to the book "Implementing CIFS: The Common Internet File System," by Christopher Hertel,

Figure 16.2 Windows Me — Later Broadcast Sample

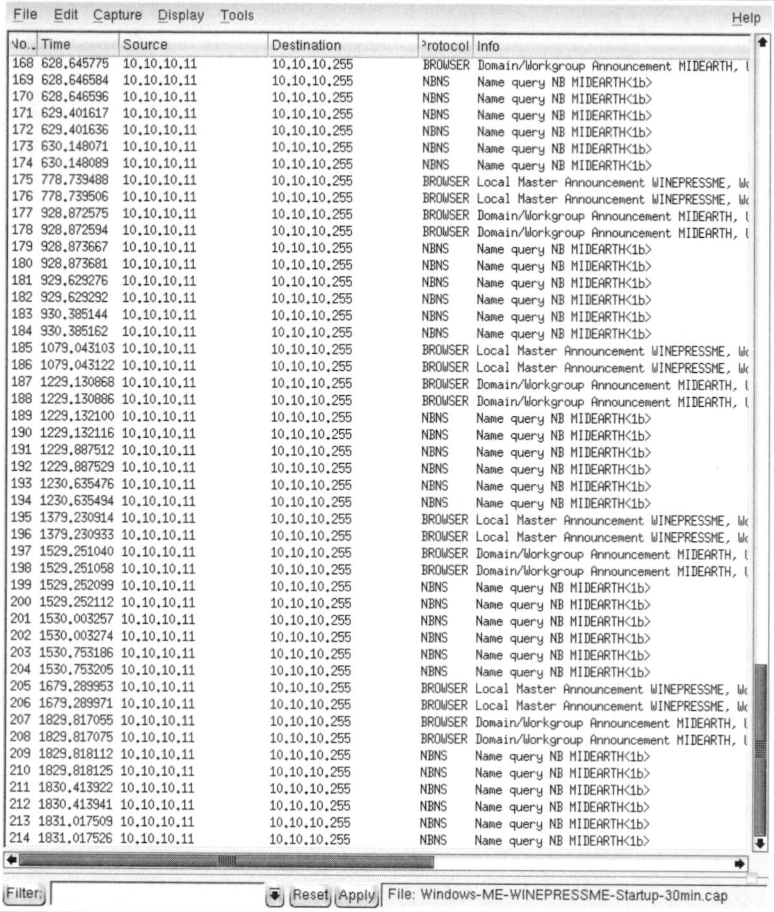

(Prentice Hall PTR, ISBN: 013047116X).

16.3.2   Second Machine Startup Broadcast Interaction

At this time, the machine you used to capture the single-system startup trace should still be running. The objective of this task is to identify the interaction of two machines in respect to broadcast activity.

Monitoring of Second Machine Activity

1. On the machine from which network activity will be monitored (using **ethereal**), launch **ethereal** and click **Capture → Start**. Click:

   (a) Update list of packets in real time

   (b) Automatic scrolling in live capture

Table 16.1 Windows Me — Startup Broadcast Capture Statistics

Message	Type	Num	Notes
WINEPRESSME<00>	Reg	8	4 lots of 2, 0.6 sec apart
WINEPRESSME<03>	Reg	8	4 lots of 2, 0.6 sec apart
WINEPRESSME<20>	Reg	8	4 lots of 2, 0.75 sec apart
MIDEARTH<00>	Reg	8	4 lots of 2, 0.75 sec apart
MIDEARTH<1d>	Reg	8	4 lots of 2, 0.75 sec apart
MIDEARTH<1e>	Reg	8	4 lots of 2, 0.75 sec apart
MIDEARTH<1b>	Qry	84	300 sec apart at stable operation
__MSBROWSE__	Reg	8	Registered after winning election to Browse Master
JHT<03>	Reg	8	4 x 2. This is the name of the user that logged onto Windows
Host Announcement WINE-PRESSME	Ann	2	Observed at 10 sec
Domain/Workgroup Announcement MIDEARTH	Ann	18	300 sec apart at stable operation
Local Master Announcement WINEPRESSME	Ann	18	300 sec apart at stable operation
Get Backup List Request	Qry	12	6 x 2 early in startup, 0.5 sec apart
Browser Election Request	Ann	10	5 x 2 early in startup
Request Announcement WINE-PRESSME	Ann	4	Early in startup

   (c) Enable MAC name resolution

   (d) Enable network name resolution

   (e) Enable transport name resolution

Click **OK**.

2. Start the second Windows 9x/Me machine. Let it run for 15 to 20 minutes. While monitoring, do not press any keyboard keys, do not click any on-screen icons or menus, and do not answer any dialog boxes.

3. At the conclusion of the capture time, stop the capture. Be sure to save the captured data so you can examine the network data capture again at a later date should that be necessary.

4. Analyze the capture trace, taking note of the transport protocols used, the types of messages observed, and what interaction took place between the two machines. Leave both machines running for the next task.

16.3.2.1   Findings

Table 16.2 summarizes capture statistics observed. As in the previous case, all announcements used UDP/IP broadcasts. Also, as was observed with the last example, the second Windows 9x/Me machine broadcasts its name on startup to ensure that there exists no name clash (i.e., the name is already registered by another machine) on the network segment. Those wishing to explore the inner details of the precise mechanism of how this functions should refer to "Implementing CIFS: The Common Internet File System."

Table 16.2 Second Machine (Windows 98) — Capture Statistics

Message	Type	Num	Notes
MILGATE98<00>	Reg	8	4 lots of 2, 0.6 sec apart
MILGATE98<03>	Reg	8	4 lots of 2, 0.6 sec apart
MILGATE98<20>	Reg	8	4 lots of 2, 0.75 sec apart
MIDEARTH<00>	Reg	8	4 lots of 2, 0.75 sec apart
MIDEARTH<1d>	Reg	8	4 lots of 2, 0.75 sec apart
MIDEARTH<1e>	Reg	8	4 lots of 2, 0.75 sec apart
MIDEARTH<1b>	Qry	18	900 sec apart at stable operation
JHT<03>	Reg	2	This is the name of the user that logged onto Windows
Host Announcement MILGATE98	Ann	14	Every 120 sec
Domain/Workgroup Announcement MIDEARTH	Ann	6	900 sec apart at stable operation
Local Master Announcement WINEPRESSME	Ann	6	Insufficient detail to determine frequency

Observation of the contents of Host Announcements, Domain/Workgroup Announcements, and Local Master Announcements is instructive. These messages convey a significant level of detail regarding the nature of each machine that is on the network. An example dissection of a Host Announcement is given in Figure 16.3.

16.3.3   Simple Windows Client Connection Characteristics

The purpose of this exercise is to discover how Microsoft Windows clients create (establish) connections with remote servers. The methodology involves analysis of a key aspect of how Windows clients access remote servers: the session setup protocol.

CLIENT CONNECTION EXPLORATION STEPS

1. Configure a Windows 9x/Me machine (MILGATE98) with a share called `Stuff`. Create a *Full Access* control password on this share.

2. Configure another Windows 9x/Me machine (WINEPRESSME) as a client. Make sure that it exports no shared resources.

Figure 16.3 Typical Windows 9x/Me Host Announcement

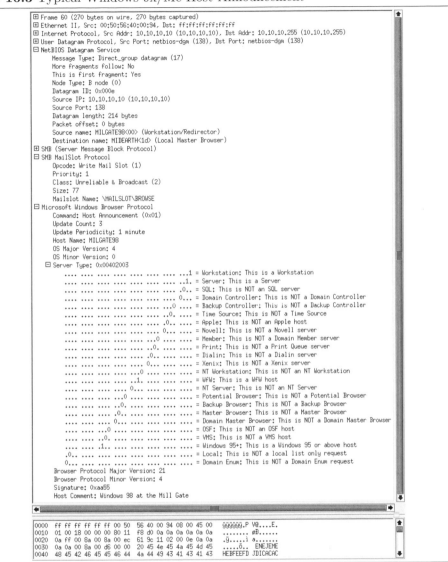

```
⊞ Frame 60 (270 bytes on wire, 270 bytes captured)
⊞ Ethernet II, Src: 00:50:56:40:00:94, Dst: ff:ff:ff:ff:ff:ff
⊞ Internet Protocol, Src Addr: 10.10.10.10 (10.10.10.10), Dst Addr: 10.10.10.255 (10.10.10.255)
⊞ User Datagram Protocol, Src Port: netbios-dgm (138), Dst Port: netbios-dgm (138)
⊟ NetBIOS Datagram Service
      Message Type: Direct_group datagram (17)
      More fragments follow: No
      This is first fragment: Yes
      Node Type: B node (0)
      Datagram ID: 0x000e
      Source IP: 10.10.10.10 (10.10.10.10)
      Source Port: 138
      Datagram length: 214 bytes
      Packet offset: 0 bytes
      Source name: MILGATE98<00> (Workstation/Redirector)
      Destination name: MIDEARTH<1d> (Local Master Browser)
⊞ SMB (Server Message Block Protocol)
⊟ SMB MailSlot Protocol
      Opcode: Write Mail Slot (1)
      Priority: 1
      Class: Unreliable & Broadcast (2)
      Size: 77
      Mailslot Name: \MAILSLOT\BROWSE
⊟ Microsoft Windows Browser Protocol
      Command: Host Announcement (0x01)
      Update Count: 3
      Update Periodicity: 1 minute
      Host Name: MILGATE98
      OS Major Version: 4
      OS Minor Version: 0
   ⊟ Server Type: 0x00402003
         .... .... .... .... .... .... ...1 = Workstation: This is a Workstation
         .... .... .... .... .... .... ..1. = Server: This is a Server
         .... .... .... .... .... .... .0.. = SQL: This is NOT an SQL server
         .... .... .... .... .... .... 0... = Domain Controller: This is NOT a Domain Controller
         .... .... .... .... .... ...0 .... = Backup Controller: This is NOT a Backup Controller
         .... .... .... .... .... ..0. .... = Time Source: This is NOT a Time Source
         .... .... .... .... .... .0.. .... = Apple: This is NOT an Apple host
         .... .... .... .... .... 0... .... = Novell: This is NOT a Novell server
         .... .... .... .... ...0 .... .... = Member: This is NOT a Domain Member server
         .... .... .... .... ..0. .... .... = Print: This is NOT a Print Queue server
         .... .... .... .... .0.. .... .... = Dialin: This is NOT a Dialin server
         .... .... .... .... 0... .... .... = Xenix: This is NOT a Xenix server
         .... .... .... ...0 .... .... .... = NT Workstation: This is NOT an NT Workstation
         .... .... .... ..1. .... .... .... = WFW: This is a WFW host
         .... .... .... 0... .... .... .... = NT Server: This is NOT an NT Server
         .... .... ...0 .... .... .... .... = Potential Browser: This is NOT a Potential Browser
         .... .... ..0. .... .... .... .... = Backup Browser: This is NOT a Backup Browser
         .... .... .0.. .... .... .... .... = Master Browser: This is NOT a Master Browser
         .... .... 0... .... .... .... .... = Domain Master Browser: This is NOT a Domain Master Browser
         .... ...0 .... .... .... .... .... = OSF: This is NOT an OSF host
         .... ..0. .... .... .... .... .... = VMS: This is NOT a VMS host
         .... .1.. .... .... .... .... .... = Windows 95+: This is a Windows 95 or above host
         .0.. .... .... .... .... .... .... = Local: This is NOT a local list only request
         0... .... .... .... .... .... .... = Domain Enum: This is NOT a Domain Enum request
      Browser Protocol Major Version: 21
      Browser Protocol Minor Version: 4
      Signature: 0xaa55
      Host Comment: Windows 98 at the Mill Gate
```

```
0000  ff ff ff ff ff ff 00 50  56 40 00 94 08 00 45 00   ÿÿÿÿÿÿ.P  V@....E.
0010  01 00 18 00 00 00 80 11  f8 d0 0a 0a 0a 0a 0a 0a   ........  øÐ......
0020  0a ff 00 8a 00 8a 00 ec  61 9c 11 02 00 0e 0a 0a   .ÿ...ì   a.......
0030  0a 0a 00 8a 00 d6 00 00  20 45 4e 45 4a 45 4d 45   .....Ö..   ENEJEME
0040  48 45 42 46 45 45 46 44  4a 44 49 43 41 43 41 43   HEBFEEFD JDICACAC
```

3. Start both Windows 9x/Me machines and allow them to stabilize for 10 minutes. Log on to both machines using a user name (JHT) of your choice. Wait approximately 2 minutes before proceeding.

4. Start ethereal (or the network sniffer of your choice).

5. From the WINEPRESSME machine, right-click **Network Neighborhood**, select **Explore**, select **My Network Places** → **Entire Network** → **MIDEARTH** → **MILGATE98** → **Stuff**. Enter the password you set for the Full Control mode for the Stuff share.

6. When the share called `Stuff` is being displayed, stop the capture. Save the captured data in case it is needed for later analysis.

7. From the top of the packets captured, scan down to locate the first packet that has interpreted as `Session Setup AndX, User: anonymous`; `Tree Connect AndX, Path: \\MILGATE98\IPC$`.

8. In the dissection (analysis) panel, expand the `SMB, Session Setup AndX Request, and Tree Connect AndX Request`. Examine both operations. Identify the name of the user Account and what password was used. The Account name should be empty. This is a `NULL` session setup packet.

9. Return to the packet capture sequence. There will be a number of packets that have been decoded of the type `Session Setup AndX`. Locate the last such packet that was targeted at the `\\MILGATE98\IPC$` service.

10. Dissect this packet as per the previous one. This packet should have a password length of 24 (characters) and should have a password field, the contents of which is a long hexadecimal number. Observe the name in the Account field. This is a User Mode session setup packet.

16.3.3.1   Findings and Comments

The `IPC$` share serves a vital purpose[3] in SMB/CIFS-based networking. A Windows client connects to this resource to obtain the list of resources that are available on the server. The server responds with the shares and print queues that are available. In most but not all cases, the connection is made with a `NULL` username and a `NULL` password.

The two packets examined are material evidence of how Windows clients may interoperate with Samba. Samba requires every connection setup to be authenticated using valid UNIX account credentials (UID/GID). This means that even a `NULL` session setup can be established only by automatically mapping it to a valid UNIX account.

Samba has a special name for the `NULL`, or empty, user account: it calls it the *guest account*. The default value of this parameter is `nobody`; however, this can be changed to map the function of the guest account to any other UNIX identity. Some UNIX administrators prefer to map this account to the system default anonymous FTP account. A sample NULL Session Setup AndX packet dissection is shown in Figure 16.4.

When a UNIX/Linux system does not have a `nobody` user account (`/etc/passwd`), the operation of the `NULL` account cannot validate and thus connections that utilize the guest account fail. This breaks all ability to browse the Samba server and is a common problem reported on the Samba mailing list. A sample User Mode session setup AndX is shown in Figure 16.5.

The User Mode connection packet contains the account name and the domain name. The password is provided in Microsoft encrypted form, and its length is shown as 24 characters. This is the length of Microsoft encrypted passwords.

---

[3]TOSHARG2, Sect 4.5.1

Figure 16.4 Typical Windows 9x/Me NULL SessionSetUp AndX Request

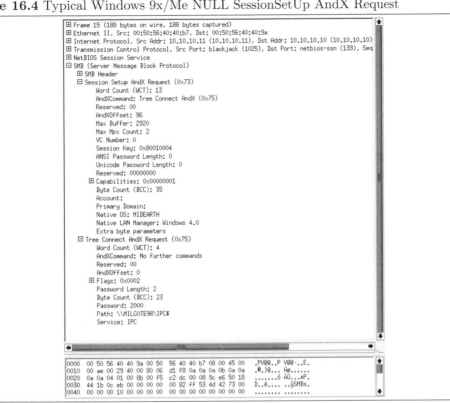

16.3.4   Windows 200x/XP Client Interaction with Samba-3

By now you may be asking, "Why did you choose to work with Windows 9x/Me?"

First, we want to demonstrate the simple case. This book is not intended to be a detailed treatise on the Windows networking protocols, but rather to provide prescriptive guidance for deployment of Samba. Second, by starting out with the simple protocol, it can be demonstrated that the more complex case mostly follows the same principles.

The following exercise demonstrates the case that even MS Windows XP Professional with up-to-date service updates also uses the NULL account, as well as user accounts. Simply follow the procedure to complete this exercise.

To complete this exercise, you need a Windows XP Professional client that has been configured as a domain member of either a Samba-controlled domain or a Windows NT4 or 200x Active Directory domain. Here we do not provide details for how to configure this, as full coverage is provided earlier in this book.

STEPS TO EXPLORE WINDOWS XP PRO CONNECTION SET-UP

1. Start your domain controller. Also, start the ethereal monitoring machine, launch ethereal, and then wait for the next step to complete.

Figure 16.5 Typical Windows 9x/Me User SessionSetUp AndX Request

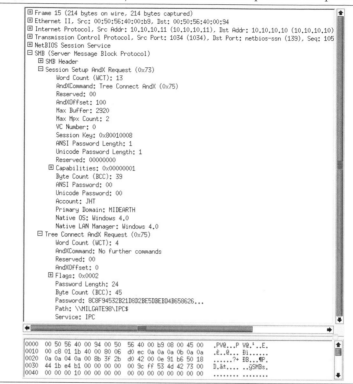

2. Start the Windows XP Client and wait 5 minutes before proceeding.

3. On the machine from which network activity will be monitored (using **ethereal**), launch **ethereal** and click **Capture → Start**. Click:

    (a) Update list of packets in real time

    (b) Automatic scrolling in live capture

    (c) Enable MAC name resolution

    (d) Enable network name resolution

    (e) Enable transport name resolution

    Click **OK**.

4. On the Windows XP Professional client, press **Ctrl-Alt-Delete** to bring up the domain logon screen. Log in using valid credentials for a domain user account.

5. Now proceed to connect to the domain controller as follows: **Start → (right-click) My Network Places → Explore → {Left Panel} [+] Entire Network → {Left Panel} [+] Microsoft Windows Network → {Left Panel} [+] Midearth → {Left Panel} [+] Frodo → {Left Panel} [+] data**. Close the explorer window. In this step, our domain

name is Midearth, the domain controller is called Frodo, and we have connected to a share called data.

6. Stop the capture on the **ethereal** monitoring machine. Be sure to save the captured data to a file so that you can refer to it again later.

7. If desired, the Windows XP Professional client and the domain controller are no longer needed for exercises in this chapter.

8. From the top of the packets captured, scan down to locate the first packet that has interpreted as Session Setup AndX Request, NTLMSSP_AUTH.

9. In the dissection (analysis) panel, expand the SMB, Session Setup AndX Request. Expand the packet decode information, beginning at the Security Blob: entry. Expand the GSS-API -> SPNEGO -> netTokenTarg -> responseToken -> NTLMSSP keys. This should reveal that this is a NULL session setup packet. The User name: NULL so indicates. An example decode is shown in Figure 16.6.

10. Return to the packet capture sequence. There will be a number of packets that have been decoded of the type Session Setup AndX Request. Click the last such packet that has been decoded as Session Setup AndX Request, NTLMSSP_AUTH.

11. In the dissection (analysis) panel, expand the SMB, Session Setup AndX Request. Expand the packet decode information, beginning at the Security Blob: entry. Expand the GSS-API -> SPNEGO -> netTokenTarg -> responseToken -> NTLMSSP keys. This should reveal that this is a User Mode session setup packet. The User name: jht so indicates. An example decode is shown in Figure 16.7. In this case the user name was jht. This packet decode includes the Lan Manager Response: and the NTLM Response:. The values of these two parameters are the Microsoft encrypted password hashes: respectively, the LanMan password and then the NT (case-preserving) password hash.

12. The passwords are 24-character hexadecimal numbers. This packet confirms that this is a User Mode session setup packet.

16.3.4.1 Discussion

This exercise demonstrates that, while the specific protocol for the Session Setup AndX is handled in a more sophisticated manner by recent MS Windows clients, the underlying rules or principles remain the same. Thus it is demonstrated that MS Windows XP Professional clients still use a NULL-Session connection to query and locate resources on an advanced network technology server (one using Windows NT4/200x or Samba). It also demonstrates that an authenticated connection must be made before resources can be used.

16.3.5 Conclusions to Exercises

In summary, the following points have been established in this chapter:

- When NetBIOS over TCP/IP protocols are enabled, MS Windows networking employs broadcast-oriented messaging protocols to provide knowledge of network services.

Figure 16.6 Typical Windows XP NULL Session Setup AndX Request

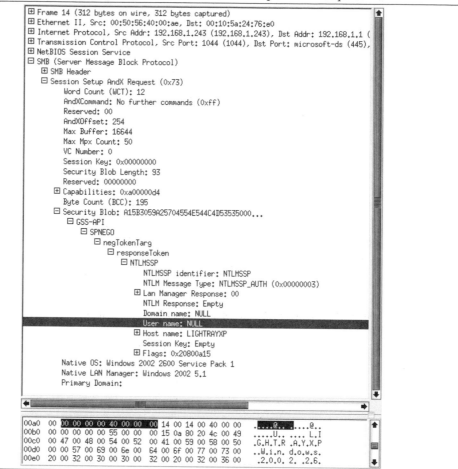

- Network browsing protocols query information stored on browse masters that manage information provided by NetBIOS Name Registrations and by way of ongoing host announcements and workgroup announcements.

- All Samba servers must be configured with a mechanism for mapping the NULL-Session to a valid but nonprivileged UNIX system account.

- The use of Microsoft encrypted passwords is built right into the fabric of Windows networking operations. Such passwords cannot be provided from the UNIX /etc/passwd database and thus must be stored elsewhere on the UNIX system in a manner that Samba can use. Samba-2.x permitted such encrypted passwords to be stored in the smbpasswd file or in an LDAP database. Samba-3 permits use of multiple *passdb backend* databases in concurrent deployment. Refer to *TOSHARG2*, Chapter 10, "Account Information Databases."

Figure 16.7 Typical Windows XP User Session Setup AndX Request

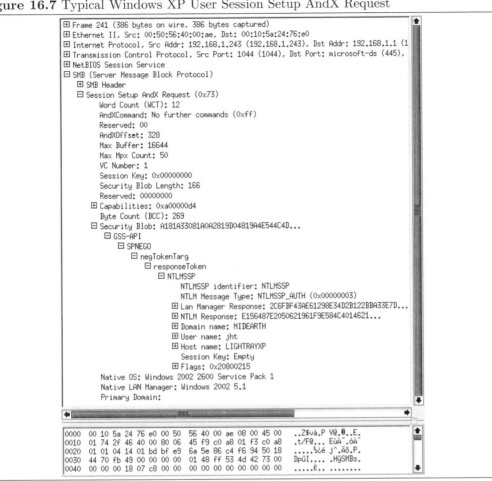

16.4   Dissection and Discussion

The exercises demonstrate the use of the `guest` account, the way that MS Windows clients and servers resolve computer names to a TCP/IP address, and how connections between a client and a server are established.

Those wishing background information regarding NetBIOS name types should refer to the Microsoft knowledgebase article Q102878.[4]

16.4.1   Technical Issues

Network browsing involves SMB broadcast announcements, SMB enumeration requests, connections to the `IPC$` share, share enumerations, and SMB connection setup processes.

---

[4]<http://support.microsoft.com/support/kb/articles/Q102/78/8.asp>

The use of anonymous connections to a Samba server involve the use of the *guest account* that must map to a valid UNIX UID.

16.5   Questions and Answers

The questions and answers given in this section are designed to highlight important aspects of Microsoft Windows networking.

F.A.Q.

1. **Q:** *What is the significance of the MIDEARTH<1b> type query?*
A: This is a broadcast announcement by which the Windows machine is attempting to locate a Domain Master Browser (DMB) in the event that it might exist on the network. Refer to *TOSHARG2,* Chapter 9, Section 9.7, "Technical Overview of Browsing," for details regarding the function of the DMB and its role in network browsing.

2. **Q:** *What is the significance of the MIDEARTH<1d> type name registration?*
A: This name registration records the machine IP addresses of the LMBs. Network clients can query this name type to obtain a list of browser servers from the master browser.

The LMB is responsible for monitoring all host announcements on the local network and for collating the information contained within them. Using this information, it can provide answers to other Windows network clients that request information such as:

- The list of machines known to the LMB (i.e., the browse list)

- The IP addresses of all domain controllers known for the domain

- The IP addresses of LMBs

- The IP address of the DMB (if one exists)

- The IP address of the LMB on the local segment

3. **Q:** *What is the role and significance of the <01><02>__MSBROWSE__<02><01> name registration?*
A: This name is registered by the browse master to broadcast and receive domain announcements. Its scope is limited to the local network segment, or subnet. By querying this name type, master browsers on networks that have multiple domains can find the names of master browsers for each domain.

4. **Q:** *What is the significance of the MIDEARTH<1e> type name registration?*
A: This name is registered by all browse masters in a domain or workgroup. The registration name type is known as the Browser Election Service. Master browsers register themselves

with this name type so that DMBs can locate them to perform cross-subnet browse list updates. This name type is also used to initiate elections for Master Browsers.

5. Q: *What is the significance of the* `guest account` *in smb.conf?*
A: This parameter specifies the default UNIX account to which MS Windows networking NULL session connections are mapped. The default name for the UNIX account used for this mapping is called `nobody`. If the UNIX/Linux system that is hosting Samba does not have a `nobody` account and an alternate mapping has not been specified, network browsing will not work at all.

It should be noted that the `guest account` is essential to Samba operation. Either the operating system must have an account called `nobody` or there must be an entry in the `smb.conf` file with a valid UNIX account, such as *guest account* = ftp.

6. Q: *Is it possible to reduce network broadcast activity with Samba-3?*
A: Yes, there are two ways to do this. The first involves use of WINS (See *TOSHARG2*, Chapter 9, Section 9.5, "WINS — The Windows Inter-networking Name Server"); the alternate method involves disabling the use of NetBIOS over TCP/IP. This second method requires a correctly configured DNS server (see *TOSHARG2*, Chapter 9, Section 9.3, "Discussion").

The use of WINS reduces network broadcast traffic. The reduction is greatest when all network clients are configured to operate in *Hybrid Mode*. This can be effected through use of DHCP to set the NetBIOS node type to type 8 for all network clients. Additionally, it is beneficial to configure Samba to use *name resolve order* = wins host cast.

NOTE

Use of SMB without NetBIOS is possible only on Windows 200x/XP Professional clients and servers, as well as with Samba-3.

---

7. Q: *Can I just use plain-text passwords with Samba?*
A: Yes, you can configure Samba to use plain-text passwords, though this does create a few problems.

First, the use of `/etc/passwd`-based plain-text passwords requires that registry modifications be made on all MS Windows client machines to enable plain-text passwords support. This significantly diminishes the security of MS Windows client operation. Many network administrators are bitterly opposed to doing this.

Second, Microsoft has not maintained plain-text password support since the default setting was made disabling this. When network connections are dropped by the client, it is not possible to re-establish the connection automatically. Users need to log off and then log on again. Plain-text password support may interfere with recent enhancements that are part of the Microsoft move toward a more secure computing environment.

Samba-3 supports Microsoft encrypted passwords. Be advised not to reintroduce plain-text password handling. Just create user accounts by running **smbpasswd -a 'username'**

It is not possible to add a user to the *passdb backend* database unless there is a UNIX system account for that user. On systems that run **winbindd** to access the Samba PDC/BDC to provide Windows user and group accounts, the *idmap uid, idmap gid* ranges set in the smb.conf file provide the local UID/GIDs needed for local identity management purposes.

8. **Q:** *What parameter in the* smb.conf *file is used to enable the use of encrypted passwords?*
A: The parameter in the smb.conf file that controls this behavior is known as *encrypt passwords*. The default setting for this in Samba-3 is Yes (Enabled).

9. **Q:** *Is it necessary to specify* encrypt passwords = *Yes when Samba-3 is configured as a domain member?*
A: No. This is the default behavior.

10. **Q:** *Is it necessary to specify a* **guest account** *when Samba-3 is configured as a domain member server?*
A: Yes. This is a local function on the server. The default setting is to use the UNIX account **nobody**. If this account does not exist on the UNIX server, then it is necessary to provide a *guest account* = an_account, where **an_account** is a valid local UNIX user account.

Appendix A

GNU GENERAL PUBLIC LICENSE

A.1 Preamble

The licenses for most software are designed to take away your freedom to share and change it. By contrast, the GNU General Public License is intended to guarantee your freedom to share and change free software - to make sure the software is free for all its users. This General Public License applies to most of the Free Software Foundation's software and to any other program whose authors commit to using it. (Some other Free Software Foundation software is covered by the GNU Library General Public License instead.) You can apply it to your programs, too.

When we speak of free software, we are referring to freedom, not price. Our General Public Licenses are designed to make sure that you have the freedom to distribute copies of free software (and charge for this service if you wish), that you receive source code or can get it if you want it, that you can change the software or use pieces of it in new free programs; and that you know you can do these things.

To protect your rights, we need to make restrictions that forbid anyone to deny you these rights or to ask you to surrender the rights. These restrictions translate to certain responsibilities for you if you distribute copies of the software, or if you modify it.

For example, if you distribute copies of such a program, whether gratis or for a fee, you must give the recipients all the rights that you have. You must make sure that they, too, receive or can get the source code. And you must show them these terms so they know their rights.

We protect your rights with two steps:

1. copyright the software, and

2. offer you this license which gives you legal permission to copy, distribute and/or modify the software.

Also, for each author's protection and ours, we want to make certain that everyone understands that there is no warranty for this free software. If the software is modified by someone else and passed on, we want its recipients to know that what they have is not the original, so that any problems introduced by others will not reflect on the original authors' reputations.

Finally, any free program is threatened constantly by software patents. We wish to avoid the danger that redistributors of a free program will individually obtain patent licenses, in effect making the program proprietary. To prevent this, we have made it clear that any patent must be licensed for everyone's free use or not licensed at all.

The precise terms and conditions for copying, distribution and modification follow.

A.2 TERMS AND CONDITIONS FOR COPYING, DISTRIBU-TION AND MODIFICATION

A.2.1 Section 0

This License applies to any program or other work which contains a notice placed by the copyright holder saying it may be distributed under the terms of this General Public License. The "Program", below, refers to any such program or work, and a "work based on the Program" means either the Program or any derivative work under copyright law: that is to say, a work containing the Program or a portion of it, either verbatim or with modifications and/or translated into another language. (Hereinafter, translation is included without limitation in the term "modification".) Each licensee is addressed as "you".

Activities other than copying, distribution and modification are not covered by this License; they are outside its scope. The act of running the Program is not restricted, and the output from the Program is covered only if its contents constitute a work based on the Program (independent of having been made by running the Program). Whether that is true depends on what the Program does.

A.2.2 Section 1

You may copy and distribute verbatim copies of the Program's source code as you receive it, in any medium, provided that you conspicuously and appropriately publish on each copy an appropriate copyright notice and disclaimer of warranty; keep intact all the notices that refer to this License and to the absence of any warranty; and give any other recipients of the Program a copy of this License along with the Program.

You may charge a fee for the physical act of transferring a copy, and you may at your option offer warranty protection in exchange for a fee.

A.2.3 Section 2

You may modify your copy or copies of the Program or any portion of it, thus forming a work based on the Program, and copy and distribute such modifications or work under the terms of Section A.2.2 above, provided that you also meet all of these conditions:

1. You must cause the modified files to carry prominent notices stating that you changed the files and the date of any change.

2. You must cause any work that you distribute or publish, that in whole or in part contains or is derived from the Program or any part thereof, to be licensed as a whole at no charge to all third parties under the terms of this License.

3. If the modified program normally reads commands interactively when run, you must cause it, when started running for such interactive use in the most ordinary way, to print or display an announcement including an appropriate copyright notice and a notice that there is no warranty (or else, saying that you provide a warranty) and that users may redistribute the program under these conditions, and telling the user how to view a copy of this License.

EXCEPTION:

 If the Program itself is interactive but does not normally print such an announcement, your work based on the Program is not required to print an announcement.)

These requirements apply to the modified work as a whole. If identifiable sections of that work are not derived from the Program, and can be reasonably considered independent and separate works in themselves, then this License, and its terms, do not apply to those sections when you distribute them as separate works. But when you distribute the same sections as part of a whole which is a work based on the Program, the distribution of the whole must be on the terms of this License, whose permissions for other licensees extend to the entire whole, and thus to each and every part regardless of who wrote it.

Thus, it is not the intent of this section to claim rights or contest your rights to work written entirely by you; rather, the intent is to exercise the right to control the distribution of derivative or collective works based on the Program.

In addition, mere aggregation of another work not based on the Program with the Program (or with a work based on the Program) on a volume of a storage or distribution medium does not bring the other work under the scope of this License.

A.2.4 Section 3

You may copy and distribute the Program (or a work based on it, under Section A.2.3 in object code or executable form under the terms of Section A.2.2 and Section A.2.3 above provided that you also do one of the following:

1. Accompany it with the complete corresponding machine-readable source code, which must be distributed under the terms of Sections 1 and 2 above on a medium customarily used for software interchange; or,

2. Accompany it with a written offer, valid for at least three years, to give any third party, for a charge no more than your cost of physically performing source distribution, a

complete machine-readable copy of the corresponding source code, to be distributed under the terms of Sections 1 and 2 above on a medium customarily used for software interchange; or,

3. Accompany it with the information you received as to the offer to distribute corresponding source code. (This alternative is allowed only for noncommercial distribution and only if you received the program in object code or executable form with such an offer, in accord with Subsection b above.)

The source code for a work means the preferred form of the work for making modifications to it. For an executable work, complete source code means all the source code for all modules it contains, plus any associated interface definition files, plus the scripts used to control compilation and installation of the executable. However, as a special exception, the source code distributed need not include anything that is normally distributed (in either source or binary form) with the major components (compiler, kernel, and so on) of the operating system on which the executable runs, unless that component itself accompanies the executable.

If distribution of executable or object code is made by offering access to copy from a designated place, then offering equivalent access to copy the source code from the same place counts as distribution of the source code, even though third parties are not compelled to copy the source along with the object code.

A.2.5   Section 4

You may not copy, modify, sublicense, or distribute the Program except as expressly provided under this License. Any attempt otherwise to copy, modify, sublicense or distribute the Program is void, and will automatically terminate your rights under this License. However, parties who have received copies, or rights, from you under this License will not have their licenses terminated so long as such parties remain in full compliance.

A.2.6   Section 5

You are not required to accept this License, since you have not signed it. However, nothing else grants you permission to modify or distribute the Program or its derivative works. These actions are prohibited by law if you do not accept this License. Therefore, by modifying or distributing the Program (or any work based on the Program), you indicate your acceptance of this License to do so, and all its terms and conditions for copying, distributing or modifying the Program or works based on it.

A.2.7   Section 6

Each time you redistribute the Program (or any work based on the Program), the recipient automatically receives a license from the original licensor to copy, distribute or modify the Program subject to these terms and conditions. You may not impose any further restrictions on the recipients' exercise of the rights granted herein. You are not responsible for enforcing compliance by third parties to this License.

A.2.8   Section 7

If, as a consequence of a court judgment or allegation of patent infringement or for any other reason (not limited to patent issues), conditions are imposed on you (whether by court order, agreement or otherwise) that contradict the conditions of this License, they do not excuse you from the conditions of this License. If you cannot distribute so as to satisfy simultaneously your obligations under this License and any other pertinent obligations, then as a consequence you may not distribute the Program at all. For example, if a patent license would not permit royalty-free redistribution of the Program by all those who receive copies directly or indirectly through you, then the only way you could satisfy both it and this License would be to refrain entirely from distribution of the Program.

If any portion of this section is held invalid or unenforceable under any particular circumstance, the balance of the section is intended to apply and the section as a whole is intended to apply in other circumstances.

It is not the purpose of this section to induce you to infringe any patents or other property right claims or to contest validity of any such claims; this section has the sole purpose of protecting the integrity of the free software distribution system, which is implemented by public license practices. Many people have made generous contributions to the wide range of software distributed through that system in reliance on consistent application of that system; it is up to the author/donor to decide if he or she is willing to distribute software through any other system and a licensee cannot impose that choice.

This section is intended to make thoroughly clear what is believed to be a consequence of the rest of this License.

A.2.9   Section 8

If the distribution and/or use of the Program is restricted in certain countries either by patents or by copyrighted interfaces, the original copyright holder who places the Program under this License may add an explicit geographical distribution limitation excluding those countries, so that distribution is permitted only in or among countries not thus excluded. In such case, this License incorporates the limitation as if written in the body of this License.

A.2.10   Section 9

The Free Software Foundation may publish revised and/or new versions of the General Public License from time to time. Such new versions will be similar in spirit to the present version, but may differ in detail to address new problems or concerns.

Each version is given a distinguishing version number. If the Program specifies a version number of this License which applies to it and "any later version", you have the option of following the terms and conditions either of that version or of any later version published by the Free Software Foundation. If the Program does not specify a version number of this License, you may choose any version ever published by the Free Software Foundation.

A.2.11   Section 10

If you wish to incorporate parts of the Program into other free programs whose distribution conditions are different, write to the author to ask for permission. For software which is copyrighted by the Free Software Foundation, write to the Free Software Foundation; we sometimes make exceptions for this. Our decision will be guided by the two goals of preserving the free status of all derivatives of our free software and of promoting the sharing and reuse of software generally.

A.2.12   NO WARRANTY Section 11

BECAUSE THE PROGRAM IS LICENSED FREE OF CHARGE, THERE IS NO WARRANTY FOR THE PROGRAM, TO THE EXTENT PERMITTED BY APPLICABLE LAW. EXCEPT WHEN OTHERWISE STATED IN WRITING THE COPYRIGHT HOLDERS AND/OR OTHER PARTIES PROVIDE THE PROGRAM "AS IS" WITHOUT WARRANTY OF ANY KIND, EITHER EXPRESSED OR IMPLIED, INCLUDING, BUT NOT LIMITED TO, THE IMPLIED WARRANTIES OF MERCHANTABILITY AND FITNESS FOR A PARTICULAR PURPOSE. THE ENTIRE RISK AS TO THE QUALITY AND PERFORMANCE OF THE PROGRAM IS WITH YOU. SHOULD THE PROGRAM PROVE DEFECTIVE, YOU ASSUME THE COST OF ALL NECESSARY SERVICING, REPAIR OR CORRECTION.

A.2.13   Section 12

IN NO EVENT UNLESS REQUIRED BY APPLICABLE LAW OR AGREED TO IN WRITING WILL ANY COPYRIGHT HOLDER, OR ANY OTHER PARTY WHO MAY MODIFY AND/OR REDISTRIBUTE THE PROGRAM AS PERMITTED ABOVE, BE LIABLE TO YOU FOR DAMAGES, INCLUDING ANY GENERAL, SPECIAL, INCIDENTAL OR CONSEQUENTIAL DAMAGES ARISING OUT OF THE USE OR INABILITY TO USE THE PROGRAM (INCLUDING BUT NOT LIMITED TO LOSS OF DATA OR DATA BEING RENDERED INACCURATE OR LOSSES SUSTAINED BY YOU OR THIRD PARTIES OR A FAILURE OF THE PROGRAM TO OPERATE WITH ANY OTHER PROGRAMS), EVEN IF SUCH HOLDER OR OTHER PARTY HAS BEEN ADVISED OF THE POSSIBILITY OF SUCH DAMAGES.

END OF TERMS AND CONDITIONS

A.3   How to Apply These Terms to Your New Programs

If you develop a new program, and you want it to be of the greatest possible use to the public, the best way to achieve this is to make it free software which everyone can redistribute and change under these terms.

To do so, attach the following notices to the program. It is safest to attach them to the start of each source file to most effectively convey the exclusion of warranty; and each file should have at least the "copyright" line and a pointer to where the full notice is found.

<one line to give the program's name and a brief idea of what it does.> Copyright (C) <year> <name of author>

This program is free software; you can redistribute it and/or modify it under the terms of the GNU General Public License as published by the Free Software Foundation; either version 2 of the License, or (at your option) any later version.

This program is distributed in the hope that it will be useful, but WITHOUT ANY WARRANTY; without even the implied warranty of MERCHANTABILITY or FITNESS FOR A PARTICULAR PURPOSE. See the GNU General Public License for more details.

You should have received a copy of the GNU General Public License along with this program; if not, write to the Free Software Foundation, Inc., 51 Franklin Street, Fifth Floor, Boston, MA 02110-1301 USA

Also add information on how to contact you by electronic and paper mail.

If the program is interactive, make it output a short notice like this when it starts in an interactive mode:

Gnomovision version 69, Copyright (C) year name of author Gnomovision comes with ABSOLUTELY NO WARRANTY; for details type 'show w'. This is free software, and you are welcome to redistribute it under certain conditions; type 'show c' for details.

The hypothetical commands 'show w' and 'show c' should show the appropriate parts of the General Public License. Of course, the commands you use may be called something other than 'show w' and 'show c'; they could even be mouse-clicks or menu items–whatever suits your program.

You should also get your employer (if you work as a programmer) or your school, if any, to sign a "copyright disclaimer" for the program, if necessary. Here is a sample; alter the names:

Yoyodyne, Inc., hereby disclaims all copyright interest in the program 'Gnomovision' (which makes passes at compilers) written by James Hacker.

<signature of Ty Coon>, 1 April 1989 Ty Coon, President of Vice

This General Public License does not permit incorporating your program into proprietary programs. If your program is a subroutine library, you may consider it more useful to permit linking proprietary applications with the library. If this is what you want to do, use the GNU Library General Public License instead of this License.

GLOSSARY

Access Control List (ACL)

A detailed list of permissions granted to users or groups with respect to file and network resource access.

Active Directory Service (ADS)

A service unique to Microsoft Windows 200x servers that provides a centrally managed directory for management of user identities and computer objects, as well as the permissions each user or computer may be granted to access distributed network resources. ADS uses Kerberos-based authentication and LDAP over Kerberos for directory access.

Common Internet File System (CIFS)

The new name for SMB. Microsoft renamed the SMB protocol to CIFS during the Internet hype in the 1990s. At about the time that the SMB protocol was renamed to CIFS, an additional dialect of the SMB protocol was in development. The need for the deployment of the NetBIOS layer was also removed, thus paving the way for use of the SMB protocol natively over TCP/IP (known as NetBIOS-less SMB or "naked" TCP transport).

Common UNIX Printing System (CUPS)

A recent implementation of a high-capability printing system for UNIX developed by Easy Software Inc.[1]. The design objective of CUPS was to provide a rich print processing system that has built-in intelligence that is capable of correctly rendering (processing) a file that is submitted for printing even if it was formatted for an entirely different printer.

Domain Master Browser (DMB)

The Domain Master Browser maintains a list of all the servers that have announced their services within a given workgroup or NT domain.

Domain Name Service (DNS)

A protocol by which computer hostnames may be resolved to the matching IP address/es. DNS is implemented by the Berkeley Internet Name Daemon. There exists a recent version of DNS that allows dynamic name registration by network clients or by a DHCP server. This recent protocol is known as dynamic DNS (DDNS).

Dynamic Host Configuration Protocol (DHCP)

---

[1] <http://www.easysw.com/>

A protocol that was based on the BOOTP protocol that may be used to dynamically assign an IP address, from a reserved pool of addresses, to a network client or device. Additionally, DHCP may assign all network configuration settings and may be used to register a computer name and its address with a dynamic DNS server.

Ethereal (ethereal)

A network analyzer, also known as a network sniffer or a protocol analyzer. Ethereal is freely available for UNIX/Linux and Microsoft Windows systems from the Ethereal Web site[2].

Group IDentifier (GID)

The UNIX system group identifier; on older systems, a 32-bit unsigned integer, and on newer systems, an unsigned 64-bit integer. The GID is used in UNIX-like operating systems for all group-level access control.

Key Distribution Center (KDC)

The Kerberos authentication protocol makes use of security keys (also called a ticket) by which access to network resources is controlled. The issuing of Kerberos tickets is effected by a KDC.

Lightweight Directory Access Protocol (LDAP)

The Lightweight Directory Access Protocol is a technology that originated from the development of X.500 protocol specifications and implementations. LDAP was designed as a means of rapidly searching through X.500 information. Later LDAP was adapted as an engine that could drive its own directory database. LDAP is not a database per se; rather it is a technology that enables high-volume search and locate activity from clients that wish to obtain simply defined information about a subset of records that are stored in a database. LDAP does not have a particularly efficient mechanism for storing records in the database, and it has no concept of transaction processing nor of mechanisms for preserving data consistency. LDAP is premised around the notion that the search and read activity far outweigh any need to add, delete, or modify records. LDAP does provide a means for replication of the database to keep slave servers up to date with a master. It also has built-in capability to handle external references and deferral.

Local Master Browser (LMB)

The Local Master Browser maintains a list of all servers that have announced themselves within a given workgroup or NT domain on a particular broadcast isolated subnet.

Media Access Control (MAC)

The hard-coded address of the physical-layer device that is attached to the network. All network interface controllers must have a hard-coded and unique MAC address. The MAC address is 48 bits long.

---

[2]<http://www.ethereal.com>

NetBIOS Extended User Interface (NetBEUI)

Very simple network protocol invented by IBM and Microsoft. It is used to do NetBIOS over Ethernet with low overhead. NetBEUI is a non-routable protocol.

Network Address Translation (NAT)

Network address translation is a form of IP address masquerading. It ensures that internal private (RFC1918) network addresses from packets inside the network are rewritten so that TCP/IP packets that lcavc thc server over a public connection are seen to come only from the external network address.

Network Basic Input/Output System (NetBIOS)

NetBIOS is a simple application programming interface (API) invented in the 1980s that allows programs to send data to certain network names. NetBIOS is always run over another network protocol such as IPX/SPX, TCP/IP, or Logical Link Control (LLC). NetBIOS run over LLC is best known as NetBEUI (the NetBIOS Extended User Interface — a complete misnomer!).

NetBT (NBT)

Protocol for transporting NetBIOS frames over TCP/IP. Uses ports 137, 138, and 139. NetBT is a fully routable protocol.

NT/LanManager Security Support Provider (NTLMSSP)

The NTLM Security Support Provider (NTLMSSP) service in Windows NT4/200x/XP is responsible for handling all NTLM authentication requests. It is the front end for protocols such as SPNEGO, Schannel, and other technologies. The generic protocol family supported by NTLMSSP is known as GSSAPI, the Generic Security Service Application Program Interface specified in RFC2078.

Server Message Block (SMB)

SMB was the original name of the protocol spoken by Samba. It was invented in the 1980s by IBM and adopted and extended further by Microsoft. Microsoft renamed the protocol to CIFS during the Internet hype in the 1990s.

The Simple and Protected GSS-API Negotiation (SPNEGO)

The purpose of SPNEGO is to allow a client and server to negotiate a security mechanism for authentication. The protocol is specified in RFC2478 and uses tokens as built via ASN.1 DER. DER refers to Distinguished Encoding Rules. These are a set of common rules for creating binary encodings in a platform-independent manner. Samba has support for SPNEGO.

The Official Samba-3 HOWTO and Reference Guide, Second Edition (TOSHARG2)

This book makes repeated reference to "The Official Samba-3 HOWTO and Reference Guide, Second Edition" by John H. Terpstra and Jelmer R. Vernooij. This publication is available from Amazon.com. Publisher: Prentice Hall PTR (August 2005), ISBN: 013122282.

User IDentifier (UID)

The UNIX system user identifier; on older systems, a 32-bit unsigned integer, and on newer systems, an unsigned 64-bit integer. The UID is used in UNIX-like operating systems for all user-level access control.

Universal Naming Convention (UNC)

A syntax for specifying the location of network resources (such as file shares). The UNC syntax was developed in the early days of MS DOS 3.x and is used internally by the SMB protocol.

SUBJECT INDEX

inform**IT**

www.informit.co

YOUR GUIDE TO IT REFERENC

Articles

Keep your edge with thousands of free articles, in-depth features, interviews, and IT reference recommendations – all written by experts you know and trust.

Online Books

Answers in an instant from **InformIT Online Book's** 600+ fully searchable on line books. For a limited time, you can get your first 14 days **free**.

POWERED
Safari
TECH BOOKS ONLI

Catalog

Review online sample chapters, author biographies and customer rankings and choose exactly the right book from a selection of over 5,000 titles.

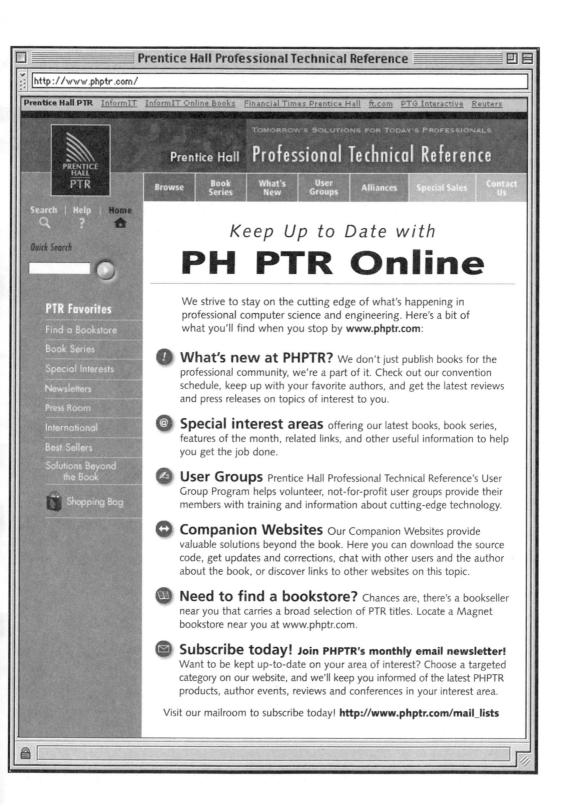

CD-ROM Warranty

Prentice Hall PTR warrants the enclosed CD-ROM to be free of defects in materials and faulty workmanship under normal use for a period of ninety days after purchase (when purchased new). If a defect is discovered in the CD-ROM during this warranty period, a replacement CD-ROM can be obtained at no charge by sending the defective CD-ROM, postage prepaid, with proof of purchase to:

Disc Exchange
Prentice Hall PTR
Pearson Technology Group
75 Arlington Street, Suite 300
Boston, MA 02116
Email: AWPro@aw.com

Prentice Hall PTR makes no warranty or representation, either expressed or implied, with respect to this software, its quality, performance, merchantability, or fitness for a particular purpose. In no event will Prentice Hall PTR, its distributors, or dealers be liable for direct, indirect, special, incidental, or consequential damages arising out of the use or inability to use the software. The exclusion of implied warranties is not permitted in some states. Therefore, the above exclusion may not apply to you. This warranty provides you with specific legal rights. There may be other rights that you may have that vary from state to state. The contents of this CD-ROM are intended for personal use only.

More information and updates are available at:
http://www.phptr.com/